REFORMING THE HOUSE OF LORDS

Reforming the House of Lords

Lessons from Overseas

MEG RUSSELL

OXFORD
UNIVERSITY PRESS

*This book has been printed digitally and produced in a standard specification
in order to ensure its continuing availability*

OXFORD

UNIVERSITY PRESS

Great Clarendon Street, Oxford OX2 6DP

Oxford University Press is a department of the University of Oxford.
It furthers the University's objective of excellence in research, scholarship,
and education by publishing world-wide in

Oxford New York

Auckland Bangkok Buenos Aires Cape Town Chennai
Dar es Salaam Delhi Hong Kong Istanbul Karachi Kolkata
Kuala Lumpur Madrid Melbourne Mexico City Mumbai Nairobi
São Paulo Shanghai Taipei Tokyo Toronto

Oxford is a registered trade mark of Oxford University Press
in the UK and in certain other countries

Published in the United States
by Oxford University Press Inc., New York

© Meg Russell 2000

ISBN 0-19-829831-5

Cover photographs: (Top) Houses of Parliament, and Big Ben

(Bottom) Gate of Houses Parliament . © Photodisc 1999.

Antony Rowe Ltd., Eastbourne

Acknowledgements

This book is the result of a study undertaken by the Constitution Unit during 1998–9, to look at second chambers in seven overseas parliaments. The study was funded by the Leverhulme Trust. We are very grateful for their support, which was essential to the project.

The work would also not have been possible without help and support from a huge number of individuals. The project relied in large part on study visits to six of the seven countries, where in most cases the second chamber and its work was poorly documented. The study was therefore wholly dependent on the co-operation of the parliamentary authorities in all the countries, and on the many people who were interviewed during the course of the research. These people, including many parliamentarians, parliamentary staff, civil servants, and academics all deserve personal thanks. They were: Valerina Agostini, Manuel Alba Navarro, Jody Blake, Jacques Blanc, Senator Nick Bolkus, Senator Pedro José Caballero Lasquibar, John Coakley, Professor Enrique Álvarez Conde, Senator Peter Cook, Senator Barney Cooney, Alain Delcamp, Cleaver Elliott, Harry Evans, Garret FitzGerald, Nadia Ganem, Pablo Garcia Mexia, Valeria Giammisso, Senator Esteban González Pons, Hans Haarmeyer, Senator Brian Harradine, Jean-Louis Hérin, Helmut Holl, John Kissane, Senator Juan José Laborda Martin, Rosemary Laing, Deirdre Lane, Jean Laporte, Professor Michael Laver, Brian Lenihan TD, Uwe Leonardy, Claire Longuet, Senator Maria Rosa Vindel López, Senator Sue Mackay, Herbert Maisl, Antonio Malaschini, Senator Maurice Manning, Angel Almendros Manzano, Francesco Marcelli, Jean Mastias, Didier Maus, Dr Mentler, Senator Gildas Molgat, Richard Mulgan, Senator Brian Mulloly, Senator Andrew Murray, John Nethercote, Úna Nic Giolla Choille, Jim O'Donnell, Jim O'Keefe TD, Senator Kathleen O'Meara, Professor Gianfranco Pasquino, Charles Powell, Senator Margaret Reid, Senator Margaret Reynolds, Maria Rosa Ripollés Serrano, Senator Carlo Rognoni, Campbell Sharman, Senator Natasha Stott-Despoja, Senator Nicholas Taylor, George Thompson, John Uhr, Jean Marc Virieux, James Warmenhoven, and Wolfgang Zeh. I am also grateful to the following, who helpfully provided contacts and proposed literature which were used in the study: Mark Audcent, Professor Sylvia Bashevkin, Professor Rodney Brazier, Paul Carmichael, Natasha Cica, David Doherty, Robert Elgie, Paul Furlong, Professor Brigid Hadfield, Professor Paul Heywood, Yvonne Galligan, David Gill, Professor Joni Lovenduski, Philippe Marliere, Professor Yves Mény, Professor Anthony Mughan, Professor Brendan O'Leary, Professor Samuel Patterson, Professor Cheryl Saunders, Jo Scard, Professor Anne Stevens, Professor Vincent Wright, and Professor Elizabeth Zoller.

Particular thanks are due to those who helped organise the programmes for the study visits, including Verona Ní Bhroinn and Stella Bianchi. Also to the many people who generously read drafts of the book, within quite unreasonable deadlines, and helped correct some of my many mistakes. These included: David Beamish, Howard Cody, Harry Evans and his team, David Hill, Pablo Garcia Mexia, Professor Ted Morton, Professor Dawn Oliver, Professor Gianfranco Pasquino, Professor Michael Rush, Campbell Sharman, Donald Shell, Paul Smith, and Damien Welfare. Three people were true heroes and helped in both these respects. These were Uwe Leonardy, Kelly Paxman, and Maria Rosa Ripollés Serrano.

The Director of the Constitution Unit, Professor Robert Hazell, painstakingly read every chapter as it came off the press, and offered constant support and encouragement. Other members of the Unit and the School of Public Policy at University College London offered help and support at different stages, and were very tolerant with me, their often absentee colleague. These included: Richard Cornes, Andrea Loux, Helen Margetts, Sara Northey, Aisling Reidy, Ben Seyd, and David Sinclair. John Louth and the team at Oxford University Press were responsible for turning the book around very quickly and efficiently.

Finally, I would like to thank my other colleagues, acquaintances, and friends, and in particular my partner Philip, for being patient during periods when I was preoccupied with study trips, research, and writing, and became a second chamber bore. I hope that some kind of normality can now resume.

Contents

List of Tables

Introduction

This book is due to be published in the midst of a national debate on reform of the House of Lords. This takes place against the backdrop of a UK constitution which has already been transformed, following the election of a Labour government in 1997. The creation of a Scottish Parliament, Assemblies in Wales, Northern Ireland and London, the establishment of Regional Development Agencies in England, and the passing of the Human Rights Act, all create a very different environment within which the Westminster parliament must operate. These factors will have an important impact on the way that reform of the House of Lords is debated and, hopefully, agreed.

The Constitution Unit, based at University College London, made its name before the 1997 election for detailed studies of many of the individual reforms which have now taken place. From the start the Unit has taken a particular interest in House of Lords reform, and the opportunities that this provides for linking together different parts of the new constitutional settlement. The Unit's first major report on the subject was published in 1996, and the second—in 1998—set out a step-by-step process for reform which has since largely been followed.[1]

Since this time, a White Paper has been published setting out the government's approach to reform of the House of Lords (Cabinet Office 1998). Legislation was been introduced to remove the right of hereditary peers to sit and vote in the house, and this completed its passage in the 1998–9 session. A Royal Commission, established to make recommendations on the second stage of reform, was given a deadline to report by the end of 1999.

However, the debate on reform of the upper house has, in general, been very insular. For example, during the two-day debate which the House of Lords held on the White Paper, no reference was made by any of the speakers to the international context or to any second chamber outside the UK. Yet bicameral (two chamber) parliaments are common around the world, and follow a diverse range of models which the UK might want to follow. Many countries began with hereditary upper

---

[1] Details of these reports may be found in the Bibliography at Constitution Unit (1996; 1998*b*).

houses, which have since been reformed. Many built their parliaments on the 'Westminster model', but these have developed over time, and diverged considerably from the original. Others start from different traditions, having second chambers which perform functions which are not currently reflected in the House of Lords. From all of these sources there is much potential for the UK to learn during its reform of the upper house.

This book therefore aims to bring a broader perspective to the British debate, and enable judgements about different options for a reformed upper house to be taken on the basis of evidence, rather than supposition. As the constitutional context in the UK changes, it is particularly important to look overseas to develop our understanding of how second chambers interact with the other parts of the constitution. The new devolved UK, with a developing rights culture, and possible changes to the electoral system yet to follow, can learn much from other countries whose systems of government already exhibit similar features. The upper house, as an organ of the national parliament, has a central role in the system and can help to underpin the rest of the new constitutional settlement.

The book considers the composition and work of seven second chambers overseas. These are in Australia, Canada, France, Germany, Ireland, Italy, and Spain. The countries chosen were intended to provide a broad range of comparators for the UK. Two are Commonwealth countries, whose parliaments were heavily modelled on the UK's, and five are European countries, with different parliamentary traditions. Three countries are federal, comprising self-governing states, whilst four are unitary—with different levels of responsibility devolved to regions or provinces. These therefore offer different examples of the directions in which the territorial nature of the UK could develop.

The chambers themselves have also been chosen for their diversity. In terms of composition they represent models which have each attracted interest as possible options for the UK upper house. One is wholly appointed, whilst two are entirely elected by the people. Three provide explicit links to other levels of government—one represents state governments, one is elected primarily by local government councillors, and one includes members elected by members of devolved assemblies. The final chamber was originally designed to represent vocational groups, rather than geographical constituencies or parties.

In terms of the powers and functions of the upper house, the seven countries also offer a range of experiences. Three of the chambers have very strong formal powers, allowing them to veto virtually all government bills. Two have moderate powers, whilst the remaining two can only delay legislation for a relatively brief time. The degree to which the chambers actually use these powers, and the factors which determine this, include important lessons for the reform of the House of Lords. A range of other duties are also carried out by the overseas upper houses, including constitutional protection, representation of state interests, parliamentary inquiries, and scrutiny of government. In these respects there are also experiences from which the UK can potentially learn.

One of the obstacles to introducing a comparative element into the Lords reform debate is that second chambers are relatively little-studied institutions. The House of Lords itself has attracted only a handful of scholars, and second chambers overseas—with a few notable exceptions—are even less well documented and understood. There are thus few texts from which British commentators have been able to draw. Until recently the one major comparative text in this area was in French (Mastias and Grangé 1987), although an informative English-language text was published recently by Patterson and Mughan (1999). However, studies to date have tended to focus on country-by-country analysis, rather than considering the composition, powers, and functions of second chambers more thematically. For UK reformers the comparative study of these elements of second chambers and their work may be instructive. Thus this book is organised thematically rather than geographically. It is hoped that the book will provide a useful addition to the comparative literature on these neglected institutions, as well as providing information of interest to those engaged in the House of Lords reform debate in the UK.

The book is intended to be accessible to different audiences, and its structure is designed accordingly. It is organised in three parts, the first of which aims to set a context, the second which discusses in detail the seven second chambers, and the third which considers the lessons that may be drawn for the reform of the House of Lords. It is intended that the three parts can be read relatively independently, and cross references have been provided where necessary, using footnotes.

Part One of the book comprises only two chapters. Chapter 1 provides some brief context about the House of Lords and its reform, including a little history and an account of recent developments. This story is later resumed in Part Three of the book. Chapter 2 provides a broad overview of second chambers around the world, considering the historical development of bicameralism and the extent of bicameral parliaments today. It looks at some of the common features of second chambers, and provides summary information about these in 20 selected countries.

Part Two forms the main body of the book. Here all aspects of the seven second chambers are considered in detail. This part of the book comprises nine chapters, each of which addresses a specific aspect of the chambers and their work.

Chapters 3 and 4 focus on the chambers' composition. Chapter 3 deals with how members of the chamber are selected, and places this in both a historical and constitutional context within each country. Chapter 4 then looks at the impact of that method of composition on the type of people who serve in the chamber—crucially in terms of their party-political balance, but also their political backgrounds, professions, gender, and age.

Chapter 5 looks briefly at organisational matters. These include the location of the chamber, how frequently it meets, and how its agenda is set. It also includes a discussion of party organisation and, importantly, of the resources provided to members—in terms of salaries and allowances, staff, and other facilities.

Chapter 6 considers the heart of the chambers' work—the scrutiny of legislation. This discussion begins with a summary of the chambers' powers over legislation, and the legislative scrutiny process in each chamber. It then looks at some of the important differences between legislative scrutiny in upper and lower houses, the innovative approaches taken in some second chambers, and the special treatment of certain kinds of legislation. The chapter also includes a discussion of the different means of resolving disputes between the two chambers over legislation, and avoiding legislative deadlock.

Chapter 7 turns to the work of committees in the chamber, and considers how upper house committees can make an important contribution to parliamentary work—in terms of legislative, oversight, and investigative functions. The role of joint committees between the chambers is also briefly considered.

The position of the chambers regarding constitutional matters is considered in Chapter 8, which demonstrates how most upper houses have considerable powers to protect the constitution. The chapter also looks at the different approaches by members of upper and lower houses to constituency work.

Chapters 9 and 10 discuss the relationship between the upper chamber and other institutions of the state. Chapter 9 looks at the relationship with government, which is often more remote in the upper than the lower house. Chapter 10 looks at the links with other levels of government, which are often—at least nominally—stronger in the upper house. This includes a discussion of the extent to which the upper house acts as a 'territorial' chamber, as well as the extent to which it helps bind the national parliament to European institutions in EU member states.

Part Two closes with Chapter 11, which attempts to evaluate public attitudes to different upper chambers, which are often open to greater criticism than lower chambers of parliament. The chapter then describes the attempts at reform in six of the seven countries, which have generally led to little or no change to the status quo.

Part Three of the book considers what can be learnt from all of this for reform of the House of Lords. The intention of these closing chapters is not to set down a blueprint or particular model for reform, but to evaluate the options in the light of the evidence from overseas. This analysis does result in certain solutions being virtually ruled out, whilst there are a number of other possibilities which might be expected to be more successful.

The main discussion in this final part is contained in Chapters 13 and 14, which cover the role and composition of the chamber respectively. Chapter 13 proposes three broad roles which a new second chamber might fulfil, each entailing a number of more detailed functions. Chapter 14 considers the options for composition of the new chamber, and how different methods of composition might help the chamber achieve the roles proposed. Chapter 12 provides a brief opening to this part of the book, and some general principles for reform which cut across the issues of role and composition. The book ends with an epilogue, Chapter 15, which attempts to predict the outcome of reform in the UK, based on history and overseas experience.

Predictions aside, only time will tell what the future of the House of Lords will be. As this text is being written, the Royal Commission is still considering its conclusions. The Commission's report is due for publication at the end of 1999, almost concurrently with this book. It should spark a national debate about the future of the upper house, not only amongst political parties, but also involving parliamentarians, representatives of devolved assemblies and local government, business and the voluntary sector, and the general public. It is hoped that this book may be of help to people in formulating their positions within that debate, and influencing the second stage of the historic reform programme which has begun.

PART ONE

———

Contexts

1

Reforming the House of Lords

The Labour government has committed itself to the reform of the House of Lords. Their manifesto for the general election of 1997 stated that:

The House of Lords must be reformed. As an initial, self-contained reform, not dependent on further reform in the future, the right of hereditary peers to sit and vote in the House of Lords will be ended by statute. This will be the first stage in a process of reform to make the House of Lords more democratic and representative. The legislative powers of the House of Lords will remain unaltered.

The system of appointment of life peers to the House of Lords will be reviewed. Our objective will be to ensure that over time party appointees as life peers more accurately reflect the proportion of votes cast at the previous general election. We are committed to maintaining an independent crossbench presence of life peers. No one political party should seek a majority in the House of Lords.

A committee of both Houses of Parliament will be appointed to undertake a wide-ranging review of possible further change and then to bring forward proposals for reform.

Significant progress towards these objectives has already been made. In particular the House of Lords Act which passed through parliament in the 1998–9 session ended the right of most hereditary peers to sit and vote in the house. This reform, which itself fundamentally changed the nature of the house, implemented stage one of the programme which the Labour Party has promised.

The House of Lords has been the subject of numerous studies. Its reform has been discussed on and off for most of this century. It is a remarkable institution, with a remarkable history, which has been ably described by many others.[1] The focus of this book, however, is the work of second chambers overseas, and what we can learn from this for the reform of the UK upper house. Before embarking on that overseas survey, this chapter runs very briefly through the essential features of the House of Lords—its composition, its work, a brief history of the

---

[1] See for example: Bogdanor (1997), Brazier (1998), Constitution Unit (1996), Dickson and Carmichael (1999), Richard and Welfare (1999), Shell (1992; 1999), Shell and Beamish (1993).

previous attempts at reform, and the new constitutional context in which the latest reforms are taking place.

THE HOUSE OF LORDS AND ITS WORK

When the House of Lords broke up in summer 1999 it comprised 1,289 members, 759 of them hereditary peers and 477 life peers. Its members also included 26 bishops and 27 current and ex- law lords, sitting in an *ex officio* capacity.[2] The house had a strong Conservative bias. In total, 471 of its members took the Conservative Party whip, 176 took the Labour Party whip and 66 the Liberal Democrat whip—the remainder adhered to no party whip, most of them sitting as 'crossbenchers'.[3]

The new parliamentary session brought a new, 'transitional' House of Lords, from which most of the hereditary peers had disappeared. This will potentially bring a fundamental change to the work of the Lords, which has developed progressively over many centuries and whose working practices have always been highly dependent on tradition and convention. The prospects for the transitional house are discussed at the end of this chapter. However, the work of the house will at least be heavily influenced by that of the chamber which preceded it.

In practice the predominantly hereditary house functioned rather better than its unwieldy size and large non-government majority would suggest. In 1998 the average attendance in the house was 428 members.[4] Convention required that policies appearing in the governing party's manifesto should be allowed to pass, and in general that government should not face unreasonable disruption. The number of defeats suffered by the Labour government in the long 1997–8 parliamentary session, though still higher than that suffered by Conservative governments, was moderate at 36 (Richard and Welfare 1999).[5]

Among those who followed the work of the House of Lords, the chamber commanded a good deal of respect. It was well accepted in parliamentary circles that the Lords made an important contribution, particularly to improving the quality of legislation. In a typical year the chamber would make between 1,500 and 2,000 amendments, the vast

[2] The *ex officio* basis for these two groups differs. Bishops sit only while they hold their posts. Law lords automatically become full voting members of the House of Lords when appointed, and hold their seats for life.

[3] The figures on party allegiance exclude 119 peers on leave or absence or without a writ of summons.

[4] *Annual Report and Accounts 1998-99*, House of Lords, 1999.

[5] For example, from 1979–97 Conservative governments suffered a total of 241 defeats in the Lords—an average of 13.4 per year.

majority of which the House of Commons would accept (Shell 1999). Studies showed that around 95 per cent of successful Lords' amendments were in fact proposed by government (Shell 1993). Many of these resulted from discussion during the passage of bills through the House of Commons—where most major legislation begins—or simply from government itself having had time to reflect. However, the care which House of Lords members could employ in scrutinising legislation also played a part. Many of the members had useful experience, from both within and outside the world of politics. Many also had greater time available than MPs for legislative work, unimpeded by constituency duties and other pressures. Consequently many detailed drafting amendments which ensured that bills 'actually fulfil their intended objectives, don't have unwanted or damaging side-effects, and are expressed in as clear and concise a way as possible' originated in the House of Lords (Shell 1998b: 23).

Aside from legislative work the predominantly hereditary House of Lords carried out many other functions which contributed to the scrutiny role of parliament. There has been no suggestion that these functions—including general debates, committee work, and questions to ministers—will change in the transitional house. Around one-sixth of the house's time was spent on oral questions to ministers, in addition to other time on ministerial statements and general debates. Around 3,000 written questions from members of the House of Lords were also answered by ministers every year. Usually most government departments included at least one minister appointed from amongst members of the Lords.

The work of House of Lords committees was also widely praised. Unlike the House of Commons the upper chamber committee system was not organised to shadow government departments, but instead around a smaller number of thematic committees. Particularly highly regarded is the European Communities Committee which, through six subcommittees involving some 70 peers, carried out selective and detailed scrutiny of proposed EU legislation. This work complemented the broader and less detailed treatment given by the equivalent House of Commons committee. The Science and Technology Committee was established in 1979 following the abolition of a similar committee in the House of Commons, and has produced reports of high quality on a range of subjects. The Delegated Powers and Deregulation Committee was initially established in 1992, with deregulation added to its remit in 1994. Although there is now a Deregulation Committee in the House of Commons, the Lords committee also considered whether the degree of delegation of power in government bills is appropriate. No parallel committee in the lower house carries out this work.

REFORM IN THE TWENTIETH CENTURY

This active House of Lords was the result a cumulative set of changes to the house and its powers during the twentieth century. The current upheaval in the chamber's membership may be seen as the latest in a long line of reforms that have edged the chamber, painfully slowly, towards becoming a modern and representative organ of parliament.

The first in this series of reforms was the 1911 Parliament Act. At the turn of the century the House of Lords, comprising only bishops, law lords and hereditary peers, numbered around 450. Its membership was overwhelmingly Conservative, and its powers to veto legislation were unlimited.[6] This inevitably led to difficulties for the reforming Liberal government elected in 1906. The crisis came when the House of Lords blocked Lloyd George's 'people's budget' of 1909. Following two general elections in which the Liberals held power, a bill to weaken the powers of the upper house passed—under the threat of swamping the Lords with Liberal appointees if they stood in its way. This bill became the Parliament Act 1911. For the first time the powers of the Lords with respect to the Commons were formally restricted. Bills could become law without the consent of the upper house following a delay of approximately two years. Furthermore a category of 'money bills' was defined which the Lords could delay for only one month. This would prevent the scenario of 1909 ever being repeated.

The next change to the power of the House of Lords was introduced by the first Labour majority government of 1945. Before the war Labour members of the House of Lords numbered only 15, and even with the addition of 44 further Labour peers the government feared that its legislative programme would be blocked (Richard and Welfare 1999). The government therefore proposed a new Parliament Bill, which limited the delaying power of the House of Lords to only one year. This eventually passed in 1949 under the provisions of the 1911 Act.

This period also saw an important change in the conventions of the house, which was probably more significant to its development than the passing of the Act.[7] In recognition of Labour's landslide victory the

---

[6] Although convention, and standing orders of the House of Commons, had since the seventeenth century given financial privilege to the lower house.

[7] Since 1949 the Parliament Acts have only run their full course on two occasions—over the War Crimes Act 1991 and the European Parliamentary Elections Act 1999. This is an

Conservative opposition in the Lords refrained from voting down proposals that were explicitly made in the Labour election manifesto. This initiative was led by the then Conservative leader in the Lords, the Marquess of Salisbury,[8] and has come to be known as the 'Salisbury convention'. It forms an important part of the informal running of the house today.

The next major change—which has also had a significant impact—was the Life Peerages Act of 1958. Until this time new additions to the house could only be made through new hereditary peerages. Life peerages were introduced by a Conservative government in an attempt to stem the inexorable rise in the size of the hereditary house. However, this actually accelerated the creation of peers—the house went on to grow by a further 50 per cent from its 1956 membership of 876. The 1958 Act also brought women into the House of Lords for the first time, and only in 1963 were women given the right to inherit a seat in the chamber, under the Peerage Act.[9] By summer 1999 still only 17 of the 759 hereditary peers were women.

Between 1963 and 1997 little real progress was made. The main milestone was the failed reform of the Wilson Labour government in 1968. This plan, which was set out in the Parliament (No. 2) Bill, would have changed the membership of the house and slightly reduced its delaying power. However, the ultimate destination of the reform would have been a wholly nominated house. This was not radical enough for the left of the parliamentary Labour Party in the Commons, whose resistance, along with Conservative members, resulted in the bill being withdrawn. This was in spite of the principles of the reform having received overwhelming support in the House of Lords itself (Shell 1992).

The removal of the hereditary peers from the house was a popular aspiration for many years. The original 1911 Parliament Act stated in its preamble that 'it is intended to substitute for the House of Lords as presently constituted a second chamber constituted on a popular instead of a hereditary basis, but such a substitution cannot immediately be brought into operation'. This has proved to be a major understatement. Despite the 1968 bill and numerous other official and unofficial proposals, this reform remained elusive for 88 years owing to

---

indication of the caution with which the unelected house used its powers, as it was perceived as increasingly unacceptable to challenge the will of the elected House of Commons.

[8] The Marquess of Salisbury was grandfather of the current Viscount Cranborne, Conservative leader in the Lords until 1998.

[9] This also gave hereditary peers the right to renounce their titles.

a failure to agree what should replace the hereditary house. This problem rests with us still.

PROGRESS SINCE 1997

Progress has been more rapid since Labour came to power in 1997. Although no action was taken in their first year of office, the House of Lords Bill, to remove the right of hereditary peers to sit and vote in the house, was introduced in the 1998–9 parliamentary session. This would form stage one of Labour's promised reform. Alongside the bill a White Paper was published, setting out the steps that the government intended to take towards stage two (Cabinet Office 1999).

Responsibility for investigating the options for reform, and coming up with initial proposals, was given to a Royal Commission. The chair of the Commission was Lord Wakeham, formerly a Conservative minister who had served at different times as both leader of the House of Commons and leader of the House of Lords. The terms of reference of the Royal Commission, as set out in the White Paper, were:

Having regard to the need to maintain the position of the House of Commons as the pre-eminent chamber of Parliament and taking particular account of the present nature of the constitutional settlement, including the newly devolved institutions, the impact of the Human Rights Act and developing relations with the European Union:

- to consider and make recommendations on the role and functions of a second chamber;
- to make recommendations on the method or combination of methods of composition required to constitute a second chamber fit for that role and those functions;
- to report by 31 December 1999.

Following the outcome of the Royal Commission, the government's plans were to establish a joint committee of both houses of parliament to 'examine the Parliamentary implications of the Commission's work'.[10] The timing of the Royal Commission would potentially allow the parties to set out their proposals for further reform in their manifestos for the next general election. Such plans could then be implemented shortly afterwards.

During the first months of the Royal Commission's life the bill was also proceeding through parliament to remove the hereditary peers. One major concession was made by the government, to ensure a smooth passage of the bill through the upper house. It was agreed that an

---

[10] Cabinet Office (1999: 35).

amendment, moved by the leader of the crossbench peers, Lord Weatherill, would be accepted if the government's plans were not disrupted. Under this plan, 92 hereditary peers would have the right to remain in the house until the second stage of reform. Seventy-five of these would be elected by the parties, in proportion to their strengths. The remainder would be certain officers of the house. The inclusion of this small number of hereditary members in the chamber would not only provide a lifeline for active hereditaries, but would also serve as a reminder to the government that the house was not fully reformed.[11]

A NEW CONSTITUTIONAL CONTEXT

The terms of reference of the Royal Commission acknowledged some of the other constitutional changes which had already come into force since the election of the Labour government, and the challenges these presented for the reform of the House of Lords. However, the Commission was given a very short time to report. Its first sitting was in March 1999, giving it less than 10 months within which to prepare its conclusions.

During the House of Lords debate on the White Paper the government leader of the house, Baroness Margaret Jay, justified the timing of the Royal Commission with the statement that:

We believe the timetable is achievable. After all, this debate has been taking place for most of this century. There is no need to undertake extensive gathering of evidence before any work can be done on the analysis of the issues.[12]

However, this rather overlooks the extent of the constitutional earthquake that has hit Britain since 1997 (Hazell 1999a; Blackburn and Plant 1999). This includes the establishment of elected assemblies in Scotland, Wales, Northern Ireland, and London, with the possibility of further devolution in the regions of England. It includes reform of the electoral system: these assemblies were elected using proportional representation (PR) and a form of PR also applied to the European elections in 1999 for the first time. These changes may be seen as a

---

[11] The 'Weatherill amendment' was the cause of a major row within the Conservative Party, when the leader of the party in the Lords, Viscount Cranborne, reached an agreement with Tony Blair that the Conservative peers would support the amendment. This was done without the consent of the Conservative leader, William Hague, and when the deal was uncovered, Cranborne was sacked. However, the Conservatives then went on to back the deal.

[12] *House of Lords Hansard*, 20 January 1999, col. 585.

testing ground for electoral reform for the House of Commons—on which the government has promised a referendum—and for local government. The Human Rights Act, incorporating the European Convention on Human Rights into UK law, reached the statute book in 1998. Experiments in local government reform are underway in many areas, including the anticipated growth of elected mayors for Britain's major cities. The UK is in the middle of what Tony Blair himself has described as 'the biggest programme of change to democracy ever proposed'.[13]

The long-term effects of these changes are hard to predict.[14] Indeed, many shorter term questions—such as whether there will be electoral reform for Westminster—remain to be answered.[15] The Scottish Parliament and Welsh Assembly elections were held on 6 May 1999, less than two months before the final deadline for submissions to the Royal Commission, and the Greater London Assembly was not due to be elected until May 2000. The Human Rights Act would not come into effect until October 2000. It was therefore very difficult for the Royal Commission to take proper account of these important developments.

Perhaps the key change in relation to reform of the House of Lords is the new territorial structure of Britain. This currently amounts to what Robert Hazell has referred to as 'quasi-federalism' (1999b: 231). As is demonstrated in Chapter 2 and subsequent chapters, the models adopted for second chambers tend to differ significantly between unitary and federal states. However, whilst Britain may be moving in a federal direction it will take many years to get there. The problems of designing a quasi-federal second chamber are addressed in Chapters 13 and 14.

THE TRANSITIONAL HOUSE

Until a second stage of reform is reached, the upper chamber will be a 'transitional' house, comprising the members left behind following the departure of most of the hereditary peers. Whilst providing a clear

---

[13] Speech to Labour Party conference, 4 October 1994.

[14] For a detailed analysis of the possible outcomes see Hazell (1999a).

[15] The Labour Party promised a referendum on a change to the voting system for Westminster, and set up a commission, chaired by Lord [Roy] Jenkins, to recommend an alternative to be put to the vote. The report of the commission (*Report of the Independent Commission on the Voting System*, Cm 4090-I, October 1998) recommended a weakly proportional system using the 'alternative vote' (AV) combined with additional members. Its proposals are not binding on the government. The outcome of any referendum is also unpredictable.

continuity with the past, this will nevertheless be a very different chamber.

The key difference, which was the main motivation for reform, will be in the balance between the parties. Of the 640 hereditary peers who were eligible to attend the house at the end of the 1998–9 session, 301 took the Conservative Party whip and only 19 took the Labour Party whip.[16] Although the Weatherill amendment results in the retention of 92 hereditary peers, at least 42 of whom will take the Tory whip, the removal of the main bulk of the hereditaries will result in a much more balanced house. This has been aided by Tony Blair's creation of an unprecedented 181 new life peers between 1 May 1997 and 5 November 1999. Eighty-eight of these were to take the Labour whip. These new creations have achieved a rough parity between Labour and the Conservatives in the transitional house. However, the balance of power will be held by a large group of peers either representing other parties, or taking no party whip at all.

An important question, which will only be answered over the passage of time, is how legitimate the new transitional house will be seen to be. This will have a crucial effect on how it uses its powers with relation to the House of Commons. Over the last decades it has been the presence of the hereditary peers that has been seen as particularly problematic and which has prevented the upper chamber from using its powers with any regularity. However the transitional house, as a wholly appointed chamber, will suffer legitimacy problems of its own when facing arguments with the elected House of Commons.

Uncertainty remains over the status that the Salisbury Convention will have in the transitional house. This convention was devised as a means of ensuring that the wholly hereditary house, dominated by the Conservatives, did not challenge the mandate of an elected Labour government. However, with the removal of most of the hereditaries there may be pressure from some quarters—most likely from the opposition in the House of Lords—to end its use. It has been suggested by some that the Salisbury Convention be put on a statutory basis in a reformed House of Lords, but it is difficult to see how this could be done in practice.[17]

Another factor which was due to influence the perceived legitimacy of the transitional house was the process of appointing new life peers. The White Paper on reform of the Lords promised that government

[16] This figure excludes 119 peers on leave or absence or without a writ of summons. Of the remainder, 22 took the Liberal Democrat whip and 217 sat on the crossbenches.

[17] This was proposed, for example, by the Labour Party in its evidence to the Royal Commission.

would 'set up an Appointments Commission to take over from the Prime Minister the function of nominating cross-bench peers', and would also have responsibility for 'vetting the suitability of all nominations to life peerages' (Cabinet Office 1999: 33). The intention of this proposal was to create a degree of transparency in appointments, and limit accusations of undue political patronage. However, by late 1999 the Appointments Commission had not yet been established. The degree of public trust in the Commission will be important to the public's general attitude to appointed upper house members.

The way in which these issues develop will have an impact on the likely longevity of the transitional house. If the public perceives the appointed house as having little legitimacy there will be pressure for continued reform. On the other hand, if the chamber is liberated by the disappearance of the hereditaries and uses its powers to challenge the government, this may spur government itself into action on stage two reform. A third option is that the transitional house plays a similar role to the one that it replaced, and goes almost unnoticed by the public. This way it could play a longer-term role, the implications of which have largely gone unconsidered.[18] As subsequent chapters—and British history—show, once a parliamentary chamber is entrenched its reform is difficult to achieve.

---

[18] For example because of the emphasis on the temporary nature of the house, little work has been done on how its membership might develop. One exception is Seyd (1999).

2

Second Chambers Worldwide

The purpose of this book is to set the reform of the House of Lords in context by looking at seven different second chambers around the world. But there is a far broader context—both historically and geographically—to the development of second chambers worldwide.

Two chamber—or 'bicameral'—parliaments are relatively common around the world. They are particularly widespread among the larger Western democracies, and particularly among federal states. However, second chambers are far from uniform in their behaviour, composition and powers. This is partly a legacy of their history, and partly the result of local circumstances. This chapter aims to provide a broad historical and global overview of these diverse institutions.

THE ORIGINS OF SECOND CHAMBERS

The existence of multi-chamber parliaments may be traced back to ancient Greece and Rome.[1] In these systems councils of elders— generally representing wealthy and powerful classes—would sit alongside more broadly based assemblies intended to represent the citizens. The majority of second chambers of today take the name inherited from the famous council of elders of ancient Rome—the Senate.

The purpose of such multi-chamber arrangements was to represent different interests and classes, thus binding society together and creating more stable government. This principle of 'mixed government' was advocated by ancient Greek philosophers, including Aristotle, and went on to influence later parliamentary arrangements around the world.[2] As Loewenberg and Patterson (1979: 121) have noted,

---

[1] Tsebelis and Money (1997) provide an excellent description of the early development of second chambers. This is the source of much of the information in the early parts of this chapter.

[2] The Athenian people's chamber, comprising 50 representatives of each of 10 tribes, could perhaps also be seen as a precursor of modern-day federal chambers. This chamber, where the representatives of the tribes were drawn by lot, was the inspiration for one of the

'bicameralism . . . originated in the essentially pre-democratic view that the representation of the nation required both an upper and lower house, in the class-conscious sense of "upper" and "lower"'.

The more immediate predecessors of today's second chambers, which developed across Europe during medieval times, were built on a similar principle. The House of Lords itself, which emerged in the fourteenth century, is one of the earliest examples and was highly influential. The evolution of bicameralism in Britain resulted from a split in the Great Council, which met to advise the king and agree taxation. The Council had previously expanded its membership from feudal lords to include burgesses representing local communities. When these different 'estates' began to meet separately this marked the emergence of an 'upper' chamber comprising the aristocracy and bishops, sitting in their own right, and a 'lower' chamber representing the people (or 'commons').

Similar developments occurred elsewhere in Europe. The Irish and French parliaments—whose origins are discussed in the next chapter—initially had three chambers, representing the aristocracy, the clergy, and the people. In the fifteenth century the Swedish Riksdag represented four estates—the aristocracy, the clergy, the towns, and the peasantry—in four separate chambers. This was reduced to two chambers in the nineteenth century and ultimately to one in 1970.

Whilst the origins of many second chambers may be traced back to this class-based model, another later model has been equally influential. This is the system adopted in the United States' constitution at the time of federation in the late eighteenth century. The constitution brought together a collection of self-governing states—most of them having their own bicameral parliaments—but with very different populations. At the Philadelphia Convention in 1787, representatives of the states met to resolve the number of representatives per state in the new legislature. There was concern amongst smaller states that they would be outvoted in a parliament with representation based on population. The outcome was the 'Great Compromise' between larger and smaller states, using a bicameral legislature to represent their conflicting interests. The lower house represented the people on a population basis and the upper house—the Senate—represented the states. In order to protect the states each was given an equal number of representatives in the Senate. This, coupled with co-equal powers for the two chambers, meant that no measure could be agreed without the support of the majority of the people's representatives and the majority of the states' representatives.

---

less conventional proposals for reform of the House of Lords, made by Anthony Barnett and Peter Carty (1998).

Similar bicameral systems went on to be adopted in many federal countries in the years that followed. The confederations of Germany and Switzerland, for example, started out with one legislative body comprising ambassadors from the states. Both later adopted a bicameral system, adding a popularly elected lower house. We also see the influence of the US system in the parliaments of Canada and Australia, as described in Chapter 3.

THE RATIONALE FOR BICAMERALISM

The different roots of upper houses, following the British model of a 'house of review' and the US model of a 'house of the states', continue to dominate modern-day debate. These different concepts of the purpose of second chambers lead to different expectations about the role they will play in the system of government. However, the two roles need not be in conflict—in modern systems a territorial chamber may also act as a constitutional guardian and house of reflection and second thought.

In many states—particularly those which are unitary—the second chamber has conventionally been a conservative force in the system. An upper house such as the House of Lords ensured protection of the landed classes against the 'tyranny of the majority' as represented in the elected House of Commons. The conservative nature of the upper house has endured in Britain, and in other states such as France and Canada, due to the way in which the chamber is composed. This conservatism need not only be class-based, but also may be dependent on the age, experience and independence of members of the upper house. Even today an important rationale for a second chamber may be as a forum of 'sober second thought', in the words of the first Canadian Prime Minister, Sir John A. Macdonald. This may provide protection against the danger of rash judgements by an unchecked lower house.

Irrespective of the profile of the chamber, the bicameral system adds an element of 'redundancy' into the legislative process which can form an important part of the checks and balances within government (Patterson and Mughan 1999). The second chamber may look afresh at legislative proposals and uncover difficulties not noticed by the first chamber. The analogy has been made that 'in every walk of life—be it medicine, science or day-to-day family problems—the second opinion is sought and valued. So it is in government.' (Evans 1995: 11–12).

Consideration by the upper house is of course likely to introduce delay into the system. However, this may be seen as a benefit. The delay enables all parties to reconsider legislative proposals, which may have been prepared in haste. This is particularly the case today, where a minimum period of legislative delay ensures there is opportunity for public debate and input from bodies and individuals outside parliament, fuelled by media coverage.

These elements of second thought and delay may be particularly valuable where one chamber of parliament is controlled by a government majority, as lower houses frequently are. This danger was recognised by James Madison, speaking at the convention at which the US constitution was agreed, when he said that there were two purposes for a second chamber: 'first, to protect the people against their rulers, secondly, to protect the people against the transient impressions into which they themselves might be led' (quoted in Patterson and Mughan 1999: 14). The existence of a second chamber which is dominated by the same party as the lower house may offer little protection—as seen at times in the 1980s by the behaviour of the House of Lords. However, it can offer greater defence than a unicameral parliament, such as the single chamber which passed the radical welfare-reform programme in New Zealand in the 1980s (Quarmby 1997).[3]

In federal states the second chamber frequently plays another role— that of representing the states, provinces, or regions of the federation at the national level. As Carmichael and Baker put it, 'the two-tier essence of the federal principle is inevitably translated into two parliamentary chambers' (1999: 73). As in the classic model of this system, the United States Senate, the representation of territorial units may be reinforced by an equal allocation of seats to each state. But this alone may not be enough to create a genuine 'states' house'. Territorial representation is further discussed in a separate section below and in more detail in Chapter 10.

BICAMERALISM TODAY

The bicameral parliament continues to be the standard model in use by large democratic states. In May 1999 the Inter-Parliamentary Union (IPU) database contained details of 178 parliamentary democracies, of which 66 were bicameral. A total of 48 of these used the title 'Senate'.[4]

---

[3] Although it should be noted that the New Zealand electoral system has since been changed to a proportional system which provides greater safeguards. On unicameral parliaments the Constitution Unit (1998*a*: 3) have said: 'The presence or absence of a second chamber cannot determine whether a parliament will be an effective democratic institution. Unicameral parliaments can be effective if well designed.'

[4] The most recent thorough review of the global situation, which used the Inter-Parliamentary Union database, was carried out by John Coakley and Michael Laver (1997)

Although this represents less than one-third of the total IPU member states, bicameralism is closely linked to other factors. Of the 22 federal member states in 1996, 18 had two-chamber parliaments, as compared to 40 of the 156 unitary states. The remaining four federal states (Comoros, Saint Kitts and Nevis, Micronesia, and the United Arab Emirates) all had a population of under two million. In unitary states the existence of second chambers is again linked to population—the largest unicameral state in Europe is Portugal, with a population of 10 million. In 1996 the average population of bicameral states was 47 million and that of unicameral states was 24 million. However there were exceptions: unicameral China (population 1.2 billion) and bicameral Palau (17,000), Antigua and Barbuda (65,000), and Grenada (92,000) (Coakley and Laver 1997).

In several federal states, state or provincial legislatures also tend to be bicameral. For example, Nebraska, which abolished one house of its legislature in 1934, is the only unicameral state in the US.[5] Queensland is the only one of the Australian states to be unicameral, having abolished its upper chamber in 1922. In Germany the reverse is the case—all the states are unicameral, bicameral Bavaria having decided to abolish its upper house in 1998. The same is true in Canada.

The existence of second chambers is not evenly spread around the world. Those countries which were particularly influenced by the Westminster or US models are far more likely to have adopted bicameral systems. Thus as well as being concentrated in Europe bicameralism is common in the Americas and the West Indies. It is relatively less common across Asia and Africa (Patterson and Mughan 1999).

There is no clear trend either towards or away from bicameralism. It is true that several countries have abolished their second chambers in the twentieth century, but these have tended once again to be small states. Notable examples are New Zealand in 1950 (population 3.5 million), Denmark in 1953 (population 5.2 million), Sweden in 1970 (population 8.7 million), and Iceland in 1991 (population 300,000). But at the same time other countries have adopted second chambers. These include Poland in 1989, Romania in 1990, Morocco in 1996, and the Czech Republic when it formed in 1993. The new South African constitution, also adopted in 1993, included a bicameral legislature where the upper house represents the provinces. This replaced a

---

for the Irish government, at which time there were 58 bicameral parliaments worldwide. Many of the figures here are taken from this survey, updated where possible.

[5] Nebraskans now call their legislature 'the unicameral' and its members 'Senators' (Patterson and Mughan 1999).

tricameral system that was based on racial divisions. Some countries have switched back and forth between one-chamber and two-chamber systems. For example, Turkey went from unicameral to bicameral in 1961 and back again in 1982 (Shell 1998*a*). Hungary, which had a two-chamber parliament from 1609 to 1949, is considering the reintroduction of an upper house, and the same issue continues to be debated in New Zealand.[6]

The Norwegian parliament provides an unusual example which could be seen as a compromise between the unicameral and bicameral systems. Here there is only one election but members then split into two chambers for the duration of the legislature. One-quarter of members form the second chamber. Bills shuttle back and forth between the houses to reach agreement, but in the case of a deadlock the matter is settled through a joint sitting. A similar structure existed in Iceland until 1991.

FEATURES OF SECOND CHAMBERS

Second chambers take many forms, both in terms of their composition and their powers with respect to the first chamber. However, although there are diverse models in use around the world, there are also many trends and common features among second chambers. These may help put the House of Lords and its reform in context.

In the sections below some of these common features and diverse characteristics are briefly examined. This is done, where possible, with reference to the 66 second chambers around the world. However, as information is not readily available about all of these chambers, a selection of 20 second chambers have also been considered in more detail. The features of these chambers, including the House of Lords, are summarised in Tables 2.1 and 2.2. The chambers considered include all OECD member countries whose parliaments are bicameral.[7] In addition three other countries: India, South Africa, and the Russian Federation, are included. Many of the issues touched upon here are then considered in more detail in later chapters for the seven countries under consideration in the book.

---

[6] The abolition of the New Zealand upper house in 1950 was intended to be a temporary measure (Jackson 1991). There was discussion in New Zealand of having a question on reinstatement of the upper house alongside the referendum on changing the voting system in 1993.

[7] This represents 17 of the 29 OECD members. The remaining members (Denmark, Finland, Greece, Hungary, Iceland, Korea, Luxembourg, New Zealand, Norway, Portugal, Sweden, and Turkey) all have single chamber parliaments.

Composition of Second Chambers

As discussed above, the origin of second chambers was the desire to provide a different form of representation to that provided by the first chamber: be this representation of classes, territorial units, or other interest groups. Thus the most immediately apparent difference between first and second chambers is generally their composition. The composition of the 20 key second chambers under consideration is summarised in Table 2.1.

Size

An important distinguishing feature of second chambers is that they are generally smaller than first chambers. Before the 1999 reform of the House of Lords, Britain was one of only three countries in the world with a second chamber larger than the first (the others being Kazakhstan and Burkina Faso). The House of Lords had almost twice as many members as the House of Commons, and was in fact one of the largest parliamentary chambers in the world.[8] The only parliament that was bigger was the (unicameral) Chinese National People's Congress with 2,970 members. Even the new transitional House of Lords will have over 600 members. The second chamber to come nearest to this in size is the Italian Senate, currently with 326 members. Only five other second chambers—those of France, India, Japan, Spain, and Thailand have more than 200 members (Coakley and Laver 1997).

On average second chambers worldwide have around 60 per cent of the number of members of the first chamber. The average size of a second chamber for a country such as the UK with between 10 and 100 million inhabitants is 90 members (Coakley and Laver 1997). This is reflected by the chambers listed in the table—only in Spain is the second chamber more than 60 per cent of the size of the first. The biggest difference in size between the chambers is in Germany, where the second chamber is only 11 per cent of the first chamber's size.

The smaller size of second chambers is often cited as a beneficial factor that, for example, makes debates and committees more manageable than those in the first chamber. This, along with other factors such as longer terms served by members of second chambers, fosters closer working relationships. These help create the more constructive and less adversarial atmosphere which is often a hallmark of second chambers.

---

[8] Although attendance in the chamber was generally far lower than its total membership—see Chapter 1.

Table 2.1. *Composition of selected second chambers*

	Size of chamber		Composition mechanism	Term
	Lower	Upper		
Australia: Senate	148	76 *51%*	Directly elected Senators elected by single transferable vote in six states and two territories. States have 12 seats each irrespective of population. Territories have two seats each. Lower house elected by alternative vote.	Six years for state Senators (half in each state elected every three years) and three for territory Senators.
Austria: Bundesrat	183	64† *35%*	Indirectly elected Members elected by provincial assemblies—three to 12 members each depending on population. Proportional system with at least one seat for second largest party.	No fixed term—members change when provincial assemblies elected.
Belgium: Sénat	150	71† *47%*	Mixed (largely directly elected) Forty members directly elected, 25 by Flemish electoral college and 15 by French. 31 appointed by Community Councils—10 Flemish, 10 French and one German. Six co-opted by Flemish groups and four by French groups. King's children are *ex officio* members.	Up to five years (same day as lower house elections).
Canada: Senate	301	105 *35%*	Appointed Members appointed by Governor General on advice of Prime Minister. Senators nominally represent provinces—large provinces have 24 seats, smaller ones four, six, or ten. Three territories have one seat each.	Appointment is to age 75.
Czech Republic: Senat	200	81 *40%*	Directly elected Majority vote in single member constituencies. Lower house is elected by a proportional system.	Six years, one-third elected every two years.
France: Sénat	577	321 *56%*	Indirectly elected Senators are elected in 100 *départements* by an electoral college of councillors and MPs. Each has between one and 12 Senators, based on population, but rural areas are overrepresented. Additional 12 Senators are elected to represent French citizens living abroad.	Nine years, one-third elected every three years.

	Size of chamber		Composition mechanism	Term
	Lower	Upper		
Germany: Bundesrat	656[†]	69 11%	Indirectly elected Members are appointed by state governments from amongst their members. Between three and six per state, depending on population.	No fixed term, members change when state governments change.
India: Rajya Sabha	630	245 39%	Mixed (largely indirectly elected) 233 elected by state legislatures using single transferable vote, with seats based on population. President also appoints 12 'distinguished' persons in fields of literature, art, science and social service.	Six years, one-third elected/ appointed every two years.
Ireland: Seanad	166	60 36%	Mixed (largely indirectly elected) 43 members elected by councillors and members of parliament in five 'vocational' categories. Six elected by graduates of two oldest universities. Eleven appointed by the Taoiseach (Prime Minister).	Up to five years (linked to lower house elections).
Italy: Senato	630	326[†] 52%	Mixed (largely directly elected) 315 members directly elected by similar semi-proportional voting system to lower house, in regions. Each president may appoint up to five life members (currently there are eight). Ex-Presidents have *ex officio* membership (currently three).	Up to five years (same day as lower house elections).
Japan: Sangiin	500	252 50%	Directly elected 152 members elected using majoritarian system in 47 constituencies with two to eight members each. 100 members elected by PR from national lists. Lower house uses additional member system.	Six years, half elected every three years.
Mexico: Cámara de Senadores	500	128 26%	Directly elected Four members elected per state. First three on majority system, with one seat guaranteed for second ranking party. Lower house uses additional member system.	Six years. Candidates may not be re-elected for a consecutive second term.
Netherlands: Eerste Kamer	150	75 50%	Indirectly elected Elected by provincial councils, using a proportional system, from amongst their members. Number of seats depends on population.	Four-year fixed term.

	Size of chamber		Composition mechanism	Term
	Lower	Upper		
Poland: Senat	460	100 22%	Directly elected Elected in 47 constituencies returning two members each and two large cities returning three each, using majority vote. Lower house uses proportional system.	Up to four years (same day as lower house elections).
Russia: Council of the Federation	450	178 40%	Indirectly elected Two members are appointed by state government and parliament in each of the 89 territories, being the state's head of administration and the chair of the parliament.	Varies by state.
South Africa: National Council of Provinces	400	90 23%	Indirectly elected Ten members appointed from each of the nine provinces, by parties, based on strength in provincial legislature. Four may be members of that legislature, including the premier—who can designate a substitute.	Five years.
Spain: Senado	350	259† 74%	Mixed (largely directly elected) 208 members elected in provinces by semi majoritarian system, mostly four per province. Remainder indirectly elected from regional assemblies, based on population. Lower house uses proportional system.	Up to four years (to date on same day as lower house elections).
Switzerland: Ständerat	200	46 23%	Directly elected Each canton elects two members and half cantons elect one. Most cantons use a majority system. Lower house elected using proportional system.	Four-year fixed term (same day as lower house elections).
UK: House of Lords	659	1,294† 196%	Mixed In summer 1999, 759 hereditary peers, 477 appointed life peers, 27 law lords and ex-law lords and 26 bishops (*ex officio*).‡	Life membership, except bishops who sit until their retirement.
USA: Senate	435	100 23%	Directly elected Each state elects two Senators irrespective of population, by majority vote. Lower house also uses majority system.	Six-year fixed term, one-third elected every two years.

† Size of the chamber is not fixed.
‡ The transitional house will include the life peers, law lords and bishops, plus 92 hereditary peers, making the upper house roughly the same size as the House of Commons.

Methods of Selecting Members

First chambers in democracies are generally elected by the people on a broad franchise. However, second chambers will tend to use a different form of composition, which may not involve direct election. The diverse range of methods by which members of second chambers are chosen may be broadly summarised as follows:

- *Direct election*
  Despite the differences in composition mechanisms between first and second chambers, the commonest method for selecting the latter is now direct election. Of the 66 second chambers worldwide, 27 use direct election by the people as their primary means of selecting members. This is also the commonest composition method amongst the 20 countries in the table, with seven chambers entirely directly elected and three more predominantly so. However, the election of the second chamber does not mean that membership is necessarily similar to that of the lower house. Difference between the chambers is generally achieved through employment of different electoral systems or means of distributing seats. Thus in five of the countries in the table the lower house is elected using a proportional system, whilst the upper house uses a majoritarian system. In one case—Australia—the reverse is the case. In the US both chambers use a majoritarian system, but the distribution of seats and the discrepancy between the size of constituencies and the length of parliamentary terms make these very different systems in practice. In three countries both houses use a proportional system for their election. However, in Belgium directly elected members make up only part of the second chamber, and in Japan different systems, with different parliamentary terms, apply. Only in Italy are two chambers elected using very similar systems with identical parliamentary terms. The consequences of this are discussed later in the book.

- *Indirect election*
  Twenty-one countries around the world use some form of 'indirect election' as the predominant means for selecting members of the upper chamber, and this applies to eight of the 20 countries considered in the table. Indirect election takes many forms, in each of which the electorate plays a part in the process, but not a direct one. For example, in France and Ireland a mixture of councillors and MPs make up an electoral college for the upper house. In Austria and India state parliaments elect its members. In Germany state governments appoint upper house members from amongst

themselves. Some of these systems are considered in more detail in Chapter 3. In most, but not all, cases indirect election is a means for the states or provinces in federal systems to be represented in the upper house. Modes of territorial representation are considered in a separate section below.

- *Appointment*
  Sixteen countries worldwide use appointment as the predominant means of selection to the upper house. However, the only wholly appointed upper house in a Western industrial country is the Canadian Senate, which is considered in detail later in the book. The other countries with wholly appointed upper chambers are Antigua, Bahamas, Barbados, Belize, Burkina Faso, Cambodia, Fiji, Grenada, Jamaica, Jordan, Saint Lucia, Thailand, and Trinidad and Tobago. In several countries a small number of appointees are included amongst members of the second chamber. These include India, with 12 appointed members, Ireland with 11, and Italy, currently with eight. Only three countries combine a significant number of appointees with (indirectly) elected members. These are Malaysia, with 43 appointed members and 26 indirectly elected members, Swaziland, with 20 appointed members and 10 indirectly elected members, and Algeria, with 96 indirectly elected and 48 appointed members.

- *Heredity*
  The reform of the House of Lords leaves only one country in the world—Lesotho—where heredity forms the primary basis for upper house membership. In addition children of the king are entitled to sit alongside 71 other members in the Belgian upper chamber. The other remaining parliaments including a hereditary element are the unicameral chambers in Zimbabwe and Tonga.

- *Ex officio*
  In some countries certain individuals become members of the upper house automatically. The Law Lords in the UK are an example. *Ex officio* membership of the upper chamber is also automatically bestowed on ex-Presidents in some countries, including Italy, Chile, Kazakhstan, Uruguay, and Venezuela.

- *Vocational/corporate*
  In a small number of upper chambers there is an attempt to represent vocational or corporate groupings. The main example of

this is Ireland, which is considered in detail in subsequent chapters. Other examples are Morocco, where two-fifths of the upper house are selected by trade unions, industry, and agriculture, and India, where 12 members of the upper house are appointed on the basis of achievement in the arts, science, and literature. The Bavarian state upper house, which was abolished in 1998, was also elected on a corporate basis.

- *Mixed membership*
  It is relatively common for an upper chamber to include a mixture of members selected in different ways. Of the 20 countries in the table, six use some form of mixed membership for the upper house. Most mixed chambers are predominantly selected in one way, with the commonest form of mixture being a predominantly elected chamber with a relatively small number of appointed or *ex officio* members (for examples see 'appointment' above). However there are examples of other models. The most diverse mix found is in Belgium, where the new constitution of 1993 included directly elected, indirectly elected, co-opted, and hereditary members in the new second chamber. The Spanish upper house, considered in detail in later chapters, also comprises a mixture of directly and indirectly elected members. Other examples are Morocco, where 162 members of the upper house are indirectly elected by regional councils and 108 are selected by vocational groups, and Pakistan, where 79 members are indirectly elected by provincial assemblies and eight are elected by members of the lower house.

Territorial Representation

In addition to whether its members are elected, appointed, or selected in some other way, the distribution of seats in a second chamber forms an important element of its composition. Whilst direct election is now the commonest means of selecting members of the chamber, some form of territorial representation—using regions, provinces, or states—is the commonest means of distributing seats.

Territorial representation is particularly prevalent in federal states. In all federal bicameral states membership of the second chamber is based on representation of the states or regions. However, this is also true of around a quarter of unitary states (Coakley and Laver 1997).

There are various ways in which territorial units may be represented in an upper house. State representation may be of:

- *the governments*—through appointment by those governments, as in Germany;
- *the parliaments*—through election by those parliaments, as in the Netherlands, Austria, and India, and for some of the representatives in Spain;
- *the people*—through direct elections as in Switzerland, Australia, and the US, or even through appointment, as in Canada.

The classic territorial chamber, which has influenced many others, is the US Senate. A key feature of this system is the equal representation of states—all with two Senators—irrespective of differing populations. This may be important to reinforcing the territorial nature of the chamber so that support by a majority of states is needed in order for a measure to be passed. But it may also be an important way of creating difference between the two chambers, particularly where both are directly elected. Australia, discussed in detail in subsequent chapters, provides an example of this.

The principle of equal representation also applies in the federal states of South Africa, Pakistan, Mexico, and the Russian Federation, and more surprisingly in unitary Poland. In other states-based second chambers distribution of seats is based on population. This is the case, for example, in Austria. In many, representation takes some account of population but still gives relatively more seats to less populous states. This is the case in Germany and Canada, as discussed in more detail in Chapter 3.

Parliamentary Terms

Another distinguishing feature of upper houses is that members often serve longer terms of office than those in the lower chamber. Life membership of the House of Lords is obviously an extreme example of this. Amongst the countries considered in the table, six years is the commonest length of parliamentary term. This applies in six countries. One country—France—uses nine-year terms. Terms are not fixed for appointed members in Italy, hereditary members in Belgium, or appointed members in Canada (who, however, must retire aged 75).

Longer terms may be combined with a rolling membership of the chamber, so that it is never dissolved. Again the UK and Canadian systems are examples. However, such a system is also common where chambers are elected, so that longer terms are combined with relatively frequent elections. The US, where Senators serve six-year terms with one-third elected every two years, is once again the classic example. Two countries considered in later chapters—Australia and France—use similar systems. In other cases, where the upper house is indirectly elected, its membership may change gradually as elections take place in constituent territories. This applies in Germany, and also in Austria and Russia. A system of rolling membership, which often means that the constitution does not allow the chamber to be dissolved, may add to the chamber's power. It may also help build continuity of work and relationships between members—especially when coupled with long parliamentary terms.

Membership Qualifications

In many cases different membership qualifications apply to the upper and lower houses. In some countries these include property qualifications which are a hangover from a traditional class-based system. However, another common feature is a higher age qualification for membership of the upper house. Thus in 1996, 14 second chambers worldwide—including Canada, India, Mexico and the US—had a minimum age qualification of 30 to sit in the second chamber. Eight— including France—used 35, four—including Italy—used 40, and one— Congo—required members of the upper house to be at least 50 (Coakley and Laver 1997).

The Powers of Second Chambers

As well as having a distinct composition to the lower house, it is usual for an upper chamber to have different powers. In the majority of parliaments around the world the powers of the second chamber are less than those of the first. Coakley and Laver (1997) calculate that of the 58 second chambers existent in 1996 only two—in the US and Bosnia and Herzegovina—had greater powers than the lower chamber. Fifteen had roughly equal powers and 41 had fewer powers. The main powers of the 20 second chambers focused upon in this chapter are summarised in Table 2.2.

Generally, where government is subject to a confidence vote in the lower house, the same does not apply in the upper house (although Italy is an exception—this is discussed in Chapter 9). Often upper houses can also only delay, rather than veto, legislation. It is common, however, for the upper house's powers over different types of legislation to vary. Commonly differences apply to financial legislation, legislation to amend the constitution and, in federal countries, legislation affecting the powers of the states.

Table 2.2. *Powers of selected second chambers**

	Ordinary legislation	Financial legislation	Dispute resolution	Constitutional amendments
Australia: Senate	Bills are introduced in either house. Upper house may amend or reject any legislation.	Must be introduced in lower house. Upper house may not amend but may 'request' amendments, or reject.	Only means of resolving disputes is to dissolve both houses of parliament.	Must pass at least one house with absolute majority and then pass referendum by majority and with support in more than half the states.
Austria: Bundesrat	Bills are introduced in lower house. Upper house can object within eight weeks, but cannot amend.	Upper house cannot object to federal budget.	Lower house can override upper house veto.	Passed by lower house only, but if one-third of upper house members demand it, there must be a referendum.
Belgium: Sénat	Two kinds of legislation: 'ordinary' bills start in lower house and pass automatically unless 15 Senators demand a review within 15 days (Sénat then can consider for 60 days); 'bicameral' bills, covering, e.g., foreign affairs, need support of both chambers.	Treated as ordinary legislation.	Lower house can override upper house veto on 'ordinary' legislation.	Require both houses to be dissolved, and two-thirds majority in both new houses.
Canada: Senate	Bills are introduced in either house. Upper house may amend or reject any legislation.	Must be introduced in lower house. Upper house may amend but not increase costs.	No means of resolving disputes—bills may shuttle indefinitely.	Senate can only block for 180 days, but must also be agreed by legislative assemblies in two-thirds of provinces, comprising 50% of population.[†]

	Ordinary legislation	Financial legislation	Dispute resolution	Constitutional amendments
Czech Republic: Senat	Bills are introduced in lower house. Upper house has 30 days to review.	Treated as ordinary legislation.	Absolute majority of deputies can overrule upper house veto.	Must be passed by three-fifths majority in both houses.
France: Sénat	Bills are introduced in either house. Upper house has right to amend or veto any legislation.	Must be introduced in lower house. Upper house may have as few as 15 days to consider it.	After two readings in each house, or one in case of urgency, joint committee proposes a compromise, which cannot be amended. If rejected lower house has last word.	These and 'organic' laws (covering, for example, the electoral system) must pass both houses and then either a joint sitting by a three-fifths majority or a referendum.
Germany: Bundesrat	Upper house sees and comments on all legislation before introduction in lower house. After lower house reading bills return to upper house for approval.	Treated as ordinary legislation, except budget which is introduced in both houses simultaneously.	Joint committee recommends a compromise, which usually cannot be amended. Then upper house has veto on bills affecting the states (around 60% of bills), lower house has last word otherwise.	Must be passed by two-thirds majority in both houses.
India: Rajya Sabha	Bills are introduced in either house. Reviewing house has six months.	Most such bills must be introduced in the lower house, but budget is introduced in both houses simultaneously and upper house has 14 days to review (lower house is decisive).	If upper house passes unwelcome amendments, rejects the bill, or fails to consider it within six months, joint session decides.	Must be passed by two-thirds majority in both houses and majority of total membership of both houses.

	Ordinary legislation	Financial legislation	Dispute resolution	Constitutional amendments
Ireland: Seanad	Bills are introduced in either house. Upper house has 90 days to consider bills passed by lower house.	Must be introduced in lower house. Upper house has 21 days to review. Can 'suggest' amendments, but lower house may ignore.	Lower house can override upper house veto within 180 days.	Treated as ordinary legislation, but must then pass a referendum.
Italy: Senato	Both houses have equal powers to introduce, amend, and reject legislation.	Treated as ordinary legislation. Budgets introduced in two houses alternately each year.	No means of resolving disputes—bills may shuttle indefinitely.	Must pass both houses by two-thirds majority. If not by absolute majority, subject to referendum if requested by one-fifth of members of either house, 500,000 electors, or five regional councils.
Japan: Sangiin	Bills are introduced in either house. Upper house has 60 days to review legislation.	Must be introduced in lower house. Upper house has 30 days to review. Lower house has last word.	Two-thirds majority in lower house overrules upper house veto. Lower house may call a joint mediation committee, but has the last word.	Must be passed by two-thirds majority in each house.
Mexico: Cámara de Senadores	Bills are introduced in either house. Both houses may amend or reject legislation.	Must be introduced in lower house. Lower house has last word on spending and upper house on tax.	Bill shuttles twice then 'review' house has the last word.	Must be passed by two-thirds majority in both houses, and by half of all provinces.
Netherlands: Eerste Kamer	Bills are introduced in lower house. Upper house can reject, but not amend, bills.	Treated as ordinary legislation.	Upper house has last word.	Require both houses to be dissolved, and two-thirds majority in both new houses.

	Ordinary legislation	Financial legislation	Dispute resolution	Constitutional amendments
Poland: Senat	Bills are introduced in lower house. Upper house has 30 days to review legislation.	Treated as ordinary legislation.	Lower house can override upper house veto.	Must be passed by two-thirds majority in lower house and absolute majority in upper house.
Russia: Council of the Federation	Bills are introduced in lower house. Upper house cannot amend bills but may reject within 14 days.	Treated as ordinary legislation.	Joint committee recommends a compromise, which may be overridden by two-thirds majority in lower house.	Some must be passed by three-fifths majority in both houses, others treated as ordinary legislation.
South Africa: National Council of Provinces	Bills are introduced in either house. For ordinary legislation upper house members have one vote each. For bills affecting provinces each province casts one block vote.	Must be introduced in lower house, but otherwise treated as ordinary legislation.	Joint committee recommends a compromise, which may be overridden by two-thirds majority in lower house.	Must be passed by two-thirds majority in lower house and six out of nine provinces in upper house, voting as blocks.
Spain: Senado	Bills are introduced in lower house. Upper house has two months to review, or 20 days in case of urgency, and may introduce amendments with an absolute majority.	Treated as ordinary legislation.	Lower house can override upper house amendments. Upper house veto may be overridden by an absolute lower house majority, or a simple majority after two months delay.	Most changes must pass by three-fifths majority in both houses. Joint committee can propose compromise, which requires two-thirds majority in lower house and absolute majority in upper house. Also subject to referendum if requested by one-tenth of members of either house.[†]

	Ordinary legislation	Financial legislation	Dispute resolution	Constitutional amendments
Switzerland: Ständerat	Bills are introduced in either house. Both houses have veto power over legislation.	Treated as ordinary legislation.	Joint committee recommends a compromise. If this is rejected the bill fails.	Unless passed by both houses, requires a referendum.
UK: House of Lords	Bills are introduced in either house. Upper house may amend or reject legislation. However, by convention upper house does not reject legislation implementing government's manifesto commitments.	Bills classified as 'money bills' must be introduced in lower house. Upper house may only delay for one month.	Lower house can override upper house veto approximately one year after bill's introduction if reintroduced in new parliamentary session.	Treated as ordinary legislation, except bill to extend life of a parliament, which Lords can veto.
USA: Senate	Bills are introduced in either house. Senate can amend or reject any legislation.	Must be introduced in lower house, but otherwise treated as ordinary legislation.	Shuttles indefinitely, but joint committee, with non-binding outcome, may be called at any time.	Must be passed by two-thirds majority in both houses, and ratified by three-quarters of states within seven years.

* Thanks are due to David Sinclair for help in preparation of this and Table 2.1.
† Major changes are subject to a more rigorous procedure (see Chapter 8).

Ordinary Legislation

Table 2.2 illustrates some of the typical limitations of upper houses over ordinary legislation. In seven cases legislation may only be introduced in the lower house. This often signifies a weak position of the upper house, although this is not always the case. For example in Russia and Austria it indicates a clear division of responsibility between the two houses, where the upper house is the states' house. In the Netherlands although the upper house cannot initiate legislation it has an absolute veto.

In general the upper house has the power to either amend or reject legislation (subject to the dispute resolution procedure, discussed below). However, in some countries this is not the case. In Austria the upper house may not formally amend legislation, but may only 'object'. In the Netherlands and Russia the upper house may reject legislation, but cannot amend it.

In many cases the upper house has a fixed period to consider legislation. This applies to half the countries in Table 2.2. In Britain the House of Commons can override an upper house veto approximately one year after its second reading of a bill, providing this is reintroduced in a new parliamentary session. In other countries the delays which second chambers may impose vary considerably, from 30 days in Poland and the Czech Republic to six months in India. However, in other countries such as Italy, Australia, and the US, there is no time limit on consideration and the upper house has an absolute veto.

In several cases there are two major categories of legislation, aside from that dealing with financial or constitutional matters, and the upper house has different powers over each. The system in Germany, where legislation affecting the states is subject to an upper house veto, is discussed in detail in Chapter 6. Similar systems exist in Austria and South Africa. In Belgium legislation on other key matters such as foreign affairs is also subject to upper house veto.

Financial Legislation

In the UK 'money bills' must be introduced in the lower house and the House of Lords may only delay them for a month.[9] Similar limitations are relatively common overseas. Thus in addition to the seven countries in Table 2.2 where ordinary legislation must be introduced in the lower house, another nine countries apply this rule to financial legislation. In five countries the time given to the upper chamber to consider financial legislation is more limited than that for ordinary legislation; in several the powers of the upper house to amend this legislation are more limited. In only three countries in the table can financial legislation be introduced in the upper house—India, where the budget is introduced in both houses simultaneously, and Italy and Switzerland where the chambers have equal powers over all legislation.

Resolving Disputes

A key determinant of the power of an upper house is the way in which legislative disputes with the lower house are resolved. One common method is for the lower house to have the 'last word'—that is the right to override objections by the upper house. This applies to most bills in

[9] For a definition of money bills, see Chapter 6.

the UK, after approximately a year, and several countries such as Austria, Belgium, and Poland after a shorter period. In some countries, such as Japan, a qualified majority in the lower house may override an upper house veto. Spain—as discussed in Chapter 6—employs a combination of these rules.

Another common option is to use a joint committee or joint session of both houses to adjudicate. In India a joint session of both houses decides. A joint committee is used in many countries, including France and Germany (as discussed in Chapter 6). Different rules apply to the acceptance of the compromise position from the committee, with the lower house decisive in some cases—with or without a qualified majority—or the upper house retaining a veto.

The third common procedure is for bills to simply shuttle between the houses until agreement is reached. This is the case in the US, and in Canada and Italy, as discussed in Chapter 6. In the US a joint committee may also be formed at any point, but its recommendations are not binding. The final and most drastic option for resolving disputes is dissolution. This is the formal procedure in Australia, and this is also considered in Chapter 6.

Constitutional Amendments

It is usual for the upper chamber to play a more powerful role when it comes to legislation that amends the constitution. The UK is the only one of the 20 countries considered in Table 2.2 not to have a written constitution and not to use a special procedure to agree constitutional change.

The commonest procedure for constitutional amendment, which applies in 14 of the countries in the table, is to require a qualified majority vote in both houses of parliament. This may be combined with other requirements, such as approval by the states in federal systems. In both Spain and Italy members of either house may call a referendum unless a qualified majority is reached. In Austria only the lower house must approve the bill, but the upper house may call a referendum. In other countries a referendum is standard, alongside less stringent parliamentary requirements. These issues are discussed in more detail in Chapter 8.

Other Powers

In addition to legislative powers, the upper chamber may have other powers within the parliamentary system that are either unique, or shared with the lower house. Upper chambers tend to play a more restricted role in making and breaking governments, although in Italy,

Switzerland, and the US, approval of the upper house is required for appointment of ministers. In Japan the upper house is involved in election of the Prime Minister, although the lower house has the last word. Questioning of ministers in the upper house may also be more limited than in the lower house, and in some cases ministers may be members only of the lower house. Such relationships with government are discussed in more detail in Chapter 9.

In many countries the upper house has a role in other significant appointments. For example in Austria, the Czech Republic, Italy, and Switzerland the election of the President takes place in a joint parliamentary sitting. In India the two houses are part of a larger electoral college for this purpose. In many countries the members of the upper house are also involved in selecting or approving members of the highest courts. This applies in Austria, France, Germany, Italy, and Switzerland. In most countries this duty is shared with the lower house, but in others, such as the Czech Republic, Russia, and the US it belongs to the upper house alone. This is further discussed in Chapter 8.

Second Chambers: Composition and Powers

Arend Lijphart, in his classic book *Democracies* (1984) classifies the powers of second chambers in relation to first chambers as 'symmetrical', 'moderately asymmetrical', or 'extremely asymmetrical'. As we have seen there are relatively few examples of countries in the first group, where powers of two chambers are very similar. Most countries will fall either into the second, where the powers differ slightly, or into the third, where the second chamber has rather weak powers. Lijphart also classifies composition of second chambers as 'congruent' (i.e. very similar) or 'incongruent'. He then goes on to conclude that a bicameral system is most effective if the two chambers are incongruent in their composition but have symmetrical or moderately asymmetrical powers. He calls this 'strong bicameralism'. Parliaments that have only one of these characteristics exhibit 'weak bicameralism' and those which can claim neither are examples of 'insignificant bicameralism'. Sartori (1997) supports the proposition that the second chambers which will be most effective are those with dissimilar composition to the first chamber, but similar powers.

However, dissimilar composition alone is not enough. The House of Lords has a distinct composition to the House of Commons, and its powers to delay legislation are relatively great. But these powers have been infrequently used because of the perceived problem of an unelected house, including many hereditary members, challenging the will of a popularly elected house. This is recognised by Lijphart when he notes that: 'The actual political significance of second chambers depends not only on their formal constitutional powers but also on their method of selection. . . Second chambers that are not directly elected lack the democratic legitimacy, and hence the real political influence, that popular election confers' (1984: 97).

This assertion is backed up by strong evidence from the survey of second chambers carried out by Coakley and Laver (1997). Their summary of the relationship between the composition and powers of second chambers is reproduced in Table 2.3.

Table 2.3. *Composition and powers of second chambers, 1996*[†]

Method of selection	Power	Total
Direct election	Greater or equal	13
	Lesser	11
Indirect election	Greater or equal	2
	Lesser	13
Appointment	Greater or equal	2
	Lesser	13
Other	Greater or equal	0
	Lesser	4
Total	Greater or equal	17
	Lesser	41

Source: Coakley and Laver (1997)
† Based on the then total of 58 second chambers.

This is an approximation, as it is very difficult to summarise the formal and informal powers accrued by a chamber. However, it illustrates the difficulty for chambers which are not directly elected of maintaining sufficient popular support to use significant powers. It is suggested that in only two cases where the upper chamber is elected indirectly—Russia and Bosnia Herzegovina—does it assert similar powers to the lower house. After closer investigation we may want to add Germany to this list. It is also noted that only two appointed chambers—in Swaziland and Jordan—can equal the lower chamber in terms of powers. This is despite the formally equal powers held by, for example, the Canadian Senate.

These issues of composition and powers, and the critical relationship between them, will be recurrent themes in later chapters. Detailed consideration of the seven second chambers which are the subject of the book will also enable us to reflect on whether those which exhibit 'strong bicameralism' as defined by Lijphart—i.e. Germany and Australia—perform more effectively than those which would be categorised as 'weakly' or 'insignificantly' bicameral. We return to this argument in Chapter 12.

THE PECULIAR NATURE OF SECOND CHAMBERS

As is revealed in the following chapters, there are many factors beyond the formal composition and powers of second chambers that influence their effectiveness. Many of these factors mean that, despite the diverse nature of these chambers in measurable terms, there is a certain atmosphere that tends to be common to them all. This is critical to their work and the impact that they have.

Factors relating to composition help to create this. One factor is the average age of members of second chambers, which tends to be higher than that of their colleagues in the lower house. This occurs in countries like the UK and Canada where members are generally appointed at the end of their careers, and Germany and France, where membership is dependent on holding other office. In some countries, such as Italy, it is the product of a higher qualification age for the chamber. It was noted above that second chambers are generally smaller than first chambers and their members are elected for longer terms. This helps to build closer working relationships between their members. Often members of upper houses are not subject to the demands of constituents—because they are appointed and have no constituency, because they represent a large region or state, or because they do not represent voters directly. This gives them more time to devote to parliamentary work.

The powers of a second chamber also help create its personality. If government cannot be brought down by the second chamber, this makes the outcome of votes in the chamber less critical. If the powers of the chamber over legislation are also reduced, so that it may be overridden by the lower house, this is even more the case. Thus a greater degree of independence amongst members of the upper house may be fostered, and the application of party whips may be less obvious. Couple this with the fact that party leaders and senior ministers tend to be concentrated in the lower house, so this receives more media attention, and the upper house is free to pursue its parliamentary work largely undisturbed.

The combination of these factors means that upper house members tend to work more closely together, scrutinise legislation in more detail, become more expert in specialist topics and are less driven by the party whip. Many of these features are recognisable in the behaviour of the House of Lords. This special personality possessed by second chambers may not make them popular, or enable them to win high profile victories, but it does provide an opportunity for them to make a distinct and valuable contribution to parliamentary systems of government.

This being said, it is perhaps surprising that second chambers have been so little studied. As pointed out by Mughan and Patterson (1999: 336) 'with the exception of the US Senate, little is known about upper houses individually, and even less is known about them in comparison with each other'. Even countries' own literature on parliament tends to give little space to the study of the upper chamber (with notable exceptions such as Australia, where the Senate is both powerful and controversial). Part Two of this book will help to illustrate, using a diverse set of examples, the work and impact of these important institutions.

PART TWO

Seven Second Chambers

3

The Composition and Context of the Chamber

Turning our attention to the seven second chambers that are the focus of this book, we will want to look at the work of these diverse chambers, and the impacts that they make. However, it is the composition of the chamber that we turn to first, and this is the subject of the current chapter and the one that follows.

In bicameral systems it is the composition of the two chambers which is generally the first feature to distinguish them in the eye of the observer. It is the composition of the upper house which often makes it unique. For example it is the composition of the House of Lords, rather than its work, which has made it a curiosity and the subject of study and comment. The same may be said—to a lesser extent—of several of the other chambers discussed in this book. The composition of the chamber, being its most visible feature, is also generally the first target amongst its critics. Reform proposals, which are commonplace amongst the countries we are considering, tend to focus on issues of composition rather than on the powers and functions of the chamber.

However, as already indicated in Chapter 2, the powers and functions of a chamber cannot be separated from its composition. This is nowhere more true than in Britain, where consideration of the role of the House of Lords would be inconceivable without an understanding of its unusual composition. The unelected nature of the house, and its inbuilt Conservative bias, have had an immeasurable impact on its behaviour within the legislative system in the twentieth century.

This chapter considers, in turn, the composition of the seven second chambers. It attempts to place the current chamber in a historical context, in order to demonstrate the role which it was designed to play within the state. However, the chamber's role within the political system will be critically affected by the structure of that system and the other institutions within it. We therefore begin with a discussion of the political system in each of the countries being considered. The chapter ends with a discussion of one particular element of a chamber's composition—the way in which distribution of seats relates to population. This is one way in which the upper house may be based on a different notion of 'representation' to the lower house, and may even be described as 'unrepresentative'.

SEVEN POLITICAL SYSTEMS

The countries considered in this book have been chosen for their diversity. All are Western democracies, and of course all have two-chamber parliaments. But there many of the similarities end. Aside from the differences in their second chambers, there are many other key differences between the seven countries in question.

Some summary information about these countries is given in Table 3.1. This begins to demonstrate some of their diversity. They vary in size from a population of 3.5 million in Ireland to 80 million in Germany, with Australia and Canada covering a huge land mass but being fairly sparsely populated. They also vary considerably in age of the current constitution. Four of the European countries have post-war constitutions, although their histories are much longer. The two Commonwealth countries have had longer periods of unbroken democracy.

Table 3.1. *Seven states: a summary*

	Population (millions)	Date of constitution	Federal or unitary
Australia	19	1901†	federal
Canada	30	1867‡	federal
France	57	1958	unitary
Germany	80	1949	federal
Ireland	3.5	1937	unitary
Italy	58	1948	unitary
Spain	39	1978	unitary§

† The Senate has since changed both its size and electoral system.
‡ Supplemented by the Canada Act 1982, without changes to the Senate.
§ Spain is sometimes referred to as a 'union' state—see the text.

The form of the state is also important to the role of the second chamber, as this is generally a different role in federal and unitary states. Three of the countries are federations, all resulting from a coming together of self-governing states in the nineteenth century. However, the distinction between federal and unitary states is blurring—France,

Italy, and Spain are all moving in the direction of decentralisation, with regional authorities gaining powers to different degrees. Indeed Spain has undergone an asymmetrical programme of devolution similar to that which has begun in the UK, and is now often classified as a 'union' state, in recognition of the degree of devolved powers in some areas of the country (Keating 1996).[1]

Like Britain, three of the states are monarchies. The two commonwealth countries actually share the British monarch, while Spain has a monarchy that played an important role in the transition from dictatorship in the late 1970s and early 1980s. The others are republics, with varying powers given to the President. In Germany, Ireland, and Italy the President is largely a figurehead with similar powers to the British monarch. However, France has a strong 'semi-presidential' system, where the President takes a leading role in government.[2] Indeed France, unlike the other countries, also conforms to the strict US model of 'separation of powers' with ministers barred from holding seats in parliament.

Parliament itself plays a different role in the political system within the different states. It is difficult to measure with any accuracy the power of parliament, and commentators in all countries seem to lament the weakening of parliament within the system. But certainly in some countries—France and Ireland in particular—parliament is seen as a marginalised institution.[3] This of course is a critical factor in understanding the position of the upper house. The modes of election to the lower house of parliament (and upper house where appropriate) also differ widely. The Australian and Canadian systems, heavily influenced by the British, are similarly based on single member constituencies, as is the French system. The other countries use some form of proportional representation. This is summarised in Table 3.2, and discussed in more detail below.

Related to the electoral system, and the degree of devolution, is the party system. In Australia national politics is primarily dominated by

[1] For simplicity both Spain and the UK will be referred to throughout the text as unitary.

[2] The role of the French President will tend to differ depending on the balance of power in parliament. The Prime Minister and cabinet must maintain the confidence of the lower house, so must reflect party strengths there. Where the President is of the opposing political camp—during what the French call a period of 'cohabitation'—he or she will have less ability to set the political agenda. However, where President and Prime Minister are from the same camp the former will play the lead role in government.

[3] The role of the French parliament has been described as 'modest to the point of being inadequate' (Frears 1990: 32), which is echoed in the words that 'in its control over the executive and its formulation of public policy, the Irish parliament, or Oireachtas, is a woefully inadequate institution' (Dinan 1986: 71).

two main parties. This is also largely the case in the other countries—
Italy being the obvious exception with many more parties represented
in parliament. However, in decentralised states there are important
parties operating at regional level, who successfully achieve
representation in the national parliament. This is particularly the case in
Canada and Spain.

All of these differences illustrate the danger of making naive
comparisons between institutions set in different political contexts. They
also begin to demonstrate that there is no perfect comparator for
Britain. However, this being said, there remains a lot which can be
learnt for Britain by looking at other countries' systems. Given the rapid
constitutional changes in the UK—which will reshape the form of the
state—it becomes more appropriate to consider a diverse set of
comparators which may help to indicate directions in which the UK
could develop.

COMPOSITION OF THE UPPER HOUSE: A SUMMARY

The composition of second chambers around the world, including that
of the seven countries considered in this book, was briefly discussed in
Chapter 2. In particular Table 2.1 gave information regarding the
composition of these chambers. Restricting the analysis to the seven
countries considered in later chapters, Table 3.2 summarises this, with
some additional information.

Three factors are immediately apparent from the information in the
table. First, in all but one of the countries the method of composition for
the two chambers is quite distinct. Secondly, this is realised in the
majority of countries by the second chamber not being directly elected,
whilst the lower house always is. Thirdly, the upper house in all the
countries is considerably smaller than the lower house.

Italy is the only country where the composition of the two chambers
is extremely similar. Here both chambers are directly elected using a
very similar, proportional, system. The main difference between them is
that the upper house includes a very small number of appointed and *ex
officio* members. Two other countries use direct election as the primary
means of selecting members of the upper house. However, in Australia
the upper house uses a proportional representation system, based on 12
Senators elected in each state, whilst the lower house uses a
majoritarian system based on single member constituencies. This results
in a different political balance in the two chambers. In Spain it is the
upper house which uses a more majoritarian electoral system, whilst the

Table 3.2. *Composition of seven second chambers*

	Lower house	Upper house
Australia		
Name of chamber	House of Representatives	Senate
Members	148	76
Electoral system	Majoritarian (AV)[†]	Proportional (STV)[†]
Term of office	Up to three years	Six years (elected in halves)
Canada		
Name of chamber	House of Commons	Senate
Members	301	105
Electoral system	Majoritarian (FPTP)[†]	n/a—appointed
Term of office	Up to five years	n/a—retire aged 75
France		
Name of chamber	Assemblée Nationale	Sénat
Members	577	321
Electoral system	Majoritarian (double ballot)	n/a—indirectly elected
Term of office	Up to five years	Nine years (elected in thirds)
Germany		
Name of chamber	Bundestag	Bundesrat
Members	672 (not fixed)	69
Electoral system	Proportional (AMS)[†]	n/a—indirectly elected
Term of office	Up to four years	n/a—rolling membership
Ireland		
Name of chamber	Dáil	Seanad
Members	166	60
Electoral system	Proportional (STV)[†]	n/a—indirectly elected, plus 11 appointees
Term of office	Up to five years	Up to five years
Italy		
Name of chamber	House of Deputies	Senate
Members	630	326 (not fixed)
Electoral system	Proportional (AMS)[†]	Proportional (AMS)[†] for 315 members, plus life members
Term of office	Up to five years	Up to five years
Spain		
Name of chamber	Congreso de los Diputados	Senado
Members	350	259
Electoral system	Proportional (regional list)	Semi majoritarian for 208 members, 51 indirectly elected
Term of office	Up to four years	Up to four years

[†] Abbreviations for electoral systems are as follows: AMS—additional member system, AV—alternative vote, FPTP—first past the post, STV—single transferable vote. Electoral systems, which vary in their application, are described in the sections on individual countries.

lower house is elected proportionally using a list system. The upper house also includes a sizeable number of indirectly elected members.

In other countries direct election is not used for the upper house. In Canada the upper house is entirely appointed, with no element of election used at all. Elsewhere some form of indirect election is used. Two chambers—in Ireland and France—are primarily elected by a college comprising mostly of local councillors. In Ireland the members elected in this way are intended to represent 'vocational' groups, and sit alongside members elected to represent the universities, and appointed by the Prime Minister. In France elections are geographically based, using *départements*—similar to English counties. In Germany, members of the upper house represent elected state governments, but are appointed from amongst the members of these governments. The Spanish Senado also includes around one-fifth of members who are indirectly elected by regional assemblies, whilst the majority of members are directly elected to represent provinces.

The difference in size between upper and lower chambers is also clearly seen from the table. In all seven cases the second chamber is considerably smaller than the first. The largest, in relative terms, are the French Sénat and the Spanish Senado, with the latter being around 60 per cent of the size of the lower house. In both Italy and Australia the size of the upper house is intentionally fixed at half the size of the lower house (this 'nexus' is specified in the Australian constitution). In Canada and Ireland the upper house is fixed at around one-third of the size of the lower chamber. In Germany the difference in size is at its most extreme—the Bundesrat being only just over one-tenth of the size of the Bundestag.

In the following sections the composition of these seven second chambers is considered in detail, while the next chapter discusses the consequences of this in terms of the kind of people who sit in the chamber. A brief historical context is also given in each case, to help fully understand the origins of the current second chamber.

AN APPOINTED HOUSE: CANADA

The Canadian Senate is the oldest amongst the seven second chambers being considered here. It is also—by no accident—the closest in composition to the British House of Lords and very similar to the new, transitional, UK upper house. It therefore seems an appropriate starting point.

The federation of Canada was created in 1867 by the coming together of four self-governing British colonies—Ontario, Quebec, New

Brunswick and Nova Scotia. The constitution of the new state, the British North America Act, was an Act of the British parliament. The bicameral legislature which formed a key institution of the state was closely modelled on its British parent.

In the run up to federation there were lengthy discussions about the form the upper house should take. It was agreed that it should represent the provinces, and there were proposals that it be elected subject to age and property qualifications. However this was rejected in favour of an appointed house, with the same qualifications. This was intended to create a wise and conservative house, a proper forum for 'sober second thought' in the best traditions of Britain and France.

Proposals that all provinces should be given an equal number of seats in the upper house were resisted by the large provinces of Ontario and Quebec. However, the British North America Act stated that the 'divisions' of Canada would each have equal representation. Ontario and Quebec each formed a division, with the third comprising the provinces of New Brunswick and Nova Scotia. The original distribution of seats in the Senate gave 24 seats to each division, with the two smaller provinces having 12 seats each. The institution thus conformed roughly to the classic model of a federal upper house. In 1915 a fourth division was created, from the western provinces of British Columbia, Alberta, Saskatchewan, and Manitoba, which had since joined the federation. These provinces were given six seats each. When Prince Edward Island joined it was given four seats—two being taken from each of New Brunswick and Nova Scotia, and when Newfoundland joined in 1949 it was given six seats. This made up the full complement of ten provinces of Canada, but by this point any principle of equal representation had been broken. The final additions were the two territories of Yukon and the North West, each given one Senate seat in 1975, and the new territory of Nunavut, given a seat in 1999. This brought the Senate to its current total of 105 members.

The original property qualifications that applied to Senate membership are now relatively meaningless—to be a member you must have property worth $4,000 and assets of at least $4,000. You must also be at least 30 years old—compared to 18 years old for membership of the lower house—and be resident in the province that you represent.

Appointments are made by the Governor General of Canada (the representative of the Queen), but in practice are in the hands of the Prime Minister. Appointments were for life (as in the House of Lords) until 1965, when a retirement age of 75 was introduced. This reform has taken a good deal of time to work through the system—in 1997 the Senate still included one member aged 91. However, the last life

Senator—Orville Phillips—took voluntary retirement when he reached 75 in May 1999.

Unlike appointments in Britain there is no tradition in Canada for appointing from outside the governing party, and few independents are appointed. Neither are there any selection criteria, apart from the legal qualifications listed above. Senate appointments are therefore 'the choicest plum in the patronage basket' for the Prime Minister amongst his party (Jackson and Jackson 1998: 330). This has caused concern in Canada, and accusations that Senate seats are traded for party donations. Such accusations are corroborated by the fact that governments often leave Senate seats vacant for long periods—the most extreme recent example being six years—whilst potential candidates vie for attention within their party (Forsey 1988). Seats are always filled shortly before the general election if there is any danger that the government will lose power.

Because ministers must be members of the Canadian parliament, but may fulfil this through being members of the Senate, appointment is a safe means for Prime Ministers to bring unelected members into government. This route is increasingly discredited, however, due to the low esteem in which the Senate is held. Another alternative is to appoint an elder MP to the Senate in order to make room in the House of Commons for a budding minister. Prime Minister Trudeau did this mid-term in order to promote his ex-secretary Jim Coutts to the ministry in 1981. However, the Canadian electorate gave their verdict on this behaviour when Coutts lost the by-election in the previously safe Liberal seat (Landes 1987).

Although the size of the Canadian Senate is generally fixed, with a set number of Senators per province, there is a formula by which the size of the house may be extended in extreme circumstances. This allows a Prime Minister to appoint additional Senators in the event of a serious deadlock between the two chambers of parliament. In the face of consistent hostility from the Senate an additional four or eight Senators—one or two from each of the four main divisions—may be appointed. No further appointments may then be made from the provinces involved until the Senate has fallen back below its standard size. This provision has been used only once, by Conservative Prime Minister Mulroney in 1990.[4]

---

[4] See Chapter 6 for details.

A DIRECTLY ELECTED SENATE I: AUSTRALIA

Like Canada, Australia is a federation which resulted from the coming together of six self-governing British colonies: New South Wales, Victoria, Queensland, Western Australia, South Australia, and Tasmania. By the time of federation all six colonies had their own established bicameral parliaments (Sharman 1988).[5]

Thus the debates leading to federation, which were held between politicians representing governments of the future states, were influenced by both a legacy of bicameralism and a wish to protect state powers. As in the US, negotiations between small and large states were played out through the design of the bicameral system:

The single most contentious issue of the Australian founders, and the one that took up the most space in the convention debates and almost caused the break-up of both the 1891 and 1897–8 conventions, was the design of the Senate. (Galligan 1995: 75)

The four smaller states fought against the Westminster model which was proposed by New South Wales and Victoria, and would have resulted in a dominant lower house. Instead they demanded equal state representation in an upper house with equal powers, as a condition for their involvement (Chalmers and Hutchison 1983). Equal representation was grudgingly accepted by larger states as a price worth paying for federation, but the final agreement gave marginally more powers to the lower house (Cumming Thom 1988). The result is a hybrid system built on the Westminster and US models.

The Senate had six representatives elected from each state, with half elected every three years. The elections initially used the British 'first past the post' system, but changed, along with those to the lower house, to a preferential voting system in 1919.[6] Each state formed one large constituency for Senate elections, and generally returned members who all represented the same party, due to the majoritarian electoral system. This tended to result in an even larger majority for government in the Senate than in the lower house. In 1946 the Labor government had benefited from this and held 33 of the 36 seats, but feared the loss of

[5] Originally all state upper houses were designed to act as a conservative counterbalance—either being nominated or elected on a limited property-based franchise. All states now have directly elected upper houses, with the exception of Queensland which abolished its upper house in 1922 (Bennett 1992).

[6] The electoral system used for the Australian lower house is now the 'alternative vote', based on single member constituencies. In this system voters indicate their order of preference for candidates and the first to reach 50 per cent of the votes—with second and subsequent preferences transferred if necessary—wins the seat.

these seats at the forthcoming general election. The government took action to protect its Senate seats, by introducing proportional representation for the Senate, at the same time as increasing the size of the chamber to 60—with 10 members from each state. As expected the government lost the election but managed to retain most of its Senate seats. However, in doing so it had introduced a system which would fundamentally and permanently change the nature of Senate and its relationship with government. In 1983 the size of the Senate was increased again (for similar reasons) so that each state now has 12 seats. This followed the addition of two seats each for the Northern Territory and Australian Capital Territory, bringing the total number of Senators to 76.

The Senate continues to be elected in parts. State members serve fixed six-year terms, with six members returned in each state every three years (while the four territory members serve fixed three-year terms and are renewed at each election). Elections to the lower house must be held at least every three years. Governments usually work to ensure that elections to the two houses are held on the same day, in order that Senate elections cannot act as a mid-term test.[7]

The two chambers are elected using different electoral systems, which results in a much more proportional result in the Senate than the lower house. The alternative vote system used in the House of Representatives generally results in one party gaining an overall parliamentary majority, while small parties and independents have little chance to win seats. The electoral system for the Senate is a form of the 'single transferable vote', with each state or territory acting as a multi-member constituency.[8] This system tends to hand the balance of power to small parties and independents. This is discussed further in Chapter 4.

---

[7] The constitution allows elections for the Senate to take place up to one year before a Senate renewal, alongside a general election, but the old Senate will continue to sit until the end of its term. For example Senate elections were held alongside the general election of October 1998, with the new Senators not due to take their seats until 1 July 1999.

[8] The Australian Senate system is not the pure single transferable vote, since voters can opt to support ranked party lists. The pure system (as used in Ireland) does not allow this— voters must instead rank candidates in order of preference, which may encourage cross party voting and support for independents. This system was employed in Australia until 1984, when 'above the line' voting was introduced, whereby voters for the Senate can support a party list. Voters who wish to support individual candidates must now vote 'below the line', and all preferences must be used, or a ballot paper is considered spoilt. This is a strong disincentive given the large number of candidates on the ballot paper (69 in New South Wales in 1998, for example) and many voters now opt for party lists.

A DIRECTLY ELECTED SENATE II: ITALY

The Italian Senate comes from a different tradition, since modern Italy was established in 1848 as a unitary state. The parliament created was bicameral, with the lower house elected on a very limited franchise (some constituencies having as few as 30 electors) and the upper house, the *Senato del Regno*, being appointed by the king. The design of the upper house was influenced by the House of Lords—appointments were on the basis of 'specific titles', for life and with no limit on numbers (Lodici 1999). As democracy grew and the franchise was widened, the appointment of members of the Senato in practice passed over to the government.

There followed a break in parliamentary democracy during the rule of Mussolini (1922–43). During this period parliament's powers were severely curtailed, and its composition became dependent on the 'corporate' model.[9] This was a cornerstone of the fascist state and went on to influence the Irish upper house.

The new Italian constitution was agreed in 1948, following the fall of Mussolini and the Second World War. This marked a return to parliamentary democracy, and there was a desire to spread power as widely as possible and include many checks and balances in the system. Naturally this implied the re-establishment of a bicameral parliament, and it was also influential in both the choice of a highly proportional electoral system and the inclusion in the constitution of devolved powers to new regional assemblies. There were some voices in the constituent assembly who proposed that the new second chamber—the 'Senato della Repubblica'—should be based on corporate representation. This proposal was initially supported by the Christian Democrats. However, it was dropped because it was seen as too similar to the fascist regime, and too difficult to implement (Rescigno 1995). Thus the words finally included in the constitution stated that 'the Senate of the Republic is elected on a regional basis'. The membership of the Senate was to be linked to the development of autonomy in Italy's 20 regions.

However, as regional assemblies were yet to be established, it was agreed that members of the Senato would initially be directly elected

---

[9] The lower house was replaced by a chamber of 400 members, who were put to the electorate *en bloc*. These individuals had been selected by the Fascist Grand Council from a list of 1,000 names proposed by professional and social organisations. In 1939 the house ceased to be elected at all, and instead comprised members of the Grand Council and others from the National Council of Corporations. (*Historical Dictionary of Fascist Italy*, P. V. Cannistraro (ed.), Westport, Connecticut: Greenwood, 1982.)

using a list system of proportional representation, based on regional boundaries. The term of office for the Senato would be six years. This compared to five years for the *Camera dei Deputati* (lower house), which was elected using a similar proportional system based on national lists.

After 1948 the development of regional government was slow. The ruling Christian Democrats feared that regional assemblies would be dominated by the Communists, and enabling legislation to put the assemblies in place was consistently blocked in parliament (Hine 1996). In the end autonomy in all regions was not progressed until 1970.[10] By this time the directly elected Senato had become a permanent feature.

Today the upper house has 315 directly elected members—exactly half the number in the lower house. Representation of the regions is based on population, and ranges between one member for Valle d'Aosta to 47 for Lombardia. The electoral system changed following a 1993 referendum which reduced the degree of proportionality in the systems for both the upper and lower house.[11] The lower house now uses a form of 'additional member' system based on 475 single member constituencies, with 155 additional members to create proportionality allocated in 27 areas (Gambetta and Warner 1996). The system for the Senato is also based on single member constituencies, but proportionality is achieved instead through allocating seats to the 'best losers' from the under-represented parties in the 20 regions. Thus all upper house members have a link to a constituency, and some constituencies have two—or even three—representatives.

The electoral cycle has also fallen into step with that for the lower house. Although the constitution gave the upper house a six-year term and the lower house a five-year term, the Senato was dissolved a year early to coincide with the elections to the lower chamber in 1953, and again in 1958. In the end a constitutional amendment in 1963 shortened its term to five years. Consequently elections for the two chambers have always been held on the same day. Italian governments were sensitive to the same concerns as Australian governments—that upper house elections would be subject to 'mid-term blues' and result in a chamber hostile to the incumbent government.

Although it is renewed on the same day using a similar electoral system, the Senato does retain some distinctive characteristics as compared to the lower house. As in many upper houses the minimum

---

[10] Five regions with 'special' status developed their assemblies earlier: Sicily, Sardinia, Trentino-Alto Adige, Friuli-Venezia Giulia, and Valle d'Aosta.

[11] The Italians remain dissatisfied with their electoral system, and there are proposals to abolish all proportionality and move to a British-style majoritarian system. A referendum on this issue failed in April 1999 due to low turnout.

age requirement for members is higher than that for the lower house—40 as compared to 25. The voting age for the upper chamber is also higher, being 25 for the Senato, but 18 for the lower house. These result in some marginal differences. However, one of the most important differences between the composition of the chambers is that the Senato contains a small number of unelected members. These members come in two categories. First, ex- Presidents of the Republic, who are entitled by right to sit in the Senate for life. There are currently three members—Francesco Cossiga, Giovanni Leone, and Oscar Luigi Scalfaro—holding seats in this capacity. In addition each President is entitled to appoint up to five life members of the Senate, although President Scalfaro (1992–9) chose not to exercise this right, seeing it as undemocratic.[12] Currently there are eight members holding seats in this capacity, making a total of 11 unelected members in the 326-strong upper house.

The resultant membership of the Senato is very similar to that for the lower house. Perhaps the most important difference between the two is their size. The smaller size of the upper house makes its membership rather less proportional than that in the lower house, so that the Senato contains fewer representatives of small parties. It also benefits from the general attributes of smaller parliamentary chambers—operating more efficiently than the more cumbersome lower house.

Whilst the initial aspiration in Italy was to have an upper house with a distinct regional membership, a series of modifications have resulted in something which is almost a carbon copy of the lower house. This sets it apart from the Australian upper house as a very different model. This similarity between the Italian chambers also extends to their powers, as discussed in later chapters. It raises questions about the 'value added' of a second chamber too similar to the first—an issue which is discussed in Chapter 12.

THE VERY FEDERAL HOUSE: GERMANY

The German upper house was born of a federal system, but has developed in a very different way to its counterparts in Canada and Australia. Modern German federalism began in 1871, with the coming together of 25 self-governing states. However, before this the German Confederation of 1815–66 and North German Federation of 1867–71 had

---

[12] The number of appointments which a President can make has actually been disputed, as some interpret the constitution to mean that five appointed members may be included in total (Rescigno 1995).

already established a structure which is clearly visible in the upper house today.

The original federal chamber dates back to the first of these periods when it formed the only constitutional organ of the confederation. The chamber was composed of ambassadors from all the member states. Each state held between one and four votes, which were cast as blocks. A similar institution then existed after 1866, and again after 1871. The 1871 chamber was—for the first time—named the Bundesrat, literally meaning 'federal council'. It sat alongside a lower house, the Reichstag, which was elected by adult males. After the First World War the Weimar Republic again included a bicameral parliament where the upper house represented the states. In this parliament the state of Prussia was dominant, its population of 42 million entitling it to 26 of the 66 seats in the upper house (Patzelt 1999).

As in Italy the advent of fascism resulted in a dismantling of parliamentary structures. This applied not only at national level but also to state parliaments. The establishment of the modern Bundesrat therefore dates to the agreement of the post-war constitution of the Federal Republic of Germany, which reinstated national and state parliaments. This is set down in Germany's constitution, the Basic Law.[13]

The modern Bundesrat continues the tradition of being a states' house. The Basic Law states that 'the Länder [states] shall participate through the Bundesrat in the legislative process and administration of the Federation'. It is one of the five permanent constitutional bodies of the German federation—the others being the Bundestag (lower house), the federal government, the Constitutional Court and the President. The membership of the house was modified in 1990 at the time of German reunification, to accommodate the five Länder of the former East Germany. Apart from this the organisation, powers, and functions of the chamber remain as they were in 1949.

The chamber has 69 seats, which makes it only a little over one-tenth of the size of the lower house.[14] Seats are allocated to Länder in a system that takes some account of population, but is designed to prevent the

---

[13] The Basic Law is so named because the framers considered it a temporary document which awaited the reunification of Germany. In fact it remains in place post-unification.

[14] Elections for the lower house use the additional member system, with half the members representing single member constituencies, and the remainder allocated to the parties to create proportionality. If proportionality cannot be achieved through this mechanism, further additional members may be added.

dominance of the chamber by one large state, as happened previously.[15] This brought the system closer to the classic US federal model.[16] The members are appointed by state governments, from amongst their own members. These always include the Minister-President of the Land. Other members of the delegation usually include the federal affairs minister, finance minister, plus as many others as there are seats. Länder may also appoint deputy members, who have identical rights to full members whenever they deputise. Thus in practice all members of the Land cabinet will be either members or deputy members of the Bundesrat, and the seats at each plenary session will be taken by the ministers most relevant to the topic of debate.

The number of votes a Land has in the chamber is equivalent to its number of seats. However, in a system inherited from the original Bundesrat, these votes must be cast as a block by each state. This means that even coalition governments at state level—of which there are many—may not split their votes.[17] Unlike in other chambers members of the Bundesrat do not sit in party groups, but the chamber is instead organised in seating blocks that are each occupied by one state delegation. Links to the governments of the states are strengthened by the fact that the chamber is never dissolved, but membership changes on a rolling basis as membership of state cabinets changes. These are some of the factors that contribute to making the Bundesrat 'the very federal house' (Patzelt 1999).

THE HOUSE OF LOCAL GOVERNMENT: FRANCE

The origin of the French Sénat has many similarities to that of the House of Lords. The French parliament originally had three chambers, representing the aristocracy, the clergy, and the people. A break in this tradition resulted from the French revolution, which temporarily created a unicameral state, followed in 1795 by introduction of an

[15] No Land (state) has fewer than three seats in the Bundesrat, those with a population of two to six million have four, a population of six to seven million brings five, and a population of more than seven million entitles a state to six seats.

[16] At the time the Basic Law was being negotiated it was argued by the SPD (Social Democratic Party) that the US model should be more closely followed, including and upper house either elected by the parliaments of the states or directly elected by the people. This would better follow the principle of 'separation of powers' than the classic German model, which included representatives of the executives of the states in the upper house. This option, however, was rejected (Patzelt 1999).

[17] Because of this the pattern of voting in the Bundesrat can form a central part of the coalition agreement at state level. This is only one indication of the centrality of the Bundesrat to the federal system.

elected second chamber 'due to the excesses of the single house' (Mastias 1999: 163). Under this system the two houses were elected at a single election, but separated afterwards into the *Conseil des Cinq-Cents*—comprising 500 members—and the *Conseil des Anciens*—comprising 250 members who had to be over 40 years of age. The latter had the function of reviewing legislation (Smith 1996). The restoration of the monarchy also saw the restoration of the tradition of an aristocratic upper house. The *Chambre des Pairs* (Chamber of Peers) existed until 1848, and until 1830 appointments were hereditary.

After another brief period of unicameralism and another nominated upper house, the Sénat established under the third republic in 1875 became the first precursor to the modern house. The role of the third republic Sénat was to bind local and national government together, and its members were elected by members of the lower house and local councillors. The Sénat electoral college was organised by *départements* (similar to English counties), with one-third of members elected every three years. The new upper house had equal powers to the lower house (Smith 1996). It therefore became an important part of the powerful third republic parliament, which overturned cabinets at an average rate of one every eight months (Safran 1998). It was during this period that the Sénat 'became synonymous with a rural France hostile to progressive ideas'—an association which continues today (Mastias 1999: 163).

France too suffered an interruption to the functioning of its democratic structures during the Second World War. When the new post-war constitution was under discussion, the desirability of an upper house was a subject for debate. This was not favoured by the left, given the conservative influence of previous French upper houses, and the constitution that was put to a referendum in April 1946 proposed a unicameral parliament. However, this referendum failed. A second referendum was held in October that year on a redrafted constitution, this time including a bicameral parliament. It was successful. This fourth republic constitution included a powerful parliament like its predecessor, although the upper chamber, the *Conseil de la Republique*, was 'a pale copy of the Third Republic Senate' (Safran 1998: 8).

The present Sénat dates back to the fifth republic constitution of 1958, agreed under General de Gaulle. However, it owes much to the third republic constitution. The Sénat comprises 321 members, compared to 577 in the lower house, the *Assemblée Nationale*. Members of the upper house must be at least 35 years old, whilst their counterparts in the lower house may be as young as 23. Sénat elections are organised in France's 100 *départements*, with each *département* electing between one and 12 Senators, depending on population.[18] Most Senators are elected by a complex electoral college, comprising members of the lower house, regional, provincial and local councillors within each *département*.[19] One-third of Senators are elected every three years, and all Senators serve nine-year terms. Each *département* has a senatorial election every nine years, with one-third of *départements* (organised alphabetically) electing members every three years. The Sénat is thus never dissolved.

In addition to this vast majority of Senators, 12 are elected to represent French residents abroad. This is a group that is not represented in the lower house. These members are elected by the Higher Council of French People Overseas, which itself comprises 150 members who are mostly directly elected by French people living outside France.

The electoral college for the main body of Senators is heavily dominated by local councillors. France has almost 37,000 local authorities—or 'communes'—which is more than every other EU member state put together. There are around 550,000 French local councillors in total. Around 145,000 people are involved in the choice of Senators, over 95 per cent of whom are representatives of the *communes*. At the 1998 elections a typical middle-sized *département*, the Dordogne, had a total 1,299 electors—four lower house deputies, 12 regional councillors, 50 departmental councillors, and 1,233 local councillors—electing two Senators. Elections take place in September, and the relatively small number of electors allows candidates to canvass individual supporters for votes. Election day itself is a Sunday, and requires the so-called *grands électeurs* to gather in the capital of the *département* to cast their votes.

The electoral system for the Sénat is biased in many ways towards underpopulated rural areas and towards politically conservative forces. First, the smaller *communes* are over-represented in the electoral colleges. Ninety per cent of *communes* represent fewer than 2,000 inhabitants (some representing only a few dozen), whilst half the French population lives in the two per cent of largest *communes*. Hence the vast majority of councillors represent sparsely populated rural areas. The electoral college takes this into account to some extent. In the smaller *communes* which represent fewer than 9,000 inhabitants, membership of the electoral college is restricted to between one and 12 members (depending on population). For *communes* with 9,000–30,000 inhabitants, all councillors of the commune (i.e. 29 to 69 people, depending on

---

[18] These include 13 members representing overseas *départements*.

[19] Elected regional councillors were added to the college when they came into existence in 1986.

population) are part of the college. In the largest *communes* one additional delegate is allowed for each 1,000 inhabitants. This still results in greater representation in the electoral college for sparsely populated areas—more than half the electors for the Sénat represent *communes* with fewer than 3,500 inhabitants, where fewer than a quarter of the population reside (Rousseau 1995).

This system involves a two-stage election in both the smallest and the largest *communes*, where councillors are first involved in an election to choose members of the electoral college. This is where the second distortion in the system comes in. For small *communes* this election uses the classic French 'double ballot' system, which is used for the lower house and presidential elections.[20] This is a majoritarian system which effectively results in the majority group on the council choosing all the delegates. In these areas parties of the right will tend to do well. The *communes* with over 30,000 inhabitants represent the urban areas, and will thus tend to include higher representation of left-wing parties. However, here members of the electoral college are chosen using a proportional system. This does not allow the left to redress the imbalance from the small *communes*.

The allocation of Senators to *départements* further biases representation towards less populated rural areas. Representation is on the basis of one Senator for the first 150,000 population, with one additional Senator for each additional 250,000. This allocation of seats is however not based on current population, but in most areas has been fixed since 1958. Since then there has been significant movement to the towns. Although there have been reforms to increase the number of seats for underrepresented areas, no *département* has ever had its number of seats reduced.

The final distortion within the system is the complex means by which the Senators themselves are elected. In most *départements* the elections for the Sénat itself, like those for the electoral college, use a double ballot, majoritarian, system. This applies in the 85 *départements* that elect between one and four Senators. The 15 remaining *départements*, which elect five or more Senators and represent more densely populated areas, use a proportional system. This combination of factors has a major political impact on the Sénat, ensuring that it has never had a Socialist majority since its inception. These issues are further discussed in the last section of this chapter, and in Chapter 4.

---

[20] Under this system there are two rounds of voting. In the first round a number of candidates may stand. In the second round all candidates except the two with the highest number of votes are eliminated. A second ballot is then held between the two remaining candidates.

A MIXED CHAMBER: SPAIN

Over the last 200 years Spain has been through both bicameral and unicameral phases. Like France and Britain this has included a period, from 1834 to 1869, when the second chamber was an aristocratic house. Spain has also experimented, from 1869 to 1876, with a federal second chamber influenced by the US model. This gave every province of Spain four Senators, irrespective of population. In 1876 a new second chamber combined members appointed by the king with *ex officio* members and others elected by corporations and major taxpayers. The conservatism of this and previous upper houses led to a unicameral phase from 1931 under the new republican constitution (Juberías 1999). General Franco seized power in 1936 and a bicameral assembly of sorts—the lower house being a corporatist assembly in which local government was also represented, and the upper chamber representing the party elite—existed during his dictatorship.

The modern Senado dates to the new democratic constitution of 1978, agreed after the death of Franco. It is thus the youngest upper chamber considered here, and the product of a remarkable transition to democracy. During this transitional period a bicameral constituent assembly was established, and this largely set the tone for the permanent Senado which followed. The design of the transitional house owed much to the 1869 constitution, consisting largely of members directly elected from the provinces, but with one-fifth of members appointed by the king.[21]

Decentralisation of the state was one of the biggest issues during negotiation of the new constitution. This was played out partly in the design of the Senado. There was considerable pressure for a more devolved state structure, following the centralised Franco regime, with immediate demands from the three 'historic' regions of Catalonia, Galicia and the Basque Country to have their autonomy returned.[22] As

---

[21] In a situation similar to that which resulted in the Weatherill amendment (see Chapter 1) these appointed seats helped ease the passage of the new institutional structure through the conservative upper house. Upper house members co-operated in the belief that the appointed element would allow some of their number to remain. In the event very few did, and the new house which followed replaced the appointed seats by representatives of the country's new regions. In contrast the lower house, which had already been partially democratised in the 1960s and 1970s to include one-third of elected members, saw some of its members re-elected to the constituent assembly's lower house.

[22] Under the republican constitution of 1931, calls for more autonomy had been granted. A Catalan parliament was created in 1932 and a Basque parliament in 1936. A statute was also agreed for Galicia, but never enacted. All these developments were suppressed by the Franco regime (Heywood 1995).

well as the pressure from the regions themselves, the left were eager for devolution as part of a new pluralist constitution. Although they were traditionally hostile to upper chambers, given their conservative history in the Spanish state, they were prepared to accept an upper house if it represented the regions (Giol *et al.* 1990). In the end the design of the Senado, alongside the rest of the constitution, was a compromise between the interests of left and right, in order to maintain consensus and a peaceful transition.

In the end the new constitution, passed overwhelmingly in a referendum in 1978, included a Senado with a mixed membership. The constitution states that 'the Senate is the chamber of territorial representation'. Like the upper house of the constituent assembly, it included 208 members directly elected by the provinces. These would be joined by members representing the 'autonomous communities' at regional level as and when these were established.

Each of Spain's 47 mainland provinces is represented by four seats in the Senado, irrespective of population. In addition the islands elect either one or three Senators each, and the African cities of Ceuta and Melilla each elect two. Elections have so far taken place on the same day as elections to the *Congreso de los Diputados* (lower house), as both chambers must be elected at least every four years. The membership qualifications for the two houses are identical.

The lower house has 350 members.[23] Its elections also use provincial boundaries, but employ a proportional system based on party lists. Whilst all provinces have four seats in the Senado the number in the lower house ranges from one to 34. The Senado also uses a semi-majoritarian, rather than proportional, electoral system. Under this system electors have three votes and may cast them either for individuals or a party list. The three candidates with the highest number of votes are elected, and the fourth seat goes to the next highest ranking party. The combination of electoral system and distribution of seats for the two chambers makes the results quite different. As elections have always been held on the same day, the party winning the lower house elections in the province usually wins three of the four seats in the Senado (only when two parties get a very similar number of votes will the distribution be different). In the 1996 elections, for example, all 47 main provinces followed this 3:1 pattern of seats in the Senado (Juberías 1999). This tends to deliver a larger majority for the

---

[23] The number of seats in the lower house is allocated on the basis of a minimum of two seats per province (one for the cities of Ceuta and Melilla), with the number of additional seats dependent on population. Population changes may result in minor changes in the number of seats.

government in the Senado than in the lower house. However, there is also some bias in favour of the right in the upper house, due to the over-representation of rural provinces. This is discussed in Chapter 4.

In addition to the representation of provinces, the Senado now includes 51 members representing autonomous communities. These members have been added gradually as autonomy has spread from one region to the next. The constitution allowed for devolved assemblies to be created, based on one or more provinces, if certain conditions were met. However it was not anticipated that autonomous communities would spring up in every region as they have—Spain having been gripped by what has been described as 'autonomy fever' after 1979 (Heywood 1995: 144). Following the establishment of devolved assemblies in Catalonia and the Basque country in 1979, Galicia, Andalucia, Asturias, and Cantabria followed in 1981. The remaining mainland provinces achieved devolution in 1982–3, and there are now 17 autonomous communities, covering every province of Spain.[24]

Autonomous community Senators are elected indirectly, by the members of the devolved assembly. Each assembly is entitled to elect at least one member, plus one more for each million inhabitants of the region. Thus the number of Senators per autonomous community varies between one and seven. The rules for electing autonomous community Senators are devolved, and thus vary from one area to another. However, it is required that the representation of parties is proportional to that in the autonomous community assembly.[25] Eleven of the 16 autonomous communities require that their Senators are elected from amongst the members of the assembly, and of the 51 such members in September 1999, 28 were members of the assembly that elected them.[26] These members add a degree of unpredictability to the political makeup of the Senado, as they are re-elected following regional assembly elections, which are staggered.

[24] The cities of Ceuta and Melilla also became 'autonomous cities' in 1995.

[25] The degree to which this representation is proportional has been the subject of some dispute. For example, in 1991 the Popular Party (PP) formed the largest group in the assembly for the autonomous community of Madrid, but the government was formed by a coalition of the Socialist Party (PSOE) and the United Left (IU). The assembly's ruling board decided that the PSOE and PP should be given two each of Madrid's Senate seats (with the IU being given one seat), despite the greater representation of the PP. The PP took the matter to the Constitutional Court, who ruled that the representation need only be 'broadly proportional' and was thus acceptable. In the subsequent elections to the assembly the PP won 54 seats to the PSOE's 32, and took three of the five Senate seats, leaving one each for the PSOE and IU.

[26] The Basque Nationalist Party (PNV) forbid their members to sit in both the Basque chamber and the Senado, as they consider the two roles to be incompatible.

Thus the upper chamber that the Spanish have ended up with is a 'hybrid model' (Juberías 1999: 267). This is a fair representation of the current structure of the Spanish state. The traditional provinces are being overtaken by the new autonomous communities, and the process of devolution to these new territories continues. Spain is probably the closest comparator to the 'quasi-federal' state which is emerging in Britain. It is therefore highly relevant to look at the Spanish Senado when considering the reform of the House of Lords.

THE 'VOCATIONAL' HOUSE: IRELAND

The Irish parliament once again begins with a history and tradition not only similar to Britain's, but at times overlapping. The original Irish parliament which sat from 1264 was tricameral, with a House of Commons, a House of Lords and a third house representing clerical proctors. This third chamber was abolished in 1536. Thus for 300 years the British and Irish parliaments had parallel bicameral structures, each comprising a House of Commons and House of Lords. The two parliaments later became directly linked—when the Irish parliament was subsumed by Westminster in 1800. Irish representatives who took their seats in London included 28 Irish lords and four Protestant Irish bishops in the House of Lords. The advent of home rule brought the return of two-chamber parliaments to Ireland. Partition in 1920 provided both north and south with bicameral parliaments.[27]

Under the Irish Free State constitution of 1922 the Seanad (Senate) was given a role similar to that of many upper houses in federal states— the role of binding the different communities of Ireland together (Dooge 1987). Half its membership was appointed by the Taoiseach (Prime Minister) as a means of ensuring that the unionist minority were represented in parliament. The other half were intended to be directly elected, but as a transitional measure were elected by members of the lower house in 1922. However, when elections took place in 1925, they attracted so few voters that this plan was subsequently abandoned. After this the system was changed so that the electorate was the combined membership of the Dáil and the outgoing Seanad (Coakley and Laver 1997). The elections of 1925 were to be the only ones to the Irish upper house ever conducted on a universal franchise.

The nationalist Fianna Fáil government elected in 1932 faced considerable difficulties with the Seanad. The house included a number

---

[27] The Northern Irish upper house existed at Stormont until that parliament was dissolved in 1972 (Coakley and Laver 1997).

of nominees with links to the British establishment and, for example, blocked legislation to remove the parliamentarians' oath of allegiance to the king. Such were the frustrations of the government that they brought forward a Seanad Abolition Bill in 1935. This was forced through without the consent of the upper house, despite the use of its full delaying power (Dooge 1987). Thus Ireland entered a short period of unicameralism.

The current Irish constitution was passed by referendum in 1937. Due to the need to maximise support for the document amongst all communities, the government reluctantly proposed the reinstatement of a bicameral parliament. However Éamon De Valera, then Taoiseach, was not prepared to allow a hostile and powerful upper house. The design of the Seanad was influenced by a papal encyclical of 1931 which proposed 'as an alternative to class conflict, an institutionalisation of sectoral divisions based essentially on groupings of occupations and of other major social interests' (Coakley 1993: 136). At the time, such 'vocationalism' or 'corporatism' was popular across Europe, with a corporate chamber sitting in Mussolini's Italy (see above) and a similar chamber existing in Portugal. Francoist Spain would later also adopt a variation on this model.

De Valera used these models to create a new Seanad which 'paid lip-service' to vocationalism, whilst ensuring that the government would have a permanent majority in the upper house (Hussey 1993: 74). The membership of the Seanad would be in three sections. The majority, 43 of the members, would be elected to represent vocational categories. Another six would be elected to represent Ireland's two oldest universities (which had held seats in the British House of Commons until 1920 and in the Dáil under the Free State constitution). An additional 11 members would be appointed by the Taoiseach. Once combined with the electoral mechanism for the vocational seats, the appointed element would ensure a majority for the government in the 60-member house. This system remains largely unchanged today.

The 166 members of the Irish lower house, the Dáil, are elected by the 'single transferable vote' (STV) system of proportional representation. This, like the original design of the Seanad, was adopted in 1921 to ensure that Protestant and unionist majorities were represented in the lower house. The system allows voters to rank candidates in order of preference in multi-member constituencies and is associated with both pluralism and individuality of candidates. The same system is used for all elections in Ireland, including the indirect elections to the Seanad.

Seanad elections are linked to the renewal of the Dáil, and the eligibility conditions for members are identical. The constitution states that the Seanad must be elected no more than 90 days after the Dáil is dissolved. This generally results in elections to the Seanad around two months after the general election, with the appointed members being announced shortly afterwards.

Table 3.3. *Vocational panels for the Irish Seanad*

Panel name	Members elected	Min. elected from each subpanel
Language, culture, literature, art, and education	5	2
Agriculture, fisheries, and allied interests	11	4
Labour, organised and unorganised	11	4
Industry, commerce, banking, engineering, and architecture	9	3
Public administration and social services	7	3

Source: Coakley (1993).

The system of elections to the Seanad is relatively complex. There are five vocational 'panels'—listed in Table 3.3. Each of these has between five and 11 members, elected by the same electoral college. This electoral college comprises members of the new Dáil, members of the outgoing Seanad, and all local councillors in Ireland.[28] In 1997 this amounted to an electorate of 992 people (Coakley and Manning 1998). Nominations to the panels come from two sources: vocational groups themselves and members of the Dáil and Seanad. Thus each panel is divided into two 'sub-panels', generally known as the 'Oireachtas' (parliament) sub-panel and the 'nominating bodies' sub-panel. The members elected must include a minimum number from each sub-

---

[28] Prior to 1947 the electorate was limited to members of the Dáil and seven members of each county and borough council—in 1938 this was 354 people. It also treated all members of panels as one single constituency. The combination of these two meant that the electoral quota was a little over eight votes—leading to accusations of corruption. Consequently the system was changed (Coakley 1993).

panel, totalling at least 16 from each. This and the total number of members elected from each panel is shown in Table 3.3.

The 'nominating bodies' for the vocational panels consist of voluntary organisations, employers' groups, trade unions, and other non-profit making bodies. These must have objectives relating to the interests of the particular panel subject, or represent people having relevant experience or knowledge. An annually revised register of these nominating bodies is kept by the Clerk of the Seanad and in 1997 included 89 organisations. These included:

- *Culture and education panel* (32 members): Irish Georgian Society, Irish National Teachers' Organisation, Law Society of Ireland, Royal College of Surgeons in Ireland, Royal Irish Academy of Music;
- *Agriculture panel* (11 members): Irish Thoroughbred Breeders' Association, Irish Greyhound Owners and Breeders' Federation;
- *Labour panel* (two members): Irish Congress of Trade Unions, Irish Conference of Professional and Service Associations;
- *Industry and commerce panel* (35 members): Insurance Institute of Ireland, Chartered Institute of Transport, Royal Institute of Architects, Irish Hotels Federation, Irish Road Haulage Association;
- *Administration panel* (nine members): Irish County Councils General Council, Irish Kidney Association, Irish Wheelchair Association.

The number of nominating bodies for each panel varies considerably, but with members of some panels entitled to nominate more than one member, the net result is that the number of seats is considerably oversubscribed. For the Oireachtas sub-panels, a candidate must be nominated by at least four members of the incoming Dáil and outgoing Seanad, with each parliamentarian entitled to nominate only one person. Because these nominations are effectively controlled by the parties, they tend to be more closely limited to the number of seats available.[29] For example, in 1997 there were 38 Oireachtas nominees, compared with 80 from the nominating bodies. The splitting of votes between the nominating bodies' nominees, coupled with the fact that the Oireachtas nominees tend to have a higher profile, means that the latter generally win a larger number of seats.

In order to be eligible to stand for a vocational panel, a candidate must be able to demonstrate 'knowledge and practical experience' of the

[29] There is a rule that there must be at least two more nominated candidates than available seats on each sub-panel. If this is not the case—as frequently occurs on the Oireachtas panels—the Taoiseach gets to nominate others. However, these are generally 'dummy' candidates who receive no votes. This increases the likelihood of the Oireachtas nominees being elected.

relevant field. However, this rule is interpreted loosely. It is the responsibility of the Clerk of the Seanad to verify that candidates are suitably qualified. Candidates may be disqualified on this basis, but this has not happened for many years. In practice, most candidates are not subject experts, and are actually sponsored by political parties—many of them have been MPs or parliamentary candidates in the past. This is naturally the case with Oireachtas nominees, but also applies to nominees from the non-political bodies. This represents realism on the part of the nominating bodies about who will be elected by an electoral college comprising national and local politicians. Of the 992 members of the electoral college in 1997, 794 were affiliated to one of the three main parties—Fianna Fáil, Fianna Gael, or the Labour Party (Coakley and Manning 1998).

With such a political electorate, the outcome of the elections is fairly predictable. Each political nominee knows that they must seek support from their own affiliated members, and must compete with others for the votes of councillors who are independent or represent the minor parties. As this amounts to a few hundred people to canvass, candidates will make the effort to meet all electors personally. This tour around Ireland, meeting councillors from even the smallest most rural councils, has become known as the 'Seanad trail'.[30] As Hussey (1993: 76) notes: 'it is during that campaign that local councillors come into their own, as the party powerful beat a path to their doors.'

The vote itself is by postal ballot, with each panel elected separately, by single transferable vote. Although candidates' political affiliation is not listed on the ballot paper, this will generally be known, as all the parties circulate their councillors and Oireachtas members with the names of affiliated candidates. In 1997 there were only five candidates out of a total of 118 who had no political affiliation. Three candidates on the labour panel were representatives of the Labour Party, but all other candidates represented either Fianna Fáil or Fianna Gael. Independent candidates polled, as usual, very badly. For example the president of the Royal Irish Academy, who as a point of principle is always nominated by the organisation, polled three votes (Coakley and Manning 1998). The verdict of the Irish Times on the first Seanad elections under the new constitution demonstrates that this has always been the case:

One thing appears to emerge from yesterday's proceedings—namely, that the idea of electing a Senate on a vocational basis has proved futile . . . The complete defeat of nearly every representative of the learned bodies, and of

---

[30] *Irish Times*, 22 July 1997.

those who purported to represent interests other than those which are frankly political, was a marked feature of the results (*Irish Times*, 30 March 1938).

The political balance of the winning candidates mirrors that of the electoral college, and of the lower house. It has been calculated that simply asking the parties to appoint Seanad members in the same proportion as their number of seats in the Dáil would generally make a difference of only one Seanad seat (Doherty 1996).

The right of the Taoiseach to nominate members of the Seanad cements the party control and government majority in the house. Although the 'Taoiseach's eleven' could be used to appoint independent members into the house, this rarely happens. In practice the seats are used to appoint any key party representatives who slipped through the net in the Dáil and Seanad elections. No members are appointed from the opposition parties. For example in 1997 six of the seats went to Fianna Fáil and four to the Progressive Democrats—their coalition partner.[31] Only one of the eleven appointed members was an independent—Dr Maurice Hayes, the former Northern Ireland Ombudsman.

The injection of independent members into the Seanad is thus left to the final section—that elected to represent the universities. Three of these six seats are elected by each of Ireland's two oldest universities—Trinity College Dublin and the National University of Ireland (NUI).[32] The election is again conducted by postal ballot, using the single transferable vote. The electorate comprises all graduates of the universities, which in 1997 was 93,309 for NUI and 31,210 for Trinity.[33] Candidates must be nominated by two voters and endorsed by eight others, but need have no other connection with the university concerned. Although these elections are criticised as elitist—as other universities, and non graduates, are excluded—they actually offer the broadest franchise of any of the sections selected for the Irish Seanad.[34] They also generally do result in independent candidates being elected. This is discussed in more detail in Chapter 4.

[31] Seven of these had previously sat in the Dáil or Seanad (most having failed to be re-elected in 1997) and a further two had been candidates in the Dáil elections.

[32] The latter includes University College Dublin, University College Cork, University College Galway, and associated colleges elsewhere.

[33] Trinity College has always been over-represented as compared to NUI, but this was originally considered justified as it was an almost exclusively Protestant College (Hussey 1993).

[34] Only four per cent of those who can vote in Dáil elections have a vote in Seanad elections. However, most of these are involved in the election of the university seats—the panel seats are elected by 0.04 per cent of the Dáil electorate (Doherty 1996).

UNREPRESENTATIVE HOUSES?

With the exception of the Irish Seanad, all the second chambers discussed here represent in some way the territorial units of the country—be it states in Germany or Australia, provinces in Canada, regions in Italy or *départements* in France. In Spain the Senado represents at once both provinces and autonomous communities. However, in all but one of these the representation in the upper chamber is disproportionate to population. This is a common feature of second chambers and a natural result of the classic federal system of equal representation for states. It is this factor which caused Australian Prime Minister Paul Keating to famously refer to the members of his Senate as 'unrepresentative swill'.[35] Although the Australian chamber adheres to this classic federal model, similar results occur in other countries where the representation of territorial units in the upper chamber is unequal.

Table 3.4 illustrates this trait of second chambers by looking at the most under-represented and over-represented geographical areas in five countries. Italy is omitted because the representation of regions in its upper house is strictly proportional to population. Ireland is also excluded, although there are still distortions in its system, mentioned below.

In all the countries illustrated in the table representation in the upper house is proportionately greater for underpopulated areas. Taking Australia as the first example, the state of New South Wales has more than ten times the population of Tasmania, but the same number of Senate seats. In the lower house they have 50 and five seats respectively. The three-quarters of Australians who live in the three most populous states are represented by fewer than half the seats in the Senate, whilst the residents of Tasmania, who represent only 2.6 per cent of Australians, are clearly over-represented. However, this is the original intention of a system where large state interests could easily override those of Australians in less populous areas without the protection offered by the upper house.

In Canada the classic federal model is not adhered to. Nevertheless the two central provinces, Ontario and Quebec, which have almost two-thirds of the country's population, have fewer than half the seats in the upper house. The four western provinces, with 30 per cent of the country's population have 23 per cent of Senate seats. The most extreme examples of over- and under-represented areas, shown in the table, are the provinces of Prince Edward Island and British Columbia. There are

[35] Parliamentary Debates, 5 November 1992.

roughly twenty times the number of people per Senator in British Columbia than in Prince Edward Island. In Germany the state of North Rhine Westphalia has almost 30 times the population of the state of Bremen but has only double the number of Bundesrat seats. In the lower house they are represented by 148 and six members, respectively. However, the system of Bundesrat representation is organised to at least ensure that the three largest states, representing over half the population, have over one-third of the seats. This prevents them being forced into constitutional change by a collaboration amongst small states (Sturm 1992*b*).

Table 3.4. *Over-representation of geographic areas in second chambers*

	Area	Population (000s)	Seats	Population per seat (000s)
Australia (states)				
Most over-represented	Tasmania	460	12	38
Most under-represented	New South Wales	6,000	12	500
Canada (provinces)				
Most over-represented	Prince Edward Island	137	4	34
Most under-represented	British Columbia	3,900	6	650
France (départements)				
Most over-represented	Creuse	131	2	66
Most under-represented	Var	815	3	272
Germany (Länder)				
Most over-represented	Bremen	680	3	227
Most under-represented	N. Rhine Westphalia	18,000	6	3,000
Spain (aut. comms.)				
Most over-represented	Castilla-León	2,500	39	60
Most under-represented	Madrid	5,000	9	556

The over-representation of sparsely populated areas can have political consequences. This is particularly the case in France, but also to some extent in Spain. This comes, in each case, because of the tendency towards political conservatism in less densely populated rural areas.

The factors creating the over-representation of rural areas in the French Sénat were outlined above. An extreme example is shown in the table.[36] The net result across France is a Sénat dominated by the centre right, where the Socialist Party has never had a majority. The Irish electoral college, which is similar to that in France, suffers similar problems due to the differential between the proportion of population to councillors in different areas. For example Dromahaire in County Leitrim has one councillor for 913 voters, compared to Dublin's Pembroke Ward with one for every 8,376 (Hussey, 1993). Thus Dublin is under-represented amongst the Seanad electorate (Coakley 1993). Such discrepancies have the potential to create political bias in the elections to the Seanad, even though these are not based on geographic units.

The under-representation of urban areas in the Spanish Senado is amply illustrated by the figures in Table 3.4. Again the capital city is the main loser. Madrid is the most densely represented area of the country, and also the most under-represented in the upper house. This is because Madrid, whilst an autonomous community in its own right, is made up of one single province. This entitles it to only four directly elected Senators, whilst Castilla-León is comprised of nine provinces, and is thus entitled to 36 directly elected Senators—although it has only half Madrid's population (Juberías 1999). The allocation of Senators to represent the autonomous community as a whole does little to compensate the capital. As in France, this affects the political outcome of the elections, making it slightly harder for parties of the left to gain seats.

Ironically in Australia where harsh accusations have been thrown at the Senate, the over-representation of certain states has little impact on the political balance of the house. In fact the Senate is far more representative of how the country votes than is the lower house. Nevertheless the 'unrepresentative' nature of the Senate is seemingly what prevents it from taking over as the dominant parliamentary chamber.

CONCLUSIONS

This chapter has described the development, and the composition, of the seven second chambers which are the subject of this book. In doing so it has attempted to demonstrate the varied histories of second

---

[36] The *département* of Creuse had its representation in the Sénat set in 1958 and has since fallen well below the 150,000 population which is required to deserve two upper house seats.

chambers, and their varied forms of representation today. It has also attempted to show how the composition of the second chamber is bound up with the history and traditions of the state, and the political system. Thus the German and Australian upper houses represent—in very different ways—the development of the federal system. The French upper house represents the conservative interests of rural France, elected largely through its councillors. The Irish Seanad is the legacy of a system where a religious minority needed to be seen to be represented through the upper house. Only in the Italian parliament is little discernible difference found between the composition of the two chambers, partly as a result of the late development of regional government which was planned in the post-war constitution.

The chapter has also discussed how most of the second chambers are distinct from their respective first chambers through not basing distribution of seats on population. This is largely a result of the classic 'territorial' role of upper houses, particularly in federal states, and relies on a different concept of representation to that normally applied in lower houses. In a modern state the most important factor in the relations between the two chambers is their political balance. This is discussed in the next chapter.

4

Politics and Personalities in the Chamber

The way the upper house behaves, the influence it has within the political system, and the way it is viewed by the public are all critically influenced by the kind of people who sit in it. In particular the political balance of the chamber will have a big impact on the attitude it takes towards the government and its legislation. However, other factors, such as the perceived political seniority of its members, will also play a major part in its bargaining power. Consideration of the chambers' membership therefore acts as necessary background to the description of their work.

The type of people who sit in the chamber is largely a result of the way they are chosen. This was discussed in the previous chapter. But it is also heavily influenced by other factors, such as the powers which the chamber has to make a difference. Key figures are unlikely to sit in a chamber which has little influence. The powers of chambers were summarised briefly in Table 2.2, and are discussed in detail in later chapters. None the less, most of the seven second chambers considered in this book have counted amongst their members important national figures, from the composer Giuseppe Verdi—who sat in the Italian *Senato del Regno*—to the poet W. B. Yeats who sat in the early Irish Seanad. Many key political figures spent spells in these houses early in their careers, amongst them Ireland's President Mary Robinson and Taoiseach Garret FitzGerald, France's President François Mitterrand and Germany's Chancellors Willy Brandt, Gerhard Schröder, and Helmut Kohl.

This chapter discusses the type of people who sit in each of the second chambers. The first, and most important, element of the chambers' composition which is examined is political balance. Amongst political members the seniority of these individuals, their position in the party and links to other political bodies, is also discussed. This is followed by consideration of the key role played in some chambers by independent members, who represent no party. Finally, the chapter looks at the 'demography' of upper house members—for example in terms of age and gender—and reviews the impact which all these factors have on the way the chamber behaves.

POLITICAL BALANCE IN THE CHAMBER

There is little more important to the functioning of the upper chamber than its political balance. Abbé Siéyès, who wrote several draft constitutions for the French Republic after the 1789 revolution, famously said that 'if a second chamber dissents from the first, it is mischievous; if it agrees, it is superfluous'.[1] Where a second chamber either consistently agrees or consistently disagrees with the lower house, this will today tend to be a result of its party political balance. Siéyès' expression updated for modern democracies might say that where the upper chamber is controlled by the same party as the lower chamber it is liable to act simply as a 'rubber stamp', but where it is controlled by an opposing majority there is a danger of deadlock. This presents a conundrum for the design of any new or reformed second chamber.

Table 4.1. *Political balance in the lower and upper house, June 1999*

	Governing party	Proportion of seats in	
		lower house (%)	upper house (%)
Australia	Liberal/National	52	45
Canada	Liberal	51	49
France	Socialist/Communist/Green	50	29‡
Germany	SPD/Green	52	n/a†
Ireland	Fianna Fáil/Progressive Dem.	49	55
Italy	Democratic Left and others	55	59
Spain	Popular Party*	45	51
UK	Labour	63	15§

‡ Approximate—party groups in the Sénat differ from those in the lower house.
† See Table 4.2 for composition of the Bundesrat.
§ House of Lords before removal of hereditary peers. Immediately after removal of the hereditaries government held 28 per cent of seats in the transitional house.
* With parliamentary support from Catalan and Basque Nationalists
Sources: Inter-Parliamentary Union, *La Stampa* (23 October 1998), House of Lords.

[1] *Archives Parlementaires*, vol. 8, page 563, 1789.

The second chambers considered in this book represent the whole spectrum of party political balance with respect to the lower house. The proportion of members of the upper and lower house which come from the governing party or coalition are shown in Table 4.1. This represents a fairly typical snapshot of the chambers, as correct in June 1999.

The eight second chambers we are considering—including the House of Lords—may broadly be grouped in three categories. The first is one where the upper and lower chambers tend to have the same majority, which is also the majority from which the government is drawn. Into this category would fall the very different second chambers of Ireland, Spain, and Italy. In the second category, which offers a potentially much more interesting scenario, the second chamber will tend not to have a majority that matches the first. This is the case in Australia and Germany. The third category contains 'the rest'—those second chambers which will at times have a majority that concurs with the lower house and at other times will not. Both the UK (to date) and France would fall into this category, because the political control of the upper house has been constant—by the Conservative Party in the UK and the centre-right in France—whilst the control of the lower house has varied. In Canada there are also long periods of agreement between the chambers, interspersed with long periods of hostility. However, this results not from the permanent control of the chamber by one party, but from a lag in control after the government changes until the new incumbents have appointed sufficient members to gain control of the Senate. The sections below consider these different scenarios in turn.

Colluding Chambers? Spain, Ireland, and Italy

Born of completely different political traditions, the second chambers in Italy, Ireland, and Spain have one thing in common: their inbuilt tendency to have government majorities. Given the different compositions of the chambers these come about for quite different reasons.

As discussed in Chapter 3, the political balance of the Irish Seanad in favour of the government was fully intended by its designers, acting under the guidance of Éamon De Valera. Having experienced at first hand the frustrations of governing with a hostile upper house, De Valera ensured that the new Seanad—both through its composition and its powers—could not cause such problems again. The 43 'vocational' seats are monopolised by the parties, but the proportional voting system means that neither these nor the six university seats could ever be dominated by an opposition party. The inclusion of eleven seats nominated by the Taoiseach ensures that even a relatively severe deficit of government seats could be counterbalanced. Thus no new Seanad has ever sat which has a non-government majority, and the current composition, where the government have 33 seats, the opposition has 20, alongside seven independent members, is fairly typical. This is a disappointment to many Irish commentators, who note that 'Except for six members, representing most of the country's university graduates, and occasionally outstanding direct appointments by the Taoiseach, the political composition mirrors that of the Dáil' (Hussey 1993: 73).

However, the one occasion in Irish history when the government changed without an election, in 1994, began a brief period when the Seanad was not dominated by the government parties. The appointed members reflected the colour of the outgoing government, seven of them representing Fianna Fáil and four the Labour Party, but the constitution contained no provision for them to be changed. Thus the new Fianna Gael/Labour Party coalition could rely on the support of only 27 of the 60 Seanad members until the general election of 1997. Ironically, this is generally accepted—by all parties—as having been a successful period in the history of an otherwise ineffective institution. The *Irish Times* (22 July 1997) remarked that: 'As a result, the Independent Senators had their finest hour, holding the balance of power and wielding an authority they never expected.' During this period the government were forced to negotiate over legislation, and in particular to alter a controversial Universities Bill, under pressure from the university senators.

A similar period occurred in the Spanish Senado between June 1995 and the general election of March 1996. Whilst the Socialist Party was in government, controlling the lower house with parliamentary support of small nationalist parties, the opposition Popular Party (PP) gained majority control of the Senado. This occurred because the balance of regional parliaments—who elect around one-fifth of members of the Senado—had swung towards the PP. However this period—in which the Senado made decisions that were unwelcome to the government—was as yet unprecedented in its history. The semi-majoritarian electoral system for the Senado means that the proportion of seats in the house won by the government has exceeded its share of the vote in every election since 1977 (Juberías 1999). Indeed the government may have an overall majority in the Senado even when it lacks one in the lower house. For example in 1996 the PP won 45 per cent of seats in the lower house and 53 per cent of the seats in the upper house, on 39 per cent of the vote (Juberías 1999). Those that suffer are the small parties, regional parties, and the parties of the left. Socialist governments tend to have a less impressive majority in the upper house than governments of the right, due to the rural bias in the distribution of seats. The worst loser in elections to the Senado has been the far left. For example, the United Left (a coalition party including the communists) gained 21 seats in the lower house in 1996, but none in the Senado (Juberías 1999). The chamber therefore retains a traditional element of conservative bias.

In Italy the party system is very different to that in either Ireland or Spain. Governments have traditionally been large coalitions, including many smaller parties. Whilst there have been attempts to streamline this system, with the 1996 elections operating under a new electoral system and won by a more cohesive, predetermined, coalition, there are still a large number of parties represented in the Italian parliament. The similarity of the electoral systems for the upper and lower houses, and the fact that elections take place on the same day, mean that the political composition of the chambers is very similar. In practice the smaller size of the Senato makes its results slightly less proportional, and fewer parties are represented. This makes it potentially easier to control. However, this must be set against the relative independence of the Italian parliament and its members with respect of government. It has been suggested that 'members of parliament, and more precisely members of the majority, are often left to their own legislative devices. Some variously combine personal drive, institutional positioning and factional or community influence, to invent for themselves a role as political or legislative entrepreneurs' (Di Palma and Cotta 1986: 67). It would thus be quite inaccurate to consider the Italian Senato to be as compliant as its Irish or Spanish counterparts.

A Distinct Voice: the Australian and German Chambers

The directly elected Australian Senate offers quite a different model to that found in Italy or Spain. Government parties have controlled the chamber for only 12 of the 51 years since proportional representation was introduced. No government has now controlled the Senate since 1981. Instead the balance of power in this period has been held by a combination of small parties and independent Senators.

The electoral system for the Senate prior to 1948 was actually very similar to that for the Spanish Senado, but without the concession of even one seat in each multi-member constituency to the losing party. Thus in 1919 the government had a 35:1 majority in the Senate, and at the point that the system was changed in 1948 enjoyed a 33:3 majority. In these circumstances, with a majoritarian system also in operation for the lower house, there was no room for the development of small parties. However, this soon occurred after proportional representation was introduced in 1948. The first break in the hegemony of the major parties came with a split in the Labor Party in 1955. Two Senators were elected from the new 'Democratic Labor Party' that same year, and held the balance of power in the Senate until 1958. They also shared the balance of Senate power with other small groups from 1961 to 1974 (Uhr 1999).

A major development that has shaped the Senate of the last two decades was the formation of a new party, the Australian Democrats, who occupy the political centre ground. The party, which formed in 1977, was a breakaway from the main centre-right party, the Liberals. Its political stance was heavily influenced by new social movements, including feminism and environmentalism, and the Democrats' unusual blend of policies includes support for human rights and trade unionism, alongside adherence to free market principles of economics. However, the success of the party has been to position itself as an alternative to the two major parties, with its founding slogan being to 'keep the bastards honest'. This won the Democrats seats in the Senate, where they took the balance of power in 1980. Since then it is they, the Greens, and independent members who have ensured that government legislation is scrutinised carefully in the upper house. The increase in the size of the Senate in 1983 was partly designed in order to reduce the influence of minor parties. However this was unsuccessful.[2]

So whilst government has been deprived of a majority, the configuration of seats in the Senate has made it unlikely that the opposition will control the chamber. John Uhr (1999: 107) has noted that: 'it is now characteristic of Senate party representation that neither the party of the government of the day nor that of the official opposition . . . can expect to control the Senate.' The politics of the Democrats, in particular, mean that they are liable to vote against both major parties on an issue-by-issue basis. Government is constantly frustrated by the Senate, but very few bills are rejected. During the 1993–6 Keating Labor government, the Democrats voted with the government 54 per cent of the time and the Greens voted with the government 43 per cent of the time. In contrast the opposition voted with the government 28 per cent of the time.[3] During this period the government succeeded in getting 96 per cent of its legislation passed (Elliott 1997), despite Paul Keating's comment that the Senate was 'a spoiling chamber' which 'frankly, the

---

[2] At the time it was believed that a move to electing an even number of seats per state at each Senate election would result in the two major parties sharing the seats equally between them and driving out minor parties (Sharman 1986). However, in practice the drop in the electoral quota required to win a seat, from 17 per cent to 14 per cent, provided an extra boost to small party representation.

[3] Statistics Unit, Senate Table Office.

rest of us should not have to stomach'.[4] In fact the small parties have been considerably more hostile to the subsequent Liberal/National Party governments of John Howard.[5] Consequently the Senate is perhaps even less popular with these parties than with Labor.

Controversy over the politics of the Senate leads to constant arguments over the notion of political 'mandate'. The adversarial two-party system still dominates the politics of the Australian lower house and a government with a majority in that house will claim a mandate to govern. However, minor parties claim a mandate to promote the positions they committed themselves to in their own manifestos, even where this means voting against the government's programme. As Campbell Sharman has suggested, 'everyone can claim to have a mandate for something' (1998: 1). This applies particularly under the Australian electoral system, where—as in the UK—the government is liable to be elected on a minority of votes. In contrast the number of seats in the Senate is broadly proportional to votes cast. In 1998 the governing parties won 54 per cent of lower house seats on 40 per cent of the vote, but only 42 per cent of seats in the Senate. The minor parties, supported by 25 per cent of voters, were actually under-represented in the Senate result—gaining 16 per cent of seats (Sharman 1998).

Emy, who has written widely on the mandate question puts it thus:

a simple version of the mandate implies that the party which wins a majority of seats in the [lower] House is entitled to govern and implement its previously stated policies. But what does the 'right to govern' really mean? Does it confer a right on the executive to give legislative effect to all its stated policies as swiftly as possible? Or does it confer a more limited right to try and implement its policies by drawing up legislation which it must still persuade a truly bicameral parliament to pass? (1997: 65)

In Germany the politics of the upper house also require careful negotiation by government, but for rather different reasons. The Bundesrat sits at the centre of a federal system where coalition government is commonplace at both state and national level. As the representation of the states in the national parliament its members are, effectively, governments rather than individuals. Votes are cast by each state as a block on the basis of coalition agreement, which means that although German politics is dominated by two main parties—the

---

[4] *Sydney Morning Herald*, 4 March 1994.

[5] During the 1996–8 government the Democrats voted with the government only 19 per cent of the time and with the opposition 64 per cent of the time. The Greens voted with the government only three per cent of the time and with the opposition 75 per cent of the time (Statistics Unit, Senate Table Office).

Christian Democrats (CDU) and Social Democrats (SPD)—government and opposition sides in the Bundesrat are not always so clear.

Table 4.2. *Party strengths in German Länder and Bundesrat, June 1999*

Party control	Land	Bundesrat seats
CDU control		
CDU alone	Saxony	4
CSU alone	Bavaria	6
CDU/FDP	Baden-Württemberg	6
	Hessen	5
	Total	*21*
SPD control		
SPD alone	Brandenburg	4
	Lower Saxony	6
	Saarland	3
	Saxony-Anhalt	4
SPD/Green	North Rhine Westphalia	6
	Schleswig-Holstein	4
	Hamburg	3
SPD/PDS	Mecklenburg-West Pomerania	3
	Total	*33*
Neither		
CDU/SPD	Berlin	4
	Thuringia	4
SPD/CDU	Bremen	3
SPD/FDP	Rhineland-Palatinate	4
	Total	*15*

The complexity of the politics of the Bundesrat is demonstrated by Table 4.2, which shows the political control of the Länder governments, and their respective number of seats in the upper house in June 1999. This illustrates the diversity of coalitions between the CDU, SPD, Greens, FDP (centre party), PDS (ex-East German communist party) and CSU (Bavarian sister party to the CDU). In contrast, the national government elected in September 1998 was a coalition of the SPD and Green parties.

German elections at Land level have a tendency to result in a backlash against parties in power at national level. Thus through substantial parts of the long period of Christian Democrat government from 1982 to 1998 the majority of Länder were controlled by SPD coalitions.

However, the recent victory of the SPD at national level has reversed this trend. The first state elections after the general election, held in Hessen in April 1999, resulted in the replacement of an SPD/Green coalition with a CDU/FDP coalition. This was widely hailed as the point at which the government lost political control of the Bundesrat. Further state elections have brought more losses to the SPD and created a much more difficult political environment for Chancellor Schröder in the upper house.

However, Table 4.2 demonstrates that the politics of the Bundesrat is a far more complex affair than that of other upper chambers. At this time the SPD was in government nationally with the CDU and FDP forming the opposition. However, the SPD and CDU shared power in two Länder, and in a third the SPD shared power with the FDP. These three Länder were therefore unlikely to take a blanket line either in favour or against government proposals. With these Länder potentially holding the balance of power the relationship between the government and the upper house begins to look a little like that in Australia.

Although the Bundesrat is in many ways a true house of the states, as represented by their—frequently coalition—governments, there is no question that its behaviour is largely driven by party politics. The original design of the chamber, with representatives sitting and voting as state blocks, was intended to minimise the influence of parties (Ziller 1982). However, as Patzelt observes, 'the central political actors in the Bundesrat are the political parties' (1999: 60). Whilst government and opposition in the chamber may not always be a black and white affair, the Bundesrat has caused considerable difficulties for national governments at times when state governments have largely been controlled by opposition parties. This is made more serious by the considerable powers that the Bundesrat has over legislation. Thus from 1969 to 1982 there was an SPD government, whilst the CDU had effective control of the Bundesrat through their control of Länder governments. This caused increasing difficulties for national government, to the point that in the 1970s there was a 'virtual stalemate of legislation' (Kolinsky 1984: 9). The result was considerable influence for the CDU in formulation of national policy (Edinger 1986). A similar situation applied from 1990 to 1998, when the SPD had effective control of the Bundesrat and the CDU formed the national government. Chancellor Schröder may face the challenge of dealing with an unsympathetic majority in the house which German commentators often refer to not as the second chamber, but rather as the 'second government' (Patzelt 1999: 85).

The examples of Australia and Germany demonstrate that the classic view of Abbé Siéyès about second chambers which support or oppose the first chamber is an oversimplification of the picture. In modern systems where majorities are not identical in the two houses, neither must they be implacably opposed. Both of the chambers discussed here offer perfect examples of this. Thus in the design of a second chamber there is more than a simple choice between rubber stamp and deadlock. We do not, in fact, have an example of a system which demonstrates permanent deadlock, as this would be inherently unstable. However, both France and Canada have been through periods where relations between the chambers have become very difficult.

The Sénat: the Voice of Conservative Rural France

The French upper house represents local government at the centre of the political system. However, this is a very different role to that which might be played by a local government house in Britain or other countries. The enormous number of local authorities and local councillors in France, which provide disproportionate representation for thinly populated rural areas, result in the Sénat having a fixed political complexion. This fixed, conservative, nature of the Sénat does not make it unrepresentative of local government. Rather it reflects the fact that local government councillors, when aggregated nationally, are unrepresentative of the political views of the population.

The centre-right dominated Sénat has proved problematic over time to both governments of left and right. However, it has been most aggressive towards the Socialists, whose representation in the chamber has always been poor. It may also play a key role at times of 'cohabitation' when the presidency and the lower house are controlled by opposing political groups.

The first fifth republic Sénat, elected in 1959, set the tone for the political attitude of the house. General de Gaulle had taken over the presidency of the republic, and his supporters were successful in winning the control of the lower house. However, they were less successful in the local government elections, and many members of the Sénat were thus fourth republic supporters who were hostile to de Gaulle. The difficult relationship between the government and the Sénat was worsened when de Gaulle introduced direct elections for the presidency. Prior to this the President had been elected by both houses of parliament, so this weakened the powers of the Sénat.[6] The hostility

[6] The constitution requires that constitutional changes in France must be passed by both houses of parliament and then either put to a referendum or agreed at a joint parliamentary

between the President and the Sénat became such that the government began trying to downgrade the institution and call for its reform. The antagonism between government and Sénat is demonstrated by the fact that de Gaulle's Prime Minister, Georges Pompidou, never entered the chamber during his six years of office (Smith 1996). This campaign of hostility culminated in a referendum on reform of the Sénat in 1969. De Gaulle turned the referendum into a vote of confidence in his leadership, and when it failed he resigned immediately. Ironically, this required the President of the Sénat to assume his duties on a temporary basis, until Pompidou was elected as the new President of the Republic.[7]

The Sénat and the President of the Republic have been political allies for only one period. President Giscard d'Estaing, elected in 1974, came from the same centrist tradition as those that controlled the upper chamber. The Sénat therefore became 'invaluable' to him when dealing with a lower house still controlled by the Gaullists (Mastias 1999: 170). The chamber was used to give a sympathetic hearing to proposals which were likely to be rejected if introduced in the lower house.

But the election of the Socialist President Mitterrand in 1981 began a period of renewed hostility between the government and the Sénat. Mitterrand dissolved the lower house and, following fresh elections, the Socialists won a 2:1 majority. However, there was a 2:1 majority against them in the Sénat (Hayward 1983). Despite the Socialists' popular mandate, the majority in the Sénat were 'implacably opposed' to the values and policies of the new government, and not afraid to demonstrate this by their actions (Mastias 1999: 171). Legislation was frequently rejected and the government was forced to adopt procedural tactics to try to rush its bills through the upper house. The peak of the crisis came when the Sénat played a key role in the defeat of a controversial education bill in 1984.[8] The house later returned to its refereeing role when the lower house elections in 1986 began a new period of cohabitation between President Mitterrand and Gaullist Prime Minister Chirac.

The election of 1997, resulting in a new Socialist government under Prime Minister Jospin, leaves the Sénat in opposition again. Whilst the Socialists are by far the largest party in the lower house, they are outnumbered in the Sénat by Gaullist and centrist forces. Small parties, such as the Greens, are excluded from the Sénat altogether.

---

sitting. On this occasion the Sénat was particularly angered that de Gaulle flouted this rule by bypassing parliament and going straight to a referendum on the issue of a directly elected President (Hayward 1983).

[7] For a discussion of the role of the Sénat President, see Chapter 5.

[8] This is discussed in more detail in Chapter 6.

Consequently the upper house is once again causing difficulties for the governing parties, and reform is back on the agenda. Some specific examples of these problems are discussed in Chapters 6 and 8.

Canada and the Senate that Lags

Seats in the Canadian Senate are not dependent on the political views of any electorate. Instead they are wholly in the gift of the Prime Minister, and are used—almost without exception—to appoint members of the governing party.[9] The result is that the number of government members in the Senate grows over time, as existing Senators retire and are replaced by new appointees.

This has resulted in several governments being elected to face a politically hostile Senate. The most serious difficulties between the two houses followed the election of a Conservative government in 1984, after a period of 21 years of virtually uninterrupted Liberal rule. The government won the biggest House of Commons majority in Canadian history, holding 211 seats to the Liberals' 40. However the Senate, in contrast, comprised 73 Liberals, 25 Conservatives, and four independent members.

Over the preceding decades a self-denying convention had developed, whereby the unelected Senate would not use its powers to reject or seriously interfere with legislation from the Commons. However the Liberals, deprived of power after so long, chose to ignore this convention and instead use the Senate as an opposition base. Many bills were delayed and amended and the situation reached crisis point in 1988 when the Senate rejected a bill for the first time in 40 years. Prime Minister Mulroney accused the Senate of 'hijacking the fundamental rights of the House of Commons' (quoted in Franks 1999: 129). A general election was called, which was won by the Conservatives, but the warfare between the chambers continued. The Senate was particularly resistant to a bill to introduce a Goods and Services Tax, in 1990.[10] The government finally forced the bill through both houses by using an extraordinary procedure allowing more Senators to be appointed. This finally created a government majority in

---

[9] The only major deviation from this tendency was during the long period of Liberal government under Pierre Trudeau, when the number of Liberal senators became so excessive that Trudeau eventually adopted a convention of replacing outgoing Conservative senators with other Conservatives. However, even this was used on occasion to electoral advantage—for example just before the election in 1979 he appointed a Conservative MP from a marginal seat to the Senate, in order that the Liberals would win his seat, which they did (Landes 1987).

[10] This and other difficulties between the chambers are discussed in Chapter 6.

the house. However, it has been suggested that the vigorous campaign by the Senate over this unpopular tax helped bring about the eventual fall of the Conservative government (Franks 1999).

The Conservatives were swept from power in the 1993 general election with an even more dramatic swing than that which had elected them. The Liberals won 172 seats, the Conservatives were reduced to just two seats, and the Bloc Québécois became the official opposition. However, the Conservatives retained a majority in the Senate until 1997. There were some resultant difficulties for the Liberal government during this period, though not so dramatic as those the party had imposed during opposition. Since government regained control of the Senate it has reverted to its traditional more passive role, with relations between the chambers once again being relatively harmonious.

POLITICAL CAREERS AND POLITICAL TYPES

Political careers in Britain have traditionally seen representatives of the major parties move in one direction only. The typical career of an elected representative might start at local government level before progression to the House of Commons. The culmination of a career would often be appointment to the House of Lords. This progression in political careers helps define the nature of the House of Lords and the representatives within it—since many are experienced politicians, older than their House of Commons counterparts, and no longer aspiring to cabinet rank. Entry to the House of Lords involves a peerage, which debars the holder from sitting in the House of Commons, and—in the case of a life peerage—cannot be renounced. Very few individuals have therefore made the progression instead from the upper chamber to the House of Commons.[11]

With the creation of the Scottish Parliament, the assemblies in Northern Ireland, Wales, and London, and further regional chambers a possibility, this pattern of political career paths may change. The establishment of a new upper chamber might also have this effect. The other seven countries under consideration show that the British model of career progression in politics is not the only one available. The composition of the chamber, its powers, and particularly its relationship

---

[11] Only 17 hereditary peerages have ever been disclaimed. In only a few cases was this done to allow the holder to take, or retain, a seat in the House of Commons. These include Tony Benn (1963), Alec Douglas-Home (1963), Quintin Hogg (1963), and James Douglas-Hamilton (1994).

with government, all fundamentally affect the political types who sit in it. This in turn affects both its atmosphere and its effectiveness.

The Canadian Senate comes closest to the British model of appointment at the end of political careers. Individuals are generally appointed to the Senate as a reward for long service to the party. This ensures that many Senators are experienced politicians—for example, Forsey (1982) noted that the membership of the Senate included 13 former ministers, 12 ex-MPs, five provincial ex-premiers, and 11 provincial ex-ministers. This has led one commentator to describe the Senate as 'a dignified pasture for superannuated political war horses' (Franks 1987: 194).

However, the membership of the Senate is viewed less benignly by many other Canadians. The blatant political patronage involved in its appointment is the primary reason for the chamber's unpopularity. Some of these issues were mentioned in Chapter 3. Another example of the use of Senate appointments to advantage the governing party is the deployment of its members to co-ordinate election campaigns. Senators often run provincial campaigns from the comfort of the Senate, whilst drawing a salary from the public purse. Both Prime Ministers Trudeau and Mulroney also appointed their national campaign managers to the Senate.

Another allegation famously levelled at the Canadian Senate is that its members are too closely connected to business interests and thus represent a 'lobby from within' (Campbell 1978). This situation is exacerbated by the fact that commercial consultancies held by Senators are not regulated in any way (Jackson and Jackson 1998).

Whilst the upper houses of Canada and the UK tend to accommodate politicians at the end of their careers, in other countries there is more of a two-way flow of members between the houses. This is certainly the case in Ireland and Spain, and to a lesser extent in Australia. In fact upper houses seem increasingly to be providing an entry point for new aspirants to high political office.

The proximity of elections to the Irish Dáil and Seanad provides an opportunity for candidates not elected to the first to instead seek selection to the second. A growing phenomenon is for new candidates, who are not well established enough to succeed in the election to the Dáil, to start their career in the Seanad. Thus the chamber is populated by 'young politicians on the way up, old politicians on the way down or midlevel politicians whose careers have received a temporary setback' (Dinan 1986: 84). The Seanad is increasingly seen as a 'stepping-stone to the Dáil' as well as a resting place from where a Dáil career may be relaunched (Chubb, 1992: 198). In 1997, 23 of the 60 members of the new

Seanad had been candidates in the recent Dáil elections, including eight MPs who had lost their seats. Seven others had been MPs previously (Nealon 1997). In addition, 16 members of the previous Seanad were successfully elected to the Dáil. Labour's Joe Costello offers a typical example: he started his national political career as a member of the Seanad, and was then elected to the Dáil. When he lost his seat he was re-elected to the Seanad, and may well seek election to the Dáil again at the next opportunity. A seat in the Seanad allows a politician to keep up a media profile and a high-ranking position in the party whilst nursing a Dáil constituency. Senators will even compete with Dáil members of the same party for constituency work, in the hope of beating them in the single transferable vote ballot at the next general election.[12] Although around half the membership of the Seanad remains stable at each election, and some of its members are committed to the institution, 'most Senators are indistinguishable from the type of career-politician to be found in the Dáil' (Gwynn Morgan 1990: 92).[13]

An important way of keeping in touch with the electorate and local opinion formers is to hold positions on local bodies. Membership of local councils is very high amongst members of the Seanad, with over 60 per cent of those elected in 1997 also being councillors (Nealon 1997). Many members also hold positions on local health councils and other such organisations. A similar tradition is followed in France, and in both cases may appear natural as local councillors form the bulk of the electorate for the upper house. However, in both cases the tradition also applies to the lower house, and contributes to the poor attendance rates in both chambers.

In France the number of elected offices that an individual may hold was limited by law in 1985, partly for this reason. The *cumul des mandats* legislation introduced restrictions so that a member of the Sénat or *Assemblée Nationale* may hold no more than one other senior elected position, including MEP, member of regional or departmental council or mayor of a *commune* with more than 20,000 inhabitants. Members may sit as local *commune* councillors in addition. The enforcement of this legislation resulted in a considerable shake-up in the membership of

---

[12] One of the main criticisms levelled at the single transferable vote is that it encourages competition amongst members of the same party, and 'clientelism' as members try to build up a personal vote amongst the electorate.

[13] The similarity between the two chambers also extends to one of the hallmarks of Irish politics—the phenomenon of the political family. At least six Senators in 1997 were related to other parliamentarians, present or past. These included three sons of Senators or MPs (one of whom also had a brother in the Dáil and one a grandfather), two daughters of MPs, and one father of an MP (Nealon 1997).

parliament. However in January 1999, 163 of the 321 members of the Sénat held positions as local mayors. In addition 20 Senators were regional councillors and 140 were departmental councillors, including 45 regional and departmental presidents. In total around 90 per cent of parliamentarians hold at least one office at local level (Mény 1998). As this applies to both houses of parliament it does not distinguish Senators from lower house deputies.[14] However, there does appear to be more of a tendency for local mayors to sit in the lower house, whilst presidents of regions and *départements* sit in the Sénat. These positions as local *notables* give members of parliament a degree of security and freedom from the party machine, as they have strong independent local profiles. A seat in parliament, meanwhile, gives local representatives privileged access to central government, which can help in delivery of local outcomes and thus help secure their positions.

In Spain a slightly different situation applies: most members of the Senado are almost indistinguishable from their lower house counterparts, but the main exception is those holding dual mandates. The majority of Spanish Senators are directly elected to represent the provinces, and are loyal party politicians just like the members of the first chamber, the *Diputados*. If anything, members of the Senado will be of a lower rank, as 'every party has consistently placed its political leaders and heavyweights on the benches of the lower house' (Juberías 1999: 285). This is linked to the weak powers of the chamber and the fact that very few ministers are appointed from the Senado.

The members elected by autonomous community parliaments, who form around one-fifth of the membership of the Senado, are of a slightly different character. Individual traditions are developing in different regions for the election of these Senators, but the seats can offer an opportunity for senior politicians within the region to gain access to the national parliament. The autonomous community of Madrid, for example, which has six seats in the Senado, sends the president of the Popular Party in the region as one of its members. Similarly one of the two representatives of the Socialist Party is both the party secretary in Madrid and the leader of the party in the regional assembly. Members of autonomous community governments, however, will not form part of the delegation to the Senado, due to the time commitment that they must make within their region. Whilst the Irish and French parliaments

---

[14] In fact this tradition of the dual mandate in French politics extends right to the top of the profession. Jacques Chirac was mayor of Paris from 1977 to 1995 and continued in this role whilst he was Prime Minister from 1986 to 1988. Alain Juppé actually ran as mayor of Bordeaux when he was both Prime Minister and Secretary General of the Gaullist party, the RPR.

to some extent organise their timetables to allow members to be present for their duties as local councillors, even junior members of an important Spanish regional parliament will find it hard to accommodate these two roles as both chambers meet most days of the week.

The ultimate dual mandate assembly is the German Bundesrat, where all members are cabinet ministers within their state. Members of Länder governments, and particularly Minister Presidents, are often important national political figures. Most federal Chancellors in Germany have held office as Minister President before taking office. Hence most Chancellors and other senior national figures have held seats in the Bundesrat in the past, and this office gave them an increased opportunity to raise their national profile. Both Gerhard Schröder and Oskar Lafontaine were Minister Presidents in the Bundesrat until the SPD gained power nationally in 1998. The presence of such figures in the Bundesrat not only helps progress their political careers, but also helps raise the profile and the bargaining power of the institution.[15]

The senior status of Bundesrat members, and their responsibilities within their home state, raise obvious difficulties for their attendance at the federal legislature. This is accommodated by the Bundesrat in three important ways. First, plenary meetings of the chamber are held only once every three weeks. Most of the work on legislation is carried out in committees, with the full chamber meeting to endorse decisions which have already been discussed in detail elsewhere. There is little debate at these plenary meetings, which generally last only half a day. Secondly, the casting of votes as blocks by the regional delegation leader means that all members need not attend. Generally only one or two ministers from each Land will be present at the plenary. This pattern marks the Bundesrat out compared with ordinary parliamentary chambers. The other important concession that allows members to manage dual mandates is that committee meetings—which form the core of the Bundesrat's work—are almost exclusively attended by civil servants. Land ministers rarely attend, and their involvement is thus limited in practice to agreeing positions on Bundesrat matters in the Land cabinet and overseeing the work of their officials.

The federal nature of the Australian Senate, where members are directly elected, is very different. In Australia, as in Italy, the power of the chamber is close to that of the lower house, and the calibre of candidates is generally equally high. The difference is that members of the upper house will be selected by state parties, who place them on

---

[15] Members of the Bundesrat also have speaking rights in the Bundestag, which can further help an individual to raise their profile and progress their political career.

what are effectively 'closed' lists, which have been ranked by the parties before they are presented to the electorate.[16] The top position on a list for one of the main parties for the Senate thus almost guarantees election. This provides a useful route for senior members of state parties to enter the national parliament. Members of the Senate have included many secretaries of state parties. Current leader of the opposition in the Senate, John Faulkner, provides one example, having been assistant secretary of the Labor Party in New South Wales before his election. In addition many of the Labor Party's official 'factions' are led by Senators. It has thus been suggested that the Senate is more of a 'house of state parties' than a true 'house of the states'.

In the past, positions on state lists for the Australian Senate were used, like appointments to the Canadian Senate, as rewards for long service to the party. But evidence suggests that this is changing, particularly as the key work of negotiating on legislation has in many ways shifted to the upper house, where the outcome of votes is less predictable. Thus the Senate is no longer a resting place for retiring MPs and is instead becoming an opening into national politics for bright young politicians. Yet despite the centrality of the Senate to the political system, for many members there is still an aspiration to enter the lower house—particularly as the most senior ministerial appointments continue to be made from there. One example of a Senator who made the transition was Gareth Evans, who was Labor's Senate house leader under Paul Keating. Evans moved to the lower house in 1996 to pursue leadership ambitions, which were never realised. Liberal Senator Bronwyn Bishop followed the same path. But probably the most striking example of this was Cheryl Kernot, leader of the Australian Democrats in the Senate, who in 1997 announced not only her intention to run for a lower house seat but also her plan to join the Labor Party. She now holds a position on the opposition front bench in the House of Representatives. Her transition demonstrates not only the frustrations of being a Senator but that of being a representative of a small party with no hope to govern.

In the Italian Senato there is no such restriction on the ministerial office that may be held. A Prime Minister has served from the Senato as recently as 1992. There remains however a tradition of party leaders being concentrated in the lower house, where media attention is also focused. The membership of the Italian parliament has been considerably shaken up by the major events of recent years, including the political corruption scandals of the early 1990s and the change of

---

[16] For a description of the electoral system, see Chapter 3.

electoral system in 1993. More than 80 per cent of Senators are new members who have entered since 1994, and the arrival of Silvio Berlusconi's Forza Italia party has brought more business-people into the chamber. However, these changes have equally affected the lower house. Of more specific impact on the Senato is the change from a regional list system of proportional representation to a constituency based system. Whilst the list system in Australia is attracting more full-time political activists into the Senate, the same phenomenon seems to be occurring in Italy following the abolition of the list system. Whilst party lists allowed senior figures from outside the political world to be placed in winnable positions, the new electoral system requires more campaigning and constituency work from candidates for the Senate. This is said to be subtly changing the nature of the house to one which is more similar to the party-dominated lower chamber.[17]

INDEPENDENTS AND NON-ALIGNED MEMBERS

Whilst representatives of the major parties form the majority in all second chambers considered here, independent members and representatives of minor parties also play an influential role in some cases. As the retention of an independent element in the House of Lords is a stated objective of many reformers in the UK, the role of independents in other countries' second chambers may hold important lessons.

Independents and minor parties in the Australian Senate sit on the 'crossbenches'—a term clearly inherited, like many other traditions, from the British parliament. These groups are generally critical through holding the balance of power in the Senate, and the role of the minor parties was described above. However, depending on the arithmetic in the chamber, independent members may have an equally critical role.

Brian Harradine is the most important independent member of the Australian Senate, where he has represented the state of Tasmania since 1975. During this time he has shared the balance of power with minor parties on many occasions. Between 1996 and 1999 his vote, along with that of a second independent, Mal Colston, was required by the conservative government to beat the combined forces of the Labor Party, Greens, and Democrats. He is therefore possibly the best-known and most widely courted member of the Senate, as well as being its longest serving member.

[17] Note that the party organisation in the chamber is discussed in Chapter 5.

The electoral systems for both the upper and lower houses in Australia actually militate against the election of independents.[18] Generally independent members have been elected to represent one of the parties, and then broken away—as Mal Colston did from the Labor Party. These members find it hard to get re-elected. Brian Harradine in contrast has always been an independent Senator, although he originally entered the Senate after being expelled from the Labor Party in 1975. He had been prominent in the party's right wing and was General Secretary of the Tasmanian Trades and Labour Council, but his expulsion resulted from his hardline position on communist influence in the party. He has benefited from a particular political tradition in Tasmania, where the state upper house has itself always been dominated by independents (Bennett 1992).

Harradine has been able to use his key position to extract concessions from governments of both parties, and to win favourable treatment for his small home state. He has played a central role in the negotiation of many controversial bills in recent years. These include the part sale of the national telecom company in 1996, over which he won disproportionate financial benefits for Tasmania, and the Native Title Bill in 1998.[19] His main political platform is a moral one, influenced by his Catholicism, and he has used his position in the Senate to campaign against pornography, abortion and family planning, and in favour of measures to encourage mothers to stay at home. However he also remains true to some elements of Labor ideology, generally supporting trade union rights and progressive taxation. On many of these issues he has played key roles in Senate committees.

The high profile and influence of Senator Harradine create particular resource problems for him. He has the same number of staff as any backbench Senator and cannot rely on a central party secretariat or leader's staff. He must do all his own research on each issue as he is never subject to the advice of a party whip. Also, because of the value of his vote and his high profile, he receives an enormous amount of correspondence. During one controversial debate on private health insurance, where the two independents held the decisive votes, he claims to have received 2,500 letters in one day. Although he has 500 supporters who help him campaign in Tasmania and benefits from the

[18] The introduction of 'above the line' voting for the Senate in 1984 (see Chapter 3) made it potentially more difficult for independents to get elected. However, Brian Harradine got around this by forming a skeleton 'party' which allows his supporters to vote above the line.

[19] These bills are discussed in more detail in Chapter 6.

help of some volunteers in parliament, his position highlights the particular challenges that can face independent members.

The independent members of the Irish Seanad, who are generally the university Senators (sometimes alongside one appointee of the Taoiseach), are under less pressure because they have rarely held the balance of power. Indeed in resource terms the university Senators are in some ways better provided for than their fellow Senators, as they may have access to university research libraries and receive support from student volunteers. This can make a difference as facilities for members of the Irish parliament are otherwise fairly limited. In a small way this may contribute to the independent university Senators being the highest profile and most respected members of what is otherwise a chamber benefiting from little profile and little respect.

It is an interesting phenomenon of the Irish Seanad that whilst the parties have managed to monopolise the 'vocational' seats they have generally had little success amongst the six university seats. Whilst the parties have run candidates in these elections, the electorate of university graduates seem to guard the independence of their representatives fiercely. With a few notable exceptions—including Mary Robinson, who entered parliament as a university Senator in 1973 and took the Labour whip—the university Senators do not adhere to any party whip. This is currently true of all six members (although one of them, journalist Shane Ross, has previously stood as a Dáil candidate for Fianna Gael). The highest profile Senator, possibly ever, is David Norris who represents Trinity college. He has made his name as a gay rights campaigner, and also used his position in the Seanad to promote other issues such as the plight of East Timor. His popularity was demonstrated when he was re-elected in 1997 from a field of 10 candidates on the first count. The other incumbents are Mary Henry, a practising medical doctor, Feargal Quinn, owner of Ireland's largest supermarket chain, Joe O'Toole, General Secretary of the main teachers' union and Brendan Ryan, who is closely associated with homelessness issues.

Independent members play less of a role in the other chambers considered here, although all except the Bundesrat include members not affiliated to the main parties. Parliamentary rules in France, Italy, and Spain, described in the next chapter, require all members of the upper house to declare to which parliamentary (i.e. usually party) group they will belong. A minimum size is set for formation of a parliamentary group, and all party representatives unable to reach this number are forced to form a group, together with any independent members, for administrative purposes. Such groups are then entitled to representation on committees, speaking rights and a certain level of secretarial and other support. In France this 'non-affiliated' group includes seven members, and is generally occupied by Senators who have broken away from the main parliamentary groups. In Spain the nine-strong group comprises members of small parties, including one member of the United Left and several from regional parties such as the Andalucian Greens and a party campaigning for independence of the island of Lanzarote.

In Italy there is some overlap between the *gruppo misto* (mixed group) and the life members of the Senato. The mixed group comprises 33 members, many who represent minor parties. However, it also includes a number of independent members, mostly life Senators. The life Senators, currently forming an 11-strong group, have on occasion been the subject of controversy. They do not generally hold the balance of power in the chamber but on one occasion in 1994 came close to forcing a result against the government. All but one of them voted in an election for the Speaker of the chamber in support of the candidate from the left group, and the government's candidate won the position by just one vote. The controversy around the role of these appointed members is demonstrated by the refusal of the recently retired President Scalfaro to take advantage of the right to appoint Senators. Scalfaro himself now sits in the Senato on an *ex officio* basis as an ex-President.

Another ex-President, Francesco Cossiga, has none the less demonstrated that the Italians can have a high tolerance for the active participation of the life Senators in politics. Cossiga was President of Italy from 1985 to 1992, representing the Christian Democrats (a party which disbanded following the corruption scandals of the early 1990s). Following the 1996 election he formed a new group in the Senate, the *Union Democratic per la Repubblica* (UDR), comprising centre-leaning members of opposition parties. When the far left failed to support the budget in 1998, the UDR played a critical and controversial part in the formation of the new government coalition of Massimo D'Alema. Thus even as a life Senator, Cossiga was a key player in the make or break of the new government.

However Cossiga, alongside seven-times Prime Minister Andreotti, are the only truly active members amongst the group of Italian life Senators. The other members, five of them retired professors, make only occasional visits to the chamber. The youngest amongst them, and one of the best known, is 78-year-old Giovanni Agnelli, president of the Fiat car company. However, given his other responsibilities he is generally seen in parliament only two or three times a year.

THE DEMOGRAPHY OF SENATORS

The literal meaning of the word 'Senate', according to the *Oxford English Dictionary* is 'council of old men', derived from the Latin term *senex* (which is also the root of words such as 'senior' and 'senile'). Although second chambers have developed over time, a number of factors result in these chambers retaining a more mature, and often more male, membership than lower houses of parliament. This applies particularly in systems where Senators are expected to have reached senior levels in their parties after long records of achievement, building on the centuries-old tradition of sagacity in upper houses. However, this may sit uncomfortably with modern moves to make parliament more representative of the population at large.

In addition to these factors some countries actually apply a higher qualification age for members of the upper house than members of the lower house. This applies in France and Canada, where the qualification age for the Senate is 12 years higher than that for the lower house. In both cases the average age of Senators is around ten years higher, partly for this reason and partly as a result of the level of seniority which must be reached in order to be elected or appointed to the upper house. More than half the members of the French Sénat are over 60, as compared to just one in five members of the lower house.[20] A higher age qualification also applies in the Italian Senato, where membership is limited to those aged over 40. This creates a significant difference to the lower house where almost one-quarter of members are under that age. In Germany there are no additional age barriers to membership of the upper house, but restriction of members to ministers in state cabinets results in a Bundesrat with no members aged under 40 (although most Bundesrat business is in fact transacted by civil servants, whose profile is unknown). And while qualification for membership of the two houses is the same in both Australia and Spain, there is also a tradition of greater maturity in the upper house. In Spain 41 per cent of Senators are over 50 and in Australia the figure is 55 per cent. This contrasts with 30 per cent and 39 per cent in their respective lower houses.

The traditional nature of the upper house, and the connection to a record of achievement elsewhere in politics may also result in a lower proportion of women than sit in the lower house. Comparative figures for this are shown in Table 4.3.

---

[20] Most figures in this section are taken from the Inter-Parliamentary Union's database, which may be found at http://www.ipu.org/ and were correct early in 1999.

Table 4.3. *Proportion of women in upper and lower houses, June 1999*

	Proportion of women in	
	lower house (%)	upper house (%)
Australia	22	30
Canada	18	30
France	11	6
Germany	31	19
Ireland	12	18
Italy	11	8
Spain	21	13
UK	18	8†

Sources: Inter-Parliamentary Union, House of Lords.
† The proportion of women in the transitional house, following the removal of most of the predominantly male hereditaries, will be approximately 15 per cent.

A lower proportion of women is seen in the upper house in France—with the most traditional of the upper houses, in Germany—where women are under-represented in Länder governments, and also in Spain. In Spain the main contributor to this tendency is the electoral system. The lower house is elected using a proportional system based on party lists, a system which is generally recognised to favour women (Norris 1996). This is because parties tend not to want to face the electorate with all-male lists. In contrast the upper house uses a majoritarian system, with most constituencies electing fewer members. This is less favourable for women. In Australia, where it is the upper house which uses a proportional system, we see that women's representation is higher than in the lower house. The representation of women is also marginally higher in the Canadian Senate than lower house. This can probably be traced to similar roots, relying on the potential embarrassment of a party which appoints only men. Indeed one of the only positive ways in which the appointment system is presented to the public is as a means of guaranteeing seats for groups that are otherwise under-represented in politics.[21] The number of women Senators appointed has risen sharply in recent years. Nevertheless, with women still making up fewer than one in three Canadian Senators this opportunity to improve women's representation has clearly not been used to the full.

The professional background of Senators is harder to analyse accurately, and has partly been considered in previous sections. Upper house members, like other parliamentarians, tend to over-represent the professional classes and under-represent manual and clerical workers. Only in France can a notable mismatch be seen between the professional backgrounds of the two houses, with 17 per cent of Senators coming from agricultural professions compared to four per cent of lower house members (Mastias 1999). This is partly a reflection of the rural over-representation in the Sénat, and partly of the related over-representation of certain political groups (for example the concentration of teachers, who tend to represent the Socialist Party, is in the lower house).

The pace of life in the upper house may enable its members to stay more in touch with their professions. This is one of the factors that is cited in the defence of the part-time House of Lords, although the duties of members of that house have become more onerous in recent years. In Italy it is relatively common for parliamentarians to pursue other careers, particularly as lawyers or doctors. In Ireland this activity is positively encouraged by the relatively lower salary levels of members of the upper house. This indicates that in these countries, at least, there is still a belief that being a Senator can be a part-time pursuit. Issues of remuneration and other forms of support for upper house members are further discussed in the next chapter.

THE PERSONALITY OF THE HOUSE

This chapter has so far largely discussed the personalities of Senators—their politics, backgrounds, age, and gender. These factors all contribute to the image and the functioning of the house. One could say that they contribute to the personality of the house itself. As briefly discussed in Chapter 2, many second chambers have very distinct personalities as compared to lower houses, and all tend to share certain personality traits. Such traits include independence of mind, stability of character, and a capacity for high quality and detailed legislative work.

---

[21] Similar proposals have been made in relation to House of Lords reform—see Chapter 14.

There are several factors which are shared by all or most of the seven second chambers considered here. First, they are all smaller than their respective first chambers, some considerably so. This results in a more intimate atmosphere, in the chamber itself and in both party groups and committees. Coupled with longer parliamentary terms, which apply in Canada, France and Australia, this means that the members of the chamber are likely to know each other better than the members of the lower house. Once the higher average age of Senators is taken into account a picture already begins to emerge of more mature and deliberative parliamentary chambers with a less adversarial atmosphere.

The powers of the chamber, and its relationship with government, are discussed in detail in chapters which follow. However, we have already seen that in several cases the power of the upper house over legislation, and particularly over making and breaking governments, tends to be less than that of the first chamber (see, for example, Table 2.2). This means that the outcome of votes in the second chamber may be less critical, and that political leaders will tend to be concentrated in the first chamber. Even in Italy and Australia, where the power of the chambers over legislation is more or less equal, party leaders and senior cabinet members will tend to be drawn more from the lower house. These factors tend to add to a calmer, less adversarial chamber which is not under such intense media scrutiny as the lower house. This could certainly be said to apply to all the chambers considered here.

Party discipline in upper chambers may also be less strict. This particularly applies where the upper house can be overridden by the lower chamber, as has been demonstrated on occasion by the British House of Lords. But this can also be a result of the stature of upper house members. The House of Lords is an example of a chamber where members are less bound by the party whip because they are at the end of their political careers, are not subject to re-selection, and have confidence in their own mature judgement. A similar situation applies, for example, in the French Sénat, where members are mature and well-established political figures. The slower, more stately, pace of the Sénat is also influenced by the nine-year terms served by its members, and even by the relative grandeur of its surroundings in the Palais du Luxembourg (Maus 1993).[22] In Canada a similar situation applies. Here, as in Britain, France, Germany, and Australia (other than in exceptional circumstances) the chamber cannot be dissolved. This helps to give it an

---

[22] Although the independence of members from the whip is often overstated—see Chapter 5 for an account of voting in the Sénat.

independent authority. The long-serving members of the Canadian Senate are socialised over time into a less partisan culture (Kunz 1965). There is thus a higher incidence of 'cross voting' in the Senate, as compared to the lower house where party discipline is extraordinarily strict. This is one factor which makes Canadians a little more tolerant of their otherwise unpopular, unelected, Senate.

The Irish Seanad, which generally has a weak position within the parliamentary system, also exhibits similar traits. The lack of pressure and adversarialism in the Seanad, its very small size and its independent members, all help provide 'a less hurried forum for discussion of the issues facing Irish society and the implications of legislative proposals' (Government of Ireland 1996: 67). The Seanad, which is less subject to media attention, is often used to debate new and controversial issues on which the parties do not have established positions. The university Senators regularly play a leading role in such debates (Gallagher 1993a).

The Australian Senate offers a counter-example on party discipline, given that the outcome of votes in the upper house is crucial to the success of the government's legislation. The political numbers in the Senate generally mean that its members must attend every vote and stick rigidly to the party line—something which need not apply in the lower house. However, the fact that political negotiations must take place in the Senate, whilst the lower house is strictly adversarial, means that relations between its members are none the less better. The rowdy debates and question periods in the House of Representatives lead Senators to dub it 'the monkey house', whilst its members refer to the Senate as 'the mortuary' (Lucy 1993). The following quote further emphasises the distinct personality of the Australian Senate, and could refer to any one of these seven second chambers:

Candidates with Prime Ministerial aspirations, with talent for scoring points from the opposing party and divining the moods of the electorate, will recognise the House of Representatives as the place where they can shine. Candidates whose aspirations lie in the direction of independent thought and research, who really want to come to grips with the issues confronting the nation, and to do something about them will see the Senate as the place where they can be most effective (Lucy 1993: 195).

CONCLUSIONS

This chapter has illustrated how the members of second chambers may differ from their lower house counterparts in a large number of ways.

This is partly a result of the composition method used for the chamber, but also a result of the functions and status of the chamber, as well as a result of tradition.

In modern systems the most important difference between the chambers is liable to be in terms of political balance. This will have a critical impact on the relationship between the two chambers, and the relationship between the upper house and government. We have seen that there are three patterns of party balance demonstrated by the seven chambers surveyed. The first is for government to control the upper house, as well as the lower house—this is generally the case in Ireland, Italy, and Spain. This holds the danger that the upper house will simply act as a 'rubber stamp' for government decisions. In France and Canada, as in the UK, the upper house is sometimes dominated by the governing party and at other times by the opposition. This leads to the prospect of periods of great tension, interspersed with periods where the upper house does not play a particularly effective scrutiny role. The most interesting pattern is that in Australia and Germany, where neither government nor opposition generally win control of the upper house. This provides an opportunity for genuine bargaining between the upper house and the government. It will be interesting to explore in later chapters whether this creates a more effective system.

The fourth option in terms of party political balance would be for the opposition to have permanent or even semi-permanent control of the upper house. It is interesting that this applies in none of the seven countries. With a powerful upper chamber this could lead to a potentially unstable situation whereby government could not proceed with its legislative programme. Even with a relatively weak chamber it could lead to severe disruption.

In some chambers independents play a significant role. This is particularly the case in the Australian Senate, where independent members have at times held the balance of power. The experience of these members holds important lessons for the future of the crossbenchers in the House of Lords. In systems where independents hold the balance of power these members both achieve a higher profile, and have higher resource needs, than is currently provided for in the UK.

As well as the political balance of the chamber, the political 'types' who sit in it will affect the way it functions. In Germany, for example, members of the upper house hold senior positions in state governments and are influential characters. In France Senators are also important local figures, often holding positions as mayors and councillors. In some countries—notably Ireland, Australia, and Spain—the upper house is shaking off the tradition of members entering at the end of their political careers. Increasing numbers of members in these countries are serving terms in the upper house before entering the lower house. This has an important impact on the status of the chamber, and the relationship between it and the lower house.

However, the traditional nature of many upper houses means that they remain dominated by members who are more mature than those in the lower house. The background of upper house members also means that women are often more poorly represented amongst them. Whilst these factors are problematic in a time when there are demands for parliaments to become more representative, the maturity and expertise in upper houses can also be beneficial. This can result in a parliamentary chamber which is more independent of government, and gives more concentrated time and attention to detailed parliamentary work.

Organisation and Administration

When considering second chambers, their administrative arrangements are hardly the most inviting topic. However, the organisation of the chamber, and the resources available to its members, can have a major impact on the way it works and who is prepared to serve in it. The seven chambers described in this book represent the full spectrum, from cramped and poorly resourced to comfortable and well provided for. In some countries the speaker of the chamber is a major political figure whilst in others a relatively minor player. In different countries the government has varying levels of control over the agenda of the chamber which, coupled with the organisation of parties in the house, may give it a greater or lesser degree of independence. These are the issues that are briefly discussed in this chapter.

THE HOUSE AND ITS SCHEDULE

The buildings that have accommodated the seven second chambers are enormously varied—from the lavish splendour of the Palais du Luxembourg, which houses the French Sénat, to the squat and functional structure which houses the German Bundesrat in Bonn. The Bundesrat is, however, due to move in 2000 to grander surroundings in the former Prussian House of Lords in Berlin.

In Britain the Westminster complex, which follows the palatial rather than the practical model, houses both the House of Commons and the House of Lords. The two chambers are found at either end of interconnecting corridors, which join at 'central lobby'. This physical design was influential on both the Canadian and Australian arrangements. In both cases the two chambers are part of the same building, and as in Britain are distinguished by green upholstery in the lower house and red in the upper house. The Canadian building is a gothic-style design not dissimilar to Westminster itself. The Australian chambers took up residence in a huge and magnificent new Parliament House in 1988. The Irish parliament also follows the tradition of housing the chambers together, but in rather more modest surroundings. Parliament sits in Leinster House, once a grand family home in central

Dublin. The large Dáil chamber has been purpose-built whilst the smaller and more unpretentious Seanad uses what was originally the family's ballroom.

In other countries the chambers are housed separately, which has the potential to encourage greater independence amongst the members of the upper house. In Rome the stately Palazzo Madama houses the Senato, several minutes walk from the seat of the lower house. In France a trip from the Sénat to the less elaborate lower house would involve a ten-minute walk followed by a four-stop journey on the Metro. A similar arrangement applies in Spain. The new parliamentary arrangements in Berlin will separate the Bundestag and Bundesrat, which in Bonn were connected by corridors from buildings in the same precinct.

In most cases the chamber forms a hemicycle, although Canada and Australia use a more 'adversarial' format, inspired by the British parliament. In Australia the Senate, like the House of Lords, also includes 'crossbenches' where independent members and those representing small parties sit. But in all cases except for Germany the seating in the chamber accommodates members of parties sitting in blocks. In contrast the Bundesrat seating blocks represent states rather than parties. These blocks, organised from left to right alphabetically by state, all face the President of the chamber. To the President's left is a block occupied by Bundesrat staff, and to the right a block reserved for federal government. In practice most of the seats in the chamber, in all these blocks, are occupied by civil servants rather than elected politicians.

The Bundesrat also has a completely different pattern of meetings to any other chamber. Plenary sessions take place only once every three weeks, and are scheduled a year in advance. These meetings begin on Fridays at 9.30 a.m. and are generally completed by 2 p.m. The main business is the taking of formal votes on policies already discussed at length in committee. There is little time for speeches, and any debate by this point is purely ritual. Votes are cast as blocks by delegation leaders, who may be the only full members of the chamber present.

The other six chambers mostly follow a pattern of meetings similar to that in the House of Lords—slightly fewer meetings than the lower house, but with the number of sitting days generally rising.[1] In all cases there are one or two days of the week when the chamber does not meet, allowing its members to spend time away from the capital. In Australia,

---

[1] In the last full parliamentary year not disrupted by an election, 1995–6, the House of Lords sat for 136 days.

where travelling distances are greatest, sitting days are relatively few—82 in 1997. However the Senate tends to meet for a few more days a year than the lower house. This is the exception. In France and Italy the chambers have the same schedule, whilst in other countries the upper house meets less frequently than the lower house. In Canada the Senate meets on three days a week, compared to the lower house's five, and the relatively short amount of time spent in plenary session has led some commentators to ridicule the institution (Landes 1987). In Spain the Senado tends to meet for two weeks of the month, while the lower house meets for three. In Ireland the workload in the Seanad has grown considerably in recent years. During the 1970s it met on average only 37 days per year, whilst the Dáil met for 88 days. However, whilst the days spent in the Dáil have remained more or less constant, the Seanad met on average 66 days per year between 1990 and 1997.

Although upper house members will have other commitments in the house—in particular committee meetings—shorter sitting hours may enable them to take on more extra-parliamentary duties than members of the lower house. This might include paid employment or more work for their political party. Such a pattern has generally been accepted in countries such as Canada and Ireland, as it has been historically in the UK. However, a minimum level of attendance will generally be expected, even in part-time chambers. In Canada there was a recent outcry when a member of the Senate, Andrew Thompson, was found to have attended only twice in 10 years. His constitutional obligation to appear at least once during each parliamentary session had been fulfilled, but nevertheless he was suspended without pay in 1998. Ultimately he resigned. This episode led to closer records of attendance being kept, with financial penalties for Senators who do not attend regularly. This illustrates how, even in relatively traditional upper houses, the phenomenon of the part-time politician is gradually becoming more rare.

THE SPEAKER

One of the extraordinary features of the House of Lords, in an international context, is the status of the presiding officer of the chamber. Not only does the Lord Chancellor chair debates in the upper house; he also holds a seat in cabinet, runs a government department, and is head of the judiciary. As a law lord he may preside in the highest court of appeal, situated within the House of Lords itself.

This is a unique arrangement, and the other chambers considered in this book are much more reflective of normal parliamentary practice. In all but one of them the chamber's presiding officer (generally known as 'speaker' or 'president') is elected by its members. The exception is Canada where the speaker is appointed by the Governor General (unlike the speaker of the Canadian House of Commons, who is elected). In Germany, although there is a formal election, the position of Bundesrat President strictly rotates around the Länder, with each in turn holding the position for a year. The holder will be the Minister President of the relevant Land. On occasion this means that a change in Land government propels a new Minister President to the position of Bundesrat President on their first day's membership of the chamber. This occurred, for example, in April 1999 following the change of control in Hessen—the Land holding the presidency of the chamber at that time—from the SPD to CDU. The position of Bundesrat President is helpful for a state Minister President—particularly a young and ambitious one such as the new leader of Hessen—as it offers the opportunity to raise their national profile. This position was useful to Gerhard Schröder, who held it as Minister President of Lower Saxony until his appointment as federal Chancellor in 1998.

In Germany the election of the Bundesrat President is no predictor of the postholder's politics, as the successful candidate is preordained. However, in most countries this will tend to result in a speaker who reflects the political majority of the chamber. One exception is Australia, where convention has it that the Senate President will be from the government side. The same convention exists in the lower house where 'the governing party will not tolerate a very high degree of impartiality from a speaker' (Lucy 1993: 180). In the Senate, in contrast, impartiality is forced by the President's need to keep the goodwill of a chamber in which the governing party does not have a majority. In Australia and other countries the politics of the presiding officer will be counterbalanced by the election of vice-presidents, secretaries and other officers representing the other parties. The Australian convention is that the Deputy President comes from the opposition party.[2]

In many countries the position of speaker of the upper house is more senior in governmental terms than the speaker of the lower house. At the top of official rankings he or she will be vying for position with the head of state, the Prime Minister and the lower house speaker. In all seven countries the position ranks at least fourth in the national pecking

---

[2] This has, however, been broken in recent years, beginning in 1990 when the Democrats failed to back the Liberal Party candidate because of allegations that he beat his wife. They instead backed Labor's Mal Colston, resulting in both the President and Deputy President being Labor. Colston later quit the party and continued in his position as an independent Senator.

order. In Germany, France, and Italy it falls to the upper house President to deputise for the national President when he or she is unavailable. This is important, at least symbolically, in emphasising the seniority of the upper house and its President. In Italy the duty is a pure formality, as the President of the Republic is only a figurehead and the need to deputise occurs rarely. However, in Germany and France it is far more meaningful. In the former the Bundesrat President, who is already the Minister President of one of the Länder, has a relatively active role in deputising for the federal President and is sometimes known as the 'second man'. In France the President of the Sénat often has politics which are hostile to those of the government and President, but is a major political figure, who is well resourced and takes an active part in political debates. The holder of this office deputises for the powerful President of the Republic, and is constitutionally the second most senior person in France.

The power of the French Sénat and its President is perhaps best illustrated by the events of the late 1960s, during the period of hostility between the chamber and President de Gaulle.[3] In 1968 when de Gaulle announced his proposals to reform the Sénat, Gaston Monnerville—who had held the presidency of the upper house since 1946—resigned his position and embarked on a national lecture tour to oppose the proposals (Smith 1999). The failure of the referendum on Sénat reform in 1969 was seen as a vote of no confidence in de Gaulle, who promptly resigned. This victory for the Sénat allowed its new President, Alain Poher, to take over as temporary President of the Republic—from where he ran in the presidential election. Although Poher was not successful he remained Sénat President until 1992, serving a second spell as President of the Republic after the death of Georges Pompidou in 1974.

Because of the seniority and prestige of the position, the election for Sénat President can be a major political battle in France. So it was in 1998 when the sitting President, René Monory, who represented the traditional centre-right in the Sénat, was voted out of office. This sparked an extraordinary meeting of the executive committee of Monory's party to discuss the crisis (Smith 1999). The election was a historic moment, as the victor, Christian Poncelet, was a Gaullist. After the events of the 1960s this was referred to as the 'vengeance du Général' (Smith 1998). Despite his different politics, Poncelet has taken a typically hardline position against reform of the Sénat, in open hostility to the proposals of Prime Minister Jospin. This is further discussed in Chapter 11.

---

[3] The politics of this are discussed in Chapter 4.

RUNNING THE HOUSE

In most cases the organisation of the house, both in administrative and political terms, will be the formal responsibility of various committees of members, under the overall control of the speaker. In reality administrative oversight will tend to rest with the chief official of the chamber and his or her staff.

The degree of control the government has over parliamentary proceedings will depend on these arrangements and on precedent and convention. In Britain government has effective control of the parliamentary timetable, including that of the House of Lords, and the same may safely be said of countries such as France and Canada.[4] This applies even where government does not politically control the chamber. However, given that it will generally be desirable for government to maintain the goodwill of the chamber, it may manage the upper house with a lighter touch than that used in the lower house.

Where committees to co-ordinate the business of the house exist, government may rely on a majority in such committees to get its business timetabled in the chamber. In Spain the 'bureau' of each house comprises its speaker and six to eight vice-chairs and secretaries, who are elected by members of the chamber using a proportional system. This group, which is responsible for such issues as timetabling and allocating bills to committees, will therefore tend to have a government majority. The same cannot be said in Italy, where the timetable of the chamber is discussed in a weekly meeting of the *capigruppi* (leaders of parliamentary groups) which is chaired by the Senate President and also attended by the four vice-presidents. If the government does not have a majority in this group—which it often does not—it has no power to insist on its desired order of business. This same arrangement exists in the lower house, and contributes to government's general frustration with parliament. For this and other reasons the Italian parliament has one of the lowest success rates for government legislation amongst all parliaments (Cotta 1994).

In Germany the 'permanent advisory council', comprising one representative from each of the Länder, has a central role in the running of the Bundesrat. The council meets weekly and its meetings are attended by the Bundesrat Director (ie. senior official) and a representative of the federal government. Its members are the 'plenipotentiaries' of each state, who head the state 'mission' offices in

---

[4] In France government control of the timetable is guaranteed under Article 48 of the constitution.

the capital. In some states the plenipotentiary will be a minister and in others a politically appointed senior civil servant. The party balance on the permanent advisory council is important in determining the degree of co-operation between the government and the upper house.

The staff of the house will in practice be critical to its running. The number of staff working for the chamber varies considerably amongst the countries considered here, and a straight comparison between them would not be meaningful. Staffing levels are particularly hard to determine where some support services are shared between the upper and lower chambers, as in the UK. However, the most lavishly resourced chamber in staff terms is probably the French Sénat, with around 1,250 employees. This excludes members' private staff but includes around 100 people who tend the Luxembourg gardens. Such resources might be coveted by the senior official of the Australian Senate, the Clerk, whose team of 268 nevertheless manage to run the chamber efficiently and document its work scrupulously. The Clerk himself is a high-profile figure, frequently appearing in the press to defend the Senate and its work. Even more alien to the UK than the outspoken French Sénat President, it is hard to imagine an official of the British parliament taking up such a role.

PARTY ORGANISATION

The organisation of political groups in the chamber has an important impact on how it runs, both in terms of the resources available for its members to carry out their work and the extent to which party discipline affects what they do. In all second chambers considered here, except the German Bundesrat, members not only sit in party blocks but also are heavily influenced by the views of their groups. In Germany the influence of parties is at least as pervasive, but given the complexity of the Bundesrat's composition its organisation takes a different form.

Where chambers are organised in party groups there is generally a minimum number of members required in order to form a group. This feature, which applies in both the upper and lower house, is one which is not formally applied in the UK.[5] In all cases upper house members are required to specify to which parliamentary group they will belong, within a few days of joining the chamber. The numbers required to form an official group vary, from five members in the Irish Seanad to 15 members in the French Sénat (this broadly reflects the different sizes of

[5] In some countries this reflects the official status which political parties have been given in the constitution of the state.

the chambers). In France, Italy, and Spain those members who are not numerous enough to form their own party groups are required to organise together as a mixed group. The size of parliamentary groups is then used for various administrative purposes, such as allocation of speaking times in the chamber, allocation of members to parliamentary committees, and allocation of allowances, staff, and office space to group secretariats.

In countries where the two chambers are housed in one building, there is more opportunity for joint work between the party groups in respective chambers. Thus in Canada, Australia, and Ireland groups representing the same party from the two chambers meet jointly on a regular basis, as well as individually. This pattern, which is similar to that in the UK, may help to build party cohesion. In France and Italy, where the parliamentary buildings are geographically separated, such meetings are less common. The party secretariats in the chambers are also geographically separate, though they will obviously communicate with each other and with party headquarters. These factors mean that the parliamentary groups of one party in the two chambers are relatively more independent, and may develop more distinct personalities and take slightly different views on policy issues.

In France the situation is exaggerated by the comparatively high threshold for forming parliamentary groups, whilst the system for selecting upper house members discriminates against smaller parties. This results in a different configuration of groups in the *Assemblée Nationale* and the Sénat, as parties join together where necessary to reach the required minimum. Consequently although any group—including the mixed group—shares the same secretariat, they do not necessarily share the same political views. For example the Rassemblement Démocratique et Social Européen (RDSE) is a coalition group comprising, effectively, the left wing of the right group and the right wing of the left group. Although both sections descended from factions of the old Radical party, in the lower house the members of the equivalent sections are aligned with the left and right groups. Whilst the group formally operates collectively in the Sénat, it will tend to put up two speakers in each debate, to give opposing points of view, and only half the group will generally vote with the government.

This situation may add to the myth that the Sénat is far more independent of party discipline than the lower house. This is a feature generally associated with upper houses, which applies to most of these chambers to some extent, but it may easily be exaggerated (the House of Lords is a case in point). Party organisation will have an important part to play in the degree of independence which really applies to members of an upper house. But this is also—as mentioned in Chapter 4—partly a product of the powers of the chamber and the type of individuals who sit in it. In countries such as France and Ireland, party discipline may be less strict because in the end the lower house has the last word on legislation. In Canada this is the case because once members are appointed to the Senate they will stay there until they retire. There is thus little the parties can do to threaten their Senators if they break the whip. A combination of both these factors is seen in operation in the House of Lords. However, whilst debate may be less inhibited and members may express their views more freely, the outcome of votes will nevertheless almost always be predictable. This is illustrated in France by the fact that spokespeople in the poorly attended upper house generally hold and cast the votes on behalf of their entire parliamentary group.[6]

In Germany the nature of the Bundesrat, where block votes are cast by representatives of coalition governments, means party organisation is less obvious. However there is in fact a rigid structure of party organisation in which Bundesrat members and their civil servants play an active part alongside members of the Bundestag. As Länder form the building blocks of the German state, the Bundestag party groups organise by Land, so creating a perfect environment for close work with the Bundesrat. Members of both houses work with the Land 'mission' in the federal capital, which is responsible for relations between the chambers and the Land government and parliament. The mission is staffed by Land civil servants and headed by the plenipotentiary. It will act as a base for meetings between members of the Bundesrat and the Bundestag from the parties of the Land's coalition, and between them and members of the Land assembly. Each plenary session of the Bundesrat, and almost every committee meeting, will be preceded by separate meetings of the CDU-controlled Länder and the SPD-controlled Länder, attended by relevant civil servants or ministers. These meetings will seek to agree a joint position before discussion is opened with members of opposing coalitions. The meeting before the plenary session will also be attended by the chief whip from the

[6] Voting in the Sénat is by cards, which must be placed in urns indicating either support or opposition to the question being debated. Although proxy voting is strictly not allowed, in practice members of the group will leave their cards to be cast *en bloc* by whichever colleague is in the chamber. The final stage of this process in the supposedly independent chamber is the weighing of the votes by Sénat officials to calculate the result, using specially calibrated scales. A similar process of proxy voting in the lower house, which uses an electronic key system, was stamped out in 1993 in order to end the undignified spectacle of members running to turn as many keys as they could before the vote was declared closed (Stevens 1996).

Bundestag, and there will be other meetings between Bundesrat and Bundestag representatives. In particular, representatives of the mission—who effectively work for members of the Bundesrat—will attend meetings of the relevant Bundestag party groups. There are thus clear party positions taken wherever possible, facilitated by this tight network of 'organisational joints' within each of the parties (Leonardy 1997).

RESOURCES FOR MEMBERS

The support of party groups forms one of the resources available to members, all of which are crucial to their effectiveness. There are many other forms of resources, few of which currently apply to the poorly resourced members of the House of Lords. Although members of the Lords have access to libraries and restaurants, and have some limited allowances, they are lacking in one important resource—a salary— which is available to members of all seven upper chambers we are considering.

In complete contrast to the UK, the commonest practice amongst these seven upper chambers is to provide members with an identical salary to that of members of the lower house. This provision applies in Canada, France, Spain, Italy, and Australia. It signifies that members of the upper house are expected to spend as much, or almost as much, time on their duties as their lower house counterparts, and are formally considered to be of equivalent status. In Ireland, where the working week of the upper chamber is traditionally shorter than that of the lower house, its members are paid proportionately less. An Irish Senator earns around two-thirds of the salary of a Dáil deputy, although the Seanad now sits for around three-quarters of the number of days of the Dáil. This leaves Senators in 1999 with a salary of only IR£23,000— roughly equivalent to a civil service graduate recruit. Only in Germany are members of the upper house not paid a separate salary for their duties, as they are already in receipt of a salary as Länder ministers.[7]

---

[7] Dual mandates in the French Sénat, however, do not prevent members drawing more than one salary. In addition to their parliamentary salary of 32,660 Francs per month at 1999 rates, and very generous allowances, the local government positions which most Senators hold are also salaried. A local mayor will earn between 2,700 and 21,400 Francs per month, depending on the size of their *commune*. A regional or departmental councillor earns between 9,000 and 15,700 Francs, and a regional or departmental council chair earns 29,236 Francs per month. Members of either house of parliament are permitted to draw from these sources to supplement their parliamentary salary by up to 50 per cent.

In addition to salaries, upper house members will be very dependent on the allowances to which they are entitled. Again these are in some cases less than allowances to lower house members, but are in no country as minimal as allowances to members of the House of Lords. In all cases the cost of basic expenses, such as travel, telephone, and postage are met, and in some cases—notably France—generous allowances are made for attendance and overnight accommodation. Additional allowances are made in most countries to chairs of committees, as well as to the speaker of the chamber and other office holders. However, probably the most important allowance in terms of the effectiveness of members is that made for staff. This varies enormously.

In Canada members of the Senate get only half the allowance made to lower house members, which pays the salaries of four or five staff members per MP. In Ireland members of the Dáil are much more poorly resourced, with one secretary each. However, members of the Seanad are even worse off—being required to share one secretary between three. At the other end of the spectrum are France and Australia, where Senators have access to at least three members of staff each. On top of this, French Senators in 1999 were entitled to a monthly allowance of 33,000 Francs for office costs, and in both countries party groups in the upper house are very well funded. In Australia each Senator has a luxurious suite of offices housing their staff, and provided with computers, communications equipment, a photocopier, and a private kitchen and bathroom.[8] However, members—particularly those on the frontbench—may also call on the resources allocated to the leaders of their parties. Until recently even the small parties we re allocated 12 staff members each. Independent members are very much disadvantaged by this arrangement, since no such additional allowance is made to their group.[9] In France the largest parliamentary group in the Sénat, the RPR, was entitled to around 850,000 Francs per month in 1999 to fund its ample parliamentary secretariat. It is more difficult to make comparisons with Germany, as members of the Bundesrat are resourced by the civil service based in the Land capital and by their mission staff in the federal capital. Aside from this they have no specific staff on account of their membership of the Bundesrat. However, in many ways they are better resourced than their Bundestag colleagues. This puts them in a powerful position when negotiations between the chambers—

[8] Other facilities available to Senators include meals delivered on request, a pool of chauffeured cars, and a swimming pool.

[9] In France, Italy, and Spain the members of the 'mixed group', including independents, may draw on a shared secretariat which is allocated to the group on the basis of its size.

or between the upper house and the federal government—take place. Indeed many of the links between party groups in the upper and lower houses, described in the previous section, allow Bundestag members to surreptitiously draw on the resources of civil servants who are controlled by their politically sympathetic Bundesrat colleagues.

Finally, the proximity of the chambers to each other will determine the degree to which more general resources for members are shared. Such facilities include bars and restaurants, where members may mix with each other and with their counterparts from the lower chamber, and libraries, which can be an important research resource. Libraries range from the generously resourced in Australia, to the notoriously inadequate in Ireland. In the latter case this just adds to the problems of a chamber where members are badly paid, poorly staffed, and have very few powers with which to make a political impact.

CONCLUSIONS

In summary, the organisation and resources of these seven second chambers vary a great deal. This affects the way the chamber carries out its work, and in some cases will act as a constraint. The Canadian and Irish Senates stand out as far more poorly resourced than their respective lower houses. In contrast members of other upper houses— such as those in France and Germany—are in some ways better resourced than their lower house colleagues. In France the resources available to members of the Sénat are reinforced by the prestige given to the chamber by the position of its President. In Australia, Italy, and Spain the resources provided to the members of the two chambers are basically identical.

The organisation of parties in the house forms an important element of the infrastructure available to members which supports them in their work. This support is likely to be less in the case of small parties and in Australia is non-existent in the case of independent Senators. Amongst party representatives the form of party organisation may have an impact on the degree of independence and freedom they have to express their views in the chamber. In some countries such as Spain and Australia party discipline is very tight, whilst in others—such as Italy and France—it may be less so. In the latter two countries members are also more independent of their colleagues in the lower house as the party groups in the different chambers organise separately, due to the geographic distance between them. The degree of independence of the chamber as a whole to set its timetable and issues for discussion will also be affected by the degree of control which government has over the legislative agenda. The legislative work of the chamber forms the topic of discussion in the next chapter.

6

The Legislative Role of the Chamber

The scrutiny of legislation is the main function of the upper house in all the countries we are considering. One of the primary roles of the chamber is to bring a perspective to parliamentary activity which is complementary to that of the lower house, and it is to the legislative process that this will largely be applied. The upper house and its members will also often give more time to legislative activity than their counterparts in the lower house. In most cases government reports primarily to the lower house, and the members of the upper house will tend to be less burdened with constituency, campaigning, media, and other work. The consideration of legislation, as described in this chapter, therefore forms the heart of the work of each upper house.

The chapter begins with a description of the chambers' powers over legislation, which vary enormously, and have an important impact on their effectiveness. It then describes the legislative processes in the upper and lower chambers, which in some parliaments are quite distinct. The way that disagreements between the chambers are resolved, when each takes a different view on legislation, is the considered. The chapter goes on to briefly discuss particular forms of legislation which may be treated differently in the upper house, before analysing the overall impact of each of the chambers over legislation.

THE POWERS OF THE CHAMBER OVER LEGISLATION

The influence of the upper house in the political system is very dependent on its formal legislative powers. Amongst the seven second chambers these powers vary considerably, covering the full spectrum from relative insignificance to complete equality with the lower house. These powers were summarised for 20 countries around the world—including these seven—in Table 2.2.

In Chapter 2 we saw that Arend Lijphart (1984) has classified the balance of power between chambers in bicameral systems as symmetrical, moderately asymmetrical, or extremely asymmetrical. Lijphart applies this classification to *de facto* powers, which depend upon the extent to which formal powers may realistically be used.

However, the same classification might be applied to purely formal legislative powers.

Symmetrical Formal Powers: Italy

The only truly 'symmetrical' system amongst the countries we are considering is Italy.[1] Here bills may be introduced in either the *Camera dei Deputati* or the *Senato*. Any bill, including the budget, may be amended or rejected by either chamber. Unless a bill is agreed in identical wording by both chambers, it cannot become law—if they cannot reach agreement, the bill will simply shuttle between them until they do, or until it is dropped.

Moderately Asymmetrical Formal Powers: Canada, Australia, and Germany

The powers of the Italian Senato are highly unusual. More commonly the upper house has powers over legislation which are inferior in some way to those of the lower house. Three of the chambers considered here could be said to have 'moderately' asymmetrical powers, at least according to their formal constitutional position. These countries are Canada, Australia, and Germany.

In Canada and Australia there are only minor differences between the formal powers of the chambers. These only apply to financial legislation and to constitutional amendments.[2] Otherwise, the two chambers have the same power to introduce, amend, or reject ordinary bills. In both cases the failure of the chambers to agree a bill can lead to serious problems. There is no easy means, in either system, for the lower house to impose its will on the upper house.

The chambers in Germany may also be said to have 'moderately' asymmetrical powers over legislation, as the Bundesrat has an absolute veto over around half of all bills. The upper house thus 'acts as a formidable hurdle to be negotiated if the federal government is to implement its legislative programme' (Smith 1992: 46). The chamber's consent is required on all bills which either affect the finances of the Länder, or cover matters under their administrative control. Given the nature of devolved powers in Germany this second category covers a vast range of subjects—in most cases the federal level has the power of legislation and the Länder the power of administration. The reach of the Bundesrat is particularly wide, since bills which include even one clause

[1] The symmetry in the Italian parliament unusually also extends to the power of the chambers over the executive. This is discussed in Chapter 9.

[2] Financial legislation is discussed later in this chapter. Constitutional bills are discussed in Chapter 8.

falling within the Länder's influence are subject to veto. In the 1994–7 session of parliament these 'consent' bills made up 61 per cent of all legislation.[3]

The legislative powers of the Bundesrat are not confined to 'consent' bills. The chamber has the right to examine all other legislation discussed at federal level and can 'object' to bills on issues—such as foreign affairs and penal law—which fall outside the administrative control of the Länder. In this case the upper house cannot veto legislation, but may delay it by requesting mediation on points of disagreement and requiring the bill to be returned to the lower house for another affirmative vote.

In practice there are relatively frequent disputes about whether bills fall into the 'consent' or 'objection' category—i.e. whether they impact on the competencies of the Länder. If such disputes are not resolved they may be referred to the Constitutional Court.[4] On occasions where government wishes to prevent the Bundesrat having a veto over a bill it may attempt to draft it in two parts, one of which requires consent and the other of which does not. However, this is likely to aggravate the upper house, and there are obviously limits to what the federal government can succeed in promoting in this way.[5]

Extremely Asymmetrical Powers: Ireland and Spain.

In Ireland and Spain the powers of the upper chamber are amongst the weakest that can be found. It has been said, for example, that the Irish Seanad is 'so subservient to the Dáil that its independent existence is currently hard to justify' (Laver 1996: 532). In both cases the upper chamber has only a very limited period in which it may consider legislation, and any upper house amendments or veto may be easily reversed by the lower house. Thus the only inconvenience which can be caused is a relatively short delay to bills. On certain kinds of legislation,

---

[3] The proportion of bills requiring Bundesrat consent has risen steadily since the first parliamentary session (1949–53) when these represented only 42 per cent of bills. This is partly because there has been a tendency for the federal state to enact more framework type legislation, with detail to be decided in the Länder. The Länder's access to decision making is therefore increasingly through the Bundesrat.

[4] It is the job of the promoter of the bill—which may be government, a group of lower house members or a Land government—to state in drafting whether the Bundesrat must consent or not. The role of the Constitutional Court is briefly discussed in Chapter 8.

[5] An example of the use of such provisions was a health reform bill in the last years of the Kohl government. This was initially drafted as a consent bill, but was vetoed by the Bundesrat. The government then revised the bill and brought it back as an objection bill. But some key parts of it had been lost.

such as financial bills and government decrees, the powers of the upper house are even more limited.

In both countries the upper house has additional formal powers, which are in practice never—or only rarely—used. If they were they could considerably strengthen the status of the chamber. In Ireland the Seanad has the power to request a referendum if a bill it has rejected is felt to contain a proposal of 'national importance'. If the Dáil passes a bill which has been rejected by the Seanad, this provision, included in Article 27 of the constitution, allows a majority of Senators to petition the Irish president within four days. If used it could be effective in counteracting the power the lower house has to overrule the Seanad. However, such a petition has never been presented. In fact the upper house has not rejected a government bill since 1964 (Gwynn Morgan 1990), and thus the conditions for such a referendum have rarely been met. It must be remembered that government has an inbuilt majority in the Irish upper house. In these circumstances even limited powers are unlikely to be used.

The same situation applies in Spain, where the weak powers of the chamber are not in practice used against the government—which tends to have a majority. Here the upper chamber is nominally one of 'territorial representation', comprising representatives of provinces and autonomous communities. In recognition of this fact it was given limited additional powers over territorial matters. However these— unlike the considerable powers of the German Bundesrat over state issues—have proved relatively meaningless in practice. The narrow categories of legislation concerned have included very few instances of bills.[6]

Not Moderate, but far from Insignificant: France

The final chamber under consideration is the French Sénat, which has relatively weaker legislative powers than its counterparts in Australia, Canada, Germany, and Italy, but is by no means as powerless as the chambers of Ireland and Spain. Unlike the last examples there is no time limit within which the Sénat must discuss legislation, although the government does have a high degree of control over the parliamentary timetable. This means the chamber and its committees may give more leisurely and considered scrutiny to legislative proposals—committees alone have three months to consider each bill. Also, the Sénat cannot be automatically overridden by the lower house, although this may happen if the mediation process between the chambers fails. The Sénat can thus

---

[6] This is discussed in more detail in Chapter 10.

cause considerable delay to government bills, and is likely to do so when controlled by a hostile majority. This gives it substantial bargaining power in the legislative process. Whilst its powers are less than 'moderately symmetrical' in relation to the lower house, its ability to influence legislation is far from insignificant.

As discussed in Chapter 2, the powers exercised by the chamber in practice may differ from its formal powers. This depends on other factors such as the political balance of the chamber, and the legitimacy which it possesses to exercise its powers. The formal powers themselves are highly dependent on the process which exists within parliament to resolve disputes between the chambers, and whether the lower house ultimately has the last word. All these issues are further examined later in the chapter. However, we first turn our attention to the legislative process in the upper house, and how that may differ to the lower house.

THE LEGISLATIVE PROCESS IN SUMMARY

The actual process by which legislation is agreed differs from one country to another, and in many cases differs between the two chambers of parliament. This is the case in the UK, for example, where most government bills are discussed in standing committees in the House of Commons, but take their committee stage on the floor of the House of Lords. The legislative process for ordinary government bills in the seven parliaments we are considering is summarised in Table 6.1. In some cases this bears a strong resemblance to the process in Britain, and in others is quite different.

The first point to note is where legislation is introduced. In Britain, and in five of the seven countries considered here, a bill may be introduced either in the upper or the lower chamber. The introduction of bills in the upper house may help to ease the legislative burdens on the lower house, and increase the legislative output of parliament. However, even in those countries where bills may be introduced in the upper house, the lower house normally initiates the majority of bills.

One reason for this is the concentration of ministers in the lower house (discussed in Chapter 9). In Australia, for example, around one-third of ministers are members of the upper house, and around one-third of bills are introduced there. This is because ministers will

Table 6.1. *Summary of the legislative process*

	Bills introduced in	Lower house process	Upper house process
Australia	Either house	Introduced in plenary, all stages generally taken on the floor of the house, though committee stage sometimes taken in 'main committee', comprising all members of the house	Scrutiny of Bills committee first, plus around one-third of bills considered in specialist committee—usually before plenary consideration
Canada	Either house	Introduced in plenary, then considered in committee, then returns to plenary	Same as lower house
France	Either house	Starts in committee, then considered in plenary	Same as lower house
Germany	Upper house	Introduced in plenary then considered in committee, then returns to plenary, then to upper house again	Starts in committee, then considered in plenary
Ireland	Either house	Introduced in plenary then considered in committee, then returns to plenary	Same as lower house, but committee stage taken on the floor of the house
Italy	Either house	Starts in committee, where it is either finally agreed, or sent on to plenary	Same as lower house
Spain	Lower house	Starts in plenary, then sent to committee, where it is either finally agreed, or sent back to plenary	Starts in committee, where it is either finally agreed, or sent on to plenary
UK	Either house	Introduced in plenary then considered in committee, then returns to plenary	Same as lower house but committee stage generally taken on the floor of the house

generally want to introduce their own legislation in the house where they sit.[7] In Canada it is increasingly unusual for bills to be introduced in the Senate—this is partly a reflection of the fact that Senate ministers are very rare.

In Ireland the proportion of legislation introduced in the upper house is also low. However, it has steadily risen from five per cent of bills in the 1960s to 16 per cent from 1990 to 1998. This is because the benefits have increasingly been seen of introducing less controversial and more technical bills in the upper house (a similar pattern is seen in the House of Lords). A good example was the bill to introduce an Environmental Protection Agency, in 1990. This was a complex bill, and there were hundreds of amendments proposed in the Seanad. The opportunity to iron out some of the technical difficulties in the bill meant that when it was considered in the Dáil its passage was relatively smooth.

In France, the proportion of bills introduced in the Sénat has fluctuated, largely as a result of the changing political balance in the two chambers. For example in 1968, when the government were seeking to marginalise the chamber, the proportion of bills introduced there was only five per cent. During the presidency of Giscard d'Estaing, when the political support of the Sénat was important to the government, this rose sharply, reaching 45 per cent in 1975. It then dropped again during the Mitterrand years. In the 1996–7 session, just before the new Socialist government was elected, the proportion of bills introduced in the upper house reached 52 per cent, exceeding for the first time the proportion introduced in the lower house.

Germany is a highly unusual example, as all bills start out in the upper house, and then return there again after consideration in the lower house. The recommendations made during the first passage through the Bundesrat thus form a central part of the discussion when the bill reaches the Bundestag. Because the bill has been public ever since it was introduced in the Bundesrat several weeks before, its introduction in the lower house 'lacks all drama' (Loewenberg 1966: 300).

Table 6.1 also summarises the legislative process in each chamber. There are two basic models for this. Those countries which have been most influenced by the British parliamentary tradition—Australia, Canada, and Ireland—use a similar process to that used in the UK. This includes several stages, starting with a formal first reading in plenary, a second reading on the principles of the bill, and then a committee stage

---

[7] In Australia, as in the UK, ministers may only attend and speak in the chamber where they are a member. In other countries the same rule does not apply. These issues are explored in Chapter 9.

during which the details of the bill are discussed. Finally the bill is discussed and voted on in a plenary session. The 'committee stage' of the bill is not necessarily taken in a committee—the alternative is for this discussion to take place in a 'committee of the whole', on the floor of the chamber (or in Australia, in the 'main committee', which sits in parallel to the chamber). The alternative process to the British model is that employed in Italy and France. Here the first consideration of the bill—in each house—takes place in committee. The bill will not be introduced in the plenary chamber until the committee has deliberated and reported. Indeed in Italy and Spain the bill may never be sent to the plenary after committee consideration, as parliamentary committees have powers delegated to them to agree most legislation.[8] The exceptions in each case include constitutional amendments and bills on the budget and foreign affairs.[9]

As the table shows, the legislative process in both chambers may not be the same. For example in Australia the House of Representatives rarely considers bills in specialist committees, whilst the Senate often does so. In addition there are other important committees in the Senate which examine all bills, and do not exist in the lower house. In Ireland it is the lower house which more often employs committees, whilst all legislative stages in the Seanad are taken on the floor of the house. In Spain, the first plenary reading of a bill takes place only in the lower house, with upper house consideration starting in committee. Otherwise the processes are identical. In Canada, France, and Italy the legislative process in both chambers is virtually the same. However, the power of committees to agree legislation in Spain and Italy may in practice result in differences. Because the two houses act independently in deciding whether a bill is passed in plenary or in committee, a bill may be finalised in committee in one house, but discussed in plenary in the other. In Spain it is far less common for bills to be agreed in committee in the Senado than in the lower house, because the rules in the two chambers governing which bills are eligible for this treatment differ slightly.[10]

---

[8] This unusual feature is one of the many similarities between the Italian and Spanish constitutions. In Italy the practice of agreeing legislation in committee was adopted in 1939, during the fascist regime. It was retained in the new constitution due to the need to pass large volumes of post-fascist legislation rapidly (D'Onofrio 1979). In Spain the practice dates back to the Franco regime (Soto 1997).

[9] Also, in Italy a bill which has been referred to a committee for agreement must be referred back to the full chamber if this is requested by one-tenth of members of the chamber or one-fifth of members of the committee.

[10] The standing orders of the lower house state that this will happen unless the plenary expressly state their desire to see the bill. In the Senado, on the other hand, legislative

More than anywhere else, the legislative process in Germany is very different in the two chambers. Here the lower house uses a process similar to that in the UK, with a first reading before the bill is sent to committee. However, in the Bundesrat the bill is sent straight to committee, where it must be considered quickly, according to a strict timetable, before returning to the chamber for a vote. This elaborate process is considered in the next section, alongside the scrutiny processes in the six other upper houses.

SCRUTINY IN THE UPPER HOUSE

The previous section demonstrated that there are many ways in which the legislative processes in second chambers overseas differ from that in the House of Lords. However, in most cases the legislative procedures within the two chambers of a parliament are similar. Rather than consider all aspects of legislative scrutiny in upper houses, this section focuses on the particular ways in which upper houses treat legislation differently. This extends beyond issues of procedure because, even where legislation goes through identical processes in the two chambers, legislative outcomes will not necessarily be the same. The ways that the chambers consider legislation will be heavily influenced by their composition and their powers. Differences in size, political balance, and types of members in the chambers—as described in Chapters 3 and 4— may mean that bills receive very different treatment in the upper and lower houses.

The section is broken into three subsections which reflect three of the key differences between the upper and lower houses when scrutinising legislation. One of these relates to the differing powers of the chamber, the second to their differing composition, and the third discusses the different legislative scrutiny processes adopted in two of the upper houses.

Time Allowed for Consideration of Bills

One of the features of upper houses is that they often have defined time limits within which to consider legislation. This can present significant challenges. In the lower houses of these seven countries—as in the UK House of Commons—there is no set maximum in terms of the time that

---

powers will not be delegated to a committee without a vote in plenary to explicitly allow this.

may be taken considering a bill. However, in several cases the same luxury does not apply to the upper house.

In Spain the upper house has only two months to consider a bill which has come up from the lower house, or 20 days if government has defined the bill as urgent. A similar system exists in Ireland, where the Seanad has a maximum of 90 days. In Germany the Bundesrat has six weeks to consider a government bill on first reading (three weeks if it is urgent) and only three weeks when it returns from the lower house. In each case the chamber must be efficiently organised in order to schedule each bill—if it fails to comment within the time available it loses the chance altogether.

In addition to the general constraints on time for the upper house, the ability for government to classify certain bills as 'urgent' can further limit the powers of the upper house. This urgency procedure applies in Spain, Germany, and France (where it affects the number of times the chamber may see the bill, rather than the time available). In all cases the use of the rule is the subject of frequent dispute—oppositions in all these countries tend to claim that governments overuse it. In Spain a recent example of a dispute was over a 1997 bill to liberalise the telecommunications industry. The bill was declared urgent by government, giving the Senado only 20 days to consider it, despite the bill having been considered in the lower house for more than six months. Government claimed that the delays which had already occurred in the passage of the bill meant it must now be passed quickly. In Germany such disputes were common during the last months of the Kohl government, as the CDU sought to rush legislation through before the election. In France the proportion of 'urgent' bills has been very high when the political majorities of the two chambers have been opposed. For example during the Socialist governments of 1981–5 and 1988–92 the proportion of urgent bills reached 43 per cent.[11]

Returning to the Spanish Senado, even non urgent bills must be considered within two months. This requires quick and efficient work on the part of the upper house. When the bill arrives, members of the house have 10 days to submit any amendments (lower house members have at least 15 days when they receive the bill). If amendments are tabled the bill is sent to a committee for these to be considered. The committee must work fast in order to report back to the chamber in time for a vote before the deadline. Whilst committees in the lower house will generally take evidence from interested parties, this is unusual in the Senado, because of the pressure of time. Instead

---

[11] Even during the 1993–7 parliament the proportion of urgent bills was 26 per cent.

committee members will sometimes use the transcripts of hearings from the lower house committee to inform their decisions. As in the lower house the work of the committee is generally led by a working group (*ponencia*) made up of spokespeople from the parties on the committee. This group is required to report to the full committee, but is able to work in a more concentrated way (because it is the only part of the process which is closed to the media, this is where much of the real negotiation goes on). The committee itself, having received this report, will use it to inform their report to the chamber.

In Germany the consideration of legislation by the Bundesrat is dictated by a rigid timetable. This is organised around the meetings of the full chamber which take place regularly every third Friday. Between these sessions there is a constant cycle of committee and other meetings in which Länder governments decide their positions on federal bills.

Each bill is sent to the Bundesrat for its first reading before it is presented to the lower house. The chamber generally has six weeks (two full cycles of meetings) to consider the bill, or three weeks if it is deemed urgent.[12] After the plenary session of the upper house has considered the bill, it is then sent to the lower house. Following consideration there it returns again to the Bundesrat, which this time has three weeks to give its final views. Therefore all committee meetings of the Bundesrat—where detailed consideration of bills takes place—are organised on a three-week cycle. This rigid timetable is made considerably easier to manage by the fact that few members of the Bundesrat are actually involved in committee meetings. Most committees are attended by Länder civil servants, who represent the views of their states based on instructions from state governments.

In Australia, the Senate does not suffer from any such curtailment of debate. Indeed pressure from small parties in the Senate has led to changes to the legislative timetable which have ensured that bills have proper time for consideration in both chambers. Until 1986 Senators were frustrated that they were often forced to rush through bills at the end of the session, because they were not sent up from the lower house in adequate time. A Democrat Senator moved a motion, now known as the 'Macklin motion', which stated that the Senate would only consider bills in a given sitting if they were received by a set deadline. This motion was agreed. However, following the introduction of the rule, Senators remained concerned that bills were rushed through the lower house, in order to meet the Senate deadline. Thus in 1994 the Senate forced government to accept a proposal, this time moved by the Green

---

[12] The chamber also has the right to request an additional three weeks to consider a bill.

Party, which required bills to have been introduced in the lower house four weeks before the Senate deadline. In this way members of the Senate succeeded in devising not only the timetable for their own house, but the restrictions in the lower house as well. This meddling in the affairs of the lower house was described by Prime Minister Keating as an act of 'vandalism' on the part of the Senate (quoted in Mulgan 1996: 194). However, the action of the Senate set a framework which facilitates more detailed parliamentary scrutiny of bills in both chambers.

The Ethos of the House and its Committees

Many of the classic features of second chambers will have an important impact on the way in which they treat legislation. These include the smaller size of upper houses, the greater maturity of their members, and greater time they have available for legislative work, alongside the relatively weaker powers of the chamber, which often results in lighter whipping and a more independent ethos. Crucially the party balance in the chamber—which is often different to that in the lower house—will also be a key factor. Thus even where there is a virtually identical legislative process in both houses, other factors in the upper house can make important differences to the quality of legislative scrutiny.

In all seven parliaments, even where the upper house has less time available for legislative consideration than the lower house, it generally has a reputation for more detailed scrutiny. This is a product both of the chamber's composition and its powers. The concentration of party leaders and ministers in the lower house, and consequently the focus of media attention on that chamber, means that lower houses tend to focus on big political issues, and high-profile point-scoring and debate. Thus although most bills may start their legislative passage in the lower house, many details often remain ill-considered when they reach the upper house. Meanwhile, by the time the bill arrives, groups both inside and outside of parliament will have had time to consider its detail and bring forward proposed amendments. These will often be debated in the less frenetic atmosphere of the upper house.

The fact that the upper house has lesser powers than the lower house also places it, at times, in a stronger position to negotiate legislative changes. Whilst members of the lower house must toe the party line, and government defeats may be seen as a confidence issue, the same pressure does not apply in the upper house. Thus even members of the government side in the second chamber may be more prone to question the content of bills, and threaten to vote against the government. In upper houses where government does not have a majority, the threat of defeat is very real. Although the chamber may have only a limited delaying power, the inconvenience and embarrassment which is caused by government defeats may result in compromise. Governments will, in any case, often make concessions more easily in the upper house than they can in the lower house, where every amendment may be viewed by the media as a defeat or a U-turn. For all of these reasons the upper house is often the site of genuine negotiation between the parties, and a higher degree of consensus than is generally found in the lower house.

The size of the chamber can also help to promote a less adversarial atmosphere and more effective work. Where there are fewer members of the house they are liable to know each other better and treat each other with greater respect. Political groups and debates are more manageable and efficient. This is particularly the case in upper house committees, which in most chambers play an important role in the scrutiny of legislation. In France, Italy, and Spain committees are the first port of call when a bill arrives in the chamber, and in Canada they give detailed scrutiny to bills later in the process. In all these cases the committees, which are structured to shadow government departments in both chambers, are smaller in the upper than the lower house.[13] They tend to be more effective bodies than lower house committees, and this too has a positive impact on the scrutiny of legislation in the chamber. In Canada, for example, Senate committees have only 12 members and are generally better attended than the larger lower house committees—whose members are overwhelmed by constituency casework and other duties. The quality of work in Senate committees is often praised, whilst 'Commons committees continue to prove disappointingly unimportant' (J. Smith, 1994: 170). Senate committees are consequently the site of more genuine deliberation and the originators of more amendments than their shadows in the lower house (Franks 1987).

Distinct Scrutiny Processes

Whilst the legislative process in Canada, France, Italy, and Spain[14] is largely identical in the two houses—except for factors such as those discussed above—the process in the remaining three countries differs in more significant ways. In Australia and Germany, in particular, the

---

[13] The size, structure and membership of committees is discussed in more detail in the next chapter.

[14] One difference between the upper and lower houses in Spain, which ought to be important in terms of legislative scrutiny, is the existence of the General Committee for the Autonomous Communities in the Senado. This was established in 1994 in an attempt to enhance the territorial role of the chamber, but its legislative achievements are unproven. The committee is discussed in more detail in Chapter 10.

legislative process in the upper chamber has developed very differently. It is thus much easier to see the distinct influence which the upper house has on the legislative outcome in these cases.[15]

The Australian Senate

The most influential factor in the treatment of legislation in the Australian upper house is the political balance of the chamber. Whilst the lower house includes a government majority, the Senate tends to be more evenly balanced, with small parties and independents generally holding the balance of power. It is primarily this fine political balance which has led to closer scrutiny of legislation in the Senate, and development of different procedures to the lower house.

In particular the Australian Senate has developed a sophisticated committee system for the scrutiny of legislation, whilst the House of Representatives uses specialist committees only rarely, and continues to take the committee stage of most bills on the floor of the house or in the 'main committee'. Although the lower house has developed a system of legislation committees since 1994—largely in response to the developments in the Senate—lower house committees remain 'very much junior and poor relations' to their counterparts in the upper house (Mulgan 1996: 201).

The legislative process in the Senate starts with consideration by two committees which still do not exist in the lower house. The first—the Scrutiny of Bills Committee—is unique amongst the countries considered in this study. This committee was inspired by the Regulations and Ordinances Committee, established many years before, which very effectively scrutinised delegated legislation.[16] Believing that delegated legislation was receiving better scrutiny than primary legislation, Senators pressed for creation of a new committee—which happened in 1981. The Scrutiny of Bills Committee now meets weekly, and discusses all bills as soon as they are introduced in parliament. If a bill is introduced in the lower house the committee will therefore normally look at it before it formally reaches the Senate. The committee has a limited remit, which focuses on the need to ensure that new legislation does not infringe personal liberties and civil rights. Scrutinising each bill against a list of criteria set down in its terms of reference, the committee prepares a weekly report which is circulated to Senators. It is assisted in this process by its own secretariat and a

---

[15] The legislative process also differs in the two chambers in Ireland, because bills are considered in committee in the lower house but on the floor of the Seanad. The role of committees in Ireland is briefly discussed in Chapter 7.

[16] The Regulations and Ordinances Committee is discussed later in the chapter.

professional legal adviser. Where issues of concern are contained within a bill, the committee will write to the relevant minister asking for a response, which will also be reported to the Senate. Sometimes this will result in government making amendments to the legislation, or sometimes to members of the Senate using the committee's report to propose amendments themselves when the legislation reaches the Senate. Potential problems are identified in around 40 per cent of bills (Uhr 1998).

The other legislative committee which is not paralleled in the lower house is the Selection of Bills Committee. This was established in 1989 because, despite the establishment of a committee system in the 1970s, relatively few bills were being sent to these committees. The Selection of Bills Committee, which includes representatives of all party groups, specifies which policy committee(s) should look at the bill. Any member may propose that a bill is sent to a particular committee, suggesting a reason, a reporting date, and possible witnesses. The Selection of Bills Committee makes recommendations to the plenary session, which are generally accepted. Since the establishment of this committee, the proportion of bills being referred to policy committees has risen steadily, reaching 39 per cent in 1998.[17] In contrast, the number of bills considered by the lower house in committee is no more than a handful every year.

As well as discussing which bills should be sent to committee for detailed consideration, the Selection of Bills Committee decides at what stage in the process this should happen. Unlike in other parliamentary systems, this element is not fixed. Initially, when the committee system was newly established, bills were sent to committee for their 'committee' stage—after their second reading in the chamber. However, this led to complaints about delay. In response to this the referral to committees has become more flexible. It is now common for the 'provisions' of the bill, rather than the bill itself, to be referred to committee. This allows a Senate committee to consider the bill whilst it is still being debated in the lower house. In 1996–7 nine out of ten bills in committee were considered at this stage (Paxman 1998). This has led to some complaints about a blurring of roles between the two chambers, but has reduced the delay which was a previous cause of concern.

The committee system itself comprises eight sets of committees in the upper house, each of which shadows two or three government departments. In each subject area there is both a 'legislation' committee, and a 'references' committee, with the latter (as discussed in the next

---

[17] *Business of the Senate 1 January to 31 December 1998*, Department of the Senate.

chapter) generally responsible for enquiries. The two have an overlapping membership. On the whole bills will be referred to legislation committees, although occasionally they are sent to references committees.[18]

One of the main reasons that the committee system was set up was to allow outside bodies to participate in the law-making process through taking hearings on bills. This forms a major part of the work of Senate committees. Such hearings are a feature of legislative consideration in most countries considered here, taking place in both houses of parliament in Canada, Italy, and France, and in the lower house in Spain and Germany. In Australia a Senate committee will normally advertise for submissions on a bill—for example placing adverts in the press and on the internet—and may write to specific interest groups inviting them to submit views. There will then be public hearings, which will often involve the committee travelling to different cities around Australia. The committee looking into the Workplace Relations Bill in 1996, for example, held 18 public hearings in 13 cities (Paxman 1998).

Australian Senate committees do not have the power to amend a bill, but their report to the full chamber will be influential. This is normally discussed during the committee of the whole debate on the bill. The recommendations of the committee will be used by members to draft amendments themselves. Senators who were on the committee will often take the lead in this. Committees also frequently produce minority reports, which can be critical in the case of legislation committees, because the minority in the committee will be the majority on the floor of the chamber. These minority reports—generally drafted by the opposition and the Democrats—are used by members, including the ill-resourced Greens and independents, to put amendments to the bill. However, although legislation committees have a government majority, official committee reports are not always uncritical of government proposals. For example in February 1999 the government-chaired Senate Legal and Constitutional Affairs Committee published a critical report on the proposed overhaul of the Human Rights and Equal Opportunities Commission—rejecting, for example, the proposal that the Commission should in future have to seek the approval of the Attorney General before getting involved in court action.

---

[18] Legislation committees have a built-in government majority, whereas references committees have inbuilt majorities against the government. Thus the tactic of sending bills to references committees is likely to be used for controversial bills. A recent example was the government's proposals in 1996 to part privatise the national telecom company, Telstra, which were sent to the references committee on Environment, Recreation, Communications and the Arts. This episode is further discussed in the final section of this chapter.

The German Bundesrat

In Germany the legislative process in the two houses is utterly different, as a result of the very different memberships of the Bundesrat and Bundestag. The process in the Bundesrat is shorter, as we have seen. It is also far more regulated. This is not entirely to the cost of the Bundesrat, as it allows busy state ministers to have a structured input into the federal legislative process. Upper house members also benefit from the fact that they see all bills before they are introduced in the Bundestag, and again after Bundestag consideration.

The Bundesrat has six weeks to consider each new bill, and three weeks to consider a bill which has been passed by the Bundestag. Thus as soon as a bill is ready it is sent to the Länder 'missions' in Bonn, from where it will be sent to all relevant government departments in each Land capital. Before discussion by the chamber in plenary the bill is discussed in one or more of the Bundesrat's policy committees. There are 13 of these committees in total, which will all meet in the first week of the chamber's three-week cycle. The committees shadow federal government departments, and are mirrored by a similar set of committees in the Bundestag. It is normal (as it is in other countries such as Italy and France) for a bill to be considered by more than one policy committee at once.[19]

Each Bundesrat committee comprises one member from each state, who is normally the relevant departmental minister. The federal government is also represented. In practice both state and federal representatives attending Bundesrat committees are officials, with the possible exception of the chair which is generally taken by a minister. The members of the committees are thus expert in their subject area— more so than committee members in most other parliamentary chambers. Representatives of the Länder are intimately acquainted with the problems of implementing policy in their departments, and are well qualified to raise technical and administrative problems with the bills which require their consent.[20] However, members will also approach bills from their own political perspective, which in many cases will be different from that of the federal government.

Recommendations from all the committees must be ready at least two weeks before a bill is considered in plenary session. In this two-week period the bill, and the committees' recommendations, will be

[19] During the 1990–4 parliament an average of 8.5 committees were involved in scrutinising key bills in the Bundestag (Von Beyme 1998). This pattern is mirrored in the Bundesrat.

[20] On complex technical matters committees can set up subcommittees which involve more specialist staff where required.

considered by individual Länder governments. This process will involve a web of meetings, between groups of officials and groups of ministers both within and across states. As well as Länder cabinets considering the proposals individually, representatives of the SPD-controlled Länder and CDU-controlled Länder will meet separately, in order to try and agree unified positions. Thus by the time the plenary itself arrives most of the negotiations will have taken place. This enables the plenary to run smoothly and efficiently, with the outcome of votes being almost entirely predictable. Indeed, many items on the agenda of the plenary session are agreed *en bloc*, with only the most controversial issues discussed or voted on separately.

After the first reading of a bill in the Bundesrat, the chamber's recommendations are sent to the government. Government then formulates a response to the points and this is sent, alongside the bill and the Bundesrat recommendations, to the lower house. The Bundestag has a more flexible and relaxed timetable within which to consider bills, which may remain there for several months. Bundestag committees take evidence from outside parties, and this may include inviting Länder representatives to attend and explain their position. In fact these members need not wait to be invited, as Bundesrat members have the right to attend and speak in the Bundestag and its committees. They can thus be influential on the committees' recommendations on a bill.

Because the Bundesrat has only three weeks to consider a bill when it returns from the lower house, representatives of the Länder may continue to negotiate with federal government whilst the bill is in the Bundestag. Länder civil servants from the Bonn missions will also keep a close eye on the progress of the bill in the Bundestag and its committees, in preparation for its return.

When the bill does return it will be considered again by the Bundesrat committees, who will pay particular attention to whether their original recommendations have been implemented. They will also review any new items which have been added to the bill by the lower house. Once again the plenary session will vote on the bill, following the usual round of meetings. At this point it becomes critical whether the legislation is a 'consent' bill, on which the Bundesrat has a veto, or an 'objection' bill, where the powers of the chamber are weaker. Where the bill is passed this will not be a particular issue. However, if the Bundesrat wishes to reject the bill, or insist on its amendments, the next stage is to initiate the dispute resolution process between the chambers, which involves a joint parliamentary committee. This and dispute resolution procedures in the other six bicameral systems are the subject of the next section.

RESOLVING DISPUTES OVER ORDINARY LEGISLATION

In a bicameral parliament there will usually come times when the two chambers disagree with each other over a bill. This may be the result of different political majorities, or simply of different perspectives. The way that such disputes are resolved is critical to the power and influence of the upper chamber. In some cases it may simply be overridden by the lower house, whereas in others it may impose its will through an absolute veto. In many countries the actual position is a compromise between these two extremes.

In the UK there is a degree of compromise, although the House of Commons may generally have the last word in the end. The most that the House of Lords can usually do is impose a period of delay. The terms of the Parliament Acts 1911 and 1949 provide, in summary, that an ordinary bill which originates in the House of Commons may receive Royal Assent without the House of Lords' agreement if it is passed in two consecutive sessions by the lower house with an interval of at least a year between.[21] Until this point the bill may shuttle back and forth between the chambers while a compromise is sought. In practice, partly due to the House of Lords' awareness of its own lack of legitimacy, disagreements have tended to be resolved more easily than this. Since 1949 the Parliament Act procedures have only run their full course on two occasions—over the War Crimes Act 1991 and the European Parliamentary Elections Act 1999. If the procedures had been used more often they could have caused much more serious disruption to governments' legislative programmes than the House of Lords has actually inflicted.

This dispute resolution procedure is unique. It is common overseas for lower houses to have the last word, but this is more usually after the upper house has had a set period to discuss a bill. These periods of delay vary considerably.[22] Another common method is for a joint committee of the two houses to be charged with finding a compromise acceptable to both houses. Alternatively, the upper house may retain an absolute veto, in which case government's only options are to dissolve the upper house or drop the legislation. The seven countries considered

---

[21] There are exceptions to this. In particular 'money bills' (certified by the Speaker) are subject to only one month's delay; bills to extend the life of a parliament, and delegated legislation, are subject to an absolute veto by the House of Lords. These forms of legislation in other parliaments are discussed in the next section. Additionally the Parliament Acts do not apply to bills introduced in the House of Lords.

[22] For a more detailed discussion of methods of resolving disputes in bicameral systems around the world, see Russell (1999).

here include examples which use each of these methods. These are discussed below. A summary of dispute resolution procedures in these and 13 other countries may also be found in Table 2.2.

Lower House Decisive

In Ireland and Spain the upper house generally has little power with which to enforce its view on the lower house. In each case the Senate has a limited period—two months in Spain and three in Ireland—to give its opinion on a bill, after which time it passes to the lower house. Here the recommendations of the upper house may simply be rejected, and the bill become law without further consultation with the upper house.

In Ireland the lower house must pass a motion, within 180 days of the Seanad's judgement on the bill, to overrule the upper house's position. However in practice such powers rarely need to be used, as the government almost always has a majority in the Seanad. The chamber's recommendations therefore tend to be uncontroversial. Where there are disagreements the Dáil has not always insisted on its rights to reject the Seanad's view, and a compromise may be found (Doherty 1996). In fact the provision exists for the formation of a joint committee to resolve a disagreement, but this has only once been used, in 1942 (Gwynn Morgan 1990).

In Spain a Senado amendment to most legislation may be overridden by a simple lower house vote. The Senado may also veto a government bill with the support of an absolute majority of members, but this may be overridden by an absolute majority in the lower house. In this case the Senado's position is rejected immediately. Alternatively, if this condition is not met, the lower house may vote again two months later, when a simple majority of those voting is sufficient to override the Senado's view. As in Ireland this procedure is rarely used, because the government normally has a larger majority in the Senado than in the lower house. This means that it generally has no difficulty getting its legislation agreed there. For limited categories of legislation Spain also has a joint committee procedure, but this has also rarely been used.[23]

Endless Shuttle

In Italy there is no such mechanism. The upper house has the right to amend or reject ordinary bills, and cannot be overruled by the lower house at any point. Furthermore there is no formal procedure, such as a

---

[23] The joint committee procedure applies, for example, to constitutional amendments and to limited categories of legislation with regional significance. However, it has only been used on one or two occasions, over the agreement of international treaties.

joint committee between the chambers, through which a compromise may be negotiated. This opens up the possibility of total deadlock between the chambers.

A bill must be agreed by the two chambers in precisely the same words, and there is no method of speeding up this process or reaching compromise. Bills simply shuttle back and forth until agreement is reached. Such legislative 'ping-pong' is common practice. There is also no rule requiring a bill to fall at the end of a parliamentary term, hence the shuttle may potentially continue for many years. The only solution is for the sponsor of the bill to withdraw it, or for the members of the houses to somehow finally agree. Sometimes agreement is reached, even after very long delays. For example a bill amending the law on rape was agreed in 1995 having shuttled between the chambers for 17 years.

Adding New Members to the House

In Canada the same difficulties apply. However, disagreements between the Senate and the House of Commons have tended to be rare. This is largely because the unelected Senate has been cautious in the use of its powers against the elected lower house. However, there have been exceptions. In particular the period in the late 1980s, when a new Conservative government faced a Liberal-dominated Senate, involved many disagreements (these are discussed in more detail at the end of the chapter). Many bills shuttled back and forth, while the government tried to persuade the Senate to change its position. In several cases government was forced to accept unwelcome amendments in order to get its legislation through.

Eventually things came to a climax in 1990, when the government sought to pass a controversial Goods and Services Tax. Prime Minister Mulroney, faced with likely opposition in the upper house, turned to a constitutional clause which had as yet never been used since 1867. This allowed the appointment of eight additional Senators—two from each of the four geographic 'divisions'—and could be used to create a government majority. Under this provision the number of Senators may increase temporarily by either four or eight, with no new appointments allowed from a province before its total has reduced to the standard level. This allowed the Conservative government to achieve a majority in the Senate, and pass the disputed bill.

Double Dissolution

Where the upper house has the power to veto legislation, the only solution to disagreement may be to dissolve both houses of parliament and call an election, potentially enabling political control of the chambers to change. This is not an option in Canada, where the upper house can never be dissolved, but it is the formal procedure for resolving deadlock in Australia.

A double dissolution in Australia may only be triggered in certain circumstances. A bill must be amended or rejected by the Senate, and the Senate's proposals be rejected by the lower house. After this, three months must elapse before the Senate restates its position and this is rejected again in the lower house. At this point the Prime Minister may request that the Governor-General dissolve both chambers and call elections. If the dispute persists after the elections the final decision on the bill may be taken by a joint sitting. In such a sitting lower house members outnumber Senators by two to one; thus the bill is likely to pass.

A double dissolution is a drastic measure, and has serious political consequences. The risks are high both for the government and the Senate. The public may not welcome the cost and upheaval of an election. Thus the Senate—and the small parties which hold the balance of power there—may risk their popularity if they force such an event too often. For the governing party there is the threat that the elections will force them out of power. Even where this seems unlikely, the elections will probably result in a Senate which is more hostile to the government than before. This is because a double dissolution involves re-electing the whole Senate, rather than only half of Senators, as in a normal election. Consequently the result is more proportional, with the small parties and independents being the beneficiaries.[24] Thus although the short-term problem may be solved, the government is even less likely to be able to get future bills through the upper house.

Nevertheless, Australian governments have resorted to double dissolutions six times this century—in 1914, 1951, 1974, 1975, 1983, and 1987.[25] Despite all the difficulties of double dissolutions they are frequently threatened by governments in response to blockages in the Senate.

Joint Committees

The use of a joint committee to resolve differences over bills has a greater potential to allow compromise to be reached, and for both

---

[24] At a regular 'half Senate' election the proportion of votes a party needs to win a seat is 14 per cent. At a double dissolution this drops to seven per cent.

[25] On three of these occasions the incumbent government was returned to power. Only in 1974 was a joint sitting held in order to pass the disputed legislation.

chambers to have some say in the outcome. In a joint committee, members of the two houses can engage directly in a discussion with each other over a disputed bill, and potentially negotiate a position which is acceptable to all. Taking this discussion off the floor of the house can also help—creating a more constructive and less confrontational atmosphere, which may be closed to public view. Such committees—often known as 'conference committees'— are in common use overseas, including in Japan, Russia, South Africa, and the USA.

Joint committees also form a critical part of the procedure for resolving disputes in France and Germany.[26] The two systems are very different, and the German committee is far more successful than the French committee at facilitating a compromise between the chambers. A discussion of the two systems should help to clarify why this is the case.

In France the committee is called the *Commission Mixte Paritaire*. It may be called if a bill has been considered twice by each chamber with no agreement reached (or once if the bill has been classified as urgent). It is the responsibility of government to convene the committee, which comprises seven members from each house. These members will have a political balance which reflects that of their chamber, and will be drawn from the policy committees which considered the bill. Their job is to devise a compromise position, which will be voted on by both chambers. In doing this they are confined to discussion of the particular clauses which remain in dispute.

Government retains considerable power over the process. Not only is government responsible for calling the committee, but it also has the power to decide whether or not to accept their conclusions, before these are put to either house. If government rejects the proposals of the committee, it may instead require that the original text of the bill is put to the vote in both chambers. The Sénat is in a weak position at this point because if it does not accept the proposals before it—which it is not at liberty to amend—the lower house may take the decision alone.

In the early years of the fifth republic, the use of the joint committee was relatively rare. For example from 1958 to 1962 committees were called on only 13 occasions, only five of which resulted in the last word going to the lower house. This gave the lower house the last word on only two per cent of legislation. However, as time has gone by both the number of occasions on which the joint committee has been called, and the proportion of legislation over which the lower house has been decisive, has steadily increased. This has been particularly prevalent

---

[26] A joint committee procedure also applies to certain legislation in Spain, and procedures to call joint committees exist in Canada and Ireland, but in practice are never used.

when the political balance of the two chambers has been opposed. For example from 1981 to 1985, when the Socialists had control of the lower house and the presidency, joint committees were called on 202 occasions. This represented disputes on more than half the eligible bills under discussion. During the 1997–8 session the committee were able to make proposals which were accepted only 29 per cent of the time—the rest of the time the committee failed to agree, or the government or lower house rejected its proposals. This handed the last word to the lower house.

In practice the French joint committee has become more politicised over time, and its power as an institution has been gradually eroded. Very often the opposing majorities in the two chambers will result in deadlock within the committee itself, which will fail to agree a solution. The respect given to the committee, and the stigma of not reaching agreement or of government giving the lower house the last word, have all but disappeared. Thus the committee is increasingly just an obstacle in a system, similar to that in the UK, Spain, and Ireland, where the lower house has the last word.

The German mediation committee—the *Vermittlungsausschuss*—is more successful, primarily because it has more power.[27] Its objective—to come up with a compromise which is acceptable to both chambers—is identical to that of the French committee. But its organisation is very different. Around one in ten bills on average is sent to the mediation committee. As in France the tendency for the committee to be called, and to reach a compromise which is acceptable to both chambers, will fluctuate according to the political control of the chambers. In the last session of the Kohl government, from 1994 to 1997, the committee was called on around 14 per cent of bills.

Unlike the French Sénat, the Bundesrat has an absolute veto over more than half of federal bills. Thus in the case of a 'consent' bill, for which Bundesrat approval is essential, the joint committee must come up with a proposal which is acceptable to the upper house. If its proposals are not acceptable, they may simply be rejected. The system allows the committee to be called twice, but if its recommendations are rejected a second time, the bill dies. This creates a powerful incentive for government and the lower house to compromise.

A second difference from the French system lies in the power to call the committee. In France this is in the sole power of the government. But in Germany if the Bundesrat is unhappy with a bill, it may call the

---

[27] The German committee was based on the powerful model used in the US Congress (Loewenberg 1966). It in turn influenced the design of the French system.

committee itself. Alternatively, if it rejects the bill altogether, or rejects the proposals of the joint committee, the government or the Bundestag may call the committee.

The committee's strength is bolstered by its membership. It is made up of 16 members of each chamber, who are appointed for a full parliamentary session. Thus it has the same stability as a permanent legislative committee. The disadvantage is that members may not be familiar with the technicalities of bills they are sent. However, this problem is outweighed by the advantages. Members of the committee—like those of other permanent committees—can develop effective working relationships, which are less likely on *ad hoc* committees. Members know that they must co-operate with each other, in order to win concessions in the future, and an atmosphere of trust and confidentiality is built up. Even where the bill under discussion is an 'objection' bill, and the Bundesrat does not have a veto, the representatives of the upper chamber will therefore be listened to in committee.

The status of committee members is also very different to that in France. The Bundesrat is represented on the committee by one member from each of the Länder, who will be senior members of state governments. Bundestag representatives are also senior figures within their parties. This means that members of the committee broker deals at the highest level. This strength is boosted by the fact that, unlike the committee in France, the German committee may be referred the entire text of the bill, rather than just the disputed clauses. This allows further scope for trading between different groups on the committee over amendments, if necessary bringing different clauses into the negotiations.[28] The disadvantage is that it can breed resentment amongst other parliamentarians if issues which they believed were resolved are reopened and changed. The status of the committee, and its power to take the final decision over legislation, has caused it to sometimes be dubbed the 'third chamber' (Tsebelis and Money 1997). Its powerful role further entrenches the position of the upper house, such that 'the Bundesrat and the conciliation committee are now the central institutions for the management of consensus politics in Germany' (Sturm 1992*a*: 109).

---

[28] The scope of the joint committee to discuss additional issues was tested to the limits in the 1980s, when an agreement reached over a budget bill included the addition of a totally new clause on an issue not previously covered by the bill. This led to much controversy, and the decision was referred to the Constitutional Court which ruled in 1986 that the committee's action be upheld but that it was 'close to the limit of the legally acceptable' (Tsebelis and Money 1997).

OTHER TYPES OF LEGISLATION

Before turning to consider the overall legislative impact of the chamber, consideration of its legislative role would not be complete without briefly discussing its input into other types of bills. In most countries, as in Britain, the role of the upper house differs depending on the type of legislation. In particular it is common for second chambers to have relatively fewer powers over financial legislation, and relatively more over bills which amend the constitution. Whilst the latter of these is considered separately in Chapter 8, the chamber's role in financial legislation is summarised below. Also considered is the involvement of the chamber in scrutinising delegated legislation, and its role in promoting non-government legislation, including that proposed by upper house members themselves.

Financial Legislation

In Britain the House of Lords has less power over financial legislation than over ordinary bills. After the rejection of the Liberal budget in 1909, the Parliament Act of 1911 introduced a category of 'money bills' over which the upper chamber would have fewer powers.[29] These may only be delayed by the House of Lords for a maximum of a month. Such reduced powers over financial legislation are relatively common in other second chambers.

Restrictions on the treatment of financial bills apply in five of the seven countries. In Australia, Canada, France, and Ireland, financial bills may only be introduced in the lower house.[30] In France all financial bills are classified as 'urgent', and so are considered only once by each chamber. Consideration of the budget may be very rushed in the upper house. The lower house is limited to 40 days for scrutiny of budget bills, and if all this time is taken the Sénat will be left with as few as 15 days. Consequently, the weeks around the budget are a period of intense activity in the upper house.

The power of the upper house to amend bills on financial matters is also often limited. In Ireland the Seanad cannot pass amendments to any bill which would raise taxes or spending, and the chamber is completely excluded from consideration of the annual budget estimates which are laid before the Dáil (Doolan 1994). In addition money bills—which are classified by the speaker of the Dáil—may not be rejected or

---

[29] According to the Parliament Acts money bills must deal exclusively with 'charges'. Thus Finance Bills to implement the Budget are not always classified in this way.

[30] This also applies in Spain, as it does to all ordinary bills.

amended by the Seanad. Instead the upper house has up to 21 days (compared to the usual 90 days) in which it may make 'recommendations', on these bills. Such recommendations may be rejected by the Dáil, but in practice they are rarely made. There have only ever been eight money bills on which the Seanad has made recommendations, and none at all since 1979 (Government of Ireland 1996). Some similar restrictions apply in Canada—here the Senate may pass amendments to financial bills, but not if these would increase either taxes or spending. However, the Senate may reject such bills.

Australia is formally subject to some of the same limitations which apply in Canada and Ireland. Appropriation bills may only be initiated in the lower house, and the Senate may only 'request' amendments, rather than amend such bills. However, the Senate retains the power to veto all bills, including financial bills. The biggest constitutional crisis in Australia's history was sparked in 1975 when the Senate consistently refused to deal with legislation allowing government expenditure. This caused a furious row, with government claiming that the Senate was breaching the spirit of the constitution—because of its reduced powers over financial bills—and the Senate insisting that it was acting fully within its rights. In the end the crisis was only resolved when the Governor-General acted unilaterally and called a double dissolution of parliament, against the wishes of the Labor Prime Minister. Labor lost the election by a landslide (Sharman 1988). Ever since these events controversy has raged in Australia over the powers of the Senate, and in particular over its powers in relation to financial bills. However, the upper house has continued to assert its right to consider financial matters, and has gone on to implement a powerful process of hearings on the twice-yearly financial estimates, which are not mirrored by any similar consideration in committee in the lower house.

In Italy and Germany the power of the upper chamber over financial legislation is the same as that over any other bills. In the Italian parliament the symmetry between the chambers in all matters is such that the introduction of the annual budget alternates between one chamber and the other from year to year. In Germany financial bills are subject to the same test as other bills to decide whether they require Bundesrat consent. However, given that the Länder are responsible for collecting many forms of taxes, and anyway are greatly affected by the levels of taxation and spending. Bundesrat consent is required on virtually all financial bills (Leonardy 1999). The budget bill itself is always an 'objection' bill and therefore subject to Bundesrat veto.

Delegated Legislation

One of the matters on which the House of Lords has a reputation for outstripping the Commons is the scrutiny of delegated legislation. The House of Lords has equal powers with the House of Commons over the agreement or rejection of such legislation.[31] Members of the Lords take part in the Joint Committee on Statutory Instruments, and the chamber spends more time debating delegated legislation than the House of Commons. In addition the House of Lords has a powerful committee for scrutiny of Delegated Powers and Deregulation, which considers whether new bills delegate powers inappropriately. No single committee takes on the equivalent role in the House of Commons.

In other countries the upper chamber often takes a greater interest in delegated legislation than the lower house. In some cases this results in the upper house being quite interventionist in this area, and having a direct impact much beyond that which applies in the House of Lords. The two clearest examples of this are Australia and Germany.[32]

The Australian Senate Standing Committee on Regulations and Ordinances has operated since 1932, and for 50 years it was the main legislative scrutiny committee in parliament. It has been suggested 'that the Senate's pioneering role in the scrutiny of delegated legislation is . . . a rare and early example of an Australian parliamentary institution leading the world' (Uhr 1998: 122). There is still no parallel institution operating in the lower house.

The committee scrutinises all forms of delegated legislation, including regulations, determinations, instruments, directions, by-laws, and notices. It has a strict set of criteria, which are set down in the Senate's standing orders. These are to ensure that each item:

- is in accordance with the governing statute;
- does not trespass unduly on personal rights and liberties;
- does not unduly make citizens' rights and liberties dependent upon administrative decisions which cannot be reviewed by a judicial or other independent tribunal;
- does not contain matter more appropriate for primary legislation.

---

[31] However, the power to reject an order has only ever been used by the House of Lords on one occasion, over the Southern Rhodesia Sanctions Order in 1968.

[32] In Ireland the Seanad was the first chamber to set up a committee on delegated legislation. This was established in 1948 as the Senate Select Committee on Statutory Rules, Order and Regulation, and from 1951 was known as the Select Committee on Statutory Instruments. However it ended its work in 1981, following a reorganisation of the parliamentary committee system (Gwynn Morgan 1990). There is now no committee in either chamber with responsibility for scrutinising the hundreds of orders which are issued every year.

The committee therefore has a clear human rights focus, as well as considering whether the objectives of an instrument fit appropriately within the remit of delegated legislation. In 1981 the committee effectively spawned a sister committee, with very similar terms of reference, to consider ordinary legislation. The Scrutiny of Bills Committee—described above—also considers whether bills inappropriately delegate legislative powers.

The Regulations and Ordinances Committee has an efficient organisation, supported by a secretariat and a legal adviser, and meets weekly. Any potential problems identified with new instruments will be taken up with the relevant minister. If concerns are serious the chair of the committee will table a motion to disallow the instrument, which may be withdrawn later if suitable assurances are received. The committee also publishes a weekly bulletin, which allows Senators to keep up to date with instruments received. In 1996–7 the committee considered 1,791 different instruments. In total, 32 undertakings were received from ministers to amend instruments or their parent acts.[33]

The committee has a good reputation. So much so that the Senate has always rejected an instrument where this is proposed by the committee. In contrast, instruments are hardly ever disallowed by the lower house. The committee retains the support of Senators by sticking rigidly to its terms of reference and not getting embroiled in primarily political disputes over regulations (although the publication of its bulletin does equip others to do so). In 1998 four instruments were rejected in the Senate, none of them on the direct initiative of the committee.[34]

Over time the committee has achieved changes to rules which would have reduced a person's right to trial by jury, allowed officials other than judicial officials to issue search warrants, and enabled officials to enter premises without identification (R. Smith 1994). It has also achieved improvements in the delegated legislation process, including better drafting and ensuring that all such legislation is accompanied by explanatory statements.

In Germany the upper house is equally active on delegated legislation, which is considered in detail in the Bundesrat and rarely in the lower house. This is because most such legislation relates to the administrative competencies of the Länder. The Bundestag is involved in consideration of delegated legislation only on the rare occasions that it covers certain specifically defined areas, such as foreign trade. There will normally be more administrative regulations considered by the

---

[33] *Annual Report 1996–97*, Senate Standing Committee on Regulations and Ordinances.
[34] *Business of the Senate 1998*, Department of the Senate.

Bundesrat than there are bills—around 200 per year. The chamber has the power to amend these regulations, or reject them outright—the mediation committee does not apply as it does to ordinary legislation. The minister concerned therefore has no choice but to listen to the voice of the Bundesrat, even where this means dropping a regulation altogether. Amendments from the chamber may be extensive. For example a regulation on cleaning up contaminated land, which was considered by the Bundesrat in April 1999, had 98 amendments proposed by five policy committees—on the environment, agriculture, economic affairs, home affairs, and housing. They ranged from demands for more radical action to concerns that the regulation was impractical to implement. In such situations government is forced to rewrite regulations in a form which the Länder are prepared to execute.

Non-government Bills

In every country considered here, the majority of legislation passed comes from government. However in all cases there are opportunities for bills to be initiated by parliamentarians, and sometimes by others. In Italy and Spain legislation may even be introduced to parliament by 'popular initiative', through collection of sufficient signatures. It may also come from regional government. However in neither of these countries is there any particular link between legislation proposed by the regions and the nominally regional upper house.

In Germany the situation is different, since state governments are represented directly in the Bundesrat. Members of the upper house may introduce legislation on behalf of their states, and frequently do so. This action is balanced by the right of Bundestag members to introduce private members' bills.[35] Such Bundesrat legislation accounts for only five per cent of successful legislation, whereas 77 per cent comes from government and 18 per cent from the lower house (Patzelt 1999). However, the states have a powerful opportunity through this route to force government action. This is discussed in Chapter 10.

In other countries the type of legislative initiatives from upper house members are more similar to private members' bills in the UK. These bills are rarely successful, when proposed by members of either chamber.[36] For example there has only been one example of a bill

---

[35] In the Bundestag there is no opportunity for individual members to propose bills, as in Britain. Instead a bill must be supported by five per cent of Bundestag members to qualify for consideration. In many cases such bills are promoted by a parliamentary group (Von Beyme 1998).

[36] In Italy the proportion of private members' bills agreed is rather higher than other countries (Cotta 1994), but essentially similar in both chambers.

initiated by Irish Senators reaching the statute book, in 1963 (Gwynn Morgan 1990). In Australia, the success rate is also low, but some important initiatives have resulted from private Senators' bills. These include the Smoking and Tobacco Products Advertisements (Prohibition) Act 1989, which banned advertising in the print media, and the Electoral (Compulsory Voting) Act 1924, which introduced the compulsory voting which is a hallmark of Australian elections.

THE LEGISLATIVE IMPACT OF THE CHAMBER

Having discussed the formal powers of the chamber over legislation, we now turn from to the overall legislative impact of the chamber. This is dependent on far more than the chamber's formal powers. As the discussion will show, the impact which the upper house makes will also depend on its party political balance (and other factors relating to its membership) and the legitimacy which it is seen to have in the eyes of the public.

The impact of the chamber differs a great deal from one country to the next. The countries under consideration can be divided into three broad groups: Spain, Ireland, and Italy, where the second chamber has limited impact; Canada and France where it scores occasional victories; and Germany and Australia, where the second chamber has a powerful role at the heart of decision making. These three groups of chambers are discussed below.

Chambers with Limited Impact: Spain, Ireland, Italy

In countries where the formal powers of the upper house are weak, there will be few examples of major legislative change which result directly from its work. This is also the case where the upper house is controlled by a government majority. However—irrespective of these factors—the chamber's impact in terms of detail may be great. Whilst the lower house will focus on the big political issues—often in the glare of media spotlight—the upper house will often concentrate on the detail of bills. This is precisely the pattern which is seen in the House of Lords.

Of the countries we are considering, it is Ireland and Spain where the chambers' impact is most obviously limited to this role. In both countries it is widely felt that legislation is considerably improved—in its technical detail if not in its general direction—by scrutiny in the upper house. This is a major achievement given that, in both cases, Senators have a far shorter time to consider legislation than their lower house colleagues. However, in neither case is there much opportunity for the upper house to alter the direction of policy, as the government has a virtually permanent majority. Attention therefore focuses on detailed legislative scrutiny, and most amendments which are passed prove to be acceptable to the lower house.[37] Many of these amendments may come from government, in response to points raised in the lower house or by outside bodies during the passage of the bill. Disputes between the chambers are unlikely because any amendments which are unwelcome to government will be defeated in the upper house. At times government may even block friendly amendments in the Seanad, to avoid the delay caused by the amended bill having to return to the Dáil. This weakens the power of the upper house to even improve the detail of bills.

In Spain the Senado has never rejected a bill, as government generally has a larger majority here than in the lower house. Its contribution is generally, like the Irish Seanad, to improve the quality of bills through detailed scrutiny and amendment. The exception was the period in 1995–6 when government temporarily lost its majority, due to the replacement of autonomous community Senators after regional elections. At this time government was promoting a controversial bill, which would have widened the qualifying criteria for legal abortion to allow this on grounds of the mother's economic status. The bill passed the lower house towards the end of the parliamentary term. Government asked the Senado to consider it as a matter of urgency, but the bureau of the chamber rejected this request. Consequently the bill fell, as elections were called soon afterwards. These elections resulted in the loss of the Socialist party majority and the bill was therefore not reintroduced.

The Irish Seanad went through a similar period from 1994 to 1997, when government lost its majority in the upper house for the first time. The focus of legislative activity in the chamber changed, given that the Seanad now had the opportunity to defeat the government. Although the government could overturn any such defeats in the lower house, the time lost to the legislative programme had the potential to cause problems. As Coakley and Laver have noted, even 'the threat of a 90 day delay may be sufficient annoyance to the Dáil and the government to try and avoid this by taking the views of the Seanad on board'(1997: 62). During this period the Seanad's main achievement was changes to the Universities Bill, which was subject to around 300 amendments in the chamber. The Senators elected to represent the universities were

---

[37] For example there were 241 bills considered by the Irish Seanad in the period 1985–94, of which 31 were amended. In only four cases did the Dáil object to any of the amendments (Government of Ireland 1996).

particularly active participants in the debate. Government was forced to accept the Seanad's amendments, partly due to the short time left before the general election.

The Seanad has passed all government bills within their 90-day deadline since 1964. In that year it failed to pass the Pawnbrokers Bill, which was a relatively minor measure. However, the only other occasion when this happened may have had a more serious impact. In 1959 the Seanad failed to pass a bill which proposed to change the electoral system. This was due to the illness of two government Senators. Only a relatively short delay was caused, but this may have been enough to change the public mood. The measure was eventually passed by the Dáil and approval was sought through a referendum. However, the referendum failed. The debate and delay in the Seanad 'may have sounded alarm bells and tipped the scales of popular support narrowly against the bill' (Gwynn Morgan 1990: 90). This demonstrates how even a second chamber with weak formal powers can make a major impact on legislative outcomes at times.

It is appropriate also to discuss the role of the Italian Senato here. This is the upper chamber with the most far-reaching powers, but it too makes a limited distinct contribution to legislation. This is due to the overlapping responsibilities of the two chambers of parliament—in Italy the upper house has no clear responsibilities of its own. Legislation shuttles back and forth indefinitely, and bills are subject to amendments in both chambers. In this process, individual parliamentarians act far more independently of party groups than they do in the UK, in both chambers. Effectively legislation passes through an almost identical process twice, through two chambers where the party balance is very similar. The Senato contributes as much to legislation as the lower house, but it is hard for the public to discern its distinct contribution. Deadlock between the chambers is as likely to be caused by differences between a few influential members as between coherent groups holding to distinct principles. In these circumstances the legislative output of parliament might actually be improved if it comprised only one chamber. Ironically, if that happened, the better chamber to keep would probably be the upper house—where it is widely appreciated that legislative scrutiny is generally more thorough, due to factors such as its smaller size and more mature membership. Despite its formal powers, the Italian Senato—or more properly bicameralism in Italy—might be said to be of limited impact.

Occasional Victories: Canada and France

The Canadian Senate has generally fallen into the bracket of second chambers whose impact is on the detail rather than the direction of government legislation. The Senate works under less time pressure than the lower house, and considers bills which have usually been subject to lengthy scrutiny by MPs—and outside organisations—by the time they arrive. Many amendments therefore tidy up outstanding details on bills, largely in response to issues which have been raised during this process. For over 30 years the Senate did not reject any bill which had been passed by the House of Commons. Eugene Forsey wrote in 1982 that 'the veto power has now become little more than a reserve power, analogous to the reserve powers of the Crown: a power only used in exceptional circumstances' (p. 272).

However, this situation changed almost overnight when the Conservative government of 1984 was elected. This began a six-year period of legislative clashes with the Liberal-dominated Senate. The Liberals had lost power after over 20 years of almost uninterrupted government, and the Senate became their opposition base. Under the leadership of Allan MacEachen, an experienced ex-cabinet minister, Liberal Senators caused difficulties with a number of bills.

This began in 1985 with a borrowing bill which made an unprecedented request for borrowing authority covering two fiscal years, without tabling the spending estimates for the second year. The Senate protested and would not pass the bill, but finally backed down when the government tabled the estimates. The problems continued with the Drug Patent Act, which shuttled back and forth between the chambers for a year from 1986 to 1987, and by further difficulties over bills on copyright and immigration in 1988 (Franks 1999).

The first major crisis came when the Senate refused to pass the Free Trade Agreement with the US, on the basis that this had not been in the Conservative manifesto. They claimed—despite their traditional support for free trade—that the agreement should be subject to approval at a general election. The Senate did not actually defeat the measure, but simply referred it to a committee, where it remained until the election. When the election came it was won comfortably by the Conservatives, and the legislation passed smoothly soon afterwards (Franks 1999).

However, in the new parliament the problems continued. A special Senate committee was very critical of the government's Unemployment Insurance Bill in 1989, proposing many amendments. This continued interference frustrated government, and caused one minister to comment that 'we're not going to have this unelected coterie of

Trudeauites decide what the policy of Canada is to be in 1990' (Franks 1999: 133). The bill shuttled back and forth for over two years until the Senate finally backed down.

The final crisis was in 1990, over a bill introducing a controversial Goods and Services Tax (GST). When the bill arrived in the Senate it was sent to the Banking Committee, which proposed that it be scrapped. Anticipating trouble the Prime Minister took the unprecedented step of appointing additional Senators to create a government majority.[38] The bill was finally passed 18 months after it had first been introduced in the Commons. However, by this point opinion polls showed that 75 per cent of Canadians were against it. It has been suggested that opposition to the GST bill by the Senate contributed to the defeat of the Conservatives in the 1993 election—which saw them reduced to only two seats in the House of Commons (Franks 1999).

Contrary to expectations, the behaviour of the Senate did not revert to full support for the Conservative government after they gained control of the chamber in 1990. Later that year came the first outright rejection of a bill in the Senate for over 30 years. This was a bill on abortion, which fell because seven Conservative Senators voted against the government. This pattern was repeated in 1993 when a bill on streamlining federal agencies was defeated in the Senate. After the Liberals had returned to government, and the Senate was controlled by the Conservatives, the chamber defeated another bill in June 1996. This proposed to end an airport privatisation which had been implemented by the previous government. Under both Conservative and Liberal control it appears that the Canadian upper house has grown accustomed to its new interventionist role, following a period when it was 'more active and influential in Canadian politics than at any other time in its history' (Franks 1999: 121).

The situation in France, where the upper house is occasionally opposed to the government, bears some similarities to the Canadian situation. Here the Sénat, like other second chambers, acts as an effective filter for the detail of legislation, whilst the lower house tends to focus on big political issues. As one expert on the French system has put it: 'if the purpose of a second chamber is to perfect legislation technically, then the [French] Senate serves this purpose' (Mastias 1999: 177). The Sénat proposes around 2,000 amendments each year, many of which serve to tidy up the details of legislation. However, as in Canada, the role of the upper house depends very much on the political balance

---

[38] See section on 'Resolving Disputes', above.

of the two chambers. At times the French Sénat plays a far more active part in the policy-making process.

When the Sénat has a similar political viewpoint to the government it tends to be a co-operative partner. Under President Giscard d'Estaing in the 1970s it was the more sympathetic chamber to government, and was frequently used to initiate bills which were less liable to be welcomed by the lower house (Smith 1999). Although controlled by the centre-right, it has also been relatively dormant in periods—at least since the 1970s—when the Gaullists have been in power. However, the level of legislative activity in the Sénat has always stepped up a gear when the Socialists are in government.

The first evidence of this was seen in the 1980s. President Mitterrand was elected in 1981 and early elections for the lower house resulted in a Socialist majority. Whilst this situation continued, the differences between the chambers were no longer focused on points of detail, but shifted to fundamental political issues. Subjects which the two houses disagreed on included reorganisation of the social security system, nuclear armament, civil liberties, and nationalisation. The Sénat took an increasingly oppositionalist line and eventually became unafraid of taking whatever action it could to disrupt the government's programme (Mastias 1999). The height of these disagreements related to a bill concerning state support for private schools, in 1984. This was a controversial bill, fiercely opposed by the middle classes. Although the Sénat did not have the power to stop the bill, its opposition leader Charles Pasqua launched a highly successful campaign which captured the public mood. The opposition of the Sénat to the bill was presented as a defence of essential personal liberties. Public opposition grew, and culminated in demonstrations on the streets, one attended by an estimated 800,000 people. Eventually the government dropped the bill and was voted out of office in 1986.

The Socialist government of 1988–93 also faced difficulties with the Sénat, and similar problems have afflicted the government of Lionel Jospin, elected in 1997. One recent major dispute was over the legislation to introduce a 35-hour working week—a key plank of the Jospin government's programme. The majority in the Sénat were implacably opposed to this bill. When the initiative was launched the Sénat set up a special investigative committee on Working Time which sought to expose the weaknesses of the proposals. When the bill itself reached the chamber it was so extensively amended that even Socialist Senators voted against it. The issue was sent to a joint mediation committee, which failed to reach agreement. Consequently the bill was eventually passed by the lower house alone. This follows a pattern where a hostile majority in the Sénat results in more legislation being forced through in this way.[39] However, events of the 1980s show that although the Sénat cannot formally block government bills, the disruption and delay which it can cause may help mobilise public opinion against governments, in ways which potentially damage them electorally.

Powers to be Reckoned with: Australia and Germany

In Australia the veto of the Senate extends to all ordinary and financial bills. As described in the section on financial legislation, the greatest constitutional crisis of Australia's history resulted from the Senate's treatment of financial bills. This led to the fall of the government in 1975, and fuelled controversy over the powers of the Senate, which continues today. As John Uhr (1999: 94–5) has said, the Senate has 'proven its capacity to bring down government and, with that power as a threat, to transform the policy substance as well as the administrative style of governments'.

However, the Senate has also proved itself to be a more effective parliamentary institution in considering the detail of legislation than the lower house. Through its network of committees, from the Scrutiny of Bills Committee and Regulations and Ordinances Committee—which concentrate particularly on human rights issues—to the policy committees where expert Senators consider bills in detail and hear evidence from outside groups, legislative scrutiny in the upper house is taken very seriously. In contrast the lower house, with its permanent government majority, has a much inferior committee system and often rushes through bills with far less consideration.

In the 1993–6 parliamentary session, 157 of a total 482 bills were amended in the Senate, with a total of 1,812 Senate amendments passed. Over 70 per cent of these amendments were from government. Many of these will follow issues raised in Senate committee hearings, or modify bills in ways which make them more palatable to minority parties, whilst still receiving the backing of government. However, this leaves 30 per cent of amendments which were not government sponsored. The majority—267—of these came from the opposition, with another 159 originating from the Australian Democrats, and 78 from the Greens and independents (Uhr 1999). In addition to this, seven bills were rejected by the Senate in this period (Evans 1997). Such activity by non-government forces in the Senate causes considerable frustration to governments. The makeup of the Senate means that day-to-day

---

[39] See the section above on 'Resolving Disputes'.

negotiation is required over most major bills, and there are occasional disputes between the chambers where government bills face rejection. Gareth Evans, leader of government in the Senate during this period is recorded as saying that the Senate 'made my life an absolute and unequivocal misery' and that negotiating with other parties there was 'the sort of thing that made grown men weep and jump off tall buildings' (quoted in Beahan 1996: 89).[40]

Labor governments have certainly had difficulties persuading the Senate to pass all their legislation; although the above figures show that the vast majority of legislation is passed, around two-thirds of it unamended. One important example of legislation blocked by the Senate was the proposal in 1986 to introduce a national photographic identity card. The idea of the 'Australia Card' was initially popular, and was a high-profile part of the government's programme. However, the bill to introduce it was vetoed twice in the Senate, by the combined forces of the Liberal/National opposition and the Australian Democrats. These defeats meant that the conditions to trigger a double dissolution of parliament had been met, and an election was called by the Labor government. New elections were held for both chambers in 1987, and Labor was re-elected to government. However, by the time parliament had reconvened the Australia Card proposals had become so unpopular that the government chose not to reintroduce them.[41] As in cases described above in France and Canada, the delay caused by the Senate had allowed the public to re-evaluated the proposals, and prevented legislation being passed which might have become unpopular later.

One of the most controversial bills held up in the Senate during the 1993–6 session was the Native Title Bill. This followed a ruling in the High Court which stated for the first time that Australian aboriginal people retain the rights to native land which was seized from their ancestors by settlers. This was clearly a very difficult issue to resolve, as it brought into question the ownership of land which had now been in white hands for generations. The possibilities for increased racial tensions were considerable. The bill sought to provide a statutory framework for deciding questions left unanswered by the High Court decision, including the creation of bodies to determine native title

---

[40] Evans moved into the lower house at the 1996 general election, to (unsuccessfully) pursue leadership ambitions.

[41] The government was also aware that the introduction of the system would require regular delegated legislation to update. Given the power of the Senate over delegated legislation government had also come to realise that this might cause insuperable practical difficulties.

claims and compensation. It received extensive scrutiny in the Senate. The Senate Legal and Constitutional Affairs Committee held a series of hearings, which resulted in five volumes of submissions and a four volume report. The record of the 'committee of the whole' debate on the bill, which discussed the committee's recommendations, ran to 450 pages in Hansard. There were 88 amendments from government, many of which responded to the committee's report. In addition there were 25 amendments accepted from the Democrats and eight from the Greens. The Liberal/National coalition remained opposed to the bill on principle, and voted against it, but the other parties supported it as amended. It passed the lower house with the Senate amendments intact (Uhr 1998). This is an extreme example of how the Australian Senate tends to shoulder most of the burden for legislative scrutiny. Senator Meg Lees, leader of the Australian Democrats, has referred to the Senate as the 'legislative powerhouse of the parliament'.[42] It is also a forum where broad support can be negotiated over difficult political issues.

Australian conservative governments, as well as Labor governments, have faced difficulties with contentious legislation in the Senate. One example was the 1996–8 government's controversial proposals to privatise the national telecom company, Telstra. The first stage of this was to part-privatisation, brought forward in the Telstra (Dilution of Public Ownership) Bill 1996. This bill was sent by the Senate to a 'references' committee—rather than a government-controlled legislation committee—which carried out an inquiry lasting many months. Seventeen amendments were made to the bill in the Senate, 15 of them from the Australian Democrats. As the Democrats opposed the bill the votes of the two independents in the Senate were crucial. The leader of the two in negotiations was Senator Harradine of Tasmania, who was initially opposed to the privatisation. However, on this occasion the government made generous concessions to Tasmania, and this eventually persuaded him to vote for the bill. A fund using privatisation income was created by the government, containing a total of $250m. Tasmania, with less than three per cent of Australia's population, received $58m of the proceeds.

The government then moved to fully privatise the company, with the Telstra (Transition to Full Private Ownership) Bill 1998. However, this time Senator Harradine stood his ground. Consequently the bill fell, becoming one of only two to be rejected by the Senate in the 1996–8

---

[42] Speech to Democrat National Convention, Jan 1999, quoted in Coonan (1999).

session.[43] Once again, an unpopular bill had been questioned, and ultimately stopped, by the upper house. The Senate, having allowed the part-privatisation, had become the site of negotiation and compromise.

The second Howard government elected in 1998 has faced similar delays and questioning by the Senate. The biggest issue to emerge in this parliament—echoing a great conflict in the Canadian Senate—was the introduction of a Goods and Services Tax. This was proposed by the Liberal/National coalition shortly before the election and opposed by the Labor Party and the Democrats—particularly in relation to tax on food and books. In an unprecedented move the Senate referred the proposals to four committees simultaneously, with co-ordination via a new select committee on the 'New Tax System'.[44] In November 1998 these committees embarked on months of hearings with high-profile witnesses, including many economists and employers who spoke against the tax. This was successful in attracting considerable media attention. In the end a compromise was reached, and the changes eventually passed in June 1999 with a tax exemption agreed in relation to food. Time will tell whether the action of Senate committees in raising public concerns about this bill could prove electorally damaging to the government in the longer term. The parallel situation in Canada, discussed above, contributed to the eventual fall of the government.

Equally influential on government legislation, though less adversarial in its approach, is the German Bundesrat. The chamber provides a forum through which the Länder bring their concerns about federal legislation to the table. It also enables the states to feed in their considerable experience in the detailed delivery of policy. In many ways the design of the upper house enables Bundesrat members to have more weight in the decision-making process than their Bundestag colleagues, due to their greater levels of expertise, and greater levels of support through the Länder civil service. Bundesrat members also have a higher status than backbench members of the Bundestag, which enables them to negotiate with federal government on a more equal basis. All of these

---

[43] The vote of Senator Harradine was also critical in the passing of a second major bill on native title, put forward by the Howard government. This sought partly to roll back the previous bill, and partly to clarify it. The new legislation was opposed by Aboriginal groups and by the Labor opposition. However it passed with the support of Senator Harradine after the negotiation of over 80 amendments. The government had threatened a double dissolution of parliament over the bill, and Senator Harradine defends his position by saying that he did not wish Australia to face a 'race-based' general election.

[44] The three permanent committees were the Community Affairs Committee; Employment, Small Businesses and Education Committee; and the Environment, Communications, Information Technology and the Arts Committee. They were all references committees, thus ensuring that they did not have a government majority.

factors, combined with the considerable formal powers of the chamber, contribute to the Bundesrat's major influence on legislation.

The effectiveness of the upper house is greatest when members use their expertise in the delivery of policy to point out technical and administrative problems with bills:

The committees of the Bundestag respect the administrative expertise of their Bundesrat colleagues, and are therefore receptive to detailed proposals for the revision of a bill on administrative grounds. But politically or regionally motivated proposals are not similarly persuasive. The Bundesrat can supply the Bundestag with effective ammunition against the bureaucratic expertise which the federal government commands. In effect it offers the Bundestag the view of a counter-bureaucracy (Loewenberg 1966: 300).

Proposals from the Bundesrat are carefully worked through by well-resourced state governments during a bill's first reading. Bundestag committees are ill-resourced in comparison, so the proposals by the upper house may be influential on the outcome of their deliberations. Amendments originating in the lower house itself will tend to be more minor (Saalfeld 1990). Where the Bundesrat has made an argument for a bill to be changed on technical grounds, this is liable to be convincing even to representatives of the governing parties in the Bundestag. Where an argument can be seen to be politically motivated this is less likely to be accepted. But this distinction may not always be straightforward—for example conservative representatives may state opposition to a bill on the basis that it has adverse financial effects on rural Länder. Thus Bundesrat members will tend to use technical arguments to cloak political objections where they can.

Given the influence of the Bundesrat's opinion on the passage through the Bundestag, and the ultimate right of the Bundesrat to veto more than half of all federal bills, government will try to anticipate the views of the chamber in advance, and avoid confrontation. Major pieces of legislation will in practice not be tabled in parliament before extensive consultations have taken place between federal and Länder governments. Draft proposals will be circulated to Länder for comment, and discussions will be held at ministerial and minister presidents' conferences. Differences will thus be thrashed out and negotiated before the bill even reaches parliament.[45] If necessary, federal government may seek deals with individual Länder—in particular those controlled by

---

[45] This is illustrated, for example, by the fact that the controversial new laws on German citizenship were passed by the Bundesrat in April 1999 with only a handful of amendments. More minor bills discussed at the same session—which were not subject to such prior negotiation—were more heavily amended.

opposition parties—to secure their support for difficult bills. This may include the use of indirect financial incentives. However, a growing independence of Länder from the centre, coupled by the post-unification increase in the number of Länder, has made such deals increasingly difficult to secure.

Where government does not take careful account of the Bundesrat's views, this can lead it into dangerous confrontations. For example the last years of Helmut Kohl's chancellorship were marked by some poor political judgements which resulted in deadlock between the chambers. The Tax Reform Bill of 1998 was a key example. It could easily have been predicted that this bill would not be acceptable to the Bundesrat, but government pressed ahead and attempted to force it through parliament. The view of the ruling CDU was that intransigence on the part of the upper house would lead the public to criticise the chamber rather than the government. However, the SPD Länder—which were in the majority in the upper house—managed successfully to present the government's plans as regressive. At the same time some CDU-controlled states which would have lost out financially were uneasy. Consequently the bill was rejected by the upper house. The disagreement continued as the bill was sent to the mediation committee, which recommended its rejection. It eventually fell, and the government was heavily criticised. The proposals had become increasingly unpopular during the delay which was caused by the bill passing back and forth. But the government was also damaged by being seen as weak for failing to get the bill through. Defeats such as this, inflicted on the federal government by SPD-controlled Länder through the Bundesrat, contributed to the dwindling popularity of the government and its eventual fall in 1998. Thus both in the day-to-day passage of legislation, and in the wider political context, the Bundesrat has shown itself to be a powerful force to be reckoned with.

CONCLUSIONS

This chapter has discussed the legislative process in upper houses, which is the most important aspect of their work. It has also examined the legislative powers of these chambers, and the impact they have on government bills.

The legislative process itself varies considerably from one upper chamber to another. In some cases it is very similar to the process in the lower house, and in others—particularly Australia and Germany—it is quite different. There are many innovative approaches followed in upper chambers overseas, which could provide useful models for the

UK. Examples are the Scrutiny of Bills committee in Australia, which looks at all bills for a human rights perspective, and the process of taking evidence on bills which applies in many countries. There are also various processes employed to resolve disputes between the upper and lower chambers over legislation. A common method is negotiation via a joint committee of both chambers. This is employed in Germany and France, and offers a potentially less adversarial resolution than simply allowing legislation to shuttle back and forth between the chambers. It can also help prevent deadlock between the chambers over bills.

The way that disputes between the chambers are resolved is an important indication of the power of the upper house. The powers of the chambers considered here vary considerably—from the right to delay legislation for only two months to the right to veto all bills. In many cases the power of the upper house is different for different kinds of bills. This particularly applies to financial bills, where second chambers generally have reduced powers. However, it can also apply, for example, to bills with particular regional impact—the German Bundesrat has an absolute veto over such bills. This categorisation cuts across those used in most parliaments, and gives the upper house a veto over much financial legislation, and delegated legislation, as well as 'ordinary' bills.

The legislative impact of the upper house is difficult to quantify, and relies on far more than its formal powers alone. It will be affected by the membership of the chamber, and in particular by its political balance. The ability of the chamber to challenge government will also depend on its popularity and perceived legitimacy.

All the chambers considered here are, like the House of Lords, valued for their detailed legislative scrutiny work. In many cases amendments proposed in the upper house will come from government, as well as from opposition parties, and may be a result of consultation on a bill, debates in the upper and lower chambers, and accommodating public opinion. Such amendments may greatly enhance the quality of legislation. Thus even a weak chamber such as the Irish Seanad may have a positive day-to-day impact on the quality of government legislation. However, when the delaying powers of the chamber are very short, and particularly where it is controlled by a government majority, there is considerably less incentive for the government or lower house to take heed of its views. Where the upper house can impose a lengthier delay, and is not controlled by government, it is in a far stronger negotiating position.

The high-profile clashes between parliamentary chambers tend to come when the upper house has considerable powers, and is not controlled by a government majority. This has happened relatively frequently in Australia and Germany, where the upper house enjoys an absolute legislative veto. The Canadian Senate possesses similar powers, but these have been used less frequently. This is primarily because the appointed Senate, like the appointed and hereditary House of Lords, does not have sufficient legitimacy to use its powers against an elected lower house. There have been occasional disputes between the chambers in Canada, primarily when the Senate has been controlled by the opposition. But generally the chamber's legitimacy problems prevent it from being a serious hurdle to government. In France, too, there have been some major showdowns between the two parliamentary chambers. These have occurred particularly when the Socialists have been in power, as the Sénat has a permanent bias towards the centre-right.

The impact of an upper chamber cannot be measured purely through the number of amendments which it introduces to government bills, or even by the number of these bills which it rejects. Even where the upper chamber does not have the formal powers to reject a bill, the delay it can cause and the debate which it can promote may prove decisive. Examples from Canada, France, and even Ireland, demonstrate that a concerted campaign by the upper house may help change public opinion, which can result in a controversial bill being amended or dropped. If government is seen to be intransigent, a battle with the upper house can damage its popularity, and even see it voted out of office. The threat of such confrontations may act as a powerful incentive to government to promote policies which are likely to meet upper house approval. Even where the powers of the chamber are limited, governments may choose to accept amendments in the upper house rather than face the prospect of defeat, and possible delay. Governments will also tend to use their knowledge of the upper house to try to avoid drafting bills which will face opposition and potentially cause embarrassment. This is one of the real, and entirely unquantifiable, powers of upper houses, and applies particularly in the case of the House of Lords. The threat of an upper house exposing government weaknesses and influencing public opinion may be enough to prevent many controversial policies ever reaching the drafting stage.

In summary we can see from this chapter that there are three factors which influence the legislative impact of an upper house. These are its political balance, its legitimacy, and its formal powers. The powers of the chamber will obviously be important in terms of the potential threat which it can pose to government if faced with legislation which it does not accept. However, legitimacy is also important. The unelected

Canadian Senate, like the House of Lords, is generally unable to use its considerable power against the elected House of Commons. But critically, political balance has at least as great an effect on an upper house's impact as either of these other two factors. It is not by accident that the description of the chambers' impact in this chapter mirrored their political balance, as it was described in Chapter 4. Upper chambers which are controlled by government will tend to be of limited impact, whilst those which are sometimes controlled by the opposition win occasional bloody victories. But an upper house will tend to be at its genuinely influential when controlled by neither government nor opposition. When the balance of power is held by other forces, government will be more inclined, and more able, to negotiate in order to secure its bills. This is seen in particular in the Australian and German upper houses. Whilst governments may find this process frustrating, a powerful upper house which is controlled by forces independent of government can help create a form of consensus politics which results in better political outcomes in the longer term.

7

Committees and Investigative Work

It is often said that 'committees are the workhorses of legislatures' (Shaw 1979: 420). Whilst the chamber itself receives more media attention, and is the site of much impassioned rhetoric, it is committees which provide the forum for much of the genuine debate and detailed scrutiny that are the heart of parliamentary work.

Second chambers often play a particularly important role in the committee work of parliaments. We have already seen in the previous chapter that some second chambers—such as the Australian Senate—have a more sophisticated committee system than their respective lower houses. Second chambers also benefit from factors such as the smaller size of committees, and the greater time available to members who serve on them. For all of these reasons committees of the upper house may make a significant contribution to the work of parliament. The House of Lords is perhaps unusual in this respect. Whilst it has a small number of specialist committees—notably the select committees on Science and Technology, European Communities, and Delegated Powers and Deregulation—a much greater number of committees is to be found in the House of Commons. This is something that might change when the membership of the upper house is reformed.

In this chapter the structure of committees in second chambers is briefly reviewed. This includes not only the types of committees that operate in the chamber, but also how their membership is made up and—crucially—their political balance. We then look at the role of joint committees—involving members of both chambers, which is significant in some countries. The final section focuses on the investigative work of upper house committees (their legislative work having been discussed in Chapter 6). The chapter ends with some conclusions about the effectiveness of upper house committees and the factors which help to create this.

THE STRUCTURE AND MEMBERSHIP OF UPPER HOUSE
COMMITTEES

Parliamentary committee systems are notoriously hard to classify, as committees take a number of forms, and carry out a vast array of duties. Shaw (1979) suggests five broad categories of committee functions: legislative, financial, investigative, administrative oversight, and housekeeping. For the sake of brevity 'housekeeping' committees will not be considered here.[1] Instead the discussion will focus on committees with more substantive functions.

All but one of the seven upper houses (the Irish Seanad being the exception) have a series of permanent committees which shadow government departments and scrutinise legislation. The number of these committees in the chamber ranges from six in the French Sénat to seventeen in the German Bundesrat.[2] The role of such policy committees is not always confined to legislation. They may stray into the field of administrative oversight by, for example, reviewing government annual reports—as in Australia, or questioning ministers—as in Italy and Spain. They may have financial responsibilities—as in France, where they consider the budget, or Australia, where they carry out estimates hearings. They may even have the right—as in Spain and France—to carry out investigations.

Most of the time the investigative function—discussed in detail later in the chapter—is carried out by a separate set of committees. In some cases these too are permanent. For example in Australia each of the eight legislation committees is mirrored by a 'references' committee in the same policy area, which is mostly concerned with investigations. In Canada legislative committees are coupled with 'standing' committees, which have a similar function to UK select committees. In addition upper chambers in all countries except Germany and Ireland have the capacity to set up *ad hoc* committees, with a limited life, to carry out specific investigations. These are generally known as 'select', 'investigative', or 'special' committees. In some cases—notably France and Italy—'special' committees may also be established for a legislative purpose; for example if a bill falls into the subject area of more than one permanent committee.

---

[1] These exist in every legislature, and cover such issues as oversight of parliamentary buildings, libraries and restaurants, or guardianship of parliamentary standing orders.

[2] In the French fourth republic there were 20 parliamentary committees, which were very powerful and frequently amended legislation heavily. The move to six large and more general committees was part of the rebalancing of power towards the executive in the fifth republic (Hayward 1983).

In most countries the structure and functions of committees in the upper house mirror those in the lower house, although other factors mean that the way these committees work can be very different. However, in some parliaments there are also major differences between the structure and functions of committees in the two chambers.

The main differences in committee structure between the houses were already becoming evident in the previous chapter. These differences occur particularly in Ireland, Germany, and Australia. In Ireland the difference is straightforward—the Seanad has no committees of its own. The current committee system of the Irish parliament centres around a set of joint committees (discussed in the next section). The lower house members of these committees form Dáil legislative committees, which are not mirrored in the upper house. The Dáil, but not the Seanad, may also set up *ad hoc* select committees.[3] Similarly in Germany, there is a more extensive committee system in the lower house than in the Bundesrat. This includes *ad hoc* committees, investigative committees, inquiry commissions, and permanent committees which have an executive scrutiny role as well as dealing with legislation (Saalfeld 1990). None of these responsibilities are shared by upper house committees, whose members have heavy responsibilities in their states. Bundesrat committees instead limit themselves to the detailed scrutiny of legislation.

In Australia there are also major differences in committee work between the two chambers. This is primarily a product of the different party balance in the two houses—since government generally has a majority in the lower house but not in the Senate. The Senate has innovative committees which consider every piece of legislation that arrives at Parliament House. The Selection of Bills, Scrutiny of Bills, and Regulations and Ordinances Committees were described in Chapter 6. The active 'legislation' and 'references' committees in the Senate contrast with a relatively inactive set of committees in the lower house. In addition the Senate sets up frequent select committees to investigate particular topics.

Spain provides the only other example of a major structural difference between the committees in upper and lower houses. This results from

---

[3] The committee system in Ireland is subject to constant change. It is relatively underdeveloped, and tends to be redesigned by each new government—scrutiny of legislation in committee has only applied systematically in the Dáil since 1995. Governments—particularly Fianna Fáil governments—have been reluctant to allow a set of committees to develop which shadow government departments. However, this was finally implemented in 1997. The impermanence of the system makes it weak, as a settled committee culture has never developed.

the new territorial focus which is being encouraged in the Senado, which led in 1994 to the establishment of a General Committee for the Autonomous Communities. This committee was charged with linking devolved governments to the national parliament and discussing regional issues. The impact of the committee is discussed in Chapter 10. It is interesting that no other upper house purporting to represent state or regional interests has set up a similar arrangement.

There can be, therefore, some important structural differences between the committee systems of upper and lower houses. In Australia, in particular, the Senate has established a far more extensive and effective set of committees than the House of Representatives. However in other countries—where the committee system in the two houses is ostensibly the same—there are also differences in practice between the operation of committees in the two houses.

An important factor is the way that membership of committees is formed. One aspect of this is the size of upper house committees, which will tend to reflect the smaller overall size of the chamber, as compared to the lower house. Since similar sets of permanent legislative committees generally exist in the two chambers, the smaller size of the upper house will result in fewer members per committee. For example each member of the French lower house serves on one, and only one, of its six policy committees. These committees have between 73 and 145 members, and are therefore quite unmanageable. They are more like mini-parliamentary chambers than effective working groups. The committees in the Sénat are structured in the same way, and whilst these are large—with between 43 and 78 members—they are certainly more workable than their lower house counterparts. Similarly in Italy there are 13 upper house committees with 26 members each, whilst lower house committees have 45 members. In Spain there are 14 upper house committees, which have 25 members each, compared to the 40 members on lower house committees. In each of these cases the smaller size of upper house committees means that their members work together more closely and effectively than members of committees in the lower house.

Another key membership issue is the party balance of committees. In most countries a rule applies stating that party balance on committees will mirror that in the chamber.[4] This applies in France, Canada, Italy, and Spain. The application of such a rule can have very different consequences in the upper and lower house. Thus in France the

---

[4] This is generally applied flexibly so that small parties are not excluded from committees. For example, in Spain all parliamentary groups are entitled to at least one representative on each committee.

government is guaranteed a majority on all lower house committees, but when government does not control the Sénat it will also not control Sénat committees. This also applies in Canada. Investigations and legislative scrutiny may thus be pursued more vigorously by upper house committees, and government may be faced with hostile committee reports and amendments. In these countries the uncomfortable relationship between government and the upper house is partly played out through its committees.

In Australia, where this relationship is at least as tense, a deal was struck between the government and the Senate over the control of committees in 1994. At this point the system was redesigned to include the current structure of legislation and references committees, operating in pairs. Prior to this all committees in both the upper and lower houses were chaired by representatives of the governing party. The new arrangement gave equal numbers of seats on all committees to government and non-government sides, with a sharing out of chairs, each of which would have a casting vote. Thus legislation committees would have a government chair, and references committees a non-government chair (Uhr 1998).[5] This notionally gave the balance of power on legislative scrutiny to government supporters and control of inquiries to non-government parties. However the chamber has sometimes bypassed this system by sending controversial bills to references, rather than legislation, committees. Committees in the lower house remain dominated by the government side and have been described as 'an extension of executive government' (Cody 1995: 24).

In Germany the organisation of committees is quite different, as the issue of equity applies between Länder rather than between parties. Thus each upper house committee has 16 members, one from each state. Each state is given the chair of one committee, whilst the chair of the seventeenth committee rotates. Two aspects of this system are particularly interesting. First, the balance of power on committees is different to that in the chamber, as it gives states equal representation, rather than the weighted votes they have in plenary sessions. Secondly, the coalition nature of state governments means that states may be represented by ministers of different parties (or more commonly their civil servants) on different committees. Each of these potentially creates a difference of opinion between the committees and the plenary chamber (Braunthal 1972). This is a very different state of affairs to that

---

[5] A similar arrangement applied to other committees. For example, the opposition were given the chair of the Scrutiny of Bills Committee, whilst government retained the chair of the Regulations and Ordinances Committee (Uhr 1998).

in the lower house, where government has a majority on all policy committees.

The party balance of the chamber itself is also important in the referral of matters to committees. Australia is a case in point. Here the chamber's consent is required to send a bill (or an issue for investigation) to a committee. This is far more readily available in the Senate than in the lower house.

Committees classically provide a more constructive forum than the plenary chamber for members to discuss the merits and detail of policy. Not surprisingly, by breaking parliamentarians into smaller, more specialist groups, which can dedicate themselves to particular bills or investigations, partisan barriers may be broken down and more genuine discussion take place. As Paul Furlong has noted with reference to Italy, there is a 'disparity between the consensual day-to-day functioning of parliament [in committee] and the formal public conflict between government and opposition' (1990: 63).

The size of committees and their party balance will have an important impact on the extent to which this consensual style of working is achieved. But there are other important factors as well. One is the profile of the house and its committees. If committees have a high media profile they may become a partisan circus in the same way as the plenary chamber. This is less likely to occur in upper houses, which have a generally lower profile. Upper house members are also likely to have a greater amount of time to devote to committee work than their lower house colleagues. Their own lower public profile, reduced amount of time spent scrutinising government (see Chapter 9) and lesser constituency duties, often make them more assiduous committee participants. Most parliaments benefit from a greater level of commitment, and often expertise, from upper house members to committee work. More time may also be spent in the upper house in committee—for example the French Sénat has traditionally spent more time in committee than in plenary session, whilst the lower house has done the opposite.

The greater concentration on committee work in the upper house may have a wider impact on the chamber. From an Australian perspective, Lucy (1993) has suggested that the time spent in Senate committees helps create a greater consensus between the parties than exists in the lower house. This factor should not be exaggerated, but may be at play in several of the examples considered here.

Returning to the four functions of committees, which were suggested at the start of this section, the legislative work of committees was largely discussed in Chapter 6. The financial function of upper house committees is generally limited, given the reduced powers of second chambers in this area. Most of the remainder of this chapter therefore focuses on the investigative role of upper house committees. But first a brief consideration is given to the role played by joint committees. In many cases this also converges with the final committee function that was suggested—that of administrative oversight.

JOINT COMMITTEES

Joint committees—made up of members of the upper and lower houses sitting together—are a common feature of bicameral systems. In the UK they are relatively little used, and the received wisdom at Westminster is that they are difficult to operate satisfactorily because the culture in the two chambers is so different. There are therefore just two permanent joint committees—on Statutory Instruments and Consolidation Bills— although *ad hoc* joint committees are occasionally established.[6] In other countries they are often more common, although their use varies from extremely rare in Germany and France to the standard committee structure in Ireland.[7]

With the exception of mediation committees to deal with disputes (see Chapter 6) it is unusual for joint committees to deal with legislation. More commonly they are associated with investigative work, and administrative oversight.

There are two particularly common duties which are delegated to joint committees. The first is constitutional reviews. In this duty joint committees can replace, or supplement, the work of other bodies such as Royal Commissions. The joint committee that will consider the proposals of the Royal Commission on the Reform of the House of Lords is an example of the UK's use of this mechanism.[8] Even in Germany, where there are generally no joint committees, one such body was established in 1992 to consider the constitutional implications of reunification. In Canada there have been large numbers of joint constitutional committees, many of them dealing with the vexed question of Senate reform. Their work is mentioned in Chapter 11. In early 1999 there were at least two joint committees on constitutional issues sitting amongst the seven countries—the All Party Oireachtas

---

[6] Examples include the Joint Committee on Parliamentary Privilege 1997–8 and the Financial Services and Markets Committee established in 1998 to consider a draft bill.

[7] Although joint committees are rarely used in Germany there is contact between the members of the houses at committee level, as Bundesrat members are entitled to attend and speak at Bundestag committees, and frequently do.

[8] See Chapter 1 for details.

Committee on the Constitution in Ireland and the Bicameral Committee on Constitutional Reform in Italy (again referred to in Chapter 11).

These joint committees will tend to have a limited life, but committees used for other purposes are often permanent. A particularly common use for these is the oversight of important statutory bodies. For example in Spain joint committees are responsible for overseeing the work of the Ombudsman and the Audit Commission. In Italy such committees are responsible for oversight of the national broadcasting company and the security services. In Australia joint committees scrutinise the work of bodies such as the National Crime Authority and the Electoral Commission.

Aside from these most common functions, joint committees may take on various other roles. For example in Australia a joint committee is responsible for scrutinising international treaties. In Canada (as in the UK) a joint committee considers delegated legislation. In several countries investigations may be allocated to a new joint committee instead of setting up a new committee in one chamber.

The rationale for appointing a joint committee to a task—rather than a committee from only one chamber—is not always clear. In the case of commissions into the constitution—which touch on parliament's role— or of the scrutiny of public bodies which report to parliament, it is a logical arrangement. However, at other times it may result less from rational factors than from competition between the chambers. Several of the joint committees in Spain—for example, those on Women's Rights and Drug Problems—began in the Senado, but became joint committees after members of the lower house began to take an interest. Thus bodies which were operating quite effectively as upper house committees (appointed on a temporary basis) have become semi-permanent joint committees.

The competition between the two parliamentary chambers is perhaps most rife in Italy, where the upper and lower houses are most similar. In addition to permanent joint committees, such as those mentioned above, there is an increasing tendency for investigations to be referred to committees comprising members of both chambers. This avoids the scenario of both chambers setting up competing committees on the same subject.[9] It also ensures co-operation, as jealousy may, for example, prevent a report from a committee in one chamber being discussed in the other. This drift towards inter-cameral working in Italy

---

[9] This tendency has at times been seen in the UK. For example the draft Freedom of Information Bill was referred to a select committee in the House of Commons in 1999. Not wishing to be outdone, the House of Lords established an *ad hoc* select committee of their own, which conducted separate scrutiny in parallel, covering much of the same ground.

has now begun to extend to permanent committees. The equivalent committees from both chambers may hold informal joint sessions, for example to avoid a minister giving separate statements to both. On occasions subcommittees from two parallel committees have joined together to form a joint subcommittee.

The parliament that most uses joint committees is in Ireland, where all permanent committees are composed in this way. These committees are responsible for a wide range of duties, including general policy, reviewing departmental annual reports, and scrutinising government agencies. They may also be asked to investigate issues and take evidence. For consideration of legislation and budget estimates the Dáil members of the committee meet alone, as a select committee of the lower house. However, even the joint committees are dominated by members of the Dáil. Party strengths on the committees are defined according to party strengths in the lower house with no reference to the Seanad. Dáil members take 14 of the 19 places on the committees and tend to hold all the (paid) positions as chair, vice chair, and whip.[10] Although members of the Seanad now have access to ministers and matters of interest through committees, these committees are clearly dominated by members of the Dáil.

The use of joint committees to carry out general parliamentary duties such as legislative and investigative scrutiny can be criticised. For example Evans (1995: 390) suggests that joint committees 'subvert the concept of bicameralism', as they blur the lines of responsibility between the two chambers. In Italy, where they are increasingly becoming the norm, their preponderance has become controversial. Placci (1993) has even suggested that they are unconstitutional, because they effectively result in unicameral decision making. It is ironic that the places where this appears the greatest danger are not only Ireland, with one of the weakest second chambers, but also Italy—with notionally one of the strongest.

INVESTIGATIVE WORK

Investigating particular events or areas of policy is one of the key functions of parliamentary committees. Committees may, for example, investigate the long-term implications of social trends, the options for

---

[10] Generally places on joint committees are allocated proportionally to the chambers on the basis of their size, so upper house members will be outnumbered on such committees. However, there are exceptions. Joint committees in Italy tend to include equal numbers from each chamber, as do some joint committees in Australia.

future government policies, or particular incidents of alleged mismanagement by government or public authorities.

In many cases upper houses are very active in this work—often more so than lower houses. In all countries barring Germany and Ireland the upper chamber has the power to carry out investigations—either in its permanent committees, or in special *ad hoc* committees, or both. The powers of these committees to summon people and papers can be considerable. In Australia and Spain witnesses may be summoned to attend, facing criminal proceedings against them if they do not. In France witnesses at parliamentary committees are required to take an oath.

In most countries the upper house can initiate an investigation— either sending it to a permanent committee or setting up an *ad hoc* committee for the purpose—if a motion is passed by the chamber. Whilst the same provision exists in the lower house, the government majority in that chamber will tend to prevent the establishment of investigations which are unwelcome to government. In upper houses the opposite may be the case. For example in Australia the Senate may pass a motion setting up a select committee, which not only defines the issue to be investigated, but also the number of members and the party balance on the committee. This gives the chamber considerable power to develop investigations that unearth matters which government would prefer to see left alone. In the lower house, in contrast, investigations are mostly initiated by government request, without any reference to the chamber (Evans 1997). In practice lower house investigations are infrequent, and most work by investigative committees takes place in the upper house.

Investigations in some upper houses may thus, at least in part, be motivated by political advantage. A recent example in the Australian Senate was the establishment in 1998 of the 'Select Committee on the New Tax System', which followed the government's announcement that it intended to introduce a Goods and Services Tax. This investigation— discussed in Chapter 6—involved four committees investigating the subject simultaneously. The select committee co-ordinated the investigations and its balance of power was held by the Australian Democrats, who were keen to cause the maximum embarrassment to government through their investigations. Similar inquiries have dogged previous Australian governments, including that of Paul Keating which was 'constantly harassed by special Senate enquiries into its alleged mistakes and misdeeds' (Evans 1999). As a consequence Keating sought not to co-operate with Senate committees, stating in 1992 that neither he nor his ministers would 'slum it' by appearing before them (quoted in Uhr 1998: 202).

Another form of investigation in Australia, which takes place twice yearly, is the 'estimates hearings' held by Senate legislative committees. These wide-ranging public hearings are held by committees into the funding and general affairs of the two or three departments which they each shadow. Generally running over two days, they allow Senators to question ministers and civil servants about the 'objectives, operations and efficiency' of their departments. However, whilst achieving a high media profile, the hearings 'typically take on the substance of an open and frequently disorganised investigation into suspicions of ministerial or bureaucratic inefficiency and maladministration' (Uhr 1998: 191). Opinions on their usefulness are mixed. Although no parallel structure exists in the lower house this has now been proposed. Lower house hearings could provide a more comfortable environment for government.

In France, Sénat investigations are generally carried out by subgroups of permanent committees. However, the chamber also has the power to create special investigative committees. These are infrequently used, but taken more seriously by the Sénat than the lower house (Stevens 1996). But Sénat investigative committees are often politically motivated. They are far more common when Socialist governments are in power. Whilst no such committees met during the Balladur and Juppé governments of 1993–7, by early 1999 there had already been four formed in reaction to the Jospin government. One example was the committee set up to investigate reductions in working time. This aimed to pre-empt the proposed government legislation to implement a 35-hour working week. The hostile Sénat used the committee to try to discredit the policy. On such occasions Senators will court media attention—for example inviting the press with them while they seek to seize documents—and may selectively invite witnesses who they suspect will back up their objections.

However, in general upper houses will pursue investigations with more rigour than lower houses, not only due to their political control but also due to their more reflective tendencies. In the same way that legislation may be scrutinised more closely in upper houses, investigations may also be followed more assiduously. Senators generally have more time, are more mature, and operate away from the glare of media publicity. This may enable them to take on more controversial subjects, which would be difficult for more politicised lower house members to deal with. For example both the Canadian and Spanish Senates have carried out committee investigations into euthanasia.[11] The Canadian committee's report, published in 1994, is highly regarded. The Spanish committee, still meeting in 1999, comprised members of the permanent committees on health and justice. The committee was taking evidence from doctors, lawyers, and many others. It planned around 100 hearings, and met for a full day once a month. Such a workload would be almost inconceivable for a committee made up of lower house members.

Upper house committees may run successful investigations, but there is always a question about what happens to their reports. If reports are not taken sufficiently seriously, significant committee findings may be lost. In many upper houses, such as the Irish Seanad, more time is devoted to the discussion of committee reports than in the lower house. Where there is little respect for the chamber this may be seen as a downgrading of committee investigations. In Canada the upper house itself carries out many important investigations, but the lack of respect for the Senate as an institution means that the impact of these is diminished. In France committee reports are not necessarily debated in either chamber, and may simply be sent to government. Given that their character is often hostile, they may never receive a response. In contrast in Australia government is required to give a response to committee reports within three months. Although the response may be brief, it will generally state a position on each of the committee's recommendations. Compliance with the three month deadline is monitored by the speaker of the chamber. In Spain the power of a committee's recommendations is strengthened by its report being put to a plenary vote in the chamber. Such a report has only failed to be endorsed on one occasion. This creates a greater pressure for government to respond. However, given that the Senado is generally heavily controlled by government parties, it is unlikely to come up with unwelcome recommendations.

CONCLUSIONS

Committee work plays an important part in the life of most second chambers. The products of committee investigations, and of scrutiny of bills in committee, can make a major impact on government policy. Second chambers, which have more time for this work and are often better suited for it, can contribute greatly. However, even more than second chambers themselves, their committees are low-profile and little-studied institutions.

---

[11] As has the House of Lords, in an investigation from 1992–4 by the Medical Ethics Committee.

Some second chambers—the notable example being the Australian Senate—have better developed systems of committee scrutiny than their equivalent lower houses. Others have the same formal system of committees, but take this work more seriously—spending more time in committee, for example, or launching more inquiries. The relatively lower media profile of upper houses can enable committees to work undisturbed, further encouraging the culture of consensus that is the strength of committee work. This, coupled with the smaller size of upper house committees, the type of members in upper houses and the greater time they have available, often means that upper house committees fulfil their role more effectively than their lower house counterparts.

A body that is not often used in the UK, but features more widely overseas, is the joint committee—involving members of both houses. This can form an appropriate forum for overseeing bodies which report to parliament, or for examining major constitutional issues. It may in fact be used to bring together members of the houses in any activity which is normally carried out in a committee. However, in countries where it has become the normal structure for ordinary committee activity—such as Italy and Ireland—it begins to blur the lines between the two chambers. Earlier chapters have suggested that it is important for the chambers to retain their identities, and too many joint committees can start to undermine this.

Shaw has defined the 'importance' of parliamentary committees as 'the ability . . . to influence or determine the outputs of the legislature and the polity' (1979: 384). It has already been suggested that upper house committees, according to this definition, can be equally or more important than their lower house counterparts. However, Shaw also observes that 'as a factor that conditions committee behaviour, party is probably more important than any other single conditioning influence' (1979: 391) . This has been seen through the examples in this chapter. In party terms, committees usually act as a mini version of the chamber, as their membership is chosen proportionally. Thus the politics of the chamber, and its attitude towards the government, will tend to be replicated in its committees. Whilst committees with government majorities—as demonstrated by select committees in the UK House of Commons—can make an important contribution, one of the strengths of upper house committees can be that they are not government controlled. This gives them a different perspective from lower house committees. Upper houses without government majorities may embark on investigations in committee which provide genuine and demanding scrutiny of policy. On the other hand they may sometimes be hijacked for oppositionalist political ends. Whilst the former can make an important contribution, the latter can be of questionable worth.

The motivation behind establishment of a committee, and the behaviour of its members, will play an important part in how its recommendations are received. Committees which are seen as driven by the opposition are unlikely to make an impact on government policy. This can act as an incentive for committee members to behave in a bipartisan way.

Once again, as with legislative scrutiny, we see that the impact of the second chamber will be crucially affected by its composition, legitimacy, and powers. If the committees of an upper house are to be taken seriously, this depends on respect for the chamber as a whole. This is an issue that is examined in Chapter 11.

8

Constitutional and Constituency Roles

Second chambers—even those which are otherwise weak—are often given particular responsibility for protecting the constitution. This responsibility flows naturally from both of the original models of second chambers—as either conservative or federal houses.

In the UK the constitutional role of the House of Lords is limited, although the Lords does have the power to veto a bill which attempts to extend the life of a parliament. However, the chamber does see one of its roles as constitutional protection, and at times has taken a particular interest in constitutional matters.[1] The house is also closely linked to the judiciary, acting—through the Law Lords—as the UK's highest court of appeal. The House of Lords, and members appointed from it to the Judicial Committee of the Privy Council, perform many of the functions which in other countries are assigned to supreme courts.

Whilst the UK's arrangements are highly unusual, strong connections between the constitution, the judiciary, and the upper chamber are common in parliaments overseas. This chapter explores such connections. It begins by considering the role played by second chambers when changes to the constitution are made. It then briefly looks at the links between the upper chamber and the judiciary—which generally comprise involvement in senior judicial appointments—and the role which second chambers occasionally play in other public appointments. It also looks at another constitutional protection role— that being the right enjoyed by members of many second chambers to seek review of potentially unconstitutional bills. Finally, it briefly looks at one of the other important aspects of parliamentary work—the extent to which members of the second chamber are involved in constituency duties.

AMENDING THE CONSTITUTION

The United Kingdom is one of only three Western democracies without a written constitution. Constitutional change therefore has a less well

---

[1] Some examples are given in Chapter 13.

defined meaning in the UK than in most other countries. The recent
changes in the UK, such as the establishment of the Scottish Parliament
and Welsh Assembly, the passing of the Human Rights Act, or the
reform of the House of Lords itself, would in most countries have
required amendments to the written constitution. Such changes would
have had to go through a more rigorous approval process than ordinary
legislation.

In the UK some limited acknowledgement is given to the importance
of constitutional bills. By convention bills considered to be 'first-class
constitutional measures' take their committee stage on the floor of the
House of Commons.[2] However, no special conditions—such as a
qualified majority, for example—need be met for such bills to pass.
With the exception of a bill to extend the life of a parliament, the House
of Lords has no more power over constitutional bills than any other.
The limited powers of parliament over these bills are a result of the ill-
defined nature of the constitution and of constitutional amendment in
the British system.

In all the countries considered here, bills to amend the constitution
are subject to a tougher approval process than ordinary legislation,
which often includes particular powers for the upper house. In all cases
the upper house either has a veto over constitutional bills, or these are
subject to other safeguards such as automatic referendums. The
arrangements for the seven countries, and for the UK, are summarised
in Table 8.1. A broader context was provided by the information in
Table 2.2.

In many cases constitutional amendments must pass in both houses,
not only by the simple majority that applies to ordinary legislation, but
by a tougher 'qualified' majority. In Italy an absolute majority (i.e. a
majority of all members of the house, not just those voting) is required,
and in Germany a majority comprising two-thirds of members of each
house is necessary. In Spain ordinary constitutional bills should pass by
a three-fifths majority in each chamber, and if this is not achieved the
bill is sent to a joint mediation committee. If after this the bill is
supported by a two-thirds majority in the lower house, it may pass with
only an absolute majority in the Senado. This still gives the upper

---

[2] Given the importance of committees—as discussed in Chapters 6 and 7—this does not
necessarily imply a better quality of scrutiny for such bills. For example, the 1997
government tried to break with convention and send the Scotland Bill and Government of
Wales Bill 1997 to standing committee. This did not happen, following opposition from the
Conservatives. Ironically, there were times during the consideration of these bills when
there were fewer members in the chamber than there would have been in a standing
committee.

Table 8.1. *The role of the upper house in passing constitutional amendments*

	Legislative process in upper house	Chamber's power to call referendum	Other safeguards
Australia	Must pass by absolute majority[†], but Senate may be overruled after a delay	None	All constitutional changes are subject to referendum
Canada	Senate can delay for only six months	None	All constitutional changes are subject to agreement by provincial legislatures
France	Pass by simple majority only, but Sénat has absolute veto[†]	None	All constitutional changes are subject to referendum, or approval by joint parliamentary sitting
Germany	Must pass by a two-thirds majority[†]	None	None
Ireland	Same as ordinary legislation	None[‡]	All constitutional changes are subject to referendum
Italy	Must pass twice, second time by an absolute majority[†]	If not passed by two-thirds majority in both houses, one-fifth of Senators may request referendum[†]	In same circumstances, referendum may also be called by 500,000 electors or five regional assemblies[§]
Spain	Must pass by a three-fifths majority[†]—or else by two-thirds majority in lower house and absolute majority in Senado*	One-tenth of Senators may request referendum within 15 days[†]	None
UK	Same as ordinary legislation, except House of Lords has veto of bill to extend life of a parliament	None	None

† Same applies in lower house.
‡ Seanad has power to petition for a referendum on any bill of 'national importance', but a referendum is automatic on constitutional change.
§ A similar provision also allows for referendums to propose the repeal of any existing law.
* Major constitutional changes, including changes to the status of the monarchy, or citizens' rights, this process must be followed by dissolution of both houses of parliament, and repeated after fresh elections. They are then also subject to a referendum.

house the opportunity to block the bill, but allows strong support in the lower house to outweigh weaker support in the upper house. In any case, a referendum may be called on a constitutional bill in Spain if one-tenth of members of either house request it within 15 days of the bill passing. A similar arrangement exists in Italy, where a referendum may be called by one-fifth of members of either house, by a petition of 500,000 electors or by five regional assemblies, unless a two-thirds majority passed the bill in both chambers.

In France, no qualified majority is required for constitutional amendments. However, the Sénat has more power in this area than over ordinary bills. Whilst the lower house may have the last word, after mediation, on ordinary bills, the Sénat has an absolute veto over constitutional bills. These are also subject to either a referendum, or a joint sitting of parliament which must pass them by a three-fifths majority. This not only applies to bills amending the constitution, but also to 'organic' bills. These are bills of a constitutional nature, which do not require an actual amendment to the constitution—a bill to change the electoral system would be an example. Similar categories of 'organic' bills exist in several other countries but are not necessarily subject to such stringent restrictions as constitutional change. In Spain the Senado actually has less power over organic bills than over ordinary legislation.

Thus in Germany, France, Italy, and Spain the upper chamber can act as a real block to constitutional change. The implications of this will be discussed shortly. However, it is also worth considering briefly the systems where the second chamber does not hold such a threat. In Canada the Senate can veto all ordinary legislation, but not constitutional bills. This arrangement was put in place in 1982, as part of the Canada Act (which provided a modernisation of the Canadian constitution), and limited the delaying power of the upper house over constitutional bills to six months. This was in fact an admission of the failure of the Senate to act as an effective territorial chamber (see Chapter 10). Instead of seeking the provinces' approval through the Senate, this approval is now required directly through provincial assemblies. The new arrangements have created a situation where the constitution is very 'rigid' and difficult to change. Attempts to reform the Senate—discussed in Chapter 11—have been frustrated by this rigidity.

The system to change the Australian constitution is quite similar to that in Canada. Unlike all other legislation, the Senate does not have a veto over constitutional change. However, this is compensated by the requirement to seek approval by the states. In Australia this is done through a referendum, which must be supported by at least half of those voting in at least four of the six states. It must also be supported by a majority of voters overall. This also creates a rigid system; of the 42 questions put to such referendums, only eight have been agreed (Parliament of the Commonwealth of Australia 1997). Similarly in Ireland a referendum is required to change the constitution. This provides a safeguard against parliament, which has no more power over constitutional changes than over other bills, taking rash or politically motivated action in this area.

Returning to the countries where the second chamber can have an impact, this has often created a real obstacle to reform. As with blocking of ordinary legislation, the chamber's behaviour over constitutional amendments will be highly dependent on its political balance. In countries such as Spain and Italy, where the second chamber tends to mirror the first, a change which has been agreed by the lower house will not generally hit problems in the upper house. However in others, such as Germany and France, the political tensions between the chambers can require careful negotiation of constitutional changes, and even result in total blockage of government proposals.

The requirement in Germany to obtain a two-thirds majority in each chamber for constitutional change is designed to ensure that such proposals have cross-party support. Except in the case of a 'grand coalition' of left and right (such as that of 1966–9), no government would hold such a large majority of seats.

Despite this stringent condition, there have been more than 40 constitutional changes agreed since 1949 (James 1998). A large proportion of these have changed the relationship and relative powers of the federal and state levels. These have generally resulted in an increase of powers to the centre (Sontheimer 1988). All these changes have had to be negotiated with state governments through the Bundesrat. Although states—and in particular their parliaments—have forfeited some powers in this process, state governments have conceded the changes, since their position in the upper house means they retain a veto on federal legislation. However, there have been clashes between the state and federal levels over constitutional change. An example was the threat from the Länder to use the Bundesrat to block constitutional changes resulting from the Maastricht treaty (this is further discussed in Chapter 10). A coalition of Länder from across the political spectrum joined together to claim rights for the states in European decision-making. The result was the inclusion in 1992 of a new article 23 of the Basic Law, giving the Bundesrat additional powers over EU matters.

This was extracted from the federal government as a condition for agreeing the changes they required (Jeffery 1998).

In France the resolution of differences between the chambers over constitutional matters has been less harmonious. The Sénat has at times used its veto to completely block government proposals. Such problems have recently troubled Lionel Jospin's Socialist government over several key proposals. One example was the government's proposed *Parité* legislation, which sought to amend the constitution to guarantee equal rights for men and women to elected office. This was given unanimous support in the lower house and received personal endorsement from the Gaullist President Chirac. The government planned to hold a joint session of parliament at Versailles on International Women's Day 1999 to endorse the change. However, these plans were thwarted when the Sénat heavily amended the proposals in January. A weakened version of the reform was eventually agreed in late June. This prompted a furious response from the press over the Sénat's conservative attitude.

Another battle between the government and the Sénat has emerged over the proposals to limit the number of elected offices which the constitution allows citizens to hold. This is an issue which cuts to the heart of French political culture, and particularly to parliament, where many members hold multiple mandates.[3] The first constitutional amendment on the *cumul des mandats* was successfully passed in 1985. This introduced a limit of two senior political positions (member of parliament, MEP, regional council member, mayor of a major *commune*, etc.) which an individual could hold at any one time. The proposal of the Jospin government is to further limit this to preclude members of parliament from holding an executive office such as mayor. This would have an impact on a large number of sitting members. The measure has been particularly opposed by the Sénat, in its notional role as the local government house. Although the legislation passed the lower house with the support of the Socialist majority, it was vigorously opposed in the Sénat. By mid-1999 these difficulties had not yet been resolved.

The Sénat's opposition to such proposals illustrates the difficulty which the government could face in implementing major constitutional change. Members of the Sénat have opposed, for example, greater devolution of powers to regional government, or rationalisation of the local government system. Crucially they are also opposed to their own reform, and have an absolute power to block it. This is further discussed in Chapter 11.

[3] See Chapter 4 for details.

JUDICIAL AND OTHER APPOINTMENTS

The House of Lords, as well as acting as a parliamentary chamber, forms the UK's highest court of appeal. The members of the chamber include up to 12 serving 'Lords of Appeal in Ordinary', commonly known as 'law lords'. As well as sitting in the House of Lords, the law lords also sit as members of the Judicial Committee of the Privy Council. These two bodies between them fulfil the roles that Constitutional and Supreme Courts serve in other countries. An additional link between the chamber and the judiciary is created by the role of the Lord Chancellor, who is not only the head of the judiciary, and a serving cabinet minister, but also acts as the presiding officer of the upper house.

It is relatively common overseas for the parliamentary upper house to have a role in overseeing the judiciary. However, other countries observe more strictly the doctrine of 'separation of powers', and do not allow dual membership of the judiciary and legislature. Instead the relationship between the parliamentary and judicial branches of government operates at arms length.

The commonest link between these branches is for upper house members to have responsibility for approving senior judicial appointments. This applies in particular to the appointment of members of Constitutional and Supreme Courts, who are the ultimate arbiters in constitutional disputes. In some countries—such as the Russian Federation and the US—this duty is borne by the upper house alone. In others it is shared equally with the lower house. Four examples of countries where the upper house shares this responsibility are Germany, France, Italy, and Spain.

In each of these countries a Constitutional Court is responsible for overseeing the protection of the constitution, and resolving constitutional disputes between different branches or levels of government.[4] The role of these bodies is further discussed in the next section. In each case the upper house plays a major part in the appointment of members of the court. Thus in Germany the two chambers each elect half the members of the court, on a two-thirds majority. This ensures that the successful candidates have broad political support. The Bundestag and Bundesrat alternate in electing the President of the court. In Spain a similar system applies, with one-third of the court elected by each chamber on a three-fifths majority. In

---

[4] In France this body is known as the 'Constitutional Council'. In other countries it is known as the 'Constitutional Court'.

France each chamber is responsible for one-third of appointments, but these are made by the President of the chamber—this is a further indication of the power of the Sénat President. In Italy the two chambers meet in a joint session to elect one-third of members of the Constitutional Court.[5]

Thus in each of these cases the upper house—and lower house—are tied into the appointment of the highest court which will at times adjudicate constitutional matters. In addition, second chambers may have other responsibilities for the judiciary. In Italy and Spain the two houses of parliament share responsibility for appointing part of the body which is responsible for day-to-day judicial oversight and appointments. In Italy a joint session of the two chambers is responsible for appointing one-third of this body, whilst in Spain the two chambers appoint one-fifth of members each. This creates an indirect line of accountability between the entire judicial system and parliament.

The upper house may also share responsibility for other public appointments and government positions. In Italy the Senato is involved in the election of the head of state—the President of the Republic is elected by a special session including members of both houses of parliament, alongside regional representatives. In Spain both houses must approve the candidate for Ombudsman (*Defensor del Pueblo*)—candidates are proposed by a joint committee, and must be approved by both houses on a three-fifths majority (Juberías 1999).[6] In Canada this responsibility extends to other public appointments, including the Official Languages Commissioner, Information Commissioner, and Privacy Commissioner, whose appointments must be approved by both houses of parliament.

[5] The German court comprises 16 judges, elected for terms of up to 12 years. The Spanish court comprises 12 members, appointed for nine years, with one-third chosen every three years. The chambers therefore approve four members each, with two of the remaining four members appointed by government and the other two by the General Council of the Judiciary. The French Constitutional Council has nine members, appointed for nine years, with one-third chosen every three years. The Presidents of the two parliamentary chambers each appoint three members, with the remaining three appointed by the President of the Republic. The Italian court comprises 15 members, appointed for nine years. Five are appointed by joint parliamentary session, five by the President of the Republic, and five by the ordinary and administrative courts.

[6] However, the lower house may have the last word on this appointment in the case of a disagreement.

PROTECTING RIGHTS AND THE CONSTITUTION

As well as blocking bills which seek to amend the constitution, some second chambers have powers to challenge the constitutionality of other bills. This operates through members of the chamber referring bills to the Constitutional Court, on the basis that they breach some provision of the constitution. In some cases this power is used frequently.

In Spain, for example, there are six routes by which a bill may be referred to the Constitutional Court. These are referral by: the Prime Minister, the Ombudsman, a judge, an autonomous community government or parliament, a group of 50 lower house members, or a group of 50 Senators. The opportunity for groups of parliamentarians to make such appeals means an opposition party may use this right, if it can find a constitutional provision which may be used to object to the bill. This can be an effective weapon against the government, and create a strong incentive for government to act within the constitution. Given the weak powers of the Senado, and its permanent government majority, it has been suggested that 'in practice [the Constitutional Court] has often become an alternative and, in some ways, more effective Second Chamber' (Newton 1997: 68–9).

Likewise the Constitutional Court in Germany can 'almost be described as a third legislative body' (Smith 1992: 45). It has a *de facto* power of amending legislation and can nullify acts which do not comply with the Basic Law. Various laws have been referred to the court by opposition parties, and struck down as a result (Sontheimer 1988). The Bundesrat has the power to make referrals to the court, as do individual Länder. However, the stronger position of the upper house in the German system means that it has recourse to the court on matters of substance less frequently than its Spanish counterpart. Because the Bundesrat has the power to veto much legislation itself, many of its referrals to the court relate simply to whether a bill is one on which its consent is required. There have been several supportive decisions in the Constitutional Court on which forms of legislation the Bundesrat can veto. This has helped increase over time the proportion of bills which require upper house consent (Jeffery 1998).

In France bills may be referred to the Constitutional Council by a group of 60 lower house members or 60 Senators, or the President of either house. As in Spain and Germany this may be used as a weapon by the opposition. For example, during the 1980s, 'recourse to the Constitutional Council became automatic when legislation was adopted against the advice of the Senate' (Mastias 1999: 172). However, where objections to a bill can be justified on constitutional grounds this can also act as an important safeguard.

Until 1974 in France the right to refer a bill to the Constitutional Council lay only with the Presidents of the two houses, rather than the members. In 1971, in a landmark case, the President of the Sénat used his power for the first time to refer a bill on the issue of freedom of association. This required an interpretation of the preamble of the constitution, which referred to the 1789 Declaration of the Rights of Man and the Citizen. The ruling, against the bill, was seen as equivalent to the establishment of a French Bill of Rights (Safran 1998).

Ever since this time the Sénat has seen itself as a protector of individual rights and freedoms, and has frequently referred bills to the Constitutional Council on these grounds (Mastias 1999). Although it has won several victories it is questionable to what extent these referrals were motivated by human rights, rather than political, objections. Whilst the Sénat has frequently sought to protect individual freedoms, it has been notably less proactive in the protection of collective rights. Referrals invariably come from the political groups, in both chambers. The Sénat's reputation as a protector of civil liberties has therefore been described as 'an exaggeration if we look closely' (Mény 1998: 74).

The same cannot be said of the Australian Senate, which has a long record of legislative scrutiny on human rights grounds, unparalleled in the lower house. Despite the absence of an Australian Bill of Rights, the Senate Standing Committee on Regulations and Ordinances has operated since 1932, scrutinising delegated legislation against a set of rights standards. It was joined in 1981 by the Senate Scrutiny of Bills Committee which scrutinises ordinary bills using a similar set of criteria. Both committees operate in a scrupulously bipartisan way, and have won many victories to protect the rights of Australians. Their work, and terms of reference, are described in more detail in Chapter 6.

CONSTITUENCY WORK

One major difference between the House of Commons and the House of Lords is the amount of time that members of the lower house devote to constituency work. This concentration on constituency work has been criticised, partly for reducing the amount of time which members have available for parliamentary duties (see, for example, Power 1998). Since members of the upper house do not represent a constituency, and are not under the same pressures, they may have more time to devote to legislative scrutiny and other parliamentary work.

There are two interlinked factors which can affect parliamentarians' tendency to get involved in constituency work. One is the electoral system (Wood 1998). Single member constituency systems are more likely to encourage a relationship between the member and the electorate, and a desire by members to maintain support by carrying out local duties. However, there is also an element of tradition, with some parliamentary systems having a stronger tradition of constituency work than others. In Britain the tradition is strong, and seemingly strengthening. A contrast is Italy, where despite a change to a single member constituency system for both houses in 1993, no comparable tradition has yet developed of MPs taking up individual cases on behalf of constituents.

In four other countries—Canada, Australia, France, and Germany—the electoral system for the lower house uses single member constituencies. Only in Germany is there no strong tradition of constituency work. Ireland's use of the single transferable vote system—which encourages competition between members in multi-member constituencies—also results in a strong tradition of constituency work.

The extent to which the constituency work tradition extends to the upper house is varied. In Ireland and France, where the upper house is elected by local government, its members are not answerable to an electorate of ordinary citizens. Irish members represent no geographical area, whilst French Senators represent an entire *département*, rather than a single constituency. The expectation would therefore be that upper house members would engage in less constituency work. However, this does not appear to be the case. French Senators are generally members of at least one local authority, and often hold an executive position such as mayor of a *commune*. They are thus closely associated with one particular local area. In order to be seen as a good local representative, and therefore stand to be elected to the Sénat, they must be seen to deliver locally. Even when elected, they retain a strong local focus and so engage in constituency work in much the same way as members of the lower house.

In Ireland the same tendency applies. Again Senators are generally local councillors, and so answerable to a local electorate. But perhaps more importantly many Senators are seeking election to the Dáil. A seat in the Seanad provides a good launch pad, as members can keep up their media profile, and their local and national networks, in preparation for the next election. Senators who plan to stand as Dáil candidates will find themselves in competition with members of their own party, as well as the opposition, and an important factor will be the amount of work they have done for the area. Thus a member of the

Seanad will often compete with local Dáil members to take on and solve constituency cases.

In Australia there is a strong constituency tradition in the lower house. However, the electoral system for the Senate should act as a barrier to upper house members' involvement in this work. Given Senators' representation of an entire, geographically vast, state, and lower house members' representation of single member constituencies, the latter are much better placed to take on this work. Thus the role of Senators in constituency activity has traditionally been minimal. However, this situation is changing, particularly among the major parties. The Labor Party, for example, now has a well-developed system for sharing constituency work amongst Senators. Members of the upper house will be encouraged to site their state office in a constituency which Labor aspires to gain in the House of Representatives. The Senator will then act as a proxy Labor MP—taking up cases on behalf of constituents, circulating information about his or her parliamentary achievements and appearing regularly in the local press. All of this activity helps prepare the seat for a Labor candidate at the next election. The Senator may also be able to cite this work when seeking reselection by the party. The Liberal Party operates a similar system, and it is only the minor parties and independents who have insufficient resources to do so. These groups, in any case, have little chance of winning lower house seats under the single member constituency system.

Only in Canada, where Senators represent similarly huge geographical areas, but have no electorate to answer to, is constituency work confined to the lower house. The appointed nature of the Canadian Senate means that there is little connection between Senators and the citizens they represent, and little respect for the Senate. The appointment of Senators until retirement means that it would be relatively hard for parties to force them to take on extra duties, as they have done in Australia. There is therefore a built-in reluctance, both by Senators and their constituents, for this type of work to be taken on. Members of the lower house, in contrast, spend so much time on their constituency work that their ability to function as legislators is often questioned. In the same way as the House of Lords, the Canadian Senate takes on a lot of the detailed legislative work that members of the House of Commons are too busy to pursue.

CONCLUSIONS

Second chambers often have a powerful constitutional role. While they are no more powerful than first chambers in this respect, they may have powers over constitutional matters which exceed their powers over ordinary bills. This is an acknowledgement of the seriousness of constitutional change, and the need to gain a broad consensus when this is planned. The veto power of the upper house—whether as a conservative house or a house representing the provinces, regions, or states—is appropriate in these circumstances.

The only truly effective territorial chamber is the German Bundesrat (this is discussed in Chapter 10). The Bundesrat's approval is required for all constitutional amendments, and this is used as a mechanism for gaining the support of the German states. This arrangement makes constitutional amendments achievable relatively quickly, whilst ensuring broad support. Other federal states such as Canada and Australia also require support from their constituent territories for all constitutional change. The fact that the upper house is not an effective territorial chamber means that they require extra-parliamentary approval mechanisms. These are cumbersome and have resulted in rigidity in these countries' constitutions. Genuinely territorial chambers might have eased this situation.

The attitude of a second chamber to constitutional amendments is liable to be shaped by its general attitude to the government. This is largely a matter of party politics. Thus a second chamber which can block constitutional change, but which is rarely controlled by government, can also introduce rigidity. This is the case in France, where the Sénat has a total veto on constitutional change. The Sénat's in-built conservative bias creates a particular problem for Socialist governments, but also results in a general inability to move beyond the old political order. Devolution to France's regions, and upper house reform, are impossible to achieve without the Sénat's consent.

The systems in Italy and Spain combine parliamentary approval of constitutional amendments with the recourse to a referendum if a significant minority of parliamentarians is opposed. However, the requirement to seek approval by the upper house is less likely to be an obstacle, as government tends to have a majority there, as well as in the lower house. In the French system the recourse to a referendum could offer a more genuinely consensual procedure than blockage by the Sénat. However, in France a referendum on constitutional change cannot be called until after both chambers have reached agreement.

Second chambers—or at least their members—may also have other methods of protecting the constitution. Frequently they are involved in the appointment of members of Constitutional Courts, which act as final arbiters in constitutional disputes. In the UK it is members of the House of Lords themselves who will be responsible for such arbitration, in the shape of the law lords. in other countries such an arrangement would not be contemplated as it would be seen as a breach of the separation of powers between parliament and the courts.

As well as being involved in the appointment of Constitutional Courts, members of upper houses may also refer matters to the courts for their consideration. In Germany, France, and Spain groups of parliamentarians from either chamber may refer legislation which they suspect breaches the constitution. Although this mechanism may be used by opposition parties to try and undermine government policy, it may also offer a real constitutional protection where the upper house cannot veto ordinary bills. It is therefore used frequently in France and Spain by members of both houses. Where a party can find genuinely constitutional—rather than purely political—grounds to oppose a law, they can be successful.

The final section of this chapter considered the constituency role played by members of upper houses. The freedom from constituency work can free up members to spend more time on parliamentary duties. However, in some systems—notably France and Ireland—the constituency tradition is so strong that it extends to members of the upper house. This helps account for poor attendance by members of the chamber. In other systems—notably Australia—members of the upper house are becoming involved in constituency work when they did not previously do so. If this engulfs as much of Senators' time as does of members of the lower house, it could threaten the traditional role of the Senate as a chamber of detailed parliamentary scrutiny.

9

Government and the Second Chamber

One of the key differences between upper and lower houses comes in their relationships with government. All the countries we are considering have 'parliamentary' systems of government (meaning that government must maintain the confidence of parliament) and scrutiny of government action is one of parliament's most important functions. There is thus a close working relationship between parliament and government, which is fraught with potential tensions. Parliament may expose government's weaknesses, reject government legislation, and ultimately even has the power to dismiss government from office.

These functions are, however, primarily the preserve of lower houses of parliament. In the majority of countries upper houses play a lesser role in the formation of government, have a junior part in its scrutiny, and do not have the power to remove it from office directly. This may be seen as a weakness of the upper house—giving it less control over the seat of real power—or alternatively as a strength. By being less associated with government an upper chamber may act more independently, and also has more time available to concentrate on its core function of scrutinising and revising legislation.

This chapter briefly summarises the position of government vis-à-vis the upper house in each of the countries we are considering. It starts by looking at the powers of the upper house in terms of making and breaking governments. It then reviews whether government members can be appointed from the upper house, and what rights of access they have to the house. Lastly it looks at forms of day-to-day government scrutiny in the upper house, particularly through questions to ministers.

MAKING AND BREAKING GOVERNMENTS

Perhaps the most striking difference between the chambers in bicameral parliaments is the lack of power which upper houses generally have to appoint and dismiss governments. Whilst parliamentary systems require government to maintain the confidence of parliament, this condition normally relates to the lower house alone.

For example in Britain, a government will fall if it loses a vote of confidence in the House of Commons. Such an event will almost certainly trigger the dissolution of the house and a general election. However, there is no parallel concept of a vote of confidence in the House of Lords. Given the past composition of the upper house, and its in-built Conservative bias, it is inconceivable that it should have had the power to dismiss the government. If it did, no Labour government could have survived. In Britain it is therefore only incumbent on government to maintain the confidence of the lower, elected, house.

Despite the greater democratic accountability of many upper houses, the same restriction applies in most other parliamentary systems. Even in Australia, where the Senate is directly elected using a proportional system, a confidence vote to bring about the fall of the government applies only in the lower house. No such mechanism exists in the Senate. Likewise in Canada, Germany, Spain, and Ireland the upper house has no power to sack the government, and the lower house alone is responsible for electing its leader.

The same system applies in France, where government may be removed by a vote of censure in the lower house, with no equivalent procedure in the Sénat. This inability of the French upper house to reject the government may be used at times to government's positive advantage. A provision applies whereby government may present its programme to the lower house, with rejection of the programme being taken as a vote of no confidence. But government may also propose its programme to the Sénat, where its rejection cannot have equivalent consequences. This allows government to test the water for controversial policies at reduced political risk. It was brought into use for the first time by President Giscard d'Estaing in 1975, when the Sénat was more supportive of his policies than the lower house. It has since been used regularly by governments of the right as a 'gesture of goodwill' to the Sénat (Mastias 1999: 182).

The exception to the rule is Italy, which is one of the only countries in the world where government may be brought down as a result of a confidence vote in the upper house. Article 94 of the Italian constitution states that government 'must enjoy the confidence of both houses'. Italy is also unusual in that the executive is in a relatively weak position with respect to parliament, and the Prime Minister does not have the power to appoint a cabinet without parliamentary approval. Thus a complete new government is subject to a vote of confidence in both chambers, which must take place within 10 days of its formation. The 'perfectly symmetrical' bicameralism of the Italian system even demands that the chambers alternate in taking this initial vote of confidence first. Either chamber may also pass a vote of no confidence in an existing government from one government to the next. Yet despite the high turnover of Italian governments, it is relatively rare for government to fail a confidence vote—such action brought down only four of the 48 governments from 1945 to 1989 (Furlong 1990).[1] On one of these occasions it was action by the Senate which did this—in the case of Giulio Andreotti's government of 1972.

In addition to separate votes of confidence, government can fall in most countries through rejection of key bills by the lower house, which may be made a matter of confidence. But in all countries except Italy a bill may be rejected in the upper house with no suggestion that this lead the government to resign. In France, for example, government may declare a bill to be a matter of confidence—in which case it becomes law unless a vote of censure is tabled in the lower house. No such power extends to the Sénat.[2]

The merits of a system where the upper house is denied the right to sack government are hotly contested by commentators. For example, in France the fact that the Sénat can reject key pieces of legislation, without bringing down the government, could be seen as demonstrating a lack of respect for the chamber's views. However, it is also seen by many as a strength, allowing the Sénat to express its opinion more freely on legislation. Whilst government can bring heavy pressure on its backbenchers in the lower house to fall into line—because a lost vote could threaten the life of the government—no similar pressure can be brought in the upper house. This boosts the independence of Senators, who may air views which are privately shared by their lower house colleagues. This is a scenario which is familiar from the bicameral system in the UK.

In Germany, France, and Canada the upper chamber is replaced in parts and can never be dissolved. In Australia this is the normal position, and may be upset only by a double dissolution. In fact in none of these seven countries can the government dissolve the upper house without also holding elections for the lower house. Thus whilst the upper house may not be able to sack government, it is also problematic—at best—for government to sack the upper house. This creates a kind of symmetry in the system, where chamber and government are encouraged to treat each other with cautious respect.

---

[1] It is more usual for the government to resign in anticipation of such a vote.

[2] This mechanism—which hands huge powers to government—provides another way for the Sénat to be bypassed. At times when the majority in the upper house has been hostile to the government it has been used surprisingly frequently. For example it applied to seven bills in 1986 alone (Frears 1990).

MINISTERS AS MEMBERS OF UPPER HOUSES

The upper house is rarely the government's creature. But this does not mean that government members are excluded from its membership. In Britain, for example, ministers must conventionally sit in parliament, but may achieve this through membership of either the House of Commons or the House of Lords. Increasingly, however, senior ministers are not drawn from the upper house. No Prime Minister has been drawn from the Lords since the nineteenth century.[3] Modern cabinets tend only to include two members of the House of Lords—those being the leader of the house and the Lord Chancellor. There is more flexibility in the appointment of junior ministers. For example, Tony Blair's government appointed in July 1999 included 13 junior ministers from the Lords out of a total of 108. It is usually the case that most government departments include at a minister drawn from the upper house.

The power to appoint to the House of Lords also allows a Prime Minister the option to bring non-parliamentarians straight into government. However, this practice is increasingly frowned upon. For example, the simultaneous appointment of businessman Gus Macdonald as a member of the House of Lords and junior Scottish Office minister caused a minor media furore in 1998.

In some respects the House of Lords is fairly typical of second chambers. In most of the countries considered here it is less common for members of government—particularly senior ministers—to be drawn from the upper house. This information is summarised in Table 9.1.

In Australia, Canada, Ireland, Italy, and Spain ministers may be drawn from either chamber, but the majority tend to come from the lower house. In Australia all governments since federation have included some ministers from the Senate. The proportion of Senator-ministers is generally a quarter to a third. The Howard ministry of 1998 was typical, including nine Senators amongst its 30 members. This gives proportional representation to Senators, who make up one-third of Australian parliamentarians. However, Australia adheres to the British tradition that the Prime Minister and finance minister will always be members of the lower house. In 1968 a Senator, John Gorton, was elected leader of the governing Liberal Party following the death of the incumbent leader. In order to take up the job of Prime Minister he resigned from the Senate and took a seat in the lower house (Uhr 1999).

---

[3] Lord Salisbury's government lasted into the twentieth century, running from 1895 to 1902.

Although many other Australian Senators have served in senior cabinet positions from the upper house, the inability to achieve the highest office from the chamber means that 'ambitious parliamentarians who want to be considered for prime ministerial office eventually have to make their way in the larger and more public world of the lower house' (Uhr 1999: 116). This has some impact on the type of politicians who sit in the upper house, as discussed in Chapter 4.

Table 9.1. *Government ministers and parliament*

	Government ministers may be members of:	Government ministers may speak in:
Australia	Either house	Only the house where they are a member
Canada	Either house—but usually only house leader sits in cabinet	Either house
France	Neither house	Either house
Germany	Lower house but not upper house	Either house
Ireland	Either house— maximum of two from the upper house, but this is rare in practice	Either house
Italy	Either house	Either house
Spain	Either house—but are mostly drawn from lower house	Either house
UK	Either house— but very limited number sit in cabinet[†]	Only the house where they are a member

† Since the 1950s Conservative cabinets have never included more than four peers and Labour cabinets not more than two (Shell 1992).

In Italy the number of ministers drawn from the Senato is also proportional to the number of Senators in parliament. Around two-thirds of ministers are usually from the lower house. However, unusually, there is no restriction on the seniority that may be reached by Senators in cabinet ranks. In the Italian system, where the two houses are equal and perform identical duties, even the Prime Minister may be drawn from the Senato. The last time this happened was in 1991, when incumbent Prime Minister Andreotti was appointed to the Senate by President Cossiga. This caused no great stir and did not result in any more attention on the Senato than usual. However, given that the Italian government may include ministers—even Prime Ministers—drawn from outside parliament altogether, this is not particularly surprising.[4] Irrespective of the origins of ministers they have the right to attend and speak in both parliamentary chambers.

In Spain, Ireland, and Canada the appointment of ministers from the upper house is far more unusual. All observe the convention that Prime Ministers are drawn from the lower house only, and the same applies to most other ministers, particularly at senior levels. Of the three, Spain has the highest incidence of ministers from the upper house, but even here the cabinet in April 1999 included no Senators.

In Ireland and Canada an increasing taboo has grown up around the appointment of ministers from the upper house. In both cases this is a reflection of the low esteem in which the chamber is held. In the wholly appointed Canadian Senate it has become common for the government house leader to be the only Senator in the cabinet. Although all Canadian ministers must be parliamentarians, it is no longer seen as acceptable to bring new members into government by appointing them to the Senate. The preferred option now is to get a potential minister to fight a by-election instead (appointing the sitting lower house member to the Senate if necessary). In the past Senators have also been used to balance the cabinet geographically, since it is important in Canada to demonstrate a fair representation of the provinces.[5] But even this practice is now increasingly rare.

In Ireland the convention of taking ministers from the lower house is even more entrenched, despite the formal constitutional position that up to two ministers (excluding the Taoiseach, deputy Taoiseach, and Finance Minister) may be appointed from the Seanad. The Government House Leader in the Seanad is not a minister, and there have only ever

---

[4] During the 1990s, for the first time, two Prime Ministers were appointed from outside parliament. The second, Lamberto Dini, formed a government which included no parliamentarians at all.

[5] For example after the 1979 election, where the Conservatives won only two seats in Quebec despite winning the election, three Quebec Senators were appointed to the cabinet (Jackson and Jackson 1998).

been two ministers drawn from the upper house—in 1957 and 1981. The second of these, James Dooge, was one of the 11 appointments made to the Seanad by Taoiseach Garret FitzGerald. He was then immediately appointed as Foreign Minister. This caused an outcry and was widely seen as a snub to the government members of the Dáil, who were assumed to have been judged unsuitable. Despite FitzGerald's intention that this move would form part of a programme to raise the profile of the Seanad, this reaction prevented him proceeding with his plan to appoint junior ministers from the upper house.

Aside from the political difficulties, practical problems would face a Taoiseach who wished to appoint Senators as ministers. This is because the Seanad elections take place some weeks after the Dáil elections. For example in 1997 the general election was held on 6 June, and the cabinet announced 20 days later. Junior ministers were all in place by 2 July. However, results of the Seanad elections were not available until mid-August, with the 11 appointed members announced a month later. It is thus quite impractical to hold ministerial positions free for members of the upper house. It has been suggested that harmonising the election dates for the upper and lower houses could help to ensure that more ministers are appointed from the Seanad (Doherty 1996).

In the remaining two countries—Germany and France—it is not permissible to appoint ministers from the upper house. In Germany this is because upper house members are already ministers in their own state governments.[6] In France it is because a strict principle of 'separation of powers' applies, with ministers in the executive being unable to be members of either chamber of the legislature. In practice most ministers in France run for election to one of the chambers, but resign their seat on appointment to government.[7] However, most members are taken from the lower house—for example, the cabinet appointed by Lionel Jospin in 1997 included 22 Deputies and only one Senator amongst its 27 members (Safran 1998).

The lack of government members in most upper houses means that flexible arrangements are needed to allow ministers to appear and speak in the chamber. The UK is unusual in not giving ministers access to both parliamentary chambers, and amongst the seven countries considered here is only joined by Australia in this respect (see Table

---

[6] State ministers are appointed to the federal government quite regularly, but this requires them to give up their state responsibilities, and thus their seats in the Bundesrat.

[7] Because of this all candidates for both the lower and upper house elections must have a running mate (*suppléant*) who will take their place in parliament in the event that they are appointed ministers. This allows most ministerial hopefuls to contest a seat, in order to give themselves added legitimacy.

9.1). In Germany and France, where there are no ministers in the upper house, access for ministers to the chamber is necessary for the smooth running of government business. However, this also operates in countries such as Ireland, where ministers could in theory be appointed from the upper house. Here ministers who are members of the lower house may attend and speak in debates in the Seanad. In practice one lower house minister will be present for most business in the Irish Seanad, including debating legislation, replying to committee reports and motions, and making government statements. Thus lack of ministerial members need not break off the links that the upper house has to government.

It has been argued that the presence of government ministers in the upper house can compromise its independence as a chamber of scrutiny. For example David Hamer, a former Australian Senator, has referred to ministers in the Senate as 'Trojan horses on behalf of the executive' (1982: 65). Instead he advocates removing the right for ministers to sit in the upper house, but still requiring them to come and answer questions in the chamber. Similarly in Canada some argue that the gradual disappearance of ministers from the Senate has helped to boost its independence (Uhr 1989). However others based in countries where the government rarely has ministers in the upper house—such as Ireland and Spain—argue that this downgrades the upper house as an institution (e.g. Juberías 1999). In Spain Senators who wish to lobby government ministers may need to make the journey across Madrid to the lower house in order to do so (Giol *et al.* 1990). The presence of ministers in the chamber may be an important symbol of its status in the eyes of politicians and the public.

HOLDING THE GOVERNMENT TO ACCOUNT

Although government may not be drawn from the upper house, or be required to maintain its support, it remains accountable to the chamber and may be subject to rigorous scrutiny there. The upper house carries out this duty through scrutiny of government legislation, which it may reject or amend, and also through the other activities described in Chapters 6–8, such as the work of investigative committees. In some cases, particularly where the upper house does not have a government majority, these activities may be pursued with greater vigour than they are in the lower house.

Another way in which government can be held to account in the chamber is through direct questions from members. The effectiveness of this mechanism may be one indication of the extent of the chamber's influence. Questions to ministers are briefly considered in this section.

In some second chambers there is no regular mechanism by which members directly question government ministers. This applies, for example, in Germany, where government is clearly accountable to the lower house only, whilst the upper house exists to review legislation.[8] However it also applies in some weak chambers, such as the Irish Seanad, where there is no opportunity for Senators to put either written or oral questions to ministers (these opportunities are both open to, and regularly used by, members of the Dáil). In Canada question time in the Senate is weekly—to the government house leader—rather than daily to all ministers, as it is in the lower house.

Even in countries where the two chambers have an equal right to question ministers, question time in the upper house will tend to be a lower key affair. In the UK question time in the House of Lords is limited to ministers who are peers, who are mostly junior ministers and answer questions on a wide brief which they may not be familiar with. In France, Italy, and Spain ministers are summoned to both chambers regularly to answer questions (irrespective of whether they are members of the chamber concerned).[9] But this will tend to attract less media attention in the upper house. This is partly a result of the seniority of the ministers who attend—the Prime Minister never attends questions in the Spanish Senado, for example, although in principle he could. But it is also a result of the seniority of those asking the questions. Even in the Italian parliament, where the Prime Minister attends both chambers, it is the lower house which attracts most attention because this is the site of clashes between the major party leaders.

However, media attention is not a measure of the quality of debate in the chamber—as demonstrated only too well by the attention given to upper and lower houses when debating legislation. The freedom from media spotlight may actually enable better government scrutiny through questions, with considered debate replacing political theatre and point-scoring. It has often been argued that this is true of the House of Lords. The same applies in Australia, where daily question time in

---

[8] Government is however required by article 53 of the constitution to 'keep the Bundesrat informed about the conduct of its business'. The same duty is followed in the lower house through question time after the weekly cabinet meeting. In the Bundesrat the procedure is for a government representative to attend the permanent advisory council, which meets on the same day. Although members of the Bundesrat may attend the lower house and participate freely in debates, they may not use this right to participate in question time.

[9] In Italy and Spain ministers may also be questioned in committee.

the Senate is far less rowdy than that in the lower house (although still very much controlled by political parties). Senate standing orders regarding questions have developed differently from those in the lower house. Constraints apply which prevent ministers turning their answers into lengthy government statements, and Senators have the opportunity to ask supplementary questions. The Senate President is less partisan than the lower house speaker, and divides questions fairly between government, opposition, and minor parties. One immediate consequence is that Senate question time allows more chances for political attack by the opposition. However, it also represents a greater hurdle for government than the question period in the lower house, and provides a greater degree of genuine scrutiny and accountability. This is typical of the work of the Australian Senate, in contrast to that of the government-controlled lower house.

CONCLUSIONS

A hallmark of upper houses is that they are less closely associated with government. Generally it is the lower house where the government must maintain a majority in order to be safe from removal from office. Only in Italy can government be removed by a vote of confidence in the upper house. Similarly, the number of ministers drawn from the upper house is generally fewer than that from the lower house, and ministers may appear less in the upper house to answer questions, make statements, or champion government bills. All of this makes for a more arms-length relationship between government and the upper house.

This raises some dilemmas. Is it better for the upper house to be close to government, but less independent of it, or further away and potentially more marginalised? These questions are the subject of debate in most of the countries discussed in this chapter. Where government is strongly represented in the chamber—as in Australia— this can be seen as compromising the independence of the chamber. If members of the upper house are seeking ministerial careers they are less likely to remain independent-minded and question the positions of their parties. However, if government appears less frequently in the upper house—as in Spain—this is criticised as a snub to Senators which demotes the importance of the chamber. The examples of these countries show, however, that the issue of ministers sitting in the chamber may be separated from that of ministers appearing there. Upper house members in Italy, for example, where the Prime Minister and all senior ministers appear before the upper house to answer questions, may be better served than members of the House of Lords, who are generally able to question only junior ministers who may be inadequately briefed.

Perhaps more important to the status of the chamber is the real power which it possesses to threaten government. In Spain these powers are slight, as the Senado cannot pass a vote of no confidence in government, and has no absolute veto over government legislation. In Italy the Senato's formal powers are great, including the unusual power to bring down the government. However, these add little to the powers of the lower house, given that the chambers generally have a similar majority.

In most countries—including Canada, Germany, and France—the upper house has no formal powers to remove the government. Likewise the government has no constitutional tool with which it can dissolve or abolish the upper house. Yet the upper house has the potential, through rejection or repeated delay of government legislation, to bring the government to its knees. Some examples were seen of this in Chapter 6. In Australia the Senate cannot formally remove the government, but through the blocking of financial legislation achieved that same end in 1975. This demonstrates how fine a line exists between the power to reject legislation—or even delay it for lengthy periods—and the power to sack the government. Effective powers over government legislation in the upper house are liable to breed respect between these two branches of the state. It is this, rather than the presence or absence of ministers in the chamber, which causes government to treat an upper chamber with care. The lack of this power—and the lack of will to use the meagre powers the chamber possesses—is the true cause of the marginal position of the upper houses in Ireland and Spain.

10

Binding Different Levels of Government Together

One of the classic roles of a second chamber is to represent the regions, provinces or states in the national parliament. The development of this model was examined in Chapter 2, where it was noted that this form of representation is now the commonest amongst upper houses around the world.

Five of the seven countries we are considering—Australia, Canada, Germany, Italy, and Spain—use their second chamber to represent regions, provinces, or states. In addition the French Sénat is used to represent primarily local government at a national level. Even the Irish Seanad, whose members do not represent geographical units, is elected predominantly by members of local government. Thus all these chambers have a potential role in binding different levels of government together.

As devolution advances in the UK, with the establishment of the new Scottish Parliament, the assemblies in Wales and Northern Ireland, and regional structures developing in England, a territorially based second chamber becomes an increasingly viable option. Devolution in the unitary states of Italy and Spain has been reflected in the membership of the upper house, whilst federal states such as Germany and Australia have long traditions of territorial upper houses. The models in these and other countries are likely to hold useful lessons for the new quasi-federal UK.

In European countries there is another dimension. Not only must the national parliament co-ordinate with sub-national assemblies, but also with the institutions of the EU. The European Communities Committee of the House of Lords does important work which is well respected both in Britain and around Europe. The continuing development of the EU is liable to make this work even more important, and this will need to be considered carefully by those reforming the House of Lords. This chapter therefore starts by analysing the role of second chambers in linking levels of government at home. But it also briefly considers the role of second chambers in EU countries in linking the national parliament with Europe.

THE UPPER HOUSE AND DIFFERENT
LEVELS OF GOVERNMENT

By way of context, it may be helpful to summarise the different levels of government which exist in each of our seven countries. These are summarised in Table 10.1. Each level of government corresponds to some kind of elected council or assembly.

Table 10.1. *Different levels of government in seven countries*

	Local	Sub-regional	Regional
Australia	municipalities and shires (750)	–	states (6) and territories (2)
Canada	municipalities (5,000)	counties (in most but not all provinces)	provinces (10) and territories (3)
France	communes (37,000)	départements (100)	regions (22)
Germany	municipalities and communes (15,000)	counties (116)	Länder/states (16)
Ireland	towns (80)	counties (29) and cities (5)	regions (8)
Italy	municipalities (8,000)	provinces (92)	regions (20)
Spain	municipalities (8,000)	provinces (50)	autonomous communities (17)

The table shows that in most countries there are three levels of government, which are classified as local, sub-regional, and regional. These would correspond, in England at least, to parish and district councils, county councils, and regions (corresponding to Regional Development Agency Areas, which may in time develop elected regional assemblies).[1]

---

[1] The structure of subnational government varies around the UK, not only because some areas have elected regional government and others do not. Also some areas have two main

The second chambers in these countries have representation which corresponds with different levels of government. In Australia, Canada, Germany, and Italy this corresponds purely with the regional level (states in Australia and Germany, provinces in Canada). In France, Sénat elections are organised using the sub-regional *départements*, but in practice are dominated by councillors from the local *communes*—regional boundaries are not used, and regional councillors make up only around one per cent of those voting in Sénat elections. In Spain the representation in the Senado is a compromise between the provincial and regional levels. As autonomous communities developed they were given seats in the upper house, which are elected indirectly, by members of the regional assemblies. However, representatives of the provinces—who are directly elected—continue to make up four out of five Senators. In Ireland there is no direct correspondence between the Seanad and local government boundaries, but local councillors make up the bulk of the electorate for the majority of upper house seats.

LINKING NATIONAL AND LOCAL GOVERNMENT: IRELAND AND FRANCE

Article 24 of the French constitution state that the Sénat 'will ensure the representation of the territorial units of the republic'. However the chamber is largely seen as representing local government.[2] The links from the chamber to local government are of two types, and outweigh the connections to other subnational institutions. First, members of the Sénat are elected by a college which is dominated by local government councillors; secondly, most members are themselves members of local authorities. For these reasons the chamber has been referred to as the 'high council of the French communes', which was the formal name of the upper house in the third republic (Mény 1998). However, it is arguable to what extent the chamber provides a genuine link even to the local level of government with which it is nominally so closely associated.

The fact that most members of the Sénat are councillors is not in itself a distinguishing feature of the chamber, as the same is also true of the lower house. However, this is more widely acknowledged in relation to the Sénat, and is influential in its image as the local government

---

tiers of local government—district and county—whilst others have single-tier unitary authorities. Local authorities throughout Scotland and Wales have a unitary structure.

[2] In the original French the constitution makes the Sénat representative of the *collectivités territoriales*. This formally includes the *communes* and *départements*, but not the regions.

chamber. Actually, both chambers are dominated by local representatives, whose dual mandates help contribute to the poor levels of attendance which afflict them both. Individual members use their positions as Senator—or Deputy—to lobby government on behalf of their particular local area. Frears has noted that '"Localism"—the practice of spending more time on local issues than being a national legislator—is one of the criticisms most frequently levelled against members of the National Assembly' (1990: 44). The same may be said about the Sénat. The prime difference between the two chambers is the political balance of the local *notables* who are elected to them. Members of the Sénat are more representative of the politics of French local government, which is dominated by conservative representatives of small towns and rural areas. In this sense at least Senators can be described as the true voice of local government.

Members of the Sénat are answerable to an electorate dominated by local councillors, and for this reason might be expected to be more responsive to local government concerns. However, it is interesting that Senators in France—and in Ireland where most of them are elected by a similar electoral college—take up cases on behalf of local residents just as readily as from local government members. In both countries there is a strong casework tradition in both houses of parliament, and to the public Senators are equally approachable as members of the lower house. Residents will tend to approach whichever local mayor or councillor holds a seat in parliament, irrespective of which chamber they belong to. The culture of localism in French and Irish politics attaches more importance—and political reward—to supporting individual local people than to supporting the local government sector strategically.

There is little evidence that the French Sénat spends more time debating issues which are the responsibility of local government—such as education—than does the lower house. If differences with the lower house do occur over such issues these are more likely to be political— over, for example, private education—than directly connected to the different perspectives of local and national government. Senators are particularly keen not to be sidelined into considering purely local issues, and some of the biggest clashes between the chambers have been over firmly national issues, such as nuclear armament or nationalisation (Mastias 1999).

The French upper house does, however, take a particular interest in debates over the structure and powers of local government. It generally claims the right to debate bills on these issues before the *Assemblée Nationale* (Mastias 1999). The Sénat has been a staunch defender of the powers of local mayors and authorities, and has fought at various times to protect or increase their financial autonomy. However, its influence has been largely conservative, protecting traditional structures and the interests of its own members. Stevens (1996: 192) argues that 'the slowness and caution with which reforms of local government in France have been approached . . . result from the strength of the links between local and central political levels'. The Sénat can shoulder at least half the blame for these delays. The chamber has been consistently opposed, for example, to the rationalisation of France's 37,000 *communes*. The attitude of Senators—whilst supportive of local powers—is also less positive towards devolution to other levels of government. When the bill to introduce regional assemblies was introduced in 1982, the Sénat supported the proposals to devolve powers to local authorities but was more lukewarm to proposals of devolution to regions. In this area, unlike others, the Sénat has the power to completely block progress, because structural changes require organic bills and constitutional amendments, on which the upper house has a veto.

It is therefore hard to argue that the Sénat fulfils its role as a chamber representative of the territorial units of France. The conservative upper house has resisted the pressures for more powers to be devolved to *départements*, although it is formally elected on the basis of these units, and has been equally unmoved by proposals to strengthen France's regions. The Sénat remains a representative of the old France, vested with a power to block developments which would weaken the outdated interests which it represents.

BINDING THE CENTRE TO THE PROVINCES, REGIONS, OR STATES

The more common pattern of territorial representation in an upper chamber is to link the national parliament to the provinces, regions or states. This is true of all upper chambers in federal countries, but also of many in unitary countries with some degree of devolution (Coakley and Laver 1997).

In a country with devolved tiers of government, there may be many benefits from using the second chamber to provide links from these to the national or federal parliament. Such an arrangement could potentially bind the nation together, minimise the dangers of fragmented decision-making and encourage common positions to be found which are to the benefit of both the nation and its component territories. The roles of a territorial upper chamber can be broken into three specific categories:

- linking the national parliament to territorial assemblies or governments;
- representing the territories and their interests at the national level;
- providing a forum for the different territorial units to debate policies and agree common positions.

However, this is the ideal. In practice the operation of territorial second chambers is often very different, as illustrated by some of the countries in this study. In this section we examine the extent to which the chambers nominally representing provincial, state, or regional government actually fulfil this role. The five countries concerned are broken into three groups—those providing no real links, some minimal links or strong and meaningful links to sub-national levels of government.

Insignificant or Non-existent Links: Canada, Australia, and Italy

The Senates of Canada, Australia, and Italy all represent the people of the country's territorial units in a direct way. The Australian and Italian second chambers are directly elected—the Australian Senate using state (and territory) boundaries and the Italian Senate using the boundaries of the regions. Members of the Canadian Senate are appointed to represent the provinces and territories of Canada, where they must reside.

In all three cases there is thus no automatic link to the territorial assemblies or governments which cover the same geographic areas. Unlike in other countries—such as those discussed below—members are not drawn from these assemblies or governments. In fact in Italy and Australia it is forbidden to run for either chamber of parliament whilst holding a seat in a regional assembly or state parliament. This has the benefit that members of the upper house are not burdened with dual mandates, and have sufficient time to devote to their national parliamentary duties. However the disadvantage is that there is no real link between Senators and devolved institutions in their area. In each case the only links will be through the party system. So for example Australian Senators may have some contact with members of the state parliament from their party, through party activities, and should also have a good relationship with the state government when their party is in control. But they will never formally appear in the state parliament and have no obligation to take its views, or the views of the state government, into account in their activities as Senators.

It is thus highly questionable whether members of the upper house in any of these countries fulfil the second criterion set out above—that of representing the interests of their province, state, or region at national level. All three systems are strongly driven by party politics, and members join a party group as soon as they enter parliament. In Australia the politics of the Senate was predicted accurately by Deakin, a member of the convention which drew up the 1900 constitution. He foresaw that 'the people will divide themselves into two parties . . . The instant Federation is accomplished the two Houses will be elected on that basis. State rights and State interests . . . will never be mentioned' (quoted in Hamer 1982: 60).

In all three countries it is very unlikely that a group of Senators from the same area might join together across party lines to defend the interests of the area. Voting in the Canadian and Australian Senates normally adheres rigidly to party lines, whilst any divergence from this in Italy is unlikely to be a result of regional concerns. This is predictable behaviour given the demands of party discipline and unity in a modern political system. In such a system negotiation of positions and expressions of dissent take place behind closed doors in party meetings, rather than in public view in parliament. The party caucus may be the only forum in which territorial concerns are expressed by members of the upper house. In Australia and Canada this can provide an important route to raise state and provincial issues. Because of the majoritarian voting system, particular states or provinces may be unrepresented amongst party caucus members from the lower house. The upper house system—particularly in Australia—ensures that Senators in the caucus include representatives of all provinces or states. This in theory prevents the major parties unintentionally devising policies which prove particularly deleterious to one or two provinces or states.

In Australia evidence suggests that the Senate is far from a champion of states' rights in general. In 1995 Wayne Goss, the premier of the state of Queensland, commented that 'none of us any longer pretend that the Senate continues to perform its political and constitutional function on behalf of the States. In fact there have been many cases in which the Senate has actively worked against the interests of the States'.[3] This hypothesis has been exhaustively tested by David Hamer, who concludes that

By any measure of public performance—amendments to Government bills, initiation of private members' bills, motions, questions to Ministers—there is no evidence that Senators have been any more diligent in protecting State interests

---

[3] *Australian*, 11 July 1995.

(real or supposed) than have the [members of the House of] Representatives: if anything, they have been slightly less diligent (1982: 60).

In defence of this claim he cites Senate opposition to a government bill in 1970 which would have given financial benefits to the states. He also carried out a survey of ministers in two different governments asking what was the greatest parliamentary pressure for states' interests. Not one respondent cited the Senate as the main source. This illustrates how in Australia—as in Italy and Canada—Senators are basically another brand of national party politician, indistinguishable in this sense from their colleagues in the lower house.

In such circumstances it is impossible for the upper house to fulfil the final function proposed above—that of providing a forum for territorial units to debate and agree policy. This is an important function, which is necessary for different regions, provinces or states to co-ordinate initiatives and reach common agreements on issues such as environmental policy, which cross their boundaries. It is also important for territorial units to have a forum through which to negotiate with national government. Such meetings are held in each country, but are completely divorced from the Senate and its members. In Italy they take place in 'state-regions' conferences, in Canada through 'federal-provincial' conferences and in Australia through state premiers' conferences, 'ministerial councils' and the 'Council of Australian Governments' which includes national, state and local government representatives. Such forums bring together the real territorial decision-makers and, ironically, further discourage any genuine territorial role for the upper house.

Struggling to Make the Links: Spain

The Spanish Senado is an unusual second chamber because it represents two distinct levels of sub-national government. The majority of members are directly elected to represent the people of Spain's 50 provinces, whilst around one-fifth of members are indirectly elected by autonomous community assemblies.

Since the Spanish constitution was agreed in 1978 there has been continuous and extensive decentralisation of the state, primarily to autonomous communities. As these have been gradually established all over Spain, the role of the traditional provinces, along with the central state, has diminished. The provincial Senators in Spain suffer from the same difficulties as the members of the Australian and Italian Senates—that as directly elected members they have no natural links with the provincial assemblies. On top of this, the growing importance of autonomous communities has obscured the need for links between the provinces and the centre.

The minority of Senators who are indirectly elected, and represent the autonomous communities, have a natural link to governmental institutions at this level. Because these Senators are elected by members of the autonomous community assemblies, they have some responsibility to serve this electorate. In addition, the majority of these Senators—28 out of 51 in September 1999—are actually members of the autonomous assemblies which elect them.

Whilst this creates a formal link between the autonomous assemblies and the Senado, the degree to which this functions in a meaningful way is limited. Senators who hold dual mandates have no requirement to report from the Senado back to their devolved assembly, or to report from their assembly to the Senado. In addition they face the difficulty of carrying out all the duties of their two roles simultaneously. This particularly affects those who represent the most powerful devolved assemblies, which meet more frequently. Because of the difficulties of managing these dual mandates it is not practically possible for frontbench members of the assemblies to take up the role of Senator. Hence members are at best backbenchers, who may have no great input into policy-making at the devolved level. At worst, autonomous community Senators are not members of their devolved assemblies at all, and have no rights to attend and speak in debates there. Their only connection to decision-making at the devolved level is therefore likely to be—as in Canada, Australia, and Italy—through their parties.

Thus the objective of creating links to devolved bodies is partially met in the Spanish system, but is not particularly effective. Less impressive is the extent to which Senators—even the minority elected by autonomous community assemblies—represent truly territorial interests. The major reason for this is the tightly disciplined and centrally controlled party system in Spain.[4] Senators' first loyalty is to their party group, whose instructions they will follow with the same loyalty as their counterparts in the lower house. Even autonomous community governments run by the major parties take many of their instructions from the national party leader. There is thus no independent party position coming from the sub-national level which Senators could seek to follow. As in Australia, Canada, and Italy, it is highly unlikely that Senators from one autonomous community would work together across the party divide. In an attempt to encourage

[4] Following the Franco dictatorship, the development of strong and disciplined parties was an explicit objective in Spain.

territorial working, the standing orders of the Senado were revised in 1982 to include the right to form 'territorial groups'. These would be granted resources and given additional speaking rights. However, these territorial groups were only permitted to be formed within existing party groups, and their contribution has consequently been described as 'meagre' (Juberías 1999: 278).

The only Senators who successfully put forward a territorial agenda are those who represent nationalist parties. These small parties, which each operate in only one autonomous community, exist purely to campaign around the rights of their area, and its difference to the rest of Spain. They are thus able to present a united front in the devolved assembly, the Senado, and the *Congreso de los Diputados*. Their party size and structures allow Senators to work closely with members of the devolved assembly, and formulate joint campaigns. This is particularly effective in the Basque country and Catalonia, where the nationalists have been in government since the devolved institutions were established.

Given that most Senators are simply national party representatives, it is difficult for the Senado to fulfil the third objective—that of operating as a forum of debate between the autonomous communities. However, this is an aspiration which is well understood in Spain—particularly given nationalist tensions—and many moves have been made to promote the Senado's role in this area. There is potential for the Senado to fill a gap, as negotiations between autonomous communities and central government have traditionally been bilateral. There are therefore many who would welcome a wider forum to debate territorial issues. There are, however, also those who would disagree. The nationalist parties remain opposed to any developments which will move Spain towards a symmetrical federal structure. They therefore oppose the system of conferences between autonomous communities which were introduced in 1992, or any increased territorial role for the Senado.

Partly because of these problems, attempts to get the Senado to fill a more territorial role have, as yet, had fairly limited success. The original design of the chamber included some responsibility for territorial affairs. This included greater powers over legislation implementing agreements between autonomous communities, and concerning the 'autonomous communities clearing fund'. But the additional powers are minimal, simply giving the Senado the right to refer such bills to a joint committee of both chambers in the event of a dispute, rather than being immediately overridden by the lower house. Bills concerning the clearing fund—designed to equilibrate between regions—must also start their passage in the upper house. However there have only ever been two such bills. Agreements between autonomous communities are generally minor matters which parliament is informed of as a pure formality. Finally, the only power the Senado has that is not shared by the lower house is to take action against an autonomous community which is 'acting against the interests of Spain'. However, this extreme sanction has never needed to be used (Juberías 1999).

Meanwhile, the Senado has taken no special role in the large volumes of legislation which has genuinely affected the autonomous communities and the shape of the Spanish state. Statutes of autonomy, for example, which devolve powers to the territorial governments, are treated as ordinary legislation so can be agreed without the consent of the Senado. The original statutes of autonomy which established the devolved assemblies were not presented to the upper house until they had already been approved in referendums (Juberías 1999). The other form of legislation which is important to autonomous communities is that which they propose themselves. Under article 87 of the constitution such bills may be presented by an autonomous community to parliament for consideration. The bill will be introduced by three members of the devolved assembly, who may speak in parliament in its support. However, such introductions take place in the lower house, rather than the Senado.

In recent years there have been more determined efforts to develop the territorial role of the upper house. These have, however, taken place within the existing constitutional powers of the chamber—which are prescribed in some detail—and have relied merely on changes to the standing orders of the Senado. The main developments were the establishment in 1994 of a General Committee for the Autonomous Communities, and the instigation of an annual debate in the upper house on the state of devolution in Spain.

The General Committee has a long list of responsibilities, which include debating territorial issues, scrutinising legislation from a territorial perspective, and scrutinising bills with a particular territorial content. The committee is double the size of others in the chamber, with 50 members, and in addition to its members it is open to any autonomous community Senator to attend and speak. The most innovative feature of the committee is that it is also open to representatives of autonomous community governments, who have the right to request that it be convened, propose issues for discussion, and attend and speak (Ripollés 1999).

In its early months the General Committee was very active, and debated issues such as how to improve the territorial role of the Senado itself. Some Senators became suspicious of the committee's wide-ranging powers and high profile, as it became dubbed the 'Senate within a Senate' (Juberías 1999). Others saw the potential for it to be used by hostile autonomous community governments to raise unwelcome issues for public discussion with government. After government announced the formation of a new committee specifically charged with reviewing the options for upper house reform (discussed in Chapter 11) the momentum behind the original committee dropped away. Nevertheless it has scrutinised numerous new statutes of autonomy, and other bills on constitutional issues such as reform of the Constitutional Court. It has also amended many other bills in terms of their territorial content. As well as this the committee has set up various working groups to investigate specific issues and make proposals to government. One important example was a group on functions of autonomous communities in relation to the EU, which met from 1994 to 1995. After hearings with various experts the group drew up a report proposing that autonomous communities have a greater role in European decision-making. However national government—reluctant to cede any of its powers in this area—had still not responded by early 1999.

The most high-profile activity of the committee has been to stage an annual debate on the 'state of autonomy' in Spain. This is attended by many members of autonomous community governments, with all presidents entitled to give an address in their regional language. The Prime Minister also makes a keynote address at the meeting, at which the cabinet, most Senators and many members of the lower house are observers. In 1994 the Prime Minister opened the meeting with a one and a half hour speech on the nature of the Spanish state, followed by speeches from all but one of the autonomous community presidents.[5] This debate was used to launch the government's initiative to reform the Senado into a more territorial house. A similar debate may also be held in the plenary session of the Senado itself, but has been less important because of the inability of autonomous community governments to take part.

However, whilst these innovations held great promise, they have been disappointing in practice. It remains the initiative of government whether 'annual' debates are held, and there were only two between 1994 and 1999. There is now a general acceptance that these well-intentioned changes are not enough to enable the Senado to fulfil its constitutional duty as the 'chamber of territorial representation'. It is particularly hard for this to work effectively whilst only 20 per cent of

---

[5] The meeting has so far been boycotted by the Basque nationalist government.

members represent the autonomous communities, and the lower house retains a veto on virtually all territorial issues. Consequently there is a general consensus that the Senado needs reform to turn it into a genuinely territorial chamber. This is discussed in Chapter 11.

Second Chamber as Fulcrum of the Federal System: Germany

In Germany the situation is very different. Like Canada and Australia, Germany is a federal system. But unlike the Canadian and Australian Senates, the Bundesrat is the 'single most important institution' of the German federal state (Patzelt 1999: 60).

It would be an understatement to say that the Bundesrat is 'linked' to state governments. Every member of a state cabinet is either a full or deputy member of the upper house. The Bundesrat is a council of state governments, creating a real and meaningful connection between them and the federal government. Federal-state links are a hallmark of the German system, so extensive and complex that they are commonly described as *politkverflechtung*—an 'entanglement' (James 1998). The Bundesrat is at the heart of this system. More formally the German system is referred to as 'co-operative federalism', reflecting the extent to which the centre and the states work together on policy issues (Sontheimer 1988).

The public are confronted with the link between federal and state politics when they vote in state elections. Because these determine the makeup of the Bundesrat as well as the state parliaments and governments, the local and the national may be blurred during the campaign. At times when the balance in the Bundesrat is close, this will be a major issue in state election campaigns. A recent example was the election in the state of Hessen in April 1999, which was dominated by debate about a controversial citizenship bill. The CDU gained control of the state, meaning that the Bundesrat was likely to take a more conservative line on the bill. Similar factors are at play in local elections in France, and regional elections in Spain, because the members elected are responsible for the choice of members of the upper house. But nowhere is the link so direct as in Germany.

The composition of the Bundesrat also creates real links between the national parliament and state parliaments. The most obvious of these is through the members of the state cabinet being responsible, and regularly reporting, to the state parliament and its committees. This reporting will include accountability for the positions they have taken in the Bundesrat, which are well publicised in the state and national press. Some state parliaments have specific Bundesrat committees, which are responsible for monitoring the work of the chamber, and their members in it. On key bills which the Bundesrat is considering, debates may be called for in state parliaments. When this seems necessary state governments will ask the federal government to extend the time available to consider a bill from six to nine weeks. This longer consideration period is automatic for constitutional bills, which will generally be debated in state parliaments before the Bundesrat decides its position (de Villiers 1999).

Given the chamber's composition, which links it firmly to both state governments and parliaments, there can be no doubt that the members of the Bundesrat represent their states. Reinforcing this is the organisation of the Bundesrat itself, which has no party groups, but seats members in state groups and requires them to vote as state blocks. Unlike members of the other four chambers discussed above, Bundesrat members representing a state therefore discuss their position amongst themselves in Land cabinets and must present a united front, due to block voting. This is of course made easier by the fact that the members are in government together—generally in coalition—and accustomed to reaching agreement. The views expressed therefore reflect the views of governments in the states, but exclude opposition voices.

As well as representing the views of individual states, which are determined by the politics of their governments, the Bundesrat does occasionally facilitate all states working together for common state interests. German commentators are keen to point out that the positions taken by Bundesrat members on most issues are influenced by party politics. The importance of political majorities in the states on the actions of the Bundesrat has been discussed in Chapters 4 and 6. However there are occasions—particularly over constitutional issues— when states with opposing majorities will unite in the Bundesrat against the federal government. One important example of this is discussed in the next section, on the Bundesrat's role in European decision-making.

Despite the central position of the Bundesrat in bringing states together, and linking them to federal decision-making, there are also many other forums where such discussions are held. These include regular minister presidents' conferences and meetings between minister presidents and the federal chancellor, meetings between state ministers and their federal counterparts, between state and federal officials, and between state and federal representatives of political parties. This system of connections is so complex that any 'attempt to pinpoint and categorise the components of the entire network of intergovernmental institutions . . . is a hazardous undertaking' (Leonardy 1999*a*: 7). However, the Bundesrat forms the apex of this system of decision-making, rather than being an institution which is divorced from it—as are the Canadian and Australian Senates. The Bundesrat is the site of final agreement on policy which has often been subject to many months of consultation between federal and state governments through these other channels. This accounts for the quick and efficient way in which Bundesrat business is despatched. Meetings between state institutions, without federal representatives present, are necessary also for reaching inter-state agreements which do not concern federal government. The meetings between the states and the centre through the Bundesrat cannot fulfil all these needs.

The Bundesrat may be used by states to propose their own legislative initiatives, which they wish to see supported at federal level. If a motion for legislation from a state or states is supported by the upper house, it is incumbent on government to respond. If a draft bill is proposed by the Bundesrat itself, government must comment on it formally in parliament within six weeks. While this system may be used for party political ends—particularly when state elections are looming—it can also be used by Länder of all political persuasions to raise state issues, or push federal policy along. One recent example was a bill on child sex abuse which was discussed in the Bundesrat in April 1999. The initiative was pursued by CSU-controlled Bavaria, who claimed that action promised by the SPD-led federal government in this area had been too slow. After several months of delay a Bavarian bill on the issue received the support of SPD Länder, who felt unable to delay matters any further. Bundesrat support for such a bill will be followed by a Bundesrat member proposing it in the lower house.

This and other mechanisms of the Bundesrat do more than simply allowing state governments to air their views on policies which they will be responsible for implementing. In the Bundesrat state governments are also entitled to give views on all areas of federal policy, and share in the responsibility of national decision-making. Over time states have ceded power upwards to the federal level, as formalised through numerous constitutional amendments. This enables federal standards to be set through which the states will operate, knowing that they retain a collective veto over such legislation through the Bundesrat. The chamber is the embodiment of the benign 'entanglement' of German federalism, which brings federal and state levels together in joint decision-making, enabling each to understand and respond to the other's point of view.

LINKING UPWARDS: EUROPE

In the UK the House of Lords has played an important part in responding to the growing parliamentary pressures resulting from membership of the EU. These pressures, affecting all member states, relate primarily to the need for mechanisms to scrutinise ever-increasing volumes of European legislation. Whilst both chambers of the UK parliament have select committees to scrutinise this legislation, the committee in the Lords carries out more selective and detailed scrutiny. It has built a strong relationship with EU institutions, and is generally highly regarded. This is partly because the House of Lords has more capacity to deal with this work than the Commons, and partly because it has many expert members who have served as members of the European Commission or as MEPs. But also the review function required by the work—with no power resting at Westminster to take final decisions—is more suited to the role and ethos of the upper house (Shell 1992).

For similar reasons, the scrutiny of European affairs was seized on more quickly in other countries by the second rather than the first chamber. For example in Italy a European Affairs Committee was established in the Senato in 1968, but not in the *Camera dei Deputati* until 1989. In France the Sénat committee was set up in 1973, and joined by a lower house committee in 1979. In Ireland the Seanad took an early interest in European Affairs, which were discussed primarily in a joint committee involving Irish MEPs. Senator Mary Robinson was 'the most expert and assiduous member ' of the committee from 1973 to 1989 (Hussey 1993: 70). The Seanad frequently debated the committee's reports, whilst there were only three such debates in the Dáil during the 18 years of the committee's existence (O'Halpin 1996).

However, as EU matters have grown in importance and profile, lower house members in all countries have been increasingly unwilling to leave them to members of the upper house. In France, Italy, Ireland, and Spain there is no longer a discernible difference between the treatment of EU matters in the two houses of parliament. The exception is Germany, where the peculiar nature of the upper house means its members bring a particular perspective to consideration of European affairs. Winning substantial powers over European matters has been one of the Bundesrat's major victories over the last 15 years.[6]

---

[6] Unlike the situation in Spain, where the upper house has yet to win this battle (see above).

In the early years of the European Community, the German Länder were frustrated by the fact that, although they were responsible for implementing much European legislation, they had no input into this at the drafting stage. The federal government was required to keep the Bundestag and Bundesrat 'informed' of European decision-making, but this would not generally afford the Länder any influence. However, in 1986 the government had to seek parliamentary ratification of the Single European Act. At this point the Bundesrat's powers allowed it to threaten to use its veto, unless government conceded the right for Länder to be fully consulted on European matters (Saalfeld 1996). The same action was repeated in 1992 when the Bundesrat's approval was required for the Maastricht Treaty. The Länder acted collectively—across party lines—to force the government to make considerable concessions. Their objectives were twofold—to restrict the federation's right to transfer their powers to European institutions, and to have a greater role in the process of European policy-making. Because the treaty required constitutional change, the federal government needed the support of two-thirds of the members of the upper house. Faced with unanimous opposition from even CDU- and CSU-controlled Länder, it was forced to devise a package of constitutional change which handed additional powers to the Länder—to be exercised through the Bundesrat (Jeffery 1998).

As a result the upper house now has a powerful role in European decision-making, largely set down in a new Article 23 of the Basic Law which was negotiated in 1992. The federal government has a constitutional duty to inform the Bundesrat 'comprehensively' and 'as early as possible' about EU matters. Draft European legislation must be considered by the chamber, giving the 'decisive' power to the upper house where the legislation affects the Länder, and the right for the Bundesrat's view to be 'taken into account' on all other matters. EU legislation is thus classified in a similar way to national legislation. It also passes through a similar process, being scrutinised by standing committees, but is then considered by the Bundesrat's powerful European Committee. At the end of this process the Bundesrat may decide that it wishes to nominate a representative of the Länder to attend meetings in Brussels alongside federal representatives, in order to ensure that government sticks to the line agreed by the chamber. Where the matter under discussion is in the exclusive control of the Länder, the Bundesrat may even nominate a member to be head of the delegation to the Council of Ministers itself. This representative, elected by the plenary meeting of the chamber, may lead the German delegation on the issue, in place of a federal representative. Thus the powers won by the upper chamber over European affairs mean it not only binds the states to the centre, but also binds the states to Europe, giving them a powerful role.

CONCLUSIONS

All seven second chambers have some degree of responsibility for creating connections between the national parliament and sub-national levels of government. However, they achieve this with very varied degrees of success. The French and Irish Senates create only tenuous links between national and local government, whilst the extents to which the Spanish, Italian, Canadian, Australian, and German chambers link to the regional level are very mixed.

To some degree the links between the upper house and devolved institutions are dependent on its method of selection. A second chamber which is indirectly elected has some automatic connection to these institutions, whilst one which is directly elected or appointed does not. In Australia, Italy, and Canada the members of the upper house have no real links with institutions at the state, regional, or provincial level. However, there are also difficulties in Ireland and France where the upper chamber does not have clear links to local government or a record of activity on issues concerning local government. This is despite the chamber being indirectly elected by an electoral college largely comprising local councillors.

In Spain it should be easier to form links between the national and regional levels, since one-fifth of members of the upper house are elected by regional assemblies. However, even here there is no formal reporting mechanism for Senators to devolved assemblies, and thus little accountability. At the same time the 'dual mandates' held by many Senators create serious time pressures. These prevent front-bench members of devolved assemblies standing for the upper house.

In all these countries members of the upper house represent their political parties far more clearly than they represent their territorial area. Territorial concerns are likely to be heard in party caucus meetings rather than on the floor of the chamber. In this respect members of the upper and lower houses behave in essentially identical ways. The only members who are seen to clearly represent territorial interests are Spanish Senators who represent nationalist parties based in particular autonomous communities. These members use the upper house to press campaigns for greater autonomy. Ironically, they also oppose the Senado becoming a more genuinely territorial house.

Germany is the only country where the upper house provides strong and genuine links between the state and national levels. The main reason for this is that its members represent governments, rather than parliaments (or citizens), and are thus the decision-makers of the state. Not only has the Bundesrat enabled state governments to have a say over national legislation, it has also enabled them to build strong links with Europe through the upper house. This has not been achieved by any of the other upper chambers.

Although the representation of governments is the key to the Bundesrat's success, there are many other features of the German system which are not dependent on this. These could be applied equally well to other second chambers. First, the German upper house is powerful. It gives state representatives a veto on legislation which affects them, and allows them to bring their own legislation to the table for debate in the national parliament. Although beginnings of this system exist in Spain, they have not been successfully applied, and such arrangements are non-existent elsewhere. Secondly, the seating in the Bundesrat organises state representatives in blocks, and they are forced to vote together as a state. In all other systems, where party blocks are formed instead, such voting behaviour would be inconceivable. Thirdly, the Bundesrat provides better links to state parliaments than exist in other countries—even in Spain where one-fifth of Senators nominally represent territorial assemblies. State parliaments scrutinise the work of the German upper house, and hold their representatives in it to account.

Any of these mechanisms—which strengthen greatly the territorial role of the German upper house—could be applied in other countries. However even in Spain, where there are real aspirations to create a true territorial chamber, they have not been put in place. This is frequently a simple failure of political will, and in Spain is coupled with nationalist tensions which make such reform look unlikely. Reform proposals—and the failure to implement them—are the subject of the next chapter.

11

Public Perceptions and Calls for Reform

House of Lords reform has been on the agenda for a long time. Removal of the hereditary peers from the house was promised as long ago as 1911—in the preamble to the Parliament Act—but was not to become a reality until 1999.[1] Yet the proposed reform had popular support. A poll late in 1998 suggested that over half the population supported the move and only around a quarter were against it. Almost half those questioned wanted to go further, and favoured an elected second chamber.[2]

However, despite the chamber's unpopular composition, there was no general clamour for its reform. The relative lack of interest in the 1999 consultation and public hearings organised by the Royal Commission on Lords reform was an illustration of this. Successive governments could afford to put reform of the upper house on the 'back burner' because the public prioritised other policies. The house itself maintained a low media profile, creating few showdowns with the elected House of Commons. It thus remains an ill-understood institution, with neither its best nor worst features widely appreciated. Only dedicated reformers, including the Conservative Party's political opponents, kept up pressure for the institution to change.

In this, as in so many ways, the House of Lords is fairly typical of second chambers. With a few exceptions these are generally low-profile institutions, often unpopular but not well understood. In most countries there are desires to reform the second chamber, but these are rarely realised. These are the issues that are explored in this final chapter of Part 2.

THE PROFILE OF THE CHAMBER

Upper chambers of parliament tend to have a much lower profile than their respective lower chambers. In most cases the upper house receives

---

[1] See Chapter 1 for a discussion of the 1911 Act.

[2] *The Guardian*, 9 December 1998. A later poll, conducted by Democratic Audit, found that the proportion of people supporting an elected chamber was 84 per cent (*The Guardian*, 17 July 1999).

less media and public attention, and is less well studied by academics and others. In many countries commentators pay little attention to the upper house when studying the work of parliament.

There are a number of reasons for this. Most important amongst them are the following three:

- *Second chambers are often not directly elected.* When the public are not involved in the selection of members of the house this will tend to attract little attention. And because the chamber is not directly accountable to the public, it receives less media coverage. This clearly applies in countries such as Canada and the UK, where members of the upper house are appointed, but also to countries such as Ireland, France, and Germany where they are indirectly elected.

- *The upper house has little power to challenge the government.* In countries such as Ireland and Spain, amendments or rejection of legislation in the upper house can simply be overturned by the lower house. In France there must be mediation first, but the lower house has the last word on most bills. Although recourse to mediation used to cause controversy in France it is now so commonplace that it no longer merits attention. Thus in these three cases the actions of the upper house may be thought of little political significance. Even in Canada, where the upper house has formal powers to reject bills, this rarely happens due to the house's lack of democratic legitimacy. In any case votes in all upper houses—except the Italian Senato—are of less consequence because they cannot bring down the government.

- *Party leaders are generally concentrated in the lower house.* Even in Italy, where the upper house is powerful and directly elected, more attention is given to the lower house. This is because the leaders of the parties are concentrated there, and it is where political deals are seen to be done. This applies to all countries, with the upper house being more concerned with detailed scrutiny and implementation.

The public profile of the chamber in any country may be predicted by considering which of these criteria apply. The Irish Seanad is indirectly elected, relatively powerless and contains no political leaders or ministers. Consequently it is little understood by the public, most of whom have no involvement in its election, and largely ignored by the media (although individual Senators may have local media profiles).

The public play no part in the selection of the Canadian Senate, and it rarely uses its blocking powers. It is therefore largely ignored, although its undemocratic composition does make it the source of controversy. Likewise in France only one in 1,500 of the population is involved in electing the Sénat, and its powers are generally limited. However, the conservative bias in the chamber is controversial, especially when used to block constitutional reforms. Additionally the Sénat President is an important figure and brings some attention to the chamber.

Undoubtedly the highest profile chambers are the Australian Senate, which is both directly elected and powerful, and the German Bundesrat, which is powerful and provides a platform for high profile Land politicians. Not only this, but the political balance in both these chambers mean that their powers to challenge government are used regularly. In Australia although party leaders are concentrated in the lower house, it is in the Senate that political deals are done. Small party Senators and independents who hold the balance of power have particularly high profiles. Generally no news programme on a legislative initiative is complete without a Senator from the Australian Democrats appearing to state how their party intends to vote.[3]

PUBLIC PERCEPTIONS OF THE CHAMBER

The low profile of most upper houses colours public perceptions. Generally these chambers are ill-understood. However, many of them arouse strong feelings which can lead to continual calls for reform.

The most embattled of the chambers is probably the Senate of Canada. Although it is responsible for much detailed legislative and investigative work, the 'accepted image of the Senate [is] as a dusty, obscure Arcadia filled with aged and retired political war horses . . . whose main concern, apart from enjoying a good, comfortable, life, is to preserve private wealth and the interests of big business' (Franks 1999: 120–1). This is an image that is perpetuated by the media, who periodically question the working hours and lifestyles of Senators. The upper house is also widely criticised by the provinces, who have no involvement in choosing its members, despite its formal role as the territorial house. These criticisms are damaging to the Senate, whose views are less likely to be listened to as a result. The results of many Senate committee investigations, for example, have been left to gather dust. As Franks has observed, 'it is clear that appointment by the Prime Minister from among party supporters has by now reduced the

---

[3] At least, this is always true when the Democrats hold the balance of power in the Senate, which they have—either with or without other minor parties and independents—for most of the time since the early 1980s.

legitimacy of the Senate to the point where it harms not only the Senate but also parliament as a whole and even the government' (1999: 156).

In Ireland 'mainstream opinion is tolerant of the Seanad rather than supportive of it' (Coakley and Laver 1997: 65). There is little to indicate that many of the public understand the chamber as 'the absence of any feeling of urgency or of momentous political cut and thrust, and the comparatively poor publicity it gets, all emphasise its lack of importance and contribute to its low prestige' (Chubb 1992: 199). However, there are times when the media focuses on the Seanad, and helps to generate negative feelings towards it. For example during the 1997 election campaign the Irish Times ran a piece entitled 'There is no point in the Seanad' and opening 'Hundreds of candidates are engaged in another frenetic election campaign, this time for a redundant institution.' It remarked that 'if there is to be no fundamental change in the Seanad's role and composition there is no reason to retain it'.[4]

Viewed as equally pointless is the powerful Italian Senate. Generally controlled by the same political parties as the lower house, and carrying out identical functions, the upper house is seen to add little to the system apart from delay. In a system where parliament is generally considered inefficient and problematic, 'the sternest criticisms of bicameralism have stemmed from its having come to be identified as one of the major causes of the malfunctioning of the whole institutional system' (Lodici, 1999: 254). Although this may not be entirely justified, 'for the most part—and here there is substantial agreement—it is the structure of a perfectly equal bicameralism that is held responsible for the crisis of representation' in Italian politics (Pasquino 1986: 119).

Of the seven chambers, the German Bundesrat is the only one that receives general public support. Germany appears to be almost unique in having no campaign that seeks to reform the upper house. In fact there are even moves to extend the structure of the Bundesrat to create second chambers in the states, attended by representatives of local government (Leonardy 1999b). This is because the Bundesrat is acknowledged as a genuine forum where state and federal interests are represented, and agreements are reached. Although disputes between the chambers can be fuelled by party politics, this is not seen as an overriding concern.

This is in stark contrast to the situation in Spain, where 'the Senate, initially intended as a chamber for territorial representation in central government, is widely seen as a useless body' (Heywood 1995: 100). Even senior officials of the upper house are prepared to admit that

---

[4] *Irish Times*, 2 July 1997.

'practically since the moment the constitution was approved, there has been talk of a less-than-ideal Senate, proposing the need for its reform, because it is felt that the chamber does not meet the requirements of full territoriality' (Ripollés 1999: 172). It had been hoped that the addition of autonomous community Senators, as devolution progressed, would strengthen the territorial basis of the house. However, these Senators make up only one in five of the total, and after almost 20 years there is a lively debate in Spain on upper house reform.

In some countries the view of the upper house is more equivocal. France is an example. Despite some attempts by the Sénat authorities to modernise its image, most commentators recognise that the upper house is essentially a conservative institution. For example, on the day after the Sénat blocked the *Parité* legislation to give women equal rights to elected office (see Chapter 8) the leader column of *Le Monde* was headed 'A Sénat from another age'. The piece said that

the Sénat boasts that it is a temple of 'wisdom' against the extremes of the [lower house] and the swings of universal suffrage. Carefully protecting a mode of scrutiny from another age, the Senators themselves are not unhappy to present themselves as the guardians of a sepia, rural, unchanging France . . . at the [Sénat], 'wisdom' becomes conservatism.[5]

These sentiments echoed the earlier comments of Lionel Jospin, who has described the Sénat as 'an anomaly amongst modern democracies'.[6]

However, the French public seem less convinced about the need to reform the upper house. The only two constitutional referendums that have ever been rejected by the French people—in 1946 and 1969—included weakening or removal of the Sénat (Maus 1993).[7] The second of these resulted in the fall of President de Gaulle. Opinion polls demonstrate that the Sénat is relatively popular. In 1990, 46 per cent of voters believed the upper house performed its role well, compared to 38 per cent who believed the same about the lower house (Rizzuto 1997). This may, however, simply indicate a lack of understanding of the work of the Sénat—because of its claimed role in protecting liberties it may be confused by some people with the Constitutional Council.

---

[5] *Le Monde*, 27 January 1999.

[6] *Le Monde*, 21 April 1998.

[7] The referendum of 1946 was on a new constitution, including a unicameral parliament. This was rejected, but a second referendum later that year—on a constitution including a bicameral parliament—was passed. In 1969 President de Gaulle staked his reputation on a referendum which would have turned the Sénat into a purely consultative body, alongside introducing regional reform, which was popular. Two months before the referendum a poll found that only seven per cent of voters wanted to see a reduced role for the upper house (Hayward 1983).

Opinions over the Australian Senate are equally split. Governments never welcome the powerful interventions of the elected Senate, which they do not politically control. However, oppositions always embrace the opportunity to use the Senate—in partnership with minor parties— to modify government proposals. Thus the major parties tend to have a schizophrenic attitude to the upper house—in government they resent its interference, but in opposition they appreciate its benefits. Prime Minister Paul Keating famously referred to members of the Senate as 'unrepresentative swill'[8] and to the house itself as a 'spoiling chamber'.[9] Nevertheless his party, upon entering opposition in 1996, began to use exactly the same tactics as the previous opposition in the Senate to rein back government. This fluctuating attitude to the upper house is shared by the press, which at times lambasts and at other times celebrates its role. Much of the debate in Australia centres around the concept of *mandate* with the government claiming that its majority in the lower house gives it a mandate to govern, and the opposition and minor parties claiming that their combined forces in the proportionally elected Senate have a mandate to question and modify government proposals. The press keenly joins in the debate, with headlines such as 'Will of the people: yes, but which people?'[10] and 'End the mandate muddle'.[11]

All the evidence suggests that voters in Australia are fairly happy with the way things are. Votes for small parties are always higher for the Senate than for the lower house, and analysis of voting patterns shows that some Australians operate 'split ticket' voting—supporting one party in the lower house elections and another in the Senate. It has been suggested that voters do this in order to ensure that, even if their own party is elected, the Senate operates as a brake on government (Bowler and Denemark 1993). When polled, 45 per cent of voters say they believe it is better when government does not control both houses of parliament, compared to 41 per cent who would prefer government to do so (Bean and Wattenburg 1998).[12]

Voter behaviour has changed over time, in a way which ensures that minor parties retain control of the Australian Senate. When the number

---

[8] Parliamentary Debates, 5 November 1992.

[9] *Sydney Morning Herald*, 4 March 1994.

[10] *The Sunday Age*, 1 November 1998.

[11] *The Sunday Telegraph*, 4 October 1998.

[12] Similar attitudes appear to apply in France. An opinion poll commissioned by the President of the Sénat after the comments of Prime Minister Jospin found that found that 57 per cent of electors said that it is a good thing for democracy if the upper and lower houses do not have the same party majority. This included 53 per cent of voters from the left and 67 per cent of voters from the right. This survey, based on interviews with 1,000 people, was quoted in a pamphlet issued by the President in defence of the Sénat.

of seats per state was increased from 10 to 12 in 1983, it was widely believed that this would make it harder for minor parties to gain seats in the upper house. Commentators believed that the election of six members per state at each half Senate election would result in the two major parties sharing the electoral spoils equally (Sharman 1986). However, the proportion of votes for small parties has continued to grow—the share of Senate votes for the two main parties has fallen, from 95 per cent in 1949 to 82 per cent in 1984 and 75 per cent in 1998 (Stone 1998). This growth has ensured that the representation of small parties in the Senate has risen, securing them a permanent refereeing role in Australian politics.

THE LONG ROAD TO REFORM

Levels of dissatisfaction with second chambers have led to calls for reform in most countries—the only upper house which has not been under such heavy attack is the German Bundesrat. Reform proposals have taken many forms, and in some cases have been pressed for many years. However, despite this the actual reforms have been few, and upper houses have remained largely as they were. There are only two minor exceptions to this: the changes to the electoral system and the number of seats in the Australian Senate—neither of which were the subject of popular demand—and the change from life appointment to a retirement age of 75 for the Canadian Senate.[13] In most countries the prospects for reform appear bleak.

Canada

The Canadian Senate is undoubtedly the chamber which has inflamed the greatest passions and inspired the longest campaign for reform. The first parliamentary debate on Senate reform was in 1874, when a Liberal Senator called for the provinces to be able to select their own candidates. As early as 1926, in *The Unreformed Senate of Canada*, Mackay wrote that 'probably on no other public question in Canada has there been so much unanimity of opinion as on the necessity of Senate reform' (p. 206).

Numerous initiatives have been taken towards Canadian Senate reform. These include proposals by two Trudeau governments in 1969 and 1978, a Senate committee in 1980, a joint parliamentary committee in 1984, and a Royal Commission in 1985. Senate reform has also

---

[13] These changes to the Australian and Canadian Senates are explained in Chapter 3.

formed part of two major packages of constitutional reform—the Meech Lake Accord of 1987 and the Charlottetown Accord of 1992—both of which failed to gain Canada-wide agreement. There has been a particularly vigorous campaign for reform in the west of Canada, driven by the right-wing Reform Party and the government of the province of Alberta. However, the possibility of a reformed Senate seems as far away as ever.

The main problem is the failure to reach a consensus on the way forward, within a context where Senate reform is linked to arguments for wider reform of the Canadian federation. What unites campaigners is opposition to the current Senate, appointed by the Prime Minister to represent the provinces. All proposals have aimed to involve the provinces in some way in the selection of their Senators, but there the similarities end. Proposals have ranged from a minimalist change— giving provinces the right to propose a shortlist of candidates to the Prime Minister—to more radical solutions leading to a directly elected upper house. Others have suggested that Canada import the Bundesrat model from Germany. Considerable attention has been given to the distribution of seats in a reformed Senate, with the provinces in the west of Canada, in particular, lobbying for greater representation. The province of Alberta has led a campaign for a 'Triple-E' Senate, inspired by the Australian and US systems. This would create a Senate which was 'elected, effective, and equal', giving the same number of seats to all provinces. This would benefit the four small provinces of the west, which have just 24 Senate seats between them, at the expense of the large provinces of Ontario and Quebec, which have 24 seats each.

The difficulty of accommodating the interests of large and small provinces has been the biggest obstacle to Senate reform. This has become bound up with other disputes between the provinces, and calls for autonomy made by Quebec. One attempt at compromise was the package contained in the Charlottetown Accord, which would have provided an elected Senate, with equal numbers of Senators per province but—in the interests of the large provinces—with considerably reduced powers. This was not seen by the west as the Triple-E Senate they wanted, since it was questionable whether it would be 'effective'. In any case a referendum on the package failed to gain sufficient support, largely due to conflicts between large and small provinces over other aspects of the constitutional reform package. The western provinces have kept up the pressure for reform, and the Alberta government has twice staged public elections for 'Senators in waiting' to force the hand of the Prime Minister in appointments. The first time, in 1989, Prime Minister Mulroney felt obliged to appoint the winning candidate, having made a commitment to provincial involvement in Senate appointments. However, two further candidates elected in 1998 have been denied seats. Liberal and Conservative Prime Ministers have been understandably reluctant to appoint Alberta's elected members as all winners so far have been from the Reform Party.

Government must take some of the responsibility for the lack of action in reforming the Canadian Senate. The report of the Joint Committee on Senate Reform, in 1984, included one of the most balanced and thoughtful sets of proposals that have been put forward (Government of Canada 1984). The permanent solution proposed was a directly elected Senate, with representation based on a compromise between equality for states and size of population (similar to the German system). The power of the Senate would be reduced to one of delay, in recognition of the greater likelihood that it would use its powers. The committee also suggested transitional arrangements for short term reform, including the introduction of nine-year terms to replace the retirement age of 75. Although the report was welcomed by government, even its transitional proposals were never put into effect. Any government would appreciate that an elected Senate—even with reduced powers—would be more likely to question its policies and enjoy public support.

Italy

Some of the themes from the reform debate in Canada are familiar in other countries, even where the existing chamber is entirely different. Italy is an example. Here reform of the upper house has been considered as part of wholesale constitutional reform, as it has at times in Canada. It has also largely focused on the need to build a genuinely territorial chamber, of the form envisaged in the Italian post-war constitution.

Formal review of the Italian constitution has taken place in several specially created parliamentary committees since the early 1980s. The most recent of these was a joint committee, created in 1997, with the task of redrafting the entire constitution. The results of the committee's work were to be debated in parliament and then put to the public in a referendum. However, due to the enormity of the task—reviewing all aspects of the constitution from parliament to the judiciary, from the degree of decentralisation to whether to adopt a presidential model of government—there were no agreed outcomes by mid-1999. Most party leaders were included on the committee.[14] However, its report was subject to over 40,000 amendments when it was tabled in the lower house in June 1997 (Senato della Repubblica 1997). Parliamentary debates on the report were inconclusive and—although the committee formally still exists—no action has been taken.

The proposals on reform of the Senato were largely in tune with those which had emerged from similar committees previously. The key objective was to make the composition and the functions of the two chambers distinctive. The new Senato would remain directly elected, but would have a rolling membership so that it could not be dissolved. It would no longer have the power to hold a confidence vote in the government, but would be compensated by additional powers over public appointments and regional issues. Under the initial proposals the main vehicle for discussion of regional issues would be a new committee (dubbed the *camerina*—little chamber) which would comprise Senators, regional presidents and representatives of the provinces and municipalities. When the proposals were amended by the lower house, this proposal was replaced with a suggestion that representatives of regions, provinces, and municipalities would become part-time Senators, and sit alongside directly elected colleagues to discuss legislation with a local or regional impact. Apart from this category of legislation there would be three others, with varying levels of involvement for the Senato. Constitutional reforms would remain subject to approval by both chambers, whilst bills on a limited number of issues—such as penal law and the judiciary—would be subject to discussion in both chambers with a joint committee introduced to resolve disputes. All other bills would be the responsibility of the lower house alone, although the Senato would be able to make non-binding recommendations.

Due to the impasse in the lower house—which centred around issues of the judiciary and the presidency—these proposals were never discussed in the Senato. However, it is hard to imagine that they would be acceptable to existing members of the upper house, as they took away many of its powers.

[14] The committee was chaired by Massimo D'Alema, then leader of the Democratic Socialist Party, and included other figures such as Silvio Berlusconi, the leader of the main opposition party, Fausto Bertinotti, the leader of the Communist Party, and Gianfranco Fini, the leader of the far-right National Alliance.

Spain

In Spain the discontent with the Senado has led to 'a veritable Babel of propositions, programmes, projects and plans' for its reform (Juberías 1999: 292). All of these have been targeted at building a more genuinely territorial upper house. Following the failure to achieve this aim through changing the standing orders of the house—in particular through the establishment of the General Committee on the Autonomous Communities in 1994—the argument has shifted to the possibilities for constitutional change. The authorities of the Senado themselves have taken a lead in this debate, publishing a series of books on reform of the upper house (e.g. Vera Santos 1997; Visiedo Mazón 1997) and hosting a conference in 1998 involving staff from many other upper houses around Europe. The subject has also been debated at other forums, including a conference of clerks of autonomous community parliaments (Pau i Vall 1996).

In 1994 the government announced its intention to reform the Senado, and an upper house committee was established to look into the options. However, despite all-party support and a series of hearings with experts—including the original drafters of the constitution—the committee was unable to agree conclusions. A new committee set up in 1995 was similarly inconclusive.

The particular difficulty in Spain is devising an upper house that reflects the new territorial politics of the state, to the satisfaction of all interest groups. The original devolution settlement envisaged greater autonomy for a few 'historic' regions (the Basque country, Catalonia, Galicia), but not for the whole of Spain. Devolution progressed at different rates in different regions, but has now enveloped the whole of Spain. What was an asymmetrical settlement has become increasingly symmetrical, as the newer autonomous communities have sought to catch up with the historic regions in terms of devolved powers. Meanwhile the historic regions have fought to retain their special status.

Thus for many people the natural development would be a Senado which took on a more federal character, representing the autonomous communities at the centre. Amongst the two main parties there is general agreement about this. To achieve this aim there is agreement that the number of autonomous community Senators should be increased, and that the chamber should be given more power over territorial matters. The Socialist Party (PSOE) has suggested that elections for the upper house be held alongside regional elections (PSOE 1998). Other suggestions have included introducing a rolling membership, so that the Senado cannot be dissolved, and representation of government members in regional delegations (Juberías 1999; Soto 1997).

But for others such solutions are unacceptable. The Basque and Catalan nationalist parties, in particular, would see this kind of upper house as a step towards a federal Spain which they completely reject. These parties (whose support the 1996 Aznar government has needed to maintain a majority in the lower house) are only interested in solutions that give greater autonomy to their regions. It is difficult to see how these demands could be met through a new upper house. Nationalist parties themselves have refused to engage in the debate on reform of the Senado. Few solutions have been suggested by others as to how Spain's asymmetrical devolution could be represented in the upper house. One proposal is for parliamentary groups to be formed, and votes to be cast, on the basis of autonomous communities rather than parties. This would mimic the Bundesrat model. An autonomous community would vote as a block in the Senado, and could have the power to veto on certain issues of particular regional importance (Caminal Badia 1996). However, even within this model it would be difficult to fully reflect regional asymmetries.

In 1996 a third upper house committee was established to look into reform of the Spanish upper house. The committee was asked to focus on three key issues: the composition of the chamber, the functions of the chamber, and reflecting the asymmetrical nature of Spanish devolution. Although progress had been made on the first two of these issues, by 1999 little had been achieved on the third, and most difficult, point. Few people expected the committee to report.

Ireland

The Irish Seanad has suffered from many of the same troubles as the Spanish Senado, being weak and generally controlled by the government. This contributes to a low public profile for the chamber, and a sense of public dissatisfaction with its work. Ever since the chamber was first established in 1937, its possible reform has been discussed.

Some proposals have focused on opportunities for gradual and minor change to improve the current representative functions of the Seanad. For example, in 1979 a constitutional referendum was passed to broaden the representativeness of the university seats in the chamber. This would allow for representation of other, newer, universities— beyond the existing two—in the upper house. However, no law has ever been passed to enact this change. Similarly there have been proposals to reform the system of electing vocational Senators, so that this is not so dominated by the parties. A 1959 commission on Seanad reform proposed that roughly half of these members should be elected by vocational bodies themselves, with politicians restricted to the election of the other half.[15] At this time, and on subsequent occasions since, opponents argued that the involvement of these bodies in the elections would result in them becoming unduly politicised. Given what the parties had to lose, it is perhaps unsurprising that they rejected the commission's report when it was discussed in the chamber. Consequently the report's recommendations were never implemented.

More recent discussions of Seanad reform have been within a context of wider constitutional review. In particular a Constitution Review Group was established in 1995, with a remit to 'review the constitution, and in the light of this review to establish those areas where constitutional change may be desirable or necessary'. Although the review group looked at the entire constitution, it devoted a sizeable portion of its final report to the reform of the Seanad. They concluded that there should be a 'a separate, comprehensive, independent examination of all issue relating to Seanad Éireann . . . If such a review does not resolve the issue of representation and other substantive issues in a satisfactory manner, serious consideration will need to be given to the abolition of the Seanad' (Government of Ireland 1996: 71).

This review was later carried out by the All-Party Oireachtas Committee on the Constitution, which was formed in 1996 to take forward the work of the Review Group. This Committee's second report, in 1997, was devoted to reform of the Seanad. It concluded that, as currently constituted, the Seanad 'does not make a useful contribution to the democratic life of the state' (Government of Ireland 1997: 6), and made a number of proposals for reform. It favoured a greater role for the upper house in neglected areas of parliamentary business, such as scrutiny of EU and delegated legislation, and organisation of committee inquiries. The legislative process would be streamlined, with the upper house playing only an 'advisory' role. The membership of the chamber would be mixed, with a quarter directly elected using European constituency boundaries and roughly a quarter each indirectly elected by lower house members and councillors. The remainder would be nominated by the Taoiseach and elected by the universities, under slight modifications to the current systems for these seats.

---

[15] The 1959 commission was established following a Dáil debate in 1957 when Dr Noel Browne moved that the Seanad should be abolished. Browne went on to become a Senator himself when he lost his seat in the Dáil in 1973 (Dooge 1987).

Following the committee's report, the 1997 general election brought a change of government. The committee was then reconstituted with a new membership and Fianna Fáil chair, Brian Lenihan. In mid-1999 this new committee was still reviewing the conclusions of the old committee, which it may or may not endorse.

France

In France the momentum for reform of the Sénat has fluctuated, depending on the relationship between the upper house and government. The breakdown in relations between the two in the 1960s led to the unsuccessful referendum of 1969.[16] With the exception of this period, pressure for reform has come when the Socialists have been in power and been plagued by hostility from the upper house.

Because of the Sénat's veto power over constitutional change, it has been necessary to try to win the support of Senators for their own reform. This means that proposals have necessarily been moderate. However, even moderate proposals have met with a chilly response in the upper house. For example in 1991 the Cresson Socialist government made some relatively minor proposals, which would have more closely related geographical representation in the upper house to population, and increased the use of proportional representation in the elections.[17] These proposals, which would have reduced the stranglehold of conservative rural areas over the Sénat, were rejected without debate in the upper house (Maus 1993).

Prime Minister Lionel Jospin announced his intention to reform the Sénat in 1998. In March 1999 a bill was published including almost identical reforms to those put in 1991. This included, for example, provision for Senators to be elected by proportional representation (PR) in *départements* with three or more seats. This would extend PR from 15 *départements* to 48. The Sénat proposed heavy amendments to the bill, although there were some indications that compromise would be possible. For example, rather than outright rejection as in 1991, the upper house proposed that PR should be used in all *départements* with four or more Senators, rather than five, as at present. By autumn 1999

---

[16] This period in the Sénat's history is discussed in Chapter 4. The referendum was also discussed above, under 'Public Perceptions of the Chamber'.

[17] The precise proposals would have been to base delegates to the electoral college which elects Senators strictly on population, with one representative per 500 inhabitants; to elect delegates to this college by proportional representation in *communes* with more than 3,500 inhabitants (rather than 30,000 inhabitants, as at present); and to elect Senators by proportional representation in all *départements* with at least three seats (rather than five seats, as at present) (Mastias 1999).

the bill had not completed its passage, and the response of the lower house to the Sénat's amendments was not clear. However, some piecemeal reform now looks possible.

Australia

In Australia, despite controversy about the role of the Senate, there have similarly been few serious attempts at reform. The reforms that have taken place—to the electoral system in 1949 and the size of the chamber in 1983—were possible within the existing constitution. All attempts to change the constitution in order to reform the Senate have failed.

The reforms which have been proposed in referendums have actually been relatively minor. A recurring proposal has been to harmonise the electoral terms of the upper and lower houses. This would result in half the Senate being elected at each lower house election, with Senators taking their seats straight away.[18] There have been four referendums on this issue, in 1974, 1977, 1984, and 1988, but these have all failed. Points made against the proposal include that it would 'enable governments to dissolve half the Senate whenever the Senate attempts to protect Australia from measures harmful to the national interest' (Parliament of the Commonwealth of Australia 1997: 104).

Other more substantial proposals have been made, but none of these have ever reached a referendum. Another recurring theme has been the desire to curb the powers of the Senate, particularly over financial legislation, following the 1975 crisis. This was the policy of the Labor Party during the 1980s and was backed by a Constitutional Commission in 1988. However, no government has had the confidence to put this issue to a referendum. Instead the parties exercise voluntary restraint, with both Labor and the Democrats having made public commitments not to block government supply bills.[19] In the 1980s Labor was also committed to removing the right of ministers to sit in the upper house, in order to reinforce the role of the lower house as the seat of government (Uhr 1989). Other proposals have included one, made in 1995 by premiers Wayne Goss of Queensland and Bob Carr of New South Wales, to reform the Senate along the Bundesrat model.

---

[18] At present Senate terms are fixed, with Senators taking their seats on 1 July. Elections can only be harmonised when the general election takes place less than a year before a due Senate election. Regular harmonisation of elections would therefore require either introduction of fixed terms for the lower house or variable terms for the Senate. At times both of these solutions have been proposed.

[19] Even 25 years after the crisis, the Liberal and National Parties have never made this commitment, which would be tantamount to admitting that their behaviour in 1975 was wrong.

Debate between the Australian parties in recent years has tended to focus on the opportunities for again reforming the Senate electoral system. Successive representatives of both major parties—when in government—have floated the idea of ending proportional representation for the upper house. This was first suggested by Labor Prime Minister Paul Keating in 1994 (Galligan 1995). Others have proposed that some proportionality be retained, but that the minimum quota to win a Senate seat be increased. This was suggested, for example, by Liberal backbencher Helen Coonan in February 1999. The objective of either of these changes—which would not require a change to the constitution—would be to reduce or eliminate the role of minor parties in the chamber. Coonan's proposal of a minimum vote share of 10 per cent to win a Senate seat would retain a nominally proportional system, whilst removing most small party representatives (Coonan 1999). However a change to the Senate electoral system for short-term political gain could backfire on government, as it did following the original adoption of PR. The danger of adopting a reform such as Coonan's would be that the Senate could then alternate between government control, acting as nothing but a rubber stamp, and opposition control, creating complete legislative gridlock. A system which allowed opposition control of the Senate in Australia's adversarial parliament could lead to regular constitutional crises of the kind which occurred in 1975.

As yet, the main opposition party has never sought to collude in Senate reform, although this remains a possibility. The Labor Party entered the 1998 elections with an open-ended manifesto commitment which would have allowed them to reform the Senate had they been in government. However, from a position of opposition they opposed Senator Coonan's proposals.

PROSPECTS FOR FUTURE REFORM

Despite widespread calls for reform, there is little progress apparent towards changing these institutions. Even in Canada, where reform debates have been live for more than a century the 'Senate remains as it has for 131 years, an anomaly, a peripheral institution of government, sometimes a nuisance, occasionally of value' (Franks 1999: 155).

There are a number of reasons for this, which again are common to several different countries. These include:

- *Territorial and other disputes.* It is very difficult in any political system to get consensus for a particular reform solution. This applies particularly where the upper house is intended to be a territorial chamber, but there are disputes between territories, or between territories and the centre, about the distribution of powers. Negotiations over the form of the upper house can become a site for arguments between competing regions which want to retain their identity and powers. This is the case in both Canada and Spain. It is difficult to see how the competing demands of the small Canadian provinces for more Senate seats and the large provinces to retain their status can ever be reconciled. Similarly in Spain there are no formal proposals as to how asymmetrical devolution can be reflected in the Senado, and it is unlikely that any such proposals could satisfy both the large national parties and the smaller nationalist groups. Any major reform of the upper house would require amendment to the constitution, and this would be likely to be used by the nationalist parties to press for greater autonomy, and even the right to secede. This tense situation, made worse by the threat of terrorist violence by the Basque nationalist group ETA, makes reform of the Senado unlikely in the short to medium term. Though less serious, the disputes between different groups in Italy—the plethora of large and small parties, of the left and the right, the competing interests of upper and lower houses, the regions and local government—resulted in a set of constitutional proposals in 1997 that were acceptable to nobody. Reform of the upper house, which is relatively low down the long list of priorities, looks unlikely at present.

• *Vested interests of government and parties.* An additional factor in most countries is the lack of incentive for government to initiate upper house reform. This is at play in Canada, where compromise proposals have been made in the past that might have secured the support of most, or all, provinces. The report of the Joint Committee on Senate Reform in 1984 formally received a warm response from government, but little was done to implement the proposals. The advantages to government of retaining an upper house which is effectively appointed by the Prime Minister, and rarely challenges policy, creates a disincentive to reform. In Ireland similar forces apply, as the upper house provides a useful repository for both failed and aspiring candidates from all parties. A genuinely vocational chamber, or one which was directly elected, would not provide the same facility for the parties and might be more difficult for government to control. This makes reform appear increasingly remote. In Australia, in contrast, the governing party has a strong incentive to reform the Senate in order to seek a majority. Both reforms to the chamber this century have resulted from a desire for short-term political advantage. Whilst government would not be able to pass such proposals through a hostile Senate, there is a danger of collusion between the two major parties to evict the minor parties from the chamber.

• *Constitutional rigidity.* It is the inability to progress other reforms to the Senate—which would require a constitutional referendum— that might drive the Australian parties to this extreme. The popularity of the Senate, and the failure of previous referendums, makes it unlikely that a poll to reduce its powers could succeed. This reflects the relative rigidity of the Australian constitution, which in this case requires that constitutional reform has popular support. However, in other states rigidity may actually prevent popular reform proposals succeeding. The Canadian constitution requires that any reform must be passed by at least two-thirds of provincial legislatures, representing half or more of the Canadian population. This is a particularly difficult hurdle for Senate reform, given that it is the subject of heated dispute between provincial governments. In France the problem is yet more fundamental—reform of the Sénat is subject to the approval of the upper house itself. In order to promote reform a government must take on not only the Sénat, but its powerful and high-profile President. This makes anything more than minor reform unlikely. The only realistic prospect for major upper house reform is an unconstitutional referendum of the kind which established the elected presidency in 1962.[20] This would however require the collusion of the President, who is responsible for calling any referendum, and is thus dependent on the prospect of a simultaneous, and determined, Socialist government and President. The stigma of past failures in referendums intended to reform the Sénat would also need to be overcome.

Aside from inaction, or reform, there is another prospect for upper houses: that of abolition. Where an upper house is ineffective and unpopular, and reform is not progressed, this can be the eventual outcome. One example was the abolition of the appointed upper

---

[20] In 1962 General de Gaulle used unconstitutional means to achieve the change to a directly elected President, as this was put to a referendum without first being agreed by parliament (Hayward 1983). It was unlikely that parliament would have passed this proposal, as parliamentarians had a major role in the previous electoral college for President. Once the change had passed a referendum it was politically impossible for it to be challenged.

chamber in New Zealand in 1950.[21] Another was the abolition of the Swedish upper house which, like the Italian Senato, carried out identical duties to the lower house.[22] Abolition of the Seanad is frequently mentioned in Ireland—it was a high profile commitment of the Progressive Democrat Party in 1988, and was suggested as an option by the Constitution Review Group in 1996. If reform does not progress— and there is little to suggest that it will—abolition of the Seanad is a real possibility. Likewise in Canada, where the reform debate has run for so long without conclusion, there are suggestions of Senate abolition. In 1999 two MPs of different parties were touring Canada gathering signatures on a petition to abolish the upper house. Although this may not be the desire of most Canadians, continued frustration with the failure to build a better Senate could ultimately lead to drastic action.

CONCLUSIONS

Despite unanimous support for the Bundesrat in Germany, and apparent public satisfaction with the Senate in Australia, upper chambers in general suffer from popularity problems. In Britain, Canada, France, Ireland, Italy, and Spain the upper house is subject to constant calls for reform. Even in Australia the frustrations of the parties lead to similar proposals being put. Mughan and Patterson summarise the situation when they describe second chambers as 'essentially contested institutions', stating that 'many countries choose not to have one, others have them but then do away with them, and still others keep them but are engaged in an apparently incessant dialogue about how they should be reformed' (1999: 338).

There are obvious shortcomings of some upper houses. For example the lack of provincial involvement and democratic mandate of the Canadian Senate, the permanent government majority in the Irish Seanad, and the dominance of conservative rural representatives in the French Sénat. However, there are other factors which make upper houses subject to criticism—and even inherently unpopular.

One difficulty is the relatively low profile of many upper chambers, and the consequent lack of understanding of their work. Where the public are not involved in the selection of a chamber's members—for

---

[21] This is described in Russell (1998) and in greater detail in Jackson (1991).

[22] When Sweden was bicameral all legislation was first considered in a joint committee, and then in both houses simultaneously. If there was no agreement it went back to the joint committee. The cabinet was responsible to both chambers (Wheare 1968). It was only a small step from this virtual unicameralism to true unicameralism in 1970.

example because it is indirectly elected—it is likely to receive little press attention. Consequently it may be thought to be doing nothing. As earlier chapters have shown, this is likely to be a false impression. Even the chambers that are least well respected, such as the Canadian Senate and Irish Seanad, make an important contribution through their legislative and investigative work. The absence of a media presence may actually help a second chamber to perform its work, if it can engage in real discussions rather than adversarial debate. However, when the chamber's profile is particularly low, its impact may be damaged. Its work may not be respected and calls for its reform, or even abolition, are likely to grow.

The second problem facing upper houses is that they may be seen as obstructive if they fulfil their basic constitutional role to delay, reflect upon and question government action. Such accusations are particularly likely from government itself, as in the Australian case. However, this is liable to influence public opinion if a popular government is prevented from implementing its programme. Again there is a difficult balance to be struck in an upper house between causing unnecessary duplication and delay, as in Italy, and being an ineffective scrutineer, as in Spain. Second chambers which do question government, such as the Australian Senate, walk a tightrope between public popularity and the threat of reform.

However, even where reform becomes desirable, it proves difficult in practice. Nowhere is this better illustrated than by the Canadian Senate—unreformed for over 100 years—or by the House of Lords itself. Overseas experience shows that it is hard to achieve consensus for reform, especially where there are disputes over the devolution of powers, and where the constitution is difficult to amend. Government may also not have sufficient will to reform a second chamber to make it more effective. This is likely, after all, to make government's life more difficult. These factors are likely to come increasingly into play in the UK, and may make the second stage of House of Lords reform difficult to achieve.

However, experience from overseas also demonstrates that there is a gradually emerging consensus about some of the features which are desirable in an upper house. As the UK enters a new reform debate, in the footsteps of others, it may be able to learn from the conclusions which have been reached in other countries. These form part of the important collection of lessons which may be drawn from overseas when considering the reform of the House of Lords. This is the subject of Part Three of the book.

PART THREE

Lessons for the UK

12

Principles of Reform

Having considered in some detail the role of second chambers overseas, we now turn our attention back to the UK, and the reform of the House of Lords. This chapter, and the ones that follow, consider what can be learnt from overseas for the design of a new second chamber.

As described in Chapter 1, the reform of the House of Lords will occur in two stages. The first—the removal of the majority of hereditary peers from the house—was completed in November 1999. The discussion in this third part of the book therefore focuses on the options for the second stage of reform—to move away from the transitional, largely appointed, chamber and towards a longer-term solution.

The chapters in Part 2 of this book reviewed the membership, powers, and functions of seven second chambers around the world. These closing chapters draw heavily on that information. However, these chapters have been designed in order that they may be read, as far as possible, independently of those that precede them. Readers may find it helpful to at least familiarise themselves with the conclusions of the earlier chapters, and with the composition of the chambers—as described in Chapter 3. But references are included throughout the closing chapters to where particular lessons from overseas are described in detail in the body of the book.

There are two key questions to be answered in designing a new second chamber. The first is: what is the chamber to do? The existing functions of the House of Lords provide a starting point, but given that the chamber—and many other parts of the British constitution—are being redesigned, it may be appropriate to change or extend these functions. These issues are considered in Chapter 13. After the functions of the chamber are clear—and only then—should the second question be addressed. That is: who should sit in the chamber? This is the subject of Chapter 14.

The intention of this opening chapter of Part 3 is therefore not to consider either the role or the membership of the new upper house in detail, but rather to set the scene, consider briefly some more general lessons which cut across these two issues, and discuss some general principles within which reform of the upper house should fit. These principles are drawn both from overseas experience, and from some of the strengths of the existing House of Lords.

LEARNING FROM OVERSEAS

Before embarking on a description of lessons from overseas, it is worth considering the merits of such an exercise for a few moments, and what we can expect to learn. It is also worth considering where the UK fits, in terms of comparison with other countries such as those whose second chambers were considered in Part 2 of the book.

The UK constitutional context is changing rapidly, as a result of the large number of reforms embarked upon since 1997.[1] The establishment of devolved assemblies has begun to introduce a new territorial politics to the UK; the Human Rights Act 1998 is starting to encourage a new rights culture; and there are many possibilities for further change, including devolution in the English regions and adoption of a more proportional voting system for Westminster. Consideration of House of Lords reform must take these new developments into account. But this is a challenging task, as it is difficult to predict their impact, which may prove to be profound (Hazell 1999a).

This in itself is an argument for considering overseas experience, drawing from countries that already demonstrate some of the characteristics that the UK is now adopting. The countries considered in this study were chosen to offer a spectrum of experience, for this very reason. The structure of their political systems was discussed briefly in Chapter 3. They represent a range of federal, devolved, and unitary states, two-party and multi-party systems, and old and new constitutions. Their second chambers have different kinds of members and responsibilities. They therefore provide a rich set of experiences from which the UK can learn.

However, the inevitable differences between countries also mean that we must be cautious in our approach. It would be foolish to expect to be able to import overseas solutions wholesale—however successful they appear to be. In many cases their success may be dependent on the political contexts and traditions within which they operate. It would be naive, for example, to expect to reproduce a German-style Bundesrat in the UK and then have that operate as successfully as it does in Germany. It would certainly be impossible—at least at present—to adopt such a chamber, since the UK does not have the federal structure

---

[1] These were discussed briefly in Chapter 1. For a more detailed discussion see Hazell (1999a).

of Germany, from which members of the upper house are drawn. Even if, over time, the chamber could be created, there is no guarantee that it would succeed. The Bundesrat's success is dependent on the strong German tradition of co-operative federalism, the German party system, and long experience of coalition government. However, at the same time, this does not preclude the UK learning much from the Bundesrat at a more detailed level.

The diversity of the seven countries considered also allows common themes to emerge. Thus in considering the prospects of an elected chamber, for example, lessons can be learnt from the well-established federation of Australia, the post-war system of unitary Italy, and the new constitution of quasi-federal Spain. Where there are common experiences across these different boundaries it may be assumed with greater confidence that applying a similar model in the UK might result in similar consequences. Some of the common themes from upper house reform debates are explored later in this chapter.

If caution is adopted, and examples are considered in the light of the UK system and its traditions, there are therefore many lessons from overseas parliaments which can be useful to the debate in the UK. These apply at both the general and the detailed level. This is the spirit of the final chapters of the book. Often these examples provide cautionary lessons about arrangements it would be advisable to avoid in the UK— based on shortcomings found overseas. Chapter 11 in particular showed that many other second chambers, like the House of Lords, suffer from popularity problems and are subject to calls for reform. The challenge for Britain is to avoid some of these pitfalls, and learn both positive and negative lessons from other countries for the design of a successful new upper house. In doing so, it will also be important to learn from some of the positive aspects of the existing House of Lords, which it may be desirable to retain. This is the subject of the next section.

BUILDING ON THE STRENGTHS OF THE LORDS

The debate on reform of the House of Lords has been driven primarily by arguments about the merits of hereditary peers sitting as members of the house. The Labour Party and a succession of centre parties, in particular, have been concerned by this issue—since it resulted in a chamber that was traditionally dominated by the Conservatives. Apart from the impact that the membership of the house has on its voting habits, little debate has focused on the way the House of Lords works, and the contribution that it makes to the UK legislature.

It is generally acknowledged that—composition method aside—the House of Lords has many strengths. Whilst there are arguments about the extent to which each of these applies, the following claims have frequently been made in defence of the House of Lords:

- Representatives of political parties in the house behave more independently than their counterparts in the House of Commons. The whipping system in the chamber is less strict—members frequently abstain, and vote against their party more often than members of the Commons. This, added to the large number of members in the house who do not adhere to any whip, leads to a more independent ethos in the chamber.

- These factors contribute to a high quality of debate in the house. Debates are less driven by party politics than those in the Commons, and include contributions from members who are expert in their fields. Debate is conducted in a more courteous and civilised fashion.

- The chamber gives more time to detailed consideration of legislation—including draft EU legislation—and proposes many useful amendments that make bills more workable in practice.

- Members of the house also contribute time to many worthwhile parliamentary inquiries and debates. Often these focus on issues that are politically sensitive, or highly technical, and which the House of Commons is less inclined to address.

To a large extent this difference between the houses is driven by their membership. For a number of reasons the members of the House of Lords have more time to devote to detailed matters, and may behave more independently than MPs generally do. Some of these factors include:

- *Independent members:* the inclusion of many independent 'crossbench' members in the upper house helps makes it distinct from the House of Commons and brings a different perspective to its work. Around 150 crossbench members will remain in the transitional, largely appointed, house.

- *Age:* the higher average age in the House of Lords means that members have more maturity and experience. In mid-1999 the average age of MPs was approximately 52, as compared to 65 in the House of Lords. The age discrepancy between the Commons and the transitional upper house will be higher still.

- *Experts:* appointed members, in particular, include many who have pursued distinguished careers before they enter the house and may be experts in their field.

- *Long terms of office:* the life terms served by members mean that they are not dependent on reselection by their party, or the electorate, and may therefore choose more freely than MPs which policies and causes to support. Life membership also means that it is in members' long-term interests to treat each other with respect.

- *More time for detailed work:* the fact that members are not elected means that they have no constituents, and are less burdened with local duties and party work than members of the Commons.

- *Political careers:* government takes most of its senior ministers from the House of Commons, so members of the Lords are less likely to pursue ministerial ambitions. In any case most members are coming to the end of their careers so may no longer be seeking advancement or promotion to government.

- *Lack of media attention:* because members do not rely on reselection or election, and are not seeking promotion, their media and public profile is low. The lack of senior ministers in the house, and the fact that it challenges government only rarely, adds to this. The low level of interest by the media and the public in the work of the house allows its members to conduct their duties largely unhindered.

These factors combine to make a chamber that is very different from the House of Commons. During the public debate on the removal of the hereditary peers from the house, many concerns were expressed that these distinct features would be lost. Such concerns will continue to be raised as the debate develops on the second stage of the chamber's reform.

However, such features are not entirely unique. Discussion in earlier chapters demonstrated that many second chambers have similar characteristics. These result from both the composition and powers of the chambers. There are therefore many lessons that can be learnt from overseas, as well as from British experience, about how the most valued characteristics of the House of Lords can be retained after its reform.

COMPOSITION, LEGITIMACY, AND POWERS

The two chapters which follow focus on the role of a new second chamber, including its powers and functions, and on the composition of such a chamber. However, it is essential to realise the extent to which these issues are interlinked. One way in which they are connected is through the importance of the perceived legitimacy of the chamber. These three features of second chambers have been a recurrent theme in the earlier chapters of the book. The relationship between them forms one of the first general lessons about the design of an effective second chamber.

Composition

One important lesson to be learnt from parliaments overseas is that the new upper house must be distinct from the House of Commons. Some of the strengths of the existing House of Lords result from its very different character to the lower house, and most people would instinctively feel that there is little point in having two chambers which simply duplicate each other. This is entirely borne out by international experience.

Amongst the second chambers considered in Part 2, there is one that is almost indistinguishable from its lower house: the Italian Senato. Here the members of the two chambers are almost identical, being directly elected on the same day using similar electoral systems. This situation is exacerbated by the fact that the two chambers have identical functions and powers. Even though the upper house is powerful, and enjoys the legitimacy brought by being directly elected, it makes little distinct impact. In fact, the inclusion of a second chamber in the system adds little except delay and confusion. This leads to intense frustration, and reform proposals targeted at either creating two distinct chambers or abolishing one of them altogether.

At present the House of Lords is distinct in membership from the House of Commons partly because of its mode of composition. Even in the new transitional house, following the removal of the hereditaries, members will remain different to those in the House of Commons, as the house will continue to include—for example—older members, and many independents. However, a distinct composition *method* does not necessarily always lead to a set of distinctive individuals in the two parliamentary chambers. For example the upper house in Ireland, which is largely indirectly elected to represent vocational groups, 'suffers from the fact that, by and large, it is merely another selection of party politicians chosen in an unnecessarily complicated and not particularly democratic manner' (Chubb 1992: 198). The inclusion of expert and independent members in the House of Lords is as much a legacy of tradition as a result of the way the chamber's members are selected. This issue will be further explored in Chapter 14.

The Irish upper house is weakened by the fact that its party balance tends to mirror that of the lower house. In a modern parliament the balance between parties will be one of the most important potential differences between the chambers. One of the successes of, for example, the Australian system is that the two chambers generally have a different party balance—despite both being directly elected. This is achieved through the use of different electoral systems, and different terms of office, for the two chambers. However, the effectiveness of the chamber is also dependent on its legitimacy and its powers.

Powers

The effectiveness of an upper chamber will obviously depend upon its formal powers, and the extent to which these enable the chamber to ask government to think again. The Australian Senate is in a strong negotiating position when it comes to legislation, because it may delay bills indefinitely or veto them altogether. In contrast, the upper houses in Ireland and Spain have only a very short time in which to study legislation, and such limited delaying powers that there is no compelling need for government to take their views seriously. This is bound up with the fact that both these upper chambers tend to have a government majority, which further weakens their ability to act.

Reduced powers in upper houses can, however, help to promote some of their valued features, such as relative independence from the party whip, lack of media scrutiny, and concentration on legislative detail. This applies in particular to the inability of most upper houses to bring down governments through votes of confidence. This makes the outcome of votes less critical, and reduces the pressure on members to conform to a party whip.

Legitimacy

As well as the composition and powers of the chamber, however, there is a third factor which crucially impacts on its effectiveness. This is the perceived legitimacy of the chamber. The House of Lords is a useful starting point for such a discussion. It is relatively powerful in theory, as it can delay ordinary bills for up to 13 months, financial bills for up to a month, and can veto delegated legislation altogether. However, the house has rarely used these powers.[2] The reason for this caution on behalf of the Lords is not that it consistently agreed with the views of the House of Commons. Far from it. The two chambers have often had very different perspectives, in particular during periods of Labour government. At times the Conservative-dominated House of Lords might be profoundly unhappy with the direction of policy, but the chamber would not go so far as to reject the government's bills. This was because of the acceptance that it would be inappropriate for the unelected, predominantly hereditary, house to challenge the will of the elected Commons.[3] The degree of subordination of the House of Lords in practice has led Vernon Bogdanor to comment that Britain has 'in effect a unicameral system of government but with two chambers of parliament' (1997: 119).

This pattern is reflected overseas, in particular in the appointed Canadian upper house:

On paper, the Canadian Senate is one of the strongest second chambers imaginable, because it has a full veto power . . . in practice it is one of the weakest legislative bodies because it has so little political credibility (J. Smith 1994: 174).

The discussion in Chapter 6 illustrated just how rarely the Canadian Senate has used its powers. Meanwhile similar powers, in the hands of the elected Australian Senate, are used relatively frequently to force government to compromise. These examples demonstrate that the *de facto* powers of a chamber may be very different from its formal powers. *De facto* powers depend on the membership of the chamber enjoying sufficient legitimacy—in the eyes of the public—to be able to use their formal powers.

'Strong Bicameralism'

A classification of two-chamber parliaments proposed by Arend Lijphart (1984) was briefly discussed in Chapter 2. This proposed that a parliament exhibits 'strong' bicameralism—i.e. a useful second chamber—if the membership of the two chambers is distinct and the

---

[2] Only twice since 1949 have the provisions of the Parliament Acts—under which the House of Commons overturns a House of Lords veto—run their full course (see Chapter 1). Only once, in 1968, has an item of delegated legislation been rejected by the house.

[3] On bills to enact manifesto commitments this acceptance was formalised in the Salisbury convention (see Chapter 1).

upper house has relatively equal powers to the lower house. A parliament exhibits 'weak' bicameralism if only one of these conditions is met. And if neither condition is met this characterises 'insignificant' bicameralism, where the upper house makes little or no impact on the work of the legislature. This echoes, in more theoretical terms, some of the observations that have been made in this section.

Amongst the parliaments considered in Part 2 of the book, there are only two that could be described as 'strongly' bicameral using Lijphart's definition. These are in Australia and Germany. In Australia the membership of the two chambers is distinct because they are elected using different electoral systems, and this results in a different party balance in each chamber. In the upper house members, at least nominally, represent the states. In Germany members of the Bundesrat are distinct because they are members of state governments, rather than nationally elected MPs. They employ different voting rules than their lower house colleagues, and often have a different party balance. In Australia the upper house is so powerful that it can veto all legislation, and in Germany this power applies to over half of all bills. Consideration of seven second chambers in previous chapters showed that the German and Australian upper houses have by far the largest impact on the work of parliament. These examples therefore back up the classification which Lijphart has proposed.[4]

However, the two chambers in question also crucially enjoy sufficient legitimacy to use their formal powers. This is in contrast to other chambers, such as the House of Lords and the appointed Canadian Senate, which have strong or moderate formal powers but by convention do not use them. This is despite their distinct forms of membership, which often result in clashing political majorities in the two chambers. The simple lack of legitimacy is enough to reduce these parliaments to the status of 'weak', or even 'insignificant' bicameralism.

Lijphart acknowledged the importance of legitimacy to the success of a second chamber. However, this was not made explicit in his classification system. In a UK context this seems particularly important. Thus in a slight revision of Lijphart's definition, it is proposed that the

---

[4] Consideration of at least four of the other five countries also backs up Lijphart's analysis. The Irish Seanad and Spanish Senado do not have a membership distinct from that of their respective lower houses, and have very weak powers. Their impact could reasonably be described as 'insignificant'. The impact of bicameralism in Italy, where the two chambers have almost identical memberships and entirely equal powers, might also be described this way. In France the Sénat has a membership that differs from the lower house, primarily in terms of party balance, and moderate powers. Its impact could be said to be 'weak', although at times the chamber has been able to cause considerable disruption to governments.

following three elements are required for 'strong' bicameralism, and a successful upper house. Lessons from overseas suggest that, if the new UK upper house is to be effective, all of these three factors will need to be built into its design:

- *Distinct composition.* There are various ways in which the membership of the new upper house can be made distinct from that of the House of Commons. The method of composition may be different, but the party balance in the chamber will also be particularly important.

- *Adequate powers:* If the new upper house is to be able to make an impact, and have bargaining power with the government and the lower house, it will need to have moderate to strong powers.

- *Perceived legitimacy:* In order to use its powers the new chamber—unlike the existing House of Lords—will need to be seen to have legitimacy, and be able to carry public support.

TOWARDS A NEW MODEL SECOND CHAMBER?

The three general requirements of a distinct composition, moderate to strong powers, and legitimacy, provide us with our overarching principles of reform. Not only are these factors recognised by political theorists, they are also demonstrated by the real world experiences of second chambers. They feature heavily in reform debates overseas which, it was seen from Chapter 11, are numerous. The debate in Italy, for example, has been driven by the desire to see a second chamber which is distinct from the first. The debate in Canada is fuelled by the perceived lack of legitimacy of the upper house. And reformers in Ireland have frequently proposed the abolition of the Seanad—which is not only weak, but also has members who are seen as too similar to those in the lower house, and who are selected through a system which is discredited.

The UK is clearly far from being alone in seeking to reform its upper house. Reform movements around the world have led to numerous parliamentary committees, Royal Commissions, study groups, conferences, and reports, which have all grappled with the question of how to design an effective upper house.[5] The proliferation of reform proposals which has resulted leads to an interesting question: is an

---

[5] Details of reform proposals overseas may be found in Chapter 11.

agreed second chamber model emerging? Are there common themes from these debates from which the UK can learn? If a consensus was developing, this could be of great use in the process of reforming the House of Lords.

Unfortunately, given the distinct political traditions in different countries, and the need to design a chamber that fits amongst the other institutions of the state, a consensus on the detail is unlikely. However, there do appear to be some features which are generally supported. These are either accepted features of existing second chambers which are seen to work successfully, or proposals which are made by reformers in other countries, or both. In many cases a feature which works in one country is proposed for introduction in another. There is a growing tendency for reformers to learn from international examples, and the UK can potentially do the same.

Some of the features which attract a large degree of support are as follows:

- *That the upper house should represent the territorial nature of the state.* Probably the most striking aspect of reform debates overseas is the extent to which there is a movement towards 'territorial' upper houses. In these systems the second chamber represents the provinces, regions, or states in the national parliament. The proposal to move towards a more territorial model has emerged in reform debates in both federal and unitary states. This remains an aspiration in Italy, for example, where the original intention that the Senato should be a house of the regions has never been realised. Even in countries where the upper house is nominally territorial—such as Canada and Spain—there is strong pressure for reform to create a more genuine connection to sub-national institutions. The Spanish example demonstrates how an opportunity can be missed to introduce a territorial chamber alongside a programme of devolution—and how this can have damaging consequences. Given the parallels between devolution in the UK and Spain, this is an issues which requires careful consideration.

- *The two chambers should have distinct functions.* It is relatively common in parliaments overseas—as at Westminster—for the lower chamber to focus on the broad direction of policy, while the upper house takes more responsibility for detailed legislative scrutiny. However, where the upper house is territorial this offers an added opportunity for specialisation, which helps make it distinctive from the lower house. Proposals in Italy and Spain, for example, would give the upper house particular responsibility for territorial matters. This builds on the German model. In Ireland it has been proposed that the upper chamber specialises by concentrating on European and delegated legislation, and detailed inquiries, whilst government ministers are restricted to membership of the lower house.

- *No powers to remove government from office.* A specialisation that receives universal support is the system whereby government must retain the confidence of the lower house only. Like the UK, most countries follow this model. The exception is Italy, where the upper house can vote government out of office. However, reform proposals include the removal of this power from the Senato.

- *Lesser powers over financial legislation, more over constitutional change.* As in Britain, most parliaments give reduced powers to the upper house over financial legislation. Australia is an exception, but since a constitutional crisis was caused by the Senate in 1975 it has been proposed that its powers be reduced in this area. On the other hand, it is common for the upper house to have powers to block constitutional change. These powers have only been weakened (for example in Canada) where other constitutional safeguards apply.

- *Government should not control the chamber.* An important way in which the two chambers may be distinct in composition is through their political balance. Government generally has a majority in the lower house, but this need not apply in the upper house. In countries where government does have a majority in the upper house— notably Ireland and Spain—the limited impact of the chamber is criticised. In contrast, the distinct political complexion of the Australian upper house adds to its impact. In Australia government is frustrated by its lack of control over the Senate, but the Australian people seem largely to support the existing party balance, which results in legislative negotiation and compromise. Polls in other countries suggest that this is a common public response.[6]

- *Direct election is supported, although indirect election may provide better territorial links.* In countries where the upper chamber is directly elected, this feature generally has public support. For example, the reform debate in Italy emphasises the importance of a distinct upper house, but few would suggest that the Senato cease to be directly

[6] Details may be found in the section on public perceptions in Chapter 11.

elected. Neither have any serious reform proposals of this type been made in Australia. Meanwhile most recent proposals in Canada have focused on the need for an elected chamber, and directly elected Senators were also included in the recent proposals in Ireland. However, in Spain, where the majority of upper house members are directly elected, it is proposed by some that territorial links would be strengthened through an expansion in the number of indirectly elected members in the chamber.

- *The second chamber should be smaller than the first.* In all countries except the UK, the second chamber of parliament is smaller than the first. This is a completely non-controversial feature, and is generally cited as one of the upper house's assets. A smaller chamber is generally more manageable and efficient, more friendly and courteous, and has smaller and more effective committees.

- *Long parliamentary terms, and a chamber renewed in parts.* Many second chambers have a membership which is renewed in parts—for example the French Sénat, where one-third of members are elected every three years, and the Australian Senate, where half are elected every three years. This means that the chamber has a rolling membership, and cannot be dissolved by government. Where this system applies it appears to be supported, and in some countries where it does not apply there are suggestions that it be introduced. For example this has been proposed in Italy, where the Senato is currently elected at the same time as the lower house, and in Spain, as a means of tying the upper house to regional elections.

In support of these arguments it is interesting to consider the German Bundesrat and Australian Senate, which are very different upper houses but are both highly effective and have general public support. Both chambers meet most of the criteria set down above. The Bundesrat is the most truly territorial of all the seven chambers, and although indirectly elected has clear legitimacy, through its representation of elected state governments. The Australian Senate has largely failed as a states' house, but carved out a distinct identity to that of the lower house by taking on many other parliamentary functions. As central sites of negotiation over policy these chambers have proved themselves to be important to the process of government, and contributed much to the impact of the legislature.

SOLVING ALL WESTMINSTER'S PROBLEMS?

Before turning our attention to some of the specifics of House of Lords reform, it is worth considering one final principle. This is the need to focus on the proper role of the second chamber at Westminster, rather than attempting to use reform to solve all of parliament's shortcomings. As the Constitution Unit have suggested:

> It is clear that many, although not all, of the reasons given for needing a second chamber are derived from the *de facto* pursuits of the House of Lords, rather than resulting from any more fundamental analysis of the necessary functions of parliamentary government. Furthermore, a number of the justifications for a second chamber in the UK represent implicit criticisms of the House of Commons . . . These are, therefore, just as much reasons for reform of the first chamber as justifications for a second chamber (1996: 29).

The reform of the House of Lords offers an unusual opportunity to look at both the composition and functions of parliament, and propose improvements. This creates a temptation to try and tackle all the perceived problems with the parliamentary system. Electoral reformers may see House of Lords reform as an opportunity to begin to introduce proportional representation at Westminster, as a precursor for House of Commons reform. Those who criticise the legislative process may see reform of the upper house as an opportunity to introduce the mechanisms and procedures which they have campaigned to have introduced in the Commons. Others who believe that additional areas of government activity should be brought under parliamentary control may propose that these responsibilities should be given to the reformed upper house. This tendency to view upper house reform as a cure-all for parliament is familiar from overseas. In Canada, for example:

> At one time, both demands for abolition and attempts at reform derived from dissatisfaction with the role and power of the Senate . . . more recent proposals . . . were predicated on the assumption that the upper house could be reshaped into an institution designed to correct perceived deficiencies elsewhere in the political system . . . reform of the Senate was viewed as a panacea for all manner of perceived ills afflicting Canadian society (Jackson and Jackson 1998: 335).

Some of the earlier sections of this chapter have demonstrated that there are many valued features of second chambers, some of which are already shared by the House of Lords. To attempt to build a new upper house which performs all the duties of an ideal House of Commons is not only unrealistic. It also threatens to damage the upper house's ability to fulfil its proper role. This consideration must be taken clearly into account when considering both the functions and composition of the new upper house.

CONCLUSIONS

This chapter has set down some of the general principles that need to be considered in the design of a new second chamber, as drawn both from overseas and UK experience. The most important principles which must be applied are that an effective second chamber will rely upon:

- a distinct membership from the House of Commons;

- moderate to strong powers to challenge government;

- sufficient legitimacy to retain the support of the public, in order to use these powers as appropriate.

Beyond this, there are a number of more detailed features of second chambers which receive considerable support overseas. These emerge from the wealth of upper house reform debates going on around the world, and were listed earlier in the chapter. Most important amongst them is the growing tendency for second chambers to be used to represent the territorial nature of the state. Experience from Spain, in particular, suggests that a failure to link House of Lords reform to the devolution settlement could be a missed opportunity.

These principles, alongside the desire to retain some of the best elements of the existing House of Lords, provide a framework within which upper house reform may be considered. This would result in a new upper house which was very different to the House of Commons—something which itself should be a key objective of reform. A chamber which sought to mirror the House of Commons, or to compensate for all the shortcomings of that chamber, would be sure to fail as an upper house. Rather, the second chamber should have a distinct role to the Commons, and a distinct membership which is appropriate to achieve this. These issues are explored in detail in the following chapters.

13

The Role and Functions of a New Chamber

Reform of the House of Lords has been driven by perceived problems with the chamber's membership. It has been the desire to remove the hereditary peers from the house, and end its Conservative bias, which has been the primary motivator for campaigners. Little has been said about what the House of Lords does, aside from how this is affected by its anachronistic membership. The role and functions of the house—and even its powers—have rarely themselves been a cause for complaint.

Nevertheless, the reform of the upper house offers an opportunity to review its purpose and the duties which it is asked to perform. Indeed a change in the chamber's membership is liable to change its character, its ability to perform its duties, and its tendency to use its powers. It would therefore be wrong to attempt to reform the membership of the house without considering, alongside this, its role and functions.

Many of the proposals for a reformed membership of the House of Lords are driven by implicit assumptions about what the house should do, and what its character should be. For example, calls for the new chamber to retain some appointed members are influenced by the desire for it to be more 'expert' than the House of Commons and able to apply this expertise to its work. Suggestions that the new upper house should have a 'territorial' membership, representing the nations and regions of the UK, are based on the presumption that there is some territorial role—currently unfulfilled—which could be played.

It is essential that the starting point for future debate should be the role which the new upper house might play at Westminster, and the functions that it might perform. Only once these are established should the membership of the house be considered, with a view to fulfilling these roles. It seems clear that many of the current functions of the House of Lords are valued, and need to be continued. This will have particular implications for the membership of the house. However, in a changing constitutional landscape, there are many additional functions that an upper house could play. The White Paper on reform of the House of Lords, published in January 1999, explicitly required the Royal Commission to take account of 'the present nature of the constitutional settlement, including the newly devolved institutions, the impact of the

Human Rights Act and developing relations with the European Union' (Cabinet Office 1999: 35). This implies a range of possible future roles for the upper house, many of which are currently performed by second chambers overseas. The experiences of these chambers, summarised in Part 2 of the book, therefore offer many lessons for the potential role of a new upper chamber in the UK.

This chapter reviews some of the possible functions that the new upper house might play in the political system, taking particular account of the new constitutional settlement. The following chapter then discusses the implications of these options for the membership of the house.

The suggested roles which a new second chamber might play are threefold, and each of these roles suggests a different set of functions. The three roles—which might be played individually or in combination—are acting as a revising and review chamber, being a constitutional guardian, and representing the new territorial nature of the UK. Each of these is discussed in turn in the sections that follow.

A REVISING AND REVIEW CHAMBER

The first classic function of a parliamentary upper house is to act as a chamber of revision and review. This is the primary role of the current House of Lords. In most modern upper houses the review role above all includes legislative work, but also extends beyond this to include other functions such as carrying out investigations or questioning ministers. All of these functions are currently carried out by the House of Lords. Whatever the roles of a reformed upper house, these functions are liable to be continued, alongside the scrutiny of ordinary government legislation, delegated legislation, and the activities and legislation of the European Union. All of these functions will—to a greater or lesser extent—be shared with the House of Commons. Whilst the upper house should not be expected to compensate for all possible failings in that house, it can considerably improve the quality and efficiency of some of this core parliamentary work.

This section considers some of the possible scrutiny functions that could be carried out by the reformed upper house. At the end of the section brief consideration is given to the kind of members who should be included in the upper house to fulfil these functions.

The Scrutiny of Legislation

The House of Lords currently spends around half its time on scrutiny of government bills. There are strong arguments for an upper house that works alongside the House of Commons on this work. The benefit of a second chamber reconsidering the decisions of the first chamber—particularly where the upper house brings a different perspective—is that a broader consensus is built for government policy. The delay involved in passing bills through the upper house may also enable a wider debate to take place on the merits of the legislation, and encourage government to think again where appropriate. Legislative scrutiny is therefore likely to remain an important function when the upper house is reformed. There are three benefits in particular which this arrangement can bring:

- *Carrying out detailed scrutiny:* Members of the House of Commons are subject to many pressures, and may have insufficient time to deal with an ever-increasing volume of legislation. They will tend to focus on the general direction of policy, and their debates are heavily whipped. This leaves a role for the upper house in scrutinising bills in detail.

- *Providing a different perspective:* If the upper house has members who represent a different set of opinions—politically, or through the representation of different constituencies such as local government, regions, or different professions—they can improve the quality of legislation by providing a broader view.

- *Asking government to think again:* In extreme circumstances, where the upper house is particularly concerned about a bill, it may want to ask government to think again. Since government is formed from a majority in the House of Commons and depends on retaining that chamber's confidence, government defeats in the lower house are rare. A voice of dissent may be more likely to come from the upper house.

The experience of overseas parliaments suggests that upper houses have an impressive record in carrying out detailed legislative scrutiny. As in Britain it is common for the upper house to complement, and greatly augment, the work carried out by pressurised lower house members. Often the upper house is responsible for introducing many detailed amendments that considerably improve the quality of government bills. This depends on upper house members having the time to devote to detailed legislative scrutiny, which in the UK would require them to remain free of many of the pressures facing members of the House of Commons.

The ability to carry out the other two functions suggested above is far more contingent on the membership of the house. In many cases—such as the Spanish and Italian parliaments—members of the upper house are largely similar to those who sit in the lower house. They therefore do not bring a very different perspective to policy making. Where upper house members do not bring a new perspective, this also affects their ability to ask government to think again. In modern parliaments the voting behaviour of a chamber is largely predictable by its political party balance. Where the balance of the two chambers is broadly similar—as in Spain, for example—disputes between the chambers are unlikely to arise. This issue of party balance is one which recurs many times in the lessons for membership of the house, and is discussed in detail in Chapter 14.

Even where membership of the two houses is similar, a different perspective on policy can be introduced through different procedures. Already in the UK the procedure for scrutiny of bills in the two houses differs, as in the Commons most bills are considered in a standing committee, whilst in the Lords they are generally considered on the floor of the house. Apart from the Delegated Powers and Deregulation Committee, which examines all bills, the current select committees of the House of Lords are not involved in legislative work. In Australia the tradition is the opposite, with the Senate having a far stronger committee system than the House of Representatives, and frequently taking evidence on bills.[1] Reform of the House of Lords might include a change in legislative processes, so that—for example—the upper house examined bills in cross-departmental policy committees, which might take evidence from outside parties. As in Australia, concerns about legislative delay could be dealt with if necessary by upper house committees examining bills which were still being debated in the lower house.[2] The upper house might also learn from the system in Germany, and many other countries, where a bill can be sent simultaneously to two or more specialist committees. Proposals such as these to improve the legislative scrutiny processes of parliament have been proposed on numerous occasions (e.g. Hansard Society 1992; Power 1996; Riddell 1998). Whilst the shortcomings of parliament cannot be entirely remedied by the reform of the House of Lords, this might be an

---

[1] This is discussed in Chapters 6 and 7.

[2] Such a proposal for the consideration of bills by House of Lords committees was made by a Lords Select Committee on Practice and Procedure in 1976 (Shell 1992).

appropriate occasion to consider how processes in the upper house can be enhanced.

To carry out their legislative functions members of the upper house must have sufficient time, resources, and powers. The questions of members' time and resources are discussed later in the chapter, and in Chapter 14. The matter of the power of the house over legislation—which is essential to its ability to ask government to think again—is considered next.

Powers over Ordinary Legislation

The powers of the House of Lords over ordinary legislation—by international standards—are fairly moderate. The provisions of the Parliament Acts allow the upper house to delay most ordinary government bills by up to 13 months after second reading in the House of Commons. In comparison the Canadian, Australian, and Italian upper houses can block all bills completely, and the German Bundesrat has this power over around 60 per cent of bills. Amongst the weaker chambers the Irish Seanad can block bills for up to three months and the Spanish Senado for only two months. The French Sénat has no fixed period of delay, but may eventually be overridden by the lower house.

However, as discussed in Chapter 12, the *de facto* power of a chamber will also depend on its membership. The House of Lords to date has used its powers to delay government legislation very rarely, because of the difficulty of challenging the elected House of Commons. The same difficulty applies, for example, to the appointed Canadian Senate. When the membership of the House of Lords changes, the attitude of members to using their powers may change with it—this may even be seen in the transitional, largely appointed, house. The Labour Party has stated that the 'legislative powers of the House of Lords will remain unaltered' after reform.[3] This would be in line with the principle set down in Chapter 12 that the powers of the new chamber should be moderate to strong. However, the interrelationship between powers and membership means that it is unwise to reform one without at least reviewing the other.

There are dangers in both a strong and a weak upper house. A chamber with an absolute veto can potentially cause legislative deadlock, and prevent government from implementing its policies. This will apply particularly if the two chambers are controlled by opposing political majorities. However, if the chamber is too weak, its views may simply be ignored by the government and the lower house—this is the

---

[3] Labour Party manifesto, 1997.

danger in countries such as Spain and Ireland. The desirable balance is a system which allows the upper house to ask government to think again on genuinely problematic bills, without providing an opportunity to disrupt the entire legislative programme.

An example of such a bill in recent political history would be the Conservative government's legislation in 1988 to introduce the local 'community charge' (generally known as the 'poll tax'). This reform of the local taxation system introduced a flat rate charge for almost all citizens, irrespective of income. Even the minister responsible for implementing the tax has since describe it as 'the single most unpopular policy any government has introduced since the War'.[4] This unpopularity was demonstrated by mass demonstrations on the streets of British cities. The community charge was, understandably in these circumstances, the subject of one of the most contentious debates in the recent history of the House of Lords. When the bill was debated in the house an amendment was moved by a Conservative peer which would have linked the charge to ability to pay. However, this amendment was defeated by 317 votes to 183, a result which was only achieved with the support of Conservative 'backwoodsmen'—hereditary members who rarely attend the house, but did so on this occasion on request of the whips. It was, at that time, the second highest recorded turnout in the chamber's history.

The House of Lords' inability to stop the community charge, which was later scrapped after only a year of operation, is often cited as a justification for reform of the house. Given that the government itself later thought better of the tax, these are surely the kind of circumstances in which an upper house should be able to influence events. So how could a repeat of this episode be avoided in the design of a new upper house? What powers would it be appropriate for the chamber to be given?

On this occasion, of course, it was not the formal powers of the house that stopped it acting—it was the membership of the house. Had the politics of the chamber been different, and the bill been blocked for a year, the tax might not have been introduced. The delay caused would have provided breathing space, in which the public and parliamentarians could debate the issue, and the government could itself reflect on the policy. Experiences in other countries such as France—as discussed in Chapter 6—demonstrate that this kind of delay can be sufficient to thwart unpopular government action. A shorter delay, on the other hand, is less likely to be effective.

[4] Chris Patten, quoted in Butler, Adonis, and Travers (1994: 1).

One of the difficulties with the current system is that the delay which can be imposed by the House of Lords is indeterminate. The Parliament Act stipulates only that a bill may be reintroduced in the next parliamentary session, if more than a year has passed since its second reading in the House of Commons. However, in practice the period of delay imposed by the upper house may be relatively short, particularly if a bill is sent to the House of Lords late in the parliamentary session.

For example, the European Parliamentary Elections Bill—to introduce a proportional voting system for European elections—was only the second bill since 1949 to be forced through the house under the Parliament Act procedures. However, objections in the House of Lords, which repeatedly tried to amend the bill to provide for 'open' rather than 'closed' lists of candidates delayed the bill by only about a month.[5] Although the bill was introduced in the House of Commons in October 1997, it did not pass to the Lords until the spring of 1998. Its third reading in the house was then not until October that year. This is when the disagreement between the chambers became clear. During the months of October and November 1998 the bill was repeatedly amended in the Lords, and shuttled back and forth to the House of Commons, where the amendments were rejected each time. The houses failed to agree by the end of the parliamentary session in November. However the bill was able to be reintroduced only eight days later, at the start of the new session. The bill's opponents in the House of Lords were, ironically, being co-operative when they ensured the bill was rejected outright in December, as it was then able to be sent for royal assent (Richard and Welfare 1999). The inconvenience caused to government by this episode in the end was relatively minor, and the elections held in June 1999 used the 'closed' list system.[6]

If the new upper house is to have a delaying power, this needs to be considerable in order to have an impact. The alternative would be to give the upper house an absolute veto—a solution effectively ruled out in the White Paper, and probably not necessary to exert pressure on government over unpopular bills. A delay of six months or a year

---

[5] The 'closed' list system which the government proposed allowed voters to choose between fixed lists of candidates which had been put forward by the parties. The 'open' list system would have instead given voters the opportunity to support individual candidates from the lists.

[6] The disruption caused on this occasion could have been far worse, because the House of Lords would have needed to delay the bill for only a little longer in order to prevent the elections being held using the new system. The Lords took the unusual step of voting against the bill at its second reading in the new session, which allowed the government to invoke the Parliament Act very quickly. Had the bill reached a third reading in the upper house it might have been too late.

would be moderate, but potentially effective. However, the current system does not guarantee this. It has been suggested that a delay of six months or a year be imposed from the first point of dispute between the chambers (e.g. Shell and Giddings 1999). This seems a very reasonable proposal. A mechanism should also be found to allow a similar fixed delay to bills which are introduced in the House of Lords. Currently there is no means to resolve disputes over such bills.

The primary reason that the powers of the House of Lords have not been much debated is that the chamber has tended to show restraint, and used its powers extremely rarely. The House of Lords' commitment to allow government legislation to pass without disruption is most clearly demonstrated by the 'Salisbury convention'. This states that the house will not block legislation which seeks to implement government manifesto commitments.[7] The convention has been brought to bear on many occasions when the house would have instinctively rejected the proposals before it—not least in 1998–9 over the bill to reform the house itself. However, the Salisbury convention remains only a convention, and it is unclear whether it will be respected in the transitional house, once the majority of hereditary peers have been removed. The Labour Party, in evidence to the Royal Commission, proposed that the convention might be formalised in the reformed house. However it is difficult to see how this could happen in practice—no such rule applies in any of the overseas chambers considered in this book.

Experience from overseas strongly demonstrates that the *de facto* powers of a second chamber over legislation depend not only on its formal powers, but also its composition and perceived legitimacy. The method of selecting members of the house, and the party balance in the chamber, will both be particularly important. These issues are discussed in Chapter 14.

Resolving Disputes Between the Chambers

Whatever the powers of the new house, a reformed membership is likely to increase the prospect that these powers are used. The current system of resolving disputes between the chambers—as demonstrated by the European Parliamentary Elections Bill, which shuttled back and forth between the chambers five times—is cumbersome and does not allow for open negotiation. Whilst many parliaments use a 'shuttle' system to resolve disputes, often with a fixed time limit or number of times each chamber can consider a bill, others use a more consensual system. In particular France and Germany—and other countries such as

[7] For the history of the convention, see Chapter 1.

the US and Japan—employ a joint mediation committee between the two chambers which tries to negotiate a compromise. If the powers of the upper house are to be significant—i.e. six months' or more delay to legislation—then it may be worth considering the introduction of a mediation committee at Westminster. This could help to break down adversarial disputes between the chambers, and result in quicker solutions involving an element of compromise.

The mediation committees in France and Germany were described in Chapter 6. This demonstrated that there are a number of factors which make the German system relatively successful, whilst the French system fails on an increasing number of occasions. If a mediation committee were to be adopted at Westminster, the following features should be considered:

- *Allow the upper house to call the committee.* In France the committee can only be called on the initiative of the government. This right should be extended to either chamber of parliament in the event of a dispute, as it is in Germany.

- *Permanent membership.* The German committee is strengthened because it is a permanent committee, set up at the start of each parliamentary session. Its members—like those of other permanent committees—can develop relationships of trust and co-operation which are more likely to result in compromise.

- *Voting rules.* Standard practice is for the party balance of representatives on the committee to mirror that of the chamber which they are drawn from. This may result in deadlock if the parties are balanced and decisions are taken by majority vote. Alternatively it may result in one party getting its way, on the basis of a majority in the committee. In the US mediation committee, the groups representing the two houses each have one block vote. This encourages compromise between the parties when the houses are controlled by different majorities.

- *Non-amendable committee proposals.* The mediation committee in France is further weakened because the government may overrule its proposals. It is more normal for committee proposals to be put to the chambers on a 'take it or leave it' basis, so that negotiation cannot be undone.

These factors may help to build the success of a mediation committee, should this be introduced at Westminster. However, ultimately the most important factor in committee success is the power of the second chamber. If the upper house has the power of veto, or significant delay, there is far more incentive for government and lower house members to listen to its views in a mediation committee. This is an important factor in both Germany and the US.

Delegated Legislation

Members of the House of Lords currently make an important contribution to the scrutiny of delegated legislation, through membership of the Joint Committee on Statutory Instruments. These instruments are also debated on the floor of the Lords far more frequently than in the Commons (Shell 1992). Although the House of Lords has the power to veto delegated legislation, this power is never used in practice.[8] However, government will sometimes redraft an instrument as a result of a hostile reception during a debate in the Lords. This additional attention given to delegated legislation in the upper house is an important contribution to the scrutiny work of parliament, and is mirrored by the work on delegated legislation in several second chambers overseas.[9] Unless the Commons is able to give more attention to this work, it is a function which the reformed second chamber will need to continue.

When the membership of the upper house changes, and there is more likelihood of the chamber using its powers, it will be appropriate to consider a change of powers over delegated legislation.[10] Based on experiences from overseas there is no reason why the functions of the upper house should not be extended to the amendment of statutory instruments, and its powers over these instruments brought into line with those over ordinary legislation. This would mirror the situation in Germany, where the power of the upper house over delegated legislation is identical to that over ordinary bills—giving the Bundesrat a veto over instruments with implications for the states. The committees of the Bundesrat regularly recommend amendments to these instruments.

[8] The one occasion when this did happen was over the Southern Rhodesia Sanctions Order in 1968.

[9] See Chapter 6.

[10] This may also become appropriate given the new category of 'section 10' remedial orders which may be introduced under the Human Rights Act, as discussed below in the section on human rights scrutiny.

The Australian Senate Standing Committee on Regulations and Ordinances may also have some features that could be adopted by a new UK upper house. This highly respected committee examines all delegated legislation against a clear set of criteria. It produces a weekly bulletin, summarising every item of legislation considered and the committee's response. This is circulated to members of the chamber to keep them up to date with developments. The bulletin may be used by members of the Senate—or the lower house—to raise any concerns about particular instruments. The committee also recommends the rejection of certain instruments to the house, and its recommendations have always been accepted. The criteria used by the committee include a particular human rights focus. This might also be adopted by the UK committee now that all legislation, primary and secondary, must comply with the Human Rights Act 1998.

The House of Lords committee for scrutiny of Delegated Powers and Deregulation also plays an important role in scrutinising all primary legislation for new delegated powers. This is another important function which must be accommodated after the house is reformed. The devolution settlement will bring a new perspective to this work, as some powers will now not be delegated to ministers, but to the Welsh Assembly. Similar arrangements might be extended over time to the English regions. The role of the committee may therefore become more complex—not only regulating the power devolved to ministers and ensuring this is limited, but also ensuring that devolved power is not unreasonably circumscribed when it is exercised by devolved institutions. This regulation function might most appropriately be carried out in a territorial second chamber, as discussed below.

European Legislation

Another important function carried out by the current House of Lords is the respected work of the European Communities Committee. This committee is responsible for detailed scrutiny of draft European legislation and for reporting on other EU policy matters. As the powers of the EU have grown, this has become an increasingly important role. The House of Lords committee is already widely regarded in Europe as one of the most effective parliamentary organs for carrying out this work, but there are concerns that far more needs to be done. The effective scrutiny of EU policy-making, and in particular the role of UK ministers in the EU, could present a major challenge for a reformed upper house.

Given the reputation of the existing committee, it is perhaps unsurprising that there is little that can be learned in this area from other EU second chambers. In most cases—as discussed in Chapter 10—the upper house carries no special responsibility for this work, which has increasingly been taken on by the lower chamber.

One idea that has been floated as a way of strengthening links between the new upper house and Europe is the greater involvement of British MEPs in the chamber's work. This was suggested as an option in the government's White Paper on reform of the Lords which stated that 'a specific role for MEPs in the second chamber might yield particular benefits' (Cabinet Office 1999: 38). The possibility of involving MEPs directly as members of the house is subject to the same difficulties of dual mandates as would apply to members of the devolved institutions.[11] Being an MEP is a full time job, and members are unlikely to be able to attend the upper chamber on a regular basis. This is liable to apply to membership of upper house committees, as well as membership of the house itself. Proof can be found in parliaments overseas—for example both the Irish and French parliaments have attempted to involve MEPs as members of committees on European affairs, but have found that their other commitments generally make them absentee members.

In Germany the upper house provides a distinct perspective on parliamentary scrutiny of draft EU legislation, because its members are representatives of the states. The Bundesrat provides an essential forum for members of state governments to have an input into formation of Germany's position on EU matters, where these affect the states. Given the European focus on the regions, this is an important role. A territorial upper house—as discussed below—could ensure that the nations and regions of the UK were involved in scrutinising EU initiatives which could have an impact on their institutions and citizens.

Investigations

Many second chambers overseas make an important contribution to parliamentary work through the staging of detailed investigations into matters of policy interest. Some examples of this work are cited in Chapter 7. Second chambers are often in a better position to carry out this work than first chambers, as their members have more time, and operate away from the public spotlight. This enables them to take on investigations which would prove politically sensitive or difficult in the highly charged atmosphere of the lower house.

The House of Lords also has a tradition of taking on such work. Investigations have included an *ad hoc* select committee on Murder and

---

[11] This is discussed in Chapter 14.

Life Imprisonment, whose 1989 report recommended an ending of the mandatory life sentence.[12] As well as *ad hoc* committees, the Science and Technology Committee carries out many investigations into sensitive scientific and ethical issues. A recent example was their November 1998 report into cannabis, which recommended that, though cannabis should remain a controlled drug, the law should be changed to allow doctors to prescribe it for pain relief.[13] The recommendations of both these committees were rejected by the government, but nevertheless provided a useful focus for debate on important issues.

Despite these examples, the number of investigations carried out by the House of Lords is currently relatively small. There is generally no more than one *ad hoc* committee per year, and most investigations are therefore confined to the subjects falling into the remit of the Science and Technology Committee. An increased role for a second chamber in investigative work could make a useful contribution. Experience from overseas suggests that it is important for the chamber itself to retain the power to embark on such investigations. It is also clear that a chamber which is overly dominated by party politics will make a less important contribution in this area, since investigations will be seen as being politically motivated—the French Sénat offers an example.[14] The success of this work will therefore depend on the party balance in the chamber and the extent to which its members are able to act in an independent way. Parliaments overseas also suggest ways in which government can be made more responsive to committee investigations in the upper house. In Spain the outcome of committee investigations are given more weight by reports being endorsed by the full chamber. In Australia the government is required to respond within three months to a committee report. Adopting either of these measures could help to strengthen the influence of the upper house.

Scrutiny of Government

The reform of the House of Lords also brings into question the relationship between the chamber and the government. This is both a matter of the functions of the house—to what extent government is accountable to the chamber—and its membership—whether members of the upper house may become ministers. These are actually two entirely

---

[12] *Report of the Select Committee on Murder and Life Imprisonment*, House of Lords, 1989.

[13] *Cannabis: the Scientific and Medical Evidence*, House of Lords Science and Technology Committee 9th Report 1997-98.

[14] See Chapter 7.

separate issues, which are often confused. However for the sake of simplicity they are considered together here.

By convention all government ministers in the UK must be members of parliament, but may fulfil this requirement by sitting in either house. Senior ministers are generally drawn from the House of Commons, and the cabinet rarely includes more than two peers—the leader of the house and the Lord Chancellor. There are two distinct reasons for this. First, the government requires the confidence of the House of Commons, but not the House of Lords, so it is appropriate for senior ministers to answer to that house. Secondly, it has become increasingly unacceptable to appoint unelected ministers to senior positions in government.

When the membership of the upper house changes, there may be pressure to reform this convention. If the new upper house were to include elected members, there would no longer be an automatic stigma attached to their appointment to cabinet positions. On the other hand if the new chamber consisted mostly of indirectly elected members—as in France or Germany—or representatives who took no party whip, it might become inappropriate for such members to be appointed to government at all.

The experience of other countries in this regard—discussed in Chapter 9—is varied. In some countries ministers may be appointed from both chambers, in some from neither, and in some from the lower house only. In several countries—such as Canada and Ireland— conventions exist which restrict the number of ministers drawn from the upper house. The only country where ministers are drawn equally from both chambers is Italy—where the two chambers are elected and largely identical.

There are benefits from excluding upper house members from ministerial positions—or at least from senior office.[15] The concentration of ministers in the lower house reinforces its position as the 'government house', and the position of the upper chamber as the chamber of review. It also creates a different career structure in the two chambers, with members of the upper house less likely to shape their behaviour around an ambition to be appointed as ministers. Upper house members are thus more likely to act independently.

Another UK convention is that ministers may only attend and speak in the parliamentary chamber where they are a member. This creates confusion between the issues of whether ministers may sit in the upper

---

[15] This has been proposed as part of the reform of the House of Lords by the Liberal Democrats, in their evidence to the Royal Commission, and by others such as Tyrie (1998) and Heathcoat Amory (1998).

house and whether they should appear there. The White Paper, for example, states that 'Most government departments are directly represented in the Lords, and those which are not have spokesmen appointed on their behalf. It would be difficult for the future second chamber to carry out its functions, in particular the revision of legislation, without access to Ministers' (Cabinet Office 1999: 38).

It is obviously important that ministers should retain access to the upper house, particularly for the presentation of government bills and statements. It also seems desirable that ministers should continue to answer questions in the upper house. However, all of these activities take place in other second chambers, irrespective of whether the ministers concerned are members of the chamber. This is because the convention barring House of Commons ministers from the House of Lords is highly unusual. In most countries ministers may speak in either chamber, irrespective of whether they are a member of that chamber. If this convention were adopted in the UK it would enable members of the upper house to question and debate with senior cabinet ministers, including possibly the Prime Minister. This could in fact improve the accountability of government to the upper house, ending the practice whereby questions are frequently answered by junior House of Lords ministers who are expected to cover an extremely wide brief.

It is worth noting here that the UK convention of government only needing to maintain the confidence of the lower house is standard practice overseas. Only in Italy is this convention not observed, and there are proposals that this situation be changed. It should not be anticipated that new UK upper house—even if wholly directly elected— be given the power to bring down the government. The inability for second chambers to topple governments actually helps boost their independence and ensure they have a distinct role from their respective lower houses.

Implications for Membership of the House

The functions of revision and review, discussed in this section, reflect many of the current activities of the House of Lords. Members of the house have found their niche in detailed scrutiny functions, and carry out many of these functions well. However in other ways the house has failed to act as an effective review chamber—particularly in respect of asking the government to think again on controversial or unpopular bills. The Conservative bias in the chamber has meant that it has failed adequately to challenge Conservative governments, whilst convention requires that Labour governments are afforded similar freedom.[16]

The reformed membership of the house offers an opportunity to build on the successes of the House of Lords, and try to improve its performance in areas where it has not performed so well. This calls for a wide range of skills in the new chamber, and a continuation of much of its ethos, which is shared with many second chambers overseas. In particular it calls for upper house members who:

- provide a distinct point of view to members of the Commons;

- represent a wide range of political views, and fields of expertise;

- are relatively independent-minded;

- have an interest in detailed policy work, including EU and delegated legislation, and capacity to carry out investigative work;

- have sufficient time and skill to devote to this work;

- enjoy the confidence of the public, in order to challenge the House of Commons over unpopular or impractical policies.

These qualities, and how they might be achieved in the membership of a new upper house, are discussed in more detail in Chapter 14.

GUARDIAN OF THE CONSTITUTION

Alongside a revising and review role, most second chambers around the world play a role as a constitutional guardian. Even chambers which have relatively weak powers with respect to ordinary legislation may have absolute powers of veto over constitutional change. The need to secure the consent of the upper house over constitutional matters reflects the importance of seeking a high degree of consensus over changes to the fundamental structure of the state. Examples of the roles of second chambers in this area were discussed in Chapter 8.

The UK system is unusual in many ways. In particular the lack of a written constitution means that no special procedures exist to ensure that constitutional arrangements are protected, and therefore broad

---

[16] Treatment has not been even-handed, as demonstrated by the number of defeats in the upper house of Conservative and Labour governments. For example, from 1979 to 1997 Conservative governments suffered a total of 241 defeats in the Lords—an average of 13.4 per year. In its first session Tony Blair's government suffered 36 defeats, despite attempts by Conservative peers to show restraint in order not to provoke calls for reform of the house (Richard and Welfare 1999).

consensus need not be sought for any change. The House of Lords has only very limited powers over constitutional matters, with the exception of its highly unusual role as the UK's highest court of appeal.

The recent swathe of constitutional changes means that the UK constitution is becoming more codified. Devolution and the Human Rights Act also signal the beginning of a new relationship between parliament and the courts. The reform of the House of Lords offers an opportunity to review the role of the upper house as a protector of the constitution, and possibly bring this more into line with international norms. Some of the new functions that might be adopted are discussed below.

Constitutional Amendments

The most basic constitutional role which a new upper house could play would be to exert a greater power over bills to amend the constitution than over ordinary bills. This is standard practice overseas. Table 2.2 considered parliamentary systems in 20 Western democracies, including the seven which are the subject of this book. It showed that, aside from the UK, the only countries where the upper house does not have special powers over constitutional amendments are those where other safeguards—such as automatic referendums on constitutional change— are built into the system. Chapter 8 discussed this aspect of the powers of second chambers in more detail.

The UK is alone amongst these countries in treating constitutional bills in the same way as ordinary legislation. Such bills may be agreed with no special procedure, beyond the convention that the committee stage of major constitutional bills is taken on the floor of the House of Commons. The one exception is the House of Lords' absolute veto over bills that seek to extend the life of a parliament. In other countries changes such as the establishment of the Scottish Parliament, the passing of the Human Rights Act, and the reform of the House of Lords itself, would have had to pass a more rigorous approval process than ordinary bills. In many cases this would have involved a key role for the upper house.

There is a strong argument that the new UK upper house should be given a role in the protection of the constitutional settlement, through having additional powers over further constitutional change. In the past such a role could not be effectively exercised, given the nature of the house's composition, although the Lords did at times try to take a stand over constitutional matters. An important example was the action of the house over legislation to abolish the Greater London Council in 1984 and 1985. The House of Lords forced the government to retreat on its intention to replace the GLC with an indirectly elected body a year before its abolition, having cancelled the elections for the authority in 1985. However, in the following year the chamber acquiesced in the GLC's abolition, which had been a government manifesto commitment (Richard and Welfare 1999; Shell 1992).

A new upper house which enjoys more public confidence could have an important role to play in scrutinising future constitutional change. Based on experience from overseas there are four ways in which the new second chamber could exercise special powers over constitutional amendments. Four options would be:

- *Legislation which seeks to alter the constitution to be passed by a qualified majority in the upper house.* Requiring the support of a qualified majority in the upper house for constitutional change is relatively common overseas. Such provisions—requiring a three-fifths or two-thirds majority—are used to ensure that constitutional amendments have cross-party support. They generally apply in both chambers to the passage of constitutional change. However in some countries, such as Spain, the majority required in the upper house may be reduced if a sufficiently high majority is obtained in the lower house.

- *The upper house to have a longer delaying power over legislation which seeks to alter the constitution.* An alternative would be for the length of time the upper house could delay constitutional legislation to be longer than that for ordinary bills. For example if ordinary bills could be delayed for six months, constitutional changes might be delayed for one or two years.[17] This would be a relatively weak form of constitutional protection by international standards.

- *The upper house to have an absolute veto over legislation which seeks to alter the constitution.* This is the most powerful and rigid form of protection which the upper house could offer. It would give the new upper house an absolute veto over constitutional change, even if it only had a suspensive veto over ordinary legislation. This would bring all constitutional legislation into line with the House of Lords' current powers over bills to extend the life of a parliament, and would be a similar system to that which applies in France. However,

[17] Another option was given in the Labour Party's 1992 manifesto, which proposed a second chamber that could 'delay, for the lifetime of a parliament, changes to designated legislation reducing individual or constitutional rights' (in contrast the Labour Party's evidence to the Royal Commission in 1999 explicitly opposed additional powers for the chamber over constitutional bills).

the French example shows that this can create difficulties in practice, as an intransigent upper house can block constitutional reform proposals even where they have popular support.

- *The upper house to be able to force government to hold a referendum on constitutional change.* A more flexible arrangement would allow a veto by the upper house on constitutional change to be overridden by government putting the proposals to a referendum.[18] This model is used in Switzerland. The benefit of this is that the upper house retains a veto, but may be less inclined to feel pressured to pass a bill if their action simply results in broader public consent being sought. The upper house would be unlikely to block a measure perceived as popular, but even if it did, the public would have the last word. An additional safeguard provided in many countries is for a fixed number of upper house members—which may fall well short of a majority—to have the power to force a referendum even a constitutional amendment has passed through parliament. This creates a greater barrier to constitutional change, but might also be considered.

The difficulty with all of these options is that they require constitutional legislation to be identified. In other countries this is straightforward, because constitutional amendments are, literally, amendments to a clearly defined constitutional document. In the absence of a written constitution no such certainty prevails in the UK. However, the identification of constitutional legislation for different treatment in the upper house is not an insurmountable problem. Important constitutional bills are already singled out in order to take their committee stage on the floor of the Commons, and a formal procedure also exists whereby the Speaker certifies 'money bills'. This category of bills, over which the House of Lords has more limited powers than over ordinary legislation, was defined in the 1911 Parliament Act. If a similar approach were adopted, a category of constitutional bills could be defined in the bill that reforms the House of Lords, with power given to the Speaker to certify such bills.[19] Such a

---

[18] This proposal was made by the Liberal Democrats in their submission to the Royal Commission.

[19] Despite the clear-cut nature of constitutional change overseas, there are also precedents in other parliaments for the upper house to have differing powers over less clearly defined categories of legislation. For example in Germany legislation affecting state interests has to be identified, as the upper house has a veto over such legislation (see Chapter 6). Similarly in France the upper house has a veto over 'organic' bills, which are less clearly defined than

definition might include, for example, legislation that alters: the status of the monarchy, the structure or powers of the legislature, the executive, and the judiciary, the existence and power of devolved assemblies, and the basic rights as set out in the Human Rights Act 1998. A broader definition might also include bills which alter: the control and organisation of political parties, the voting system, conduct of elections and referendums, the administration of justice, and the administration of local government.[20]

If it were seen as problematic for constitutional bills to be formally defined, an alternative might be to allow the upper house to call a referendum on any bill which they considered to be of constitutional status. This initiative might be subject to a simple or a qualified majority in the upper house. Such a convention would depend on the restraint of upper house members, but could serve as a powerful incentive to government to reach agreement with the chamber on constitutional issues. This would be similar to the right of the Irish upper house to request a referendum on any bill of 'national importance'.[21]

Constitutional and Human Rights Scrutiny

The adoption of the Human Rights Act 1998, which incorporates the European Convention on Human Rights (ECHR) into UK law, will have important implications for Westminster. This was acknowledged in the White Paper on reform of the House of Lords. The upper house already has a tradition of activity in human rights, driven largely by particular members with strong interests in this area. The inclusion in the house of current and retired law lords, and other senior lawyers, has resulted in it at times seeking to take a human rights protection role (Reidy 1999a). An upper house which performed the role of constitutional guardian could take lead responsibility for such matters in future.

The government has already committed itself to establishing a joint human rights committee, including members of both chambers.[22] At a minimum the new upper house will need to provide members of this committee, which will have responsibility for scrutiny of legislation and orders from a human rights perspective, and conduct of inquiries into human rights. However, the government has also indicated that the

---

constitutional bills. Where there is a dispute over the status of a bill in France or Germany, this may be referred to the Constitutional Court.

[20] These two categories correspond roughly to the categories of constitutional amendments and 'organic' bills used in other countries (see Chapter 8). In France the upper house has a veto over both these forms of legislation.

[21] See Chapter 6.

[22] For details see Reidy (1999b).

scrutiny role of the new committee may be limited. Section 19 of the Human Rights Act requires that the minister responsible for introducing a new bill must make a statement that the provisions of the bill are compatible with the ECHR, or else a statement that government wishes to proceed with the bill despite its lack of compliance. The government has indicated that the joint committee may have responsibility for scrutinising only those bills where it has not been possible to issue a statement of compliance.[23] These are likely to be rare, particularly given the likely reluctance on the part of ministers to indicate that legislation is not compatible with human rights commitments.

It could therefore be desirable for a new upper chamber, taking on a constitutional watchdog role, to establish a committee which examines all bills for compliance with the Human Rights Act. Such a committee could be built on the model of the Australian Senate Scrutiny of Bills Committee, described in Chapter 6. Under this model, the upper house committee would report its views on all bills formally to the chamber, and would take up any issues of concern with ministers, keeping the house informed of progress. Such a committee could also go further, scrutinising all bills against the government's international human rights obligations. An alternative model, which applies in many overseas parliaments, would be for the upper house to have a general constitutional committee. This could examine bills from a human rights perspective, but also consider other aspects such as their impact on the devolution settlement. Such a committee would be particularly appropriate in a territorial chamber, which is discussed below.

The formal powers of the upper house over human rights matters will also need to be considered. Protection of rights guaranteed under the Human Rights Act could form part of its constitutional protection role, as proposed above. One area where the upper house will have considerable powers is over ministerial orders under section 10 of the Human Rights Act. These may be issued where an existing Act of parliament is found to be in breach of the ECHR, allowing ministers to amend the offending Act through delegated legislation. Such orders are due to be scrutinised by the new joint committee on human rights.

---

[23] In a statement to the House of Commons announcing the establishment of the committee, Leader of the House Margaret Beckett said that the government 'envisage that the Joint Committee's terms of reference will include the conduct of inquiries into general human rights issues in the United Kingdom, the scrutiny of remedial orders, the examination of draft legislation where there is doubt about compatibility with the ECHR, and the issue of whether there is a need for a human rights commission to monitor the operation of the Human Rights Act' (*House of Commons Hansard*, 14 December 1998, Col. 604).

Under current arrangements the upper house will have a veto over section 10 orders, but no amending power. These powers might be reconsidered, in line with suggestions made above relating to delegated legislation.

The Judiciary

As well as fulfilling many of the roles of other second chambers, the House of Lords also acts as the UK's highest court of appeal, through the work of the law lords. This is a unique arrangement, as other countries employ a stricter doctrine of 'separation of powers' between the legislature and the judiciary. This is the case in all the countries considered here, which each have Constitutional or Supreme Courts that fulfil the judicial role carried out by the law lords. Many argue that a similar approach should be employed in the UK, with the removal of the law lords from the upper house and their replacement with an independent supreme court.[24]

A detailed discussion of the House of Lords' judicial role, and the future of these arrangements, is outside the scope of this study. However, if the reform of the House of Lords did involve the removal of the law lords, there are precedents from overseas for a new relationship between the upper house and the senior judiciary. These were discussed in Chapter 8. In particular the upper house might be given responsibility for appointing some or all of the members of the supreme court, maybe by a qualified (three-fifths or two-thirds) majority, to ensure consensus. This would provide a degree of continuity with the present system. If responsibility for these appointments were shared, the other possible partners would be the lower house, the government, or an independent judicial appointments commission. If such a commission was established it would also be consistent with the practice in several countries to give the upper house some responsibility for appointing its members.

Public Appointments

If the upper house were to become involved in public appointments, this principle could be extended well beyond the judiciary. As discussed

---

[24] This has been proposed by the IPPR (1991) and was argued by all-party law reform group Justice in their submission to the Royal Commission. The Liberal Democrats' submission also favoured this approach, whilst the Conservative-inspired Mackay Commission assumed that the law lords would not form part of the new house. The Labour Party submission left this matter open.

in Chapter 8, such systems exist in other countries such as Canada and Spain.

Public appointments are subject to little or no parliamentary oversight at present. Some commentators have suggested that the growth in the number of arms-length government agencies and quangos calls for greater parliamentary scrutiny, including involvement in appointment of such bodies' chief executives (e.g. Riddell 1998). This responsibility could be given to departmental select committees—in either chamber—or could develop as a new specialism of the upper house. Involvement in appointments could be limited to the highest levels, including the chief executives of key inspectorates, such as schools and prisons, and the major regulatory bodies, such as OFWAT, OFTEL, and the Rail Regulator. If the upper house had a constitutional guardian role it might be natural for it to have a greater role in the appointments of constitutional standards bodies, such as the Committee for Standards in Public Life and the Electoral Commission. This involvement might also extend to other key public positions, such as the Chair of the BBC and the Governor of the Bank of England.[25]

As well as senior appointments, there is a potential parliamentary role in the oversight of these important public bodies. In many other countries this responsibility is taken by specialist joint committees of both houses, which monitor priorities and performance.[26] If such a system were introduced in the UK, responsibility could be given to a series of joint committees, or fall to committees in the upper house alone. In either case, if parliamentary oversight is to be extended to these areas, members of the upper house could make an important contribution through such committees.[27]

Implications for Membership of the House

A role for the new upper house as guardian of the constitution would have many of the same demands on its members as the revision and review role, discussed earlier. Members must represent a range of views and areas of expertise, be able to act sufficiently independently, and have sufficient interest, time, and other resources to dedicate to their work. However, this role also suggests some additional factors to be taken into account in devising the membership of a new upper house:

[25] Such proposals form part of the Liberal Democrats' submission to the Royal Commission.

[26] See Chapter 7.

[27] A role for the new upper house in scrutiny of public bodies has been proposed by, for example, Democratic Audit (1999).

- If the chamber is to have the power to block constitutional amendments, it should be at least as representative as the House of Commons, if not more so. To avoid important constitutional decisions (such as abolition of devolved assemblies, or changes to the electoral system) being taken for party political gain, the members of the chamber must fairly reflect the political spectrum of the population. In matters of human rights it is equally important that the chamber reflects the population in other terms, including gender and ethnicity.

- In particular it is important that the chamber fairly represents all the nations and regions of the UK, as many constitutional issues are liable to refer to devolved matters. The membership of the chamber should not be seen to be biased towards any particular part of the union. This links to the question of the chamber taking on a more 'territorial' role, as discussed in the next section.

- If the law lords were removed from the house this would reduce the level of legal expertise in the chamber, which is often seen as one of its beneficial qualities. Such expertise might, however, be particularly important to the chamber's constitutional role. This could be an argument for inclusion of other senior lawyers to replace the law lords as members of the new upper house.

A TERRITORIAL CHAMBER

One of the key lessons which can be learnt from overseas, as discussed in Chapter 12, is that there is an increasing movement towards territorial second chambers. The third role which the new upper house might therefore play is a territorial one. This would be an entirely new role within the UK parliament. However, it is now more relevant, thanks to the new, and evolving, devolution settlement. A territorial role for the new upper house would bring the UK into line with international trends—territorial representation is now the commonest form of representation in second chambers worldwide. It is particularly common in federal states such as Germany and Australia, but also applies in unitary states with different degrees of regional devolution.

The design of a territorial upper house for the UK would clearly be a more difficult task than that in many other countries, because of the asymmetrical way in which devolution is developing. The White Paper on reform of the House of Lords acknowledged that a territorial role was a possibility for the new upper house but noted that 'Few countries face the situation which will be the United Kingdom's immediately after the devolved institutions take up their duties, of having a central Parliament whose powers are different in relation to different parts of their country' (Cabinet Office 1999: 37).

One country where a very similar situation did apply was Spain in the early 1980s.[28] However, the designers of the Spanish constitution failed to effectively link devolution and the new upper house. This has severely weakened the chamber, and resulted in widespread calls for its reform.[29] It has also created a missed opportunity—that of having an upper house at the heart of a devolved Spain, holding the regions, which are now increasingly fragmented, together. It has been suggested that devolution in the UK will follow a similar pattern to that in Spain, with assemblies spreading gradually until these envelop the whole of the country (e.g. Hazell and O'Leary 1999). Creation of a territorial chamber in the UK could therefore prevent a similar gap occurring to that which has emerged at the heart of devolved Spain, and help avoid some of the resulting problems seen in that country.

The potential benefits of a territorial chamber were discussed in Chapter 10. The general purpose of such an arrangement is to provide meaningful links between the national parliament and devolved parliaments or governments. This can facilitate co-ordinated decision making, complementing direct inter-governmental links such as inter-ministerial conferences. By ensuring that territorial concerns are brought to the attention of the national parliament, it can also potentially promote understanding and help to guard against the fragmentation of the state.

However, genuine connections of this kind must be carefully built into the design of a second chamber. Many supposedly territorial upper houses act as just another collection of national politicians, insufficiently connected to devolved institutions to fulfil their intended role. Canada is another country where the upper house is nominally territorial, but connections between it and provinces are weak, and have failed to protect against fragmentation and calls for secession by the province of Quebec. The extent to which different second chambers perform effectively as territorial chambers was discussed in Chapter 10.

Some of the functions which a territorial chamber might play in quasi-federal Britain are suggested below. Also discussed are the structural

---

[28] This is described in Chapter 3.
[29] See Chapter 11.

arrangements that would need to be put in place to ensure that such a chamber properly fulfilled its objectives.

The Work of a Territorial Chamber

The primary function of a territorial upper house would be to allow the concerns of the nations and regions to be fed into the work of the UK parliament. The chamber would still perform roles of scrutiny and review, and constitutional guardianship, as described above. However, it would bring to these functions the particular perspectives of the different parts of the UK. Members of the upper house would represent their nations and regions in the same way that MPs represent constituency interests. But additionally they could connect Westminster with the policies being pursued by devolved governments and parliaments.

Some suggestions have already been made as to specific ways in which a territorial perspective could be advantageous in legislative work. A territorial upper house could, for example, provide a forum for representatives of the nations and regions to feed into EU policy making, and scrutinise European legislative proposals from a territorial perspective. Consideration of the delegated powers in new primary legislation, currently scrutinised in a committee of the House of Lords, will involve determining whether appropriate powers have been delegated to the devolved assemblies or executives. This work would most appropriately be done by a body which is fully representative of the different areas of the UK.

Territorial tensions will be reduced if devolved governments, and citizens of the nations and regions, are convinced that Westminster takes their concerns into account in all its business. This particularly applies to non-devolved legislation. In Scotland many major areas of policy making are now devolved. However, in Wales—and England if devolution proceeds—devolved matters will be far more limited. In all nations and regions there would be a role for representatives at Westminster who provide input into non-devolved matters, many of which will have an indirect impact on the operation of the devolved institutions. Whilst MPs of course offer this to some extent, their representative duty is to their particular constituency, rather than their nation or region as a whole. MPs also have no formal link with the devolved institutions.

In an entirely territorial chamber, all scrutiny activities would be approached from this perspective. In the German Bundesrat, for example, all legislative committees include one representative of each of the states. However, in a chamber that was only partly territorial in its membership, specific structures might be built into the scrutiny process to consider territorial concerns. For example, an upper house committee of the nations and regions might have responsibility for reviewing all legislation to assess its territorial impact. A committee of this kind operates in the Spanish upper house.

Going further than this, some territorial upper houses—such as those in Belgium, Germany, and South Africa—have additional powers over legislation that has particular relevance to the territories. Given the asymmetrical nature of devolution in the UK, it is difficult to see how this could apply in the short term. However, if devolution develops to cover all of the English regions—as for example it ultimately did in Spain—there might be an argument for giving the upper house a veto over matters where the devolved assemblies have important responsibilities. If Westminster were responsible for agreeing framework legislation to be implemented in detail by the nations and regions, the upper house could provide the forum through which they had an input into its content.

In addition a territorial upper house might potentially be given responsibility for introducing legislation which was promoted by the nations and regions. Private members' legislation in such a chamber might naturally develop this role. However, there is also precedent overseas for members of devolved assemblies to sponsor national parliamentary bills.[30] The upper house would be the natural place for such legislation to be introduced. This proposal connects with the need to create genuine links between the nations and regions and a territorial upper house. This is considered next.

Creating Genuine Accountability

In order to carry out these territorial functions it would be essential that members of the upper house were genuine representatives of the nations and regions, rather than simply being national politicians. In many countries, such as Australia, Canada, Italy, and Spain, genuine links have not been forged between 'territorial' members of the upper house and territorial governments and parliaments in the areas that they represent. Only in Germany can it really be said that the upper house effectively binds the politics of the states to that of the national parliament.

Although it is commonly held that it is the method of composition of a chamber that defines its territorial nature, this is not necessarily the case. It is true that the nature of the German Bundesrat is heavily

---

[30] This applies in Italy, Spain, and Germany. Further details can be found in Chapter 10.

influenced by its members' dual roles as members of state governments. However, this is also amplified by some of the procedures of the house. Indirectly elected Spanish Senators, in contrast, behave in essentially the same way as their directly elected colleagues, although many of them hold dual mandates as members of regional assemblies. This demonstrates that the mode of selecting a chamber's members is not enough alone to determine their behaviour. Some of the features of the German system would almost certainly create a more territorial chamber if applied to the Spanish upper house, or indeed any territorial chamber, be it indirectly elected, directly elected, or appointed.

If there were a desire to create a territorial upper house in the UK, serious consideration should be given to the following issues.[31]

- *Methods of reporting to devolved assemblies:* In countries such as Australia, Canada, and Italy there is no link at all between members of the upper house and the devolved institutions. Even in Spain where some Senators are elected by members of regional assemblies, there is no formal reporting mechanism or accountability to these assemblies. Only in Germany does such reporting occur, because Bundesrat members' dual role as members of state cabinets means they are constantly answerable to Länder parliaments. Some state parliaments even have special Bundesrat committees to monitor the work of the upper house. There are strong arguments for members of the upper house representing the nations and regions to be required—whether or not they are members of the devolved assembly in their area—to answer regular questions in the assembly and/or account for their work in its committees. Members might also be given speaking rights in the assembly if there were issues before the upper house that they wanted to raise for debate.

- *Involving members of devolved governments in the chamber's work:* A central feature of the German system is that members of Länder governments have access to a national parliamentary platform to air their views on policy.[32] In Spain, members of regional governments have the right to speak in a special upper house committee on regional affairs, but not in the chamber itself. Such connections do not exist in other countries such as Australia and Canada. Giving the right for representatives of devolved assemblies or governments to

---

[31] All of these issues are discussed in more detail in Chapter 10 in relation to second chambers overseas.

[32] This does not only apply to the Bundesrat: members of Länder cabinets also have speaking rights in the lower house, the Bundestag.

speak in the new upper house, if properly regulated, could be an appropriate reciprocal arrangement if its members can speak in devolved assemblies.[33] This could help provide genuine links between devolved governments and Westminster, whilst avoiding members of these governments being burdened by dual mandates.

- *Territorial debates in the upper house:* If the upper house is the territorial chamber, it should also be given primary responsibility for any special debates or scrutiny on issues affecting the devolution settlement. The Spanish upper house, for example, has introduced an annual debate in the chamber on the state of devolution in Spain, attended by members of national government and all devolved governments. These initiatives have unfortunately had little impact, but with greater political will could be made to work elsewhere.

- *Absence of ministers from the upper house:* The role of government in a second chamber of revision and review was considered above. However, the inclusion of ministers in the chamber also links to the issue of creating a genuinely territorial house. In Germany the inability to appoint upper house members to the federal cabinet—because of their existing state responsibilities—ensures that the sole focus of upper house members is on matters within their states. If members of a new upper chamber were engaged in some of the activities listed above—such as addressing territorial assemblies and their committees, and scrutinising national and EU legislation from a territorial perspective—this might be more than enough to occupy their time without also taking up ministerial appointments.

If mechanisms such as these to create a genuine link between Westminster and devolved interests were not built into a territorial chamber, the danger is that it would simply become a house dominated by national party interests. In the Spanish Senado the representatives of nationalist parties are the only members who are able to present themselves as truly representing territorial views. The same pattern could easily establish itself in a devolved UK.[34]

---

[33] Speaking rules would probably be necessary, in order to ensure that these representatives did not simply abuse access to the national stage for partisan advantage. An alternative would be the German system, where speaking time is regulated by the parties. Here state representatives who speak in the Bundestag use up part of their party's quota of speaking time. The system is self-regulating, and seems to work well.

[34] The Scottish National Party are already displaying some of the tactics used by the Basque Nationalist Party in Spain with regard to the new upper house. Their submission to

Organisation of the Chamber

As well as creating links between the upper house and devolved parliaments and governments, the German Bundesrat maintains its territorial identity through particular elements of its internal organisation. If the territorial nature of a new UK upper house were to be reinforced, the following measures might also be considered.

- *Seating members in territorial groups:* In the German upper house members sit in blocks representing their states, rather than their parties. This is highly unusual—in the French, Italian, Australian, Canadian, and Spanish chambers members who nominally represent territorial units immediately form parliamentary groups on the basis of parties. In most cases they then vote consistently as party blocks. Consideration might be given to seating members of the new upper house in blocks representing the nations and regions, rather than the more traditional party groups. This would help create a distinctive character to the chamber, as compared to the House of Commons. It might also, to some extent, help foster a less adversarial atmosphere in the upper house.

- *Requiring members to vote in territorial groups:* Of course, seating arrangements alone would not prevent members of the upper house voting in party blocks. The key to state cohesion in the German upper house is that the representatives of each state are required to cast a single block vote. In this system negotiation of positions in the upper house—between members who may represent different parties—is quite natural, as these members work together in state coalition governments. However a similar arrangement applies in the South African upper house, where members represent the provinces, but are simply representatives of parties rather than provincial governments.[35] On matters of particular territorial relevance each province is required to cast one block vote, which requires negotiation between the parties in each province. Although

---

the Royal Commission on Reform of the House of Lords favoured abolition of the house. They opposed a new, territorial, house on the grounds that 'It is no secret that the Scottish National Party does not wish to strengthen the Union, and should be no surprise that we are reluctant to participate in a structure whose highest priority is to maintain the status quo.' Experience from Spain—further discussed in Chapter 11—suggests that if a territorial house is not designed from the outset, it will become more difficult to tie nationalist parties into the work of the chamber over time.

[35] Members of the South African upper house are appointed by parties in proportion to their strengths in provincial assemblies.

this system involves consensus building, and negotiation of genuinely territorial positions, it is hard to imagine this working in the new upper house, given the UK's adversarial traditions.

- *Limited vetoes for national/regional blocks:* Although voting in territorial blocks might not be practical for most legislation, it could be applied in limited circumstances. This mechanism has been proposed by reformers in Spain as a means of representing asymmetrical devolution in the upper house. Constitutional change is the most obvious example of where a territorial veto might be appropriate. For example, Westminster retains the power to abolish the Scottish Parliament, or alter its powers. The use of territorial vetoes might allow such action to be blocked by all Scottish upper house members acting together. If all parties were represented in the group, consensus amongst them would represent a powerful territorial view.[36] As suggested earlier, in discussion of the constitutional guardian role for the house, government might then seek approval through a referendum to overturn such a veto.

Implications for Membership of the House

A territorial upper house would be involved in many of the activities of revision and review, and constitutional guardianship, which were discussed in previous sections. Therefore its membership would need to be appropriate to these tasks, as already discussed. The additional property which would be required in a territorial chamber would be the ability to take a perspective particular to the nation or region, and to build links effectively with its devolved institutions. Members therefore, in addition to being national politicians, must be prepared to be active in the politics of Scotland, Wales, Northern Ireland, or their English region. Such activity would be encouraged by some of the measures already discussed. Designing the membership of a territorial chamber is the subject of separate consideration in the next chapter.

[36] If this procedure were adopted it is suggested that a consensus amongst members from the nation or region, or at least a qualified majority, should be required to cast a block vote. This would avoid vetoes being used by opposition parties who had managed to win half the seats in a territorial block.

WHAT UPPER HOUSE MEMBERS SHOULD NOT DO: CONSTITUENCY WORK

The previous sections have proposed a number of roles and functions that might be fulfilled by a new upper house. These all, in one way or another, complement the existing work of the House of Commons and would enable the upper house to retain a distinct character. The ability to remain distinct from the House of Commons will be very important to the success of the house. The range of functions proposed—even if not taken up in full—represent a challenging workload for upper house members. It is therefore important that these members have sufficient time available to devote to their parliamentary duties. The nature of the house's work also demands that members take a different perspective from members of the Commons and are not driven by parochial interests.

For all of these reasons it is important that members of the new upper house are not driven into taking on constituency work, which occupies a great deal of MPs' time. One of the strengths of the current House of Lords is that its members are free from this form of pressure, leaving more time to devote to other duties. This is because members of the House of Lords are not elected, and represent only themselves and their party. A similar tradition of no constituency work is also a strength in overseas upper houses, such as the Canadian Senate, but is becoming eroded in others such as the Australian Senate.[37] Since members of the British public are already able to contact their MP to take up particular local problems, involvement of upper house members in this work would simply cause confusion and competition between members of the two houses. It would also prevent members of the upper house from concentrating on their parliamentary work.

In designing the new upper house this factor should therefore be taken into account. One possibility would be for a convention to apply, requiring that upper house members do not become involved in constituency work. However, the Australian example shows that this could be difficult to maintain. Under some systems—such as an appointed or indirectly elected upper house—involvement in constituency work is less likely to be an issue. But there are also ways in which this danger may be minimised in a directly elected house. These issues are further discussed in Chapter 14.

---

[37] See Chapter 10.

CONCLUSIONS

This chapter has considered some of the roles and functions which might be fulfilled by a reformed upper house. The intention has not been to be prescriptive, but to set down some of the options. Of the roles and functions suggested—all of which are commonly employed in second chambers overseas—some or all might be considered appropriate for a new upper house in the UK.

In summary the three roles suggested, and their associated functions, are as follows:

Chamber of revision and review:

- The scrutiny of legislation will almost certainly continue to be the core function of the reformed upper house. This should complement the work of the House of Commons by bringing a different perspective. This function could be improved in the house through introduction of legislative procedures not currently employed in the Commons, such as committees taking evidence on bills from outside bodies.

- In order to exert sufficient pressure over government, and ask it to think again, the upper house must have considerable delaying powers—probably six months to one year—or an absolute veto.

- In order to resolve disputes between the two chambers in a more consensual way, a joint mediation committee might be established, learning in particular from equivalent committees in Germany and the US.

- The upper house will probably remain the focus for scrutiny of delegated legislation—a duty that will grow in importance as a result of devolution and the Human Rights Act. The powers of the upper house over such legislation might be brought into line with those over ordinary legislation—allowing the chamber to amend or delay, but possibly not veto, these matters.

- The upper house will also probably continue its detailed scrutiny of EU matters. If the house took on a territorial role this role could be extended to allow representatives of the nations and regions to feed in to EU policy.

- The investigative role of the upper house could be extended beyond the current occasional *ad hoc* committees and the work of the Science and Technology Committee. The upper house and its committees should retain the right to initiate investigations, as they see fit, and procedures might be adopted to make government more responsive to their findings.

- The role of ministers in the chamber will need to be reconsidered when its membership changes. It might be appropriate to end appointment of ministers from the upper house, in order to promote a distinct and independent character. The upper house could continue to scrutinise and question government if speaking rights in the chamber were extended to ministers who were members of the lower house. This is quite normal overseas.

Constitutional guardian:
- The new upper house might be given responsibility for protecting the constitutional settlement. This could be exercised through a veto, or greater delaying power, over legislation introducing constitutional change. Alternatively the upper house could have the power to require such changes to be approved in a referendum.

- The implementation of the Human Rights Act 1998 will have considerable parliamentary impact, much of which could be borne by the new upper house. Members will play a part in the joint human rights committee, and a separate human rights or constitutional committee might also be created in the upper house, to scrutinise all bills.

- The position of the law lords in the House of Lords is highly unusual by international standards. If the law lords were removed from the chamber and established as a separate supreme court, the upper house might be involved in the appointment of members of the court, and possibly other judicial appointments.

- In addition the upper house could provide scrutiny of other public appointments and public bodies, especially for those bodies which themselves involve a constitutional guardian role.

Territorial chamber:
- The upper house could be given a role as a territorial chamber, which might help to bind the nations and regions together under the

new devolution settlement. This would bring the UK upper house into line with an emerging trend amongst second chambers overseas.

- The primary function of such a chamber would be to bring regional perspectives to the legislative, investigative, and constitutional roles of the chamber.

- If the upper house was to operate as a territorial chamber it would be important to build in mechanisms whereby it was genuinely linked to the devolved institutions. Examples include requiring upper house members to answer questions in devolved assemblies and allowing members of devolved governments to speak in the upper house.

- Members of a territorial upper house might also be required to sit, and even vote, in territorial blocks.

Each of these roles has implications for the membership of the chamber, as discussed in the body of the chapter. It is particularly important that members of the upper house represent a different perspective from those of the House of Commons, and complement the members of the lower chamber in terms of their interests, skills, and experience. Members must be broadly representative of the population in terms of gender and ethnic balance, and geographical spread. They must be seen as independent-minded and be able to retain the support of the public. And they must have sufficient time to be able to devote to the considerable burden of parliamentary work which membership of the house entails. In particular they must not begin to engage in constituency work, which is a very demanding element of the work of MPs.

This chapter has attempted to outline a realistic set of responsibilities which would be appropriate for a new upper house, based on international standards. The membership which would be appropriate to perform these functions is the subject of the next chapter.

14

The Composition of a New Chamber

The composition of the upper house—who its members are—is the subject which most excites would-be reformers. Calls for House of Lords reform in the twentieth century have largely been driven by concerns about its hereditary members. The majority of these members were removed in 1999, but debates about stage two of the current reform programme tend also to be dominated by arguments about who should sit in the new upper house.

In the previous chapter the options for the role of the new house were discussed. It is the ability to carry out the house's preferred role which should drive decisions about its membership. This chapter therefore seeks to explore the options for membership of the new chamber which will enable it to carry out these functions. Particular emphasis is given to the principles which were set down in Chapter 12—in particular the need to build on the strengths of the existing House of Lords, whilst creating a chamber which has legitimacy, but remains clearly distinct from the House of Commons.

Guided by this, and by other lessons from overseas, this chapter looks in detail at the possible membership of the new house. It begins by considering some of the general aspects of the house's membership, such as its size, party balance, and the degree of independence of upper house members. It also discusses some aspects of how a territorial chamber—if that it what is desired—could be designed. Finally, the chapter considers what preoccupies many reformers—the method(s) of composition that might be employed in the new chamber. The merits of direct and indirect election, appointment, and *ex officio* membership are all considered, along with the prospects for a chamber that mixes members chosen by more than one of these methods.

THE SIZE OF THE CHAMBER

By the middle of 1999 the House of Lords, with 1,289 members, was one of the largest parliamentary chambers in the world. It was also almost double the size of the House of Commons. As discussed in Chapter 2, the average upper chamber is around 60 per cent of the size of its respective lower house. Even the transitional House of Lords, with over 600 members, is almost double the size of its nearest rival—the Italian Senato.

Many of the valued features of second chambers overseas are enhanced by their smaller size. Members of the house know each other better, and consequently work together more closely on the floor and in committees. Smaller size can help members develop a common ethos which creates a less adversarial chamber. Despite the size of the House of Lords, many of these features have traditionally been present in the house. This is for a number of reasons, some of which are discussed below. However, it is also influenced by the fact that the working membership of the house is much smaller than its total membership. In 1998 the average daily attendance in the house reached its highest ever, but was still only 428 members.[1]

As the membership of the upper house changes, attendance levels are likely to rise. Not only were many hereditary members inactive, but convention, and consciousness of the chamber's lack of perceived legitimacy, demanded that government legislation be allowed to pass. Many Conservative members, in particular, could afford to stay away on a regular basis—in government their votes were rarely needed as they vastly outnumbered the opposition, and in opposition the Conservative whips did not use their full might. As the two main parties in the chamber become more evenly matched, conventions may break down and better attendance on both sides be required by the whips. In order to enjoy the benefits of a smaller chamber, it will therefore be necessary to restrict membership of the reformed house. A membership of half the size of the House of Commons—or 330—would still make the UK upper house the largest in the world.

At present the size of the House of Lords is flexible, and this is another of its unusual features. In most other countries the size of the upper house is fixed, or fluctuates only slightly as a result of population changes or—in the case of Italy—because there are a handful of life members. If the new upper house were elected it would be natural for its size to be fixed. Even if an appointed element is retained, this seems desirable. This is discussed later in the chapter.

TERMS OF OFFICE

Another distinguishing feature of the House of Lords is the continuity in its membership. Life membership means that the annual turnover in

---

[1] *Annual Report and Accounts 1998-99*, House of Lords, 1999.

the house is very low. This is one of the features which, despite its extraordinary size, helps to build relationships in the house so that members know each other well and treat each other with respect. As one peer has stated 'Because we have hitherto thought we were together 'till death do us part, we do all learn to accept each other'.[2] This helps create a less adversarial culture. The fact that the government cannot dissolve the upper house (except, potentially, through its reform) also gives the chamber a strength, which is offset by the fact that its powers are weaker than those of the House of Commons. In Chapter 9 the symmetry in this arrangement was identified: whilst the upper house, unlike the lower house, is denied the right to dismiss the government, the government is also denied the right to dismiss the upper house.

It is common in parliaments overseas for upper houses to have a rolling membership, so that they may not be dissolved by government. As discussed in Chapter 12, this is one of the key features which is either present in most upper chambers, or proposed by reformers. Common ways of achieving this are for the chamber to be elected in parts (as in France, Germany, and Australia) or otherwise renewed in parts when state governments or parliaments change (as in Germany, and for part of the house in Spain). A rolling membership in most cases implies longer terms of office for upper house members than lower house members, and this is also seen as beneficial. For example in France Senators are elected for nine-year terms, with one-third elected every three years. Senators in Australia tend to be elected on the same day as the general election, serving terms twice as long as those in the lower house.

Given the current system of life membership of the House of Lords, a rolling membership and long terms would ensure at least some continuity with tradition. It would have other advantages as well. In particular if an elected chamber has a rolling membership, this can be used to ensure that it never has a more recent mandate than the lower house, and therefore cannot claim a greater legitimacy. It is also likely to result in a more stable party balance, making the chamber less susceptible to swings in public opinion and more likely to act as a moderating influence. The likely makeup of a chamber renewed in halves is illustrated in Table 14.2, later in the chapter.

[2] Professor the Earl Russell, quoted in Mitchell (1999: 16).

PARTY BALANCE IN THE CHAMBER

The party balance in the new chamber will be a crucial element of its composition. The British parliament—particularly the House of Commons—is dominated by the political parties. The party balance of the new chamber is likely to be a key determining factor in much of its behaviour. In Chapter 12 we saw that a different party balance in the upper house is one of the most important ways in which it may maintain an distinct character to that of the lower house.

In terms of the party balance of the new upper house, there are three possible outcomes that need to be considered.

- *Government control.* The first possibility is that government has a majority in the upper house. In some countries, particularly where the two chambers are elected at the same time, this is a regular feature of the parliamentary system. Spain, Italy, and Ireland are examples. In others, including the UK to date, this is a feature some of the time. The difficulty with government control of the chamber is that it can have a tendency to turn the upper house into a 'rubber stamp' for government policy. A government majority means that the upper house is less likely to challenge government action, even when this is unpopular. Even the chamber's committees will tend to have a government majority, which can weaken their distinct perspective.[3] The danger is that the powers of the chamber become theoretical only, and are rarely—if ever—used. Although steps may be taken to boost the independence of upper house members, and thus encourage representatives of the governing party to take a more detached view, it is difficult for a chamber with a permanent government majority to play an effective review role. As a consequence, such a chamber is unlikely to gain the respect of the public—in countries where this situation applies there tend to be movements to reform, or even abolish, the upper house.

- *Opposition control.* An opposition majority in the upper house is, however, even more likely to be problematic. This creates a potentially unstable situation, as an opposition-controlled chamber may seek to disrupt all government legislation. The House of Lords has, of course, been dominated by the opposition during all periods of Labour government. However, the conventions of the house mean

---

[3] The lack of a government majority in committees, as discussed in Chapter 7, can be one of the strengths of the upper house.

that it has not used the full force of its powers against the government. The appointed Canadian Senate has also tended to show restraint when opposition controlled, despite its formidable formal powers. In both cases this resulted from the perceived lack of legitimacy of the chamber. Other chambers which are opposition-controlled on occasion are prevented from causing legislative deadlock because their powers are limited. The French Sénat is an example. In contrast opposition control of a powerful and legitimate chamber—such as the Australian Senate—could result in serious problems for government, possibly leading to constitutional crisis. The likely party control of the new upper chamber must thus be considered alongside the perceived legitimacy of its membership, and its formal powers.

- *Neither government nor opposition control.* The third option is for neither government nor opposition to have a majority in the chamber. This balance is the stated preference of the current government, and has the implicit support of the Conservative Party.[4] It also appears to be the most effective option according to overseas experience, as discussed in Chapter 12. If no party has overall control this avoids the danger of the upper house becoming either a rubber stamp or an opposition chamber. However, it does give the balance of power in the chamber either to minor parties, independent members, or both. In Australia such a system works, and while this constantly frustrates government, it appears to be popular with the public. Even in Ireland, where the upper house has weak powers, the chamber worked effectively during one isolated period when independent members had control. In a UK context it would be necessary to consider who would hold the balance of power in a chamber where no party had an overall majority. In Australia the Democrats and Greens, who generally have this role, are opportunistic and tend to play to public opinion. This generally results in popular outcomes, which are a compromise between government and opposition positions. In Britain some of the minor parties have clear-cut political agendas. The opportunity exists for nationalist parties, or Northern Irish parties, to play this refereeing role. This could have a more difficult outcome, with such parties potentially holding the government to ransom. An alternative,

---

[4] Labour's policy is quoted in Chapter 1. The Mackay Commission set up by Conservative leader William Hague, whose report was commended to the Royal Commission by the Conservative Party, concluded that 'no one political party should have a structural majority' in the new house (Mackay 1999: 22).

attractive to many, is to design the chamber so that independent members hold the balance of power. This does however have problems of its own, which are discussed in the section that follows.

Given the importance of party balance in the chamber, the idea of designing a chamber so that a particular balance is assured seems attractive. Indeed this would appear to be the intention of the major parties, as outlined above. However, such an exercise should be approached with caution—future developments may change the party balance in the chamber in unpredictable ways. In Australia, for example, the electoral system and size of the Senate were changed in 1948, largely in order to ensure that an outgoing government retained its seats.[5] Whilst this did happen, the change also had other effects which the government did not intend. Minor parties were formed, which eventually came to hold the balance of power in the upper house. A further change in the number of Senate seats in 1983 was designed to squeeze these parties out of the system, but this failed because their share of the vote continued to increase. These parties now control the Senate more decisively than ever. This illustrates how reform of the upper house—alongside other constitutional changes—could result in changes both to voting behaviour and the party system itself. These changes are difficult to predict.[6] The only certain way of denying a majority to either government or opposition (and also denying control to one of the minor parties) may be to retain a sizeable number of independent members in the house. This is discussed in more detail in later sections.

An alternative way of changing the voting pattern of the house— which is untested in the UK setting—would be to introduce different voting rules into standing orders. Such possibilities were mentioned in Chapter 13 in relation to the constitutional and territorial roles of the house. Voting in the German Bundesrat, for example, is less predictable than in other upper houses because the members vote in blocks by state, rather than along party lines. Another example of voting rules overcoming day-to-day party balance is the requirement for qualified majorities in many chambers for specific decisions, such as public appointments or constitutional change.[7] This requires government and opposition to vote together on matters of particular national

---

[5] See Chapter 3 for details of these changes.

[6] See Mitchell and Seyd (1999) for a discussion of the possible impact of constitutional change on the party system.

[7] See Chapter 8.

importance. Either of these mechanisms could be considered for the new upper house.

INDEPENDENCE, INDEPENDENT MEMBERS, AND 'EXPERTS'

Many proposals for reform of the Lords focus on the importance of not further politicising the chamber. It is generally seen as undesirable that the upper house should become a predominantly 'party house', along the lines of the House of Commons. Here votes are heavily whipped and their outcome is largely predictable, whereas the whip is applied less rigidly in the Lords, and followed less rigidly by its members.[8] The inclusion of a large number of members who do not adhere to a party whip also helps create a very different atmosphere in the house. Many of the functions which were suggested in the previous chapter called for the upper house to have members who are freer to express independent views than their counterparts in the Commons. The extent to which this may be achieved in a reformed upper house is considered below.

Encouraging Independence

When it comes to major issues of principle, it is clear that the seven second chambers considered in this book all—to a greater or lesser extent—play the role of party houses. This is illustrated in particular by their impact on legislation, as discussed in Chapter 6. Despite the different composition mechanisms employed by these upper houses, their voting behaviour is largely determined by party balance. This is seen in the elected Australian Senate, the appointed Canadian Senate, the Sénat of France, which represents local government, and the Seanad of Ireland which nominally represents the professions. In the Spanish Senado, directly and indirectly elected members sit side by side in party groups, and behave in identical ways. Even in the Bundesrat, where there are no government and opposition sides, the chamber's behaviour is driven by complex coalition politics.[9]

None the less, a common feature of second chambers is their reputation for a greater independence of mind than lower houses. This is particularly evident in their consideration of legislative detail. Here the issues are more technical, and less subject to the whip and

---

[8] Of course the extent to which the existing House of Lords is a party house is a much debated point. This was briefly discussed in Chapters 12 and 13.

[9] See Chapter 4 for a discussion of this, and party balance in other chambers.

requirements of party loyalty. Even on bigger issues, although speaking and voting across party lines may be rare in both chambers, the threat of rebellion in the upper house may be greater, forcing government to modify its proposals and amend its bills. This pattern is seen clearly in the House of Lords.

It is partly the power and functions of the upper house which result in its members behaving more independently. For example, the fact that the upper house cannot bring down the government, and may only be able to delay—rather than veto—legislation, makes party discipline less critical. Additionally, the lack of media and public attention on the chamber leaves its members freer to speak their minds. Retaining these features in a reformed upper house could be at least as influential in promoting independence as the kind of members that sit there, and how they are selected.

However, there are factors relating to the composition of the house which may encourage its members—including those who take a party whip—to express more independent views. Some of these are as follows.

- *A rolling membership and long terms of office.* This was proposed above. If the members of the house change gradually, and serve long terms of office, this helps create strong relationships in the chamber. If government cannot dissolve the house this may also encourage members to act independently. A system of rolling membership, through partial renewal of the house, could therefore promote independence.

- *Non-renewable terms.* One of the benefits of long terms of office is that members are not forced to start thinking about reselection by their party until long after they enter the house. Members may consequently be slightly less preoccupied with party discipline. To avoid this problem altogether, members of the upper house could be permitted to serve one term only.[10] This would mirror the current situation, where members of the House of Lords never have to face reselection. However, this also risks the constant leakage of expertise from the house, and would make membership potentially less attractive (unless the fixed terms applied were very long). Non-renewable terms are not used in any of the seven countries

---

[10] This was proposed, for example, by the Mackay Commission (1999). An alternative is to retain the system of life membership of the house, but this has disadvantages—discussed elsewhere in the chapter—both in terms of the size of the chamber and in terms of its party balance.

considered in this book, although they are used in the Mexican upper house.

- *No ministers in the house.* If ministers are appointed from within the house, party representatives may enter the chamber with aspirations towards to ministerial office, and consequently be very responsive to party discipline. A house without ministers is more likely to develop an independent ethos.[11]

- *More mature members.* A common feature of upper houses, including the House of Lords, is that members are older on average than their lower house counterparts. More mature members are likely to have more expertise, greater confidence in their views, and be less likely to be seeking promotion, as they approach the end of their careers. All of these factors can encourage independence. Some composition methods, such as indirect election or appointment, are likely to result in a more mature membership in the upper house.[12] Alternatively, a direct way of ensuring that upper house members are more mature is to apply a minimum qualification age which is higher than that for the lower house. This is relatively common overseas, with a minimum age of between 30 and 40 being quite usual.[13] Setting such a limit for the new upper house would help to create a contrast to the House of Commons where the minimum age of members is 21. It would also help guard against the upper house changing from a mature chamber where members end their careers, to a junior chamber where ambitious young members begin. This pattern is developing, for example, in the Irish Seanad.[14]

Independent Members

The discussion of party balance in the chamber suggested that it may be desirable to retain independent members in the reformed upper house. Indeed the presence of a large number of 'crossbenchers' in the House of Lords, who do not take any party whip, has always been seen as one of the strengths of the chamber. Crossbenchers remain a considerable force in the transitional house, with around 150 seats at the end of 1999. Retaining an independent element in a new chamber, within a membership that can command public support, is one of the major

---

[11] The pros and cons of including ministers in the house were discussed in Chapter 13.
[12] This is discussed in Chapter 4.
[13] See Chapter 2.
[14] This has had damaging consequences for the chamber—see Chapter 4.

challenges of reform. The White Paper on reform of the House of Lords indicated that the government intended to respond to this challenge and 'is committed to maintaining a significant independent presence in the second chamber' (Cabinet Office 1999: 24).

None of the seven upper chambers which have been considered in this book includes a particularly large number of independent members. The highest proportion are the six university Senators in the Irish Seanad, representing 10 per cent of the chamber's total membership. Apart from this, a very small number of non-aligned members are included amongst the appointees in the Italian and Canadian upper houses, and the Australian Senate generally includes one or two elected independents.

The first lesson, therefore, is that independent members are very difficult to obtain—particularly through election. In most Western democracies, all elections for political office will tend to be dominated by the parties. The longest-serving independent member of the Australian upper house—Brian Harradine—is elected to represent the small state of Tasmania, which has a long tradition of independents in its state legislature. However, he is the exception—other independents in the Senate tend to have broken away from party groups in the chamber. The electoral system for the Australian Senate makes it particularly difficult for independents to get elected, being essentially based on 'closed' party lists and covering large geographical areas.[15] It is difficult for an ill-resourced independent to compete effectively in these circumstances. Other electoral systems, such as the pure single transferable vote system used in Ireland, or 'open' party lists, may make it easier for independent members to get elected. However, the most reliable means of ensuring independent members are retained in the chamber is through systems other than election. Possibilities include appointment, *ex officio* membership, vocational seats, or even random selection. These options are discussed later in the chapter.

Assuming that independent members are included in the house, there are other problems to consider. One is the prospect of independents holding the balance of power. If the desired outcome of reform is a chamber where no party has an overall majority, this may be the result. Despite the large number of crossbenchers in the House of Lords, this would, in effect, be a new situation for the UK. A combination of Conservative dominance in the chamber, and the Salisbury convention, have meant that crossbenchers seldom decide the outcome of votes.

---

[15] Formally, the Senate is elected using a single transferable vote system. However, because of the system of 'above the line' voting, most voters mark their cross against the name of a party (see Chapter 3).

However, as the parties become more evenly balanced in the house, and particularly if established conventions break down, this may happen more and more regularly—even in the transitional house.

If crossbenchers do hold the balance of power, this is likely to result in far greater attention being paid to the behaviour of particular members. Brian Harradine is perhaps the best-known of all Australian Senators, due to his decisive influence in the passage of many government bills. He has used this position to promote a highly traditional moral agenda.[16] Even in a large group of crossbench members, the majority may vote in a predictable way, leaving a small number who effectively hold the balance of power. These members could become controversial figures. This controversy would be heightened if questions can be raised about the validity of the route— for example, appointment—by which these members entered the house. It is even possible that, if the system of life appointments to the chamber continued, one or two eccentric independent members could effectively hold the balance of power for many years. This, and the need to limit the size of the chamber, suggest that it would be preferable for any appointed members to serve limited terms, as elected members do in the House of Commons.

Another factor which is illustrated by the case of Brian Harradine is the difficulty of resourcing independent members. Whilst Senator Harradine has often held the balance of power in the upper house, he has never had party structures to fall back upon, and must study each issue individually and decide how to cast his vote. This is clearly a situation that already applies to the crossbench members of the House of Lords. It is worsened by the fact that these members have to date received none of the funding which applies to party groups in the house.[17] Although the government intends to implement the recommendations of the Neill Committee, which will provide some funding to the crossbenchers, it is proposed that this funding amount to only £20,000 per year.[18] This must support the whole group, comprising approximately 150 members. This difficult situation will become less tenable if the crossbench members have a more decisive influence on the outcome of debates. Senator Harradine, for example, receives enormous volumes of mail on issues which he is likely to influence, and has no infrastructure to deal with this. It is important that independent

[16] See Chapter 4.

[17] Even the funds available to party groups is very small, compared to that in the House of Commons. In 1997–8 the two main opposition parties in the Lords received a total of £134,000.

[18] *The Funding of Political Parties in the United Kingdom*, Home Office, Cm 4413, 1999.

members in a new upper house are not placed at this kind of disadvantage compared to party representatives.

The Inclusion of 'Expert' Members

In the House of Lords it is not only the crossbench members, and the independent nature of many party members, which command respect. This is boosted by the inclusion of many members in the house who are seen as experts in their fields. These include practising academics, lawyers and judges, doctors, businesspeople, and religious leaders, as well as many who have retired from these professions, or are retired MPs, MEPs, or civil servants. It is often said that it would be impossible to maintain this tradition in an elected house, making inclusion of appointed or *ex officio* members essential.

None of the overseas second chambers studied here achieve the same reputation for expert membership as the House of Lords. Of them all it is possibly the Italian Senato—which is directly elected—that has the most similar tradition. Here the party list system for elections (which was dropped in 1993) allowed parties to place prominent figures, such as academics, lawyers, and doctors, high on their lists without entailing these individuals in arduous campaigning work. On the other hand the appointed Canadian Senate has the same potential, but this is rarely used. The Senate is largely filled with faithful party activists, many of whom have served as MPs. This demonstrates that the inclusion of expert members in an upper house can be as much a product of tradition as a result of the method of composition.

Another factor which has made it possible for experts to hold seats in the House of Lords is the traditional part-time character of the house. This allowed members who pursue other careers to attend only infrequently. With over 1,000 members the house could function with some members contributing to only the occasional debate on their subject of expertise. This is not the case in any of the overseas second chambers we have considered, and is something that is liable to change in a reformed upper house in the UK. As already discussed, a more politically balanced membership in the upper house is liable to result in a breakdown of the Salisbury convention, requiring members who take the party whip to attend more frequently. It would be difficult for active members of the professions to play a part in a full-time upper house.

In any case it has been suggested that 'the degree of specialisation [in the Lords] is often overstated. Retired grandees have not always kept up with recent thinking in their professions, and often either do not know who to ask or do not wish to ask for any briefing' (Quarmby 1997: 7). In a reformed upper house it may therefore be more effective to conform to the international norm of including experts as advisers in the house on particular bills, rather than as members of the house itself.

RESOURCES

Amongst the upper chambers considered here, the members of the House of Lords are unique in receiving no salary at all for their duties.[19] Members of the Lords also have no right to an office, office equipment, or staff. In 1998/9 they were entitled to a daily attendance allowance of £35.50, plus daily office costs of up to £34.50 (from which members must meet the cost of any secretarial assistance, equipment, postage, etc.). For a member who attended the house every day this would amount to maximum pay of £5,147 and office costs of £5,002 for an average sitting year of 145 days. In 1998/9 members based outside London were also entitled to claim travelling expenses and an overnight allowance of £80.50 for each day they attended.[20] In comparison members of the House of Commons received a salary of £45,066, an annual office costs allowance of £49,232, plus travel costs. Members representing constituencies outside central London also received an additional accommodation allowance of £12,717. MPs have an office, access to photocopiers, telephones, post-paid envelopes, and a generous pension scheme. The total costs of the two houses in 1997/8 were £40 million for the House of Lords and £241 million for the House of Commons (Richard and Welfare 1999).

The standard situation overseas is for members of the upper house to be subject to the same pay, conditions, and allowances as lower house members. The exceptions are Ireland, where the pay for upper house members is slightly lower, in recognition of shorter sitting hours, and Canada, where office allowances are smaller because members of the Senate do not deal with constituency work. However, all seven countries acknowledge that membership of the upper house is a job, and that members need to be properly remunerated for their time. It is also acknowledged that upper house members require secretarial and research support in order to carry out their duties effectively.

This is something that must be given serious consideration in designing the new UK upper house. Members of the House of Lords are increasingly expected to work full-time on their parliamentary duties,

[19] Members of the Bundesrat do not receive a salary for their federal parliamentary duties, but all are salaried members of state governments. For a discussion of salaries and allowances to upper house members overseas, see Chapter 5.

[20] *Annual Report and Accounts 1998-99*, House of Lords, 1999.

and this trend is liable to continue. It is therefore more and more unrealistic to expect members to be able to support themselves through outside employment. The current system of remuneration clearly excludes people from membership of the house unless they can earn sufficient income outside sitting hours, or are otherwise self-supporting. This prevents the house becoming fully representative of the population. The cost of introducing salaries and allowances would obviously depend on the number of members in the reformed house, as well as the level at which these allowances were set. However, for a house with 330 members—i.e. half the size of the Commons—the annual cost of paying remuneration equivalent to MPs' salaries would be £16.1 million and the cost of paying identical allowances would be roughly £20.1 million (in practice a lower allowance might be paid in recognition that upper house members should not deal with constituency work).[21] The cost of salaries and office costs would therefore be considerably higher than the cost of peers' current allowances, which stood at £9.5 million in 1998/9.[22] However, this would not bring the cost of the upper house anywhere near that of the House of Commons. In terms of other facilities, a major reduction in the size of the upper house would also make it easier to provide accommodation and services for members and their staff.

COMPOSITION OF A TERRITORIAL CHAMBER

The importance attached to territorial chambers was one of the key findings from overseas, as outlined in Chapter 12, and some of the roles which such a chamber might take on in the UK were discussed in Chapter 13. Establishment of a territorial chamber could link the reform of the House of Lords to the unfolding devolution settlement in a way which has not happened in countries such as Italy and Spain, where calls for reform have been widespread as a result.

Insofar as there is a debate about formation of a territorial chamber, this has tended to focus on the composition mechanism for such a chamber, in terms of whether it should be directly elected—to represent the people of the UK's nations and regions—or indirectly elected, to represent their assemblies or governments. The pros and cons of these

---

[21] The total cost in 1998/9 of House of Commons members' salaries was £32.2 million, of office costs allowances was £32.4 million, and of additional costs allowances was £7.8 million. These figures have simply been halved to estimate the cost of introducing them in an upper house with 330 members.

[22] *Annual Report and Accounts 1998-99*, House of Lords, 1999.

methods of selection are considered in the next section. However, the evidence from overseas suggests that this is not the key question to be answered. Far more important to creating a genuinely territorial chamber is building mechanisms that effectively tie members of the chamber into the politics of their nation or region. Some possible ways of doing this were discussed in Chapter 13. Nevertheless, there do remain other generic issues around the composition of a territorial chamber which will need to be considered, irrespective of the way its members are chosen. Two of these—the English question and the distribution of seats—are discussed here.

Anticipating Future Devolution

Although devolution applied initially to only certain parts of the UK— Scotland, Wales, Northern Ireland, and London—the territorial nature of British politics is developing. Regional Development Agencies were established in the English regions in 1999, and in the same year the European elections were fought using these regional boundaries. By mid-1999 regional chambers—comprised largely of local government councillors—had been established throughout England. Nevertheless, it was still unclear when, if ever, elected English regional assemblies would be created. The government appeared to have lost momentum for this part of the reform programme, but this may grow instead from the bottom up, over time. Experience from overseas suggests that pressure for devolution is likely to grow as English regions seek to catch up with Scotland and Wales (Hazell and O'Leary 1999). Eventually devolved assemblies may even spread to cover the whole of the UK, as they did in Spain in the 1980s.

The experience of Spain, where the upper house did not take full account of devolution, or anticipate its development, is a cautionary tale for the UK. Here the failure of the Senado to act as a territorial upper house has led to calls for reform, and done nothing to bind the fragmented regions together. This and other overseas experiences suggest that serious consideration should be given to representation of the English regions in the new upper house, in such a way that would allow a smooth transition to be made if devolution progresses. This is a consideration in each of the sections which follow. The particular challenge is finding a solution that allows for this transition to happen smoothly, but would also be robust in the short to medium term if elected assemblies are not established in all English regions. This is probably one of the most difficult issues facing UK reformers.

Another problem which has been raised in relation to the asymmetrical devolution settlement is the danger of introducing the so-called 'West Lothian question' into the upper house. This has been used as an argument against a territorial chamber (Bogdanor 1999; Richard and Welfare 1999). The West Lothian question relates to the difficulty caused by Scottish members of the house having the right to vote on English matters, when the equivalent matters in Scotland have been devolved and are no longer subject to approval by English members at Westminster. This is a problem that will need to be accommodated in both chambers. However, it does not in itself appear to be a valid argument against a territorial chamber, since the only way the problem could be avoided would be to exclude Scottish members from the upper house. This is clearly not a realistic solution. Indeed, as territorial politics develops, and sensitivities increase, it seems particularly important that any new upper house includes a fair distribution of members from all parts of the United Kingdom.

The Distribution of Seats

The question of fairness between nations and regions leads to another difficult issue—the matter of distribution of seats between different areas. This is something that has caused much debate in other countries in relation to the upper house. It is central to the upper house reform debate in Canada, for example, as discussed in Chapter 11.

The classic model for a territorial house originates from the role of such chambers in newly forming federal states.[23] This model gives equal numbers of seats to all territorial units, irrespective of population. The rationale for this is that it ensures all areas have an equal voice in one house in the legislature, in the same way that population-based representation is intended to ensure an equal voice for all citizens in the other. The aim of this was to protect the interests of citizens in less populous areas. The Australian Senate is an example of the application of this model. Here the arrangement ensures that representatives of the two largest states cannot outvote representatives of the four smaller states in the Senate, as they can in the House of Representatives. As a result the state of Tasmania, with a population of 460,000, has the same number of Senators as New South Wales, with a population of six million. Similar arrangements exist in other federal states, such as the US, and have more recently been adopted by some unitary states, such as Poland. Likewise in Spain, the provinces each have four seats in the upper house, but their representation in the lower house varies between one and 34 seats. Even where the pure model of equal representation is not applied, it is very common for less densely populated areas to be

---

[23] This was discussed in Chapter 2.

compensated for their lack of representation in the lower house through additional seats in the upper house. This applies for example in Germany and France.[24] Thus it is quite usual for the rationale behind distribution of seats to be entirely different in the upper house.

Table 14.1: *Options for distribution of seats in a territorial chamber*

	Population (000s)†	Option 1: Equality	Option 2: Population based
South West	4,841	20	20
Eastern	5, 293	20	22
South East	7,895	20	32
West Midlands	5,317	20	22
East Midlands	4,141	20	17
Yorkshire and Humberside	5,035	20	20
North East	2,600	20	11
North West	6,891	20	28
London	7,074	20	29
Wales	2,921	20	12
Scotland	5,128	20	21
Northern Ireland	1,663	20	6
TOTAL	58,801	240	240

† *Source*: Regional Trends 33, 1998.

In the UK the discrepancy between the populations of nations and regions is not so great as it is, for example, amongst Australian states. Table 14.1 shows the population of the 12 nations and regions (which in

[24] The kind of distortions this creates in terms of representation of individual citizens was discussed in Chapter 3 and illustrated in Table 3.4.

England correspond with Government Office regions, now used for elections to the European Parliament). The population of each area varies between 1.7 million inhabitants in Northern Ireland and 7.9 million in the South East of England.

The table also illustrates the impact of two different forms of distribution of seats—one based on equality and the other on the population of the nations and regions. Under the first of these models all areas are given 20 seats in the upper house, irrespective of population. This upper chamber, with 240 seats, would adhere to the classic territorial model. As the model intends, it would give an equal voice in the upper house to less populous areas, including Northern Ireland, Wales, and the North East. This is at the expense of the most populous areas, including London, the South East, and the North West, which have relatively more seats in the House of Commons.[25] The alternative to this system, which may be more intuitive in the UK, would be to base each area's representation in the upper house on its population. The results of this option are also illustrated in the table, for an upper house with 240 members. This would give six seats to Northern Ireland, 12 seats to Wales, and 32 seats to the South East of England.

There is a consequence associated with the classic territorial model of an upper house, which may be seen as potentially advantageous in the UK. Australia once again illustrates this. The Australian parliament, like Westminster, comprises a lower house elected using single member constituencies, in which the governing party tends to have a majority.[26] The Senate, which has strong, though not equal, powers is directly elected, using a proportional voting system. Under these arrangements there would appear to be a real danger that the upper house be seen as the more representative house, since it is more reflective of the country's voting habits. If it were seen this way it could challenge the supremacy of the lower house, and the right of government—often elected on a minority of the vote—to govern. However this does not happen in Australia, because the Senate does not give equal representation to all citizens, as the lower house does. The fact that the upper house instead gives equal representation to states allows it to be

---

[25] In the House of Commons, for example, the South East region has 83 MPs, Wales has 40, and Northern Ireland has 18.

[26] The electoral system for the Australian lower house is the alternative vote (AV), rather than the first past the post system used in the UK. This is explained in Chapter 3.

viewed as the 'unrepresentative' house, and helps maintain its subordinate status.[27]

Australia is unusual, however, in that equal representation of states in the upper house does not distort the party balance in the chamber. In other countries, as discussed in Chapters 3 and 4, the over-representation of less populous areas in the upper house often has this effect. Generally this favours conservative parties, which tend to have stronger support in rural areas. The overrepresentation of rural areas in the French Sénat, for example, has resulted in that chamber having a permanent centre-right bias, and never having been controlled by parties of the left.

An equal allocation of seats to all nations and regions would therefore have potential advantages, in that it would adhere to a classic upper house model, provide representation on a different basis to the House of Commons, and therefore help retain the supremacy of that house.[28] However, it might also result in difficulties. In particular if it created an inbuilt political bias in the upper house this could be a serious problem, as it would affect the position which the upper house took on legislation, and could at times alter the course of government policy.

Table 14.2 indicates the likely political outcome of elections to an upper house with seats allocated according to the two different models. This allocates seats to parties on a proportional basis, using general election results. In line with the discussion earlier in this chapter, the chamber is elected in halves, with members serving two House of Commons terms.[29]

In terms of political balance, the most obvious result is that parties based in the less populous areas of Wales and Northern Ireland would be overrepresented in a chamber where seats were allocated on an equal basis to all nations and regions. This applies particularly in Northern Ireland, where the party system is largely separate to that in the rest of the UK, and the population is particularly small. This necessarily means

---

[27] The directly elected Senate in the US is also directly elected, and based on the same principle of equal representation of states. It is not the subordinate house. However, in this case the Senate was consciously established with stronger formal powers than the lower chamber.

[28] The problem of creating an upper house which is more representative than the lower house is ignored in many proposals. For example the Liberal Democrats' submission to the Royal Commission proposed an upper house elected by PR, based on boundaries of the nations and regions, and with membership proportional to population.

[29] This is the model which is used in Australia. A new upper house might also be elected in thirds, rather than halves, and its election might be tied to elections for devolved assemblies, rather than Westminster. The model used in Table 14.2 is therefore for illustration only.

that Northern Irish parties will hold 20 seats in a chamber based on equal representation, compared with six seats in a chamber where representation is based on population. This could potentially make the difference between these parties holding, or not holding, the balance of power in the chamber. Results such as these do not occur in Australia because all parties represented in the upper house contest seats across the whole country.

Table 14.2: *Effect of distribution of seats on party balance, in a chamber elected in halves in 1992 and 1997, using a proportional system*[†]

	Option 1: Equality			Option 2: Population based		
	1992	1997	Total	1992[‡]	1997	Total
Labour	41	53	94	41	52	93
Conservative	47	34	81	53	39	92
Liberal Democrat	20	20	40	23	21	44
Scottish National Party	2	2	4	2	2	4
Plaid Cymru	1	1	2	0	1	1
Sinn Fein	1	2	3	0	1	1
SDLP	2	3	5	1	1	2
UUP	4	3	7	1	1	2
DUP	1	1	2	1	0	1
NI Alliance	1	1	2	0	0	0
TOTAL	120	120	240	122	118	240

† Seats are allocated on the basis of pure proportionality, rather than any particular electoral system. Allocation is on the basis of votes cast in the general election. Actual results would therefore be likely to differ, depending on the electoral system, and voters' responses to it.
‡ Where the number of members to be elected in an area is odd, the greater number have been allocated in 1992 and the lesser number in 1997.

The two allocations have less of an impact on the balance of representation between the three main parties. Unlike in other countries the equal allocation of seats certainly does not seem to favour the

Conservatives, who actually win fewer seats under this system than under a system based on population, in both 1992 and 1997. This is primarily because the system of equal allocation of seats results in underrepresentation of the South East of England and London—where the Conservatives win a relatively high proportion of seats. It is therefore the Conservatives who primarily lose out from the overrepresentation of Northern Ireland and Wales. However the total distortion—as in Australia—is not great. The table also indicates how electing the chamber in halves would lead to a relatively stable party balance, as the Conservative majority in 1992 is balanced by the Labour majority in 1997.

An additional complication in the UK context is the representation of nations, as opposed to regions, in the upper house. Whilst the concentration of population in England would make it impractical to give each nation equal numbers of seats, Scottish and Welsh representatives might claim that they should have more power in the upper house than a small or medium-sized English region. It has been suggested that a territorial upper house might give the nations some kind of weighted representation in recognition of their special status (Osmond 1998). However, this would obviously not be provided through giving an equal number of seats to each nation and region, whilst an allocation based on population would give relatively fewer seats to Wales and Northern Ireland. An alternative is to provide a different kind of power through limited vetoes, as discussed in the section on a territorial chamber in Chapter 13. The parallel problem of representing nations and regions in the Spanish upper house has never been solved, and remains one of the biggest obstacles to reform of the Senado.[30]

COMPOSITION METHODS

This and the preceding two chapters have set down some of the principles which must be considered before deciding on the members of the new upper house. This has demonstrated that there are many issues that must be taken into account before the composition method for the chamber is arrived at. These issues having been discussed, we finally turn our attention to the mode of selecting members of the new house.

There are broadly four ways in which members of the new chamber could be chosen:
- direct election;

---

[30] See Chapter 11.

- indirect election;

- appointment;

- other less commonly used methods, such as 'functional' or vocational selection, *ex officio* membership, or random selection.

These methods may be used singly, or be combined to create a mixed chamber. Each of these options, including the prospects for a mixed chamber, are considered in the sections that follow.

Direct Election

As shown in Chapter 2, direct election is now the commonest means of selecting members for upper houses around the world. Amongst the chambers considered in this book, it is used for all members of the Australian Senate, virtually all members of the Italian Senato, and four-fifths of members of the Spanish Senado. Reformers in the UK have grown increasingly interested in the possibility of a directly elected upper house. Evidence to the Royal Commission from the Liberal Democrats proposed a wholly elected chamber, whilst the Conservatives proposed a largely elected chamber. Many members of the House of Commons have pledged their support to the principle of a directly elected chamber.[31]

Democracy, Legitimacy, and Powers

One of the most obvious advantages of a directly elected chamber is that it would be seen to be democratic. In a modern democracy it is instinctive to expect political institutions, particularly parliament, to be elected. As a result of this, direct election a second chamber is liable to win the support of the public. Evidence from overseas, as discussed in Chapter 12, demonstrates that there are rarely calls to end direct election to a second chamber, whilst chambers which are not directly elected frequently face demands for elections to be introduced.

When the public is involved in electing members of the upper house, it is more likely to be perceived as legitimate. This in turn means that it would be more able to use its powers, whilst retaining its popularity. Elected chambers tend to enjoy considerable *de facto* powers. Whatever

---

[31] 157 MPs of all parties signed an Early Day Motion proposed by Conservative MP Andrew Tyrie in 1999 stating that 'this house believes that the composition of the second chamber should be determined by election'. The EDM attracted support from 80 Labour, 39 Conservative, 35 Liberal Democrat, and two Plaid Cymru MPs. The Scottish National Party, whose submission to the Royal Commission favoured abolition of the upper house, have also said that if the upper house remains, it should be directly elected.

powers a new directly chamber was given, it would almost certainly feel at liberty to use them when it disagreed with the lower house. The instinctive answer to this dilemma might be to limit the chamber's formal powers. However a directly elected upper house would be unlikely to settle for weak powers. Such a chamber might well press, with public support, for an increase in its powers. For example, the upper chamber in the Czech Republic was created in 1993 and given a delaying power of 30 days over legislation. The chamber has already started the process of seeking greater powers.

Crucial to the chamber's ability to use its powers is not only its legitimacy, and formal powers, but also its party balance. The directly elected upper chamber in Italy does not often clash with the lower house, because it tends to have a similar government majority. The powerful chamber in Australia forces government to think again, but this generally results in compromise because the Senate is controlled by neither government nor opposition. A directly elected chamber which was controlled by the opposition party, on the other hand, could create considerable disruption. This should be a consideration in the design of a directly elected upper house. This applies particularly to the chamber's electoral system, and the question of whether other members are included in the house who are not directly elected.

The Need for a Distinct Chamber

One of the primary dangers with a directly elected chamber is that it could be too similar to the House of Commons. The chamber would be likely to be filled by party representatives, and attract considerable media and public attention. These factors could threaten to diminish some of the valued qualities of the upper house, such as its independent ethos, and concentration on the detailed scrutiny of legislation.

It would be particularly important that the membership of a directly elected chamber was seen to be clearly distinct from that of the House of Commons. By designing a chamber with a distinct membership, some of the problems mentioned above could be minimised. In particular, in order to protect the supremacy of the House of Commons, it may be possible to design the composition of the elected second chamber so that it was seen as less 'representative' than the lower house. Measures that might be introduced include:

- *Rolling membership.* Some of the benefits of a rolling membership, whereby only a half or one-third of the chamber are elected at once, have already been discussed. In a directly elected chamber this would result in members serving longer terms than MPs, so that the

House of Commons could always claim a newer mandate than the upper house.

- *Equal numbers of seats for all nations and regions.* This was also discussed above, and is a factor in protecting the supremacy of the Australian lower house, even though the upper house is elected using a proportional system. It bases the representation in the upper house on a different principle to that used in the House of Representatives. Projections for a system such as this in the UK were shown in Tables 14.1 and 14.2.

- *Inclusion of a small number of unelected members.* This option of course breaches the principle of a wholly elected chamber. But the inclusion of a number of appointed or *ex officio* members could be used in an attempt to 'dilute' the legitimacy of an elected upper house.

Potential Difficulties with Direct Election

In designing a directly elected second chamber, there are several other factors which will need to be taken into account. These include:

- *Independent members.* There are many reasons why it could be desirable for independent members to be included in the new upper house. This was discussed earlier in the chapter. However, it was also noted that it would be difficult to design a directly elected chamber in which independent candidates would win many seats. A wholly directly elected upper house would be likely to be dominated by the parties. This could be another reason for including a small unelected element in the house.

- *Voter fatigue.* With elections for local, regional, national, and European assemblies and parliaments, there is growing concern about 'voter fatigue'. An elected upper house could add to this problem, although this would be eased by upper house elections being held on the same day as other elections. This is common overseas.

- *Constituency work.* If members of the upper house are directly elected, and therefore accountable to the public, there is a danger that the tradition of constituency work could spread to the chamber. As discussed in Chapter 13, this would not be desirable. However, this is more of a problem under some electoral systems than others.

How and When to Elect

For all the reasons outlined above, the format and timing of elections will be crucial to the character of a directly elected upper house. The design of the electoral system, and the timing of elections, will therefore need careful consideration.

The upper chamber must be clearly distinct from the House of Commons, and the immediate consequence of this is that the two chambers must be elected using different voting systems. Under the current arrangements—where the Commons is elected by first past the post—this would suggest that elections to the new upper house should use a proportional system. This would create an arrangement in the UK similar to that in Australia. The Australian system combines a majoritarian lower house with a proportionally elected Senate, with the result that parliament includes elements of both adversarial and consensus politics—and generally operates through a slightly uneasy compromise between the two. One benefit of this is that the electoral system is fairly stable—there are no serious calls for proportional representation to be introduced for the Australian lower house, as there have been in New Zealand and the UK. Were this solution to be adopted in the UK it might therefore dampen demands for electoral reform for the House of Commons. Indeed the two issues would need to be considered together, as the introduction of PR for the Commons, when the upper house was already elected this way, could result in an Italian-style situation, where the two chambers became too similar.[32]

Another consideration in the choice of electoral system is the need to discourage constituency work. This implies that, in a reverse of the arguments frequently made in relation to the electoral system for the House of Commons, it may be desirable to break the link between elected representatives and constituents as far as possible. This points strongly to a proportional system based on large multi-member constituencies, rather than a system using single member constituencies.

Unless new boundaries are to be adopted, the two most natural options for such multi-member constituencies would be to use the existing boundaries of the nations and regions, or to treat the whole of the UK as one big constituency. Elections using the boundaries of the nations and regions could use either open lists or the single transferable

---

[32] In fact the Jenkins proposals (*Report of the Independent Commission on the Voting System*, Cm 4090-I, October 1998) are only semi proportional, so could possibly be combined with a highly proportional upper house. However, if an elected upper house had sufficient powers, this could answer many of the concerns which have led to calls for reform of the House of Commons system, by acting as a check on single party governments elected on a minority of the vote.

vote system.[33] Either of these would give relatively less control to central party machines, and could even result in the election of some independent candidates. Using the whole of the UK as one single constituency, on the other hand, would involve such a large number of candidates on the ballot paper that these systems would be impractical. The only viable system in this situation—unless the chamber was very small—would be closed party lists. These are increasingly seen as undesirable, as they deny voters the opportunity to vote for particular candidates.

A rolling membership for the upper house, with only one-third or a half of members elected each time, would help ensure a manageable number of candidates appeared on the ballot paper in each nation and region. The risk of voter fatigue associated with more frequent elections could be dealt with by holding upper house elections alongside other elections. The obvious options would be to run these elections alongside general elections, as in Australia, or alongside elections to the devolved assemblies. This second option would also boost the territorial nature of the upper house, as discussed in the next section.

Direct Election and a Territorial Chamber

One of the benefits of a directly elected chamber is that it would be easy to base on the nations and regions. If these boundaries were used for elections to the upper house, this could form the seeds of a territorial chamber, which might develop over time if devolution in England progresses. Although this would provide no automatic accountability between upper house members and devolved institutions, links could be cemented using the kinds of methods discussed in Chapter 13. The main advantage, given the asymmetrical nature of the devolution settlement, would be that there was no major transition needed in order to represent England. If and when elected regional assemblies were created, members of the upper house from the English regions could simply build relationships with them. In the short term, relationships could be encouraged between members of the upper house representing English regions and the Regional Development Agencies and regional chambers.

The status of the upper house as a territorial chamber would be enhanced by two further measures, both of which have already been mentioned. The first would be equal representation for each nation and

---

[33] These were the two options proposed for an upper chamber based on the nations and regions by the Labour Party's Plant Commission on the electoral system (Labour Party 1993).

region, ensuring an equal voice for all parts of the UK. The second would be to hold upper house elections alongside those for devolved assemblies. This would link the two in voters' minds, and increase the likelihood that upper house elections would be fought on regional issues. Members of the upper house could be elected for two or three terms of each devolved assembly, which for the Scottish Parliament and Welsh Assembly would be eight or 12 years. Elections in England could be timed alongside local government elections, changing to shadow elections to regional assemblies if and when these develop.

Indirect Election

An alternative, which is also in common use overseas, is for members of the upper house to be indirectly elected. Under this system members are usually chosen by sub-national assemblies or governments, thus making the upper house a kind of territorial chamber. In the case of France and Ireland the electoral college for the upper house is instead dominated by local councillors.[34] Given the structure of the UK the options for an indirectly elected second chamber would therefore be to involve the assemblies of the nations and regions in its election, or local government councillors, or both.

Democracy and Legitimacy

An indirectly elected upper house, whilst not involving voters directly, still follows a democratic principle. This could allow the chamber to enjoy democratic legitimacy, whilst avoiding some of the potential problems of a directly elected house—such as voter fatigue and burdening upper house members with constituency work.

None the less, the upper house would be seen as less reflective of the will of the voters, and thus would be less likely than a directly elected chamber to threaten the supremacy of the House of Commons. Whilst some might see indirect election as denying voters a choice, the distinct and subordinate character of the upper house could also be seen as an advantage. Not only would this reinforce the powers of the House of Commons, it would also encourage some of the features which are valued in many upper houses. Indirectly elected chambers tend to attract less public attention, because they are not directly accountable to the public, and thus be less driven by the media agenda.[35] This can have

---

[34] Occasionally—as in these two cases—members of the lower house are also included in the electoral college for the upper house.

[35] This is discussed in Chapter 11.

benefits, particularly since members of the lower house are already subject to intense media spotlight.

A disadvantage of indirectly elected chambers is that they can result in regional or local elections becoming dominated by national issues. If members of the upper house were elected by members of the devolved assemblies, this would link elections to these assemblies with the political balance of the upper house. In countries such as Germany, with indirectly elected upper houses, this can result in national issues dominating regional election campaigns.[36]

Dual Mandates and Links to Devolved Assemblies

One advantage of an indirectly elected upper house is that this could create a tangible link from Westminster to the devolved assemblies. Members of such a chamber would be directly accountable to an electorate comprising devolved assembly members. An objection which is frequently raised, however, is that members of devolved assemblies themselves have too many responsibilities to take on national parliamentary work. In the UK such dual mandates would be a particular problem because the Scottish Parliament and Welsh Assembly—unlike devolved assemblies in some countries—have been set up as full time institutions.[37] Given the added difficulty of the geographical distances involved, it would not be possible for these members to attend Westminster regularly.

The German Bundesrat, which comprises members of state governments, avoids this problem by meeting only once every three weeks, for half a day. Between plenary meetings the detailed work of legislative scrutiny is carried out by state civil servants. Such an arrangement would not be a serious prospect in the UK, given the traditions of a neutral civil service on the one hand and a full time upper house on the other.

The alternative is for members of devolved assemblies to elect upper house members from outside their own ranks. In Spain, indirectly elected members of the Senado do not have to be members of regional assemblies, and many of them are not. The argument against this would be that only members of the assembly can provide real links with regional decision-making. However, the Spanish Senado shows that even these members do not necessarily create meaningful links. Most indirectly elected members of the Senado are junior backbenchers in

[36] This is discussed in Chapter 10.

[37] Plaid Cymru, in their submission to the Royal Commission, were prepared to accept that Welsh Assembly members could serve in the upper house, on the condition that the assembly be made larger in order to manage this.

their assemblies, and there is no formal reporting mechanism between the two. Members elected from outside assemblies could potentially create better links than this, if the measures proposed in Chapter 13 were employed. Such members would also have sufficient time to devote to national parliamentary duties. Upper house members elected by members of the devolved assemblies, rather than the general public, would have an added sense of accountability to devolved institutions.

Electing Members

As with a directly elected chamber, the system and timing used to choose members in an indirectly elected upper house would be important. Some of the same principles would apply.

If the members of the upper house were to represent the devolved assemblies, it would be natural for their election to be linked to the assemblies' electoral cycles. A new intake of upper house members could be elected at the start of each new assembly term. In chambers overseas it is usual for the party balance of indirectly elected upper house members to be designed to reflect that in each assembly. Alternatively, seats could be divided between the parties on the basis of the share of votes cast at the assembly elections, which might result in a more proportional outcome.[38] In either of these cases members of the assembly could vote in party groups in order to elect the number of members which their party had been allocated. Another option—similar to the Irish system—would be for all members of the assembly to vote together, using a proportional system. The result would then be roughly proportional to party strengths in the assembly. The use of an open list system or the single transferable vote might marginally increase the likelihood of cross-party voting and the election of independent candidates. It might even be possible to require assembly members to vote for a certain number of independent candidates, on a cross-party basis.[39]

A serious problem with elections by devolved assemblies, however, is that the pool of voters for these elections would be very small. There are 129 members of the Scottish Parliament, which is a reasonable electorate if, say, 10 members of the upper house were to be elected at any one

---

[38] For example the share of seats in the Scottish Parliament did not accurately reflect the share of the vote in 1999. The Labour Party gained 34 per cent of votes for the regional list part of the election, but 43 per cent of seats in the parliament.

[39] A system where members are elected from outside the assembly raises questions about how candidates qualify to get on the ballot paper. One option would be to require nomination by a fixed number of members of the assembly. A similar system is used amongst parliamentarians for nominations to the Irish Seanad (see Chapter 3).

time. However there are only 60 members in the Welsh Assembly and 25 in the Greater London Assembly. A rolling membership, where only one-third or a half of upper house members were elected at once would go some way towards alleviating this problem. But in London, in particular, the size of the electorate could present insurmountable difficulties.

Asymmetry and the English Question

Another obvious obstacle to an indirectly elected upper chamber is that devolved assemblies have so far only been established in four of the 12 nations and regions. In the absence of English regional government outside London, a transitional arrangement would need to be found for England.

The section earlier in this chapter on anticipating future devolution emphasised that any such arrangement would need to meet two criteria. It must offer flexibility in the event of further devolution in England, but must also be stable if this did not occur. This is a difficult demand to meet in an indirectly elected chamber, as it would be necessary to find some method of indirect election in England that could be used in the short to medium term.[40] One solution, suggested by John Osmond (1998), would be for the regional associations of local authorities to be responsible for these elections. An alternative would be for the elections to be carried out by the transitional English regional chambers, which also consist mostly of councillors. However, neither of these solutions would be likely to be viable in the long term, as these institutions themselves are indirectly elected. If English regional government did not develop there would certainly be calls for reform.

Representing Local Government

A final option for an indirectly elected chamber would be to design it as a chamber of local government, or include a number of local government representatives within it. The best existing parallels for such a system are the upper houses of France and Ireland.

These chambers demonstrate some of the difficulties of representing local government in the upper house, as neither of them reflect local government concerns particularly effectively. In both cases members are primarily party representatives, and in addition have to struggle with the problem of dual mandates—as most also serve as local councillors.

---

[40] An alternative would be to allow the chamber to be directly elected in English regions without elected assemblies. But this would create an immediate 'democratic deficit' in Scotland and Wales, and would also be politically difficult to reverse at a later date.

It is even more difficult for the upper house to link in a meaningful way to local government than it is to regional government, since local authorities are so numerous and cannot all expect to be directly represented. Accountability could instead be provided by upper house members through local authority associations. But in this case it would be easier for such associations to be responsible themselves for electing upper house members, as suggested above. Alternatively members representing these associations could serve in an appointed or *ex officio* capacity. It is to these, unelected, forms of representation that we turn in the final sections of this chapter.

Appointment

There is obviously a long tradition of appointment to the House of Lords. Whereas appointment to a parliamentary chamber would be thought unusual in many countries, appointees have formed an element of many proposals for reform of the UK upper house.

Democracy and Legitimacy

The primary cause of concern about appointments to the upper house is the impact that this would have on public opinion, and the legitimacy of the house. Unlike direct and indirect election, it may be difficult to achieve public confidence in members of the upper house who are appointed. Appointment provides no accountability for members either to the electorate or a body chosen by them. Because of this there is a danger that appointed members in the upper house could become controversial, fuelling calls for further reform, and that the legitimacy of the house might be damaged to the extent that it could not adequately fulfil its functions.

On the other hand appointed members might be included in an otherwise elected house in a conscious attempt to reduce the perceived legitimacy of the chamber. If there are fears about an elected house threatening the supremacy of the House of Commons, the inclusion of a number of appointed members might be seen to 'dilute' its legitimacy. This is further discussed below.

Representing the Under-represented

The primary arguments in favour of appointment relate to the desire to include members in the house who are unlikely to be elected. In particular, appointment is one of the only reliable methods of including independent members in the house. The inclusion of such members could be advantageous, for reasons outlined earlier in the chapter. The inclusion of expert and experienced members from all walks of life—some of whom may take a party whip—is also valued. This too may be used as an argument in favour of appointed members. However, as indicated above, other countries have traditions of high profile individuals standing for election on party lists.

Another argument which is made in favour of appointment is that it could potentially be used to boost the representation of other under-represented groups. These might be individuals from particular professions, age, or ethnic groups, for example. The White Paper on House of Lords reform suggested that appointment could be a way of improving women's representation in a reformed house (Cabinet Office 1999). However, this tool has not been used effectively in the House of Lords so far. Of a total 477 life peers in summer 1999, only 87 (18 per cent) were women. This figure has been only marginally improved by new appointments—of the 181 life peers created between May 1997 and November 1999, 36 (20 per cent) were women.[41]

A Wholly or Largely Appointed Chamber

One option is to exclude all elected elements from the new upper house, and decide on a wholly appointed chamber. The only realistic comparator for this option is Canada. There are many problems with the Canadian Senate, in particular the degree of Prime Ministerial patronage that is involved in appointments, and the lack of input from the provinces.[42] However, the Canadian experience also suggests that a wholly appointed chamber—just like the old House of Lords—would suffer legitimacy problems which prevented it from challenging the elected chamber. Thus even where government proposed unpopular action, the upper house might feel unable to stand in its way. The same problems would be liable to apply in a chamber which was largely, but not wholly, comprised of appointees.

Challenges to government by the Canadian Senate, which are rare, have led to controversy and calls to reform the chamber. It is difficult to predict how a wholly or largely appointed chamber would fare in the UK, which has different traditions to Canada. Its success would depend in part on public support for the appointments system as discussed below. All that can be said is that indications from Canada are not good. The best way of predicting the long term outcome from a wholly

---

[41] Meanwhile progress in the elected House of Commons has been rapid, with the number of women members doubling from 60 in 1992 to 120 in 1997.

[42] See Chapter 3.

appointed house will be to watch the performance of the transitional House of Lords.

Limiting the Number of Appointees

An alternative, which has been more widely supported, is the possible inclusion of a smaller number of appointees in an otherwise elected house.[43] There are precedents for this—the Italian upper house includes a small number of appointees—currently eight out of 326—and the Irish upper house includes 11 appointees in its total membership of 60. In the UK it has frequently been proposed that the number of appointees might be anything up to one-third of the members of the new chamber. This is more unusual—as indicated in Chapter 2 only Malaysia, Algeria, and Swaziland combine a sizeable number of appointees alongside elected members in the upper house.

Including a small number of appointees could help bring underrepresented groups into the chamber, whilst avoiding the potential problems of a wholly appointed house. However, this does raise some of the difficulties of a mixed chamber, which are discussed below.

If all or part of the chamber were to be appointed, it would be advisable for the number of appointees to be limited in some way. At present the chamber's open-ended size allows Prime Ministers to potentially alter its party balance, by simply adding more members. This can lead to accusations that the system is being abused for political advantage, which is liable to damage the legitimacy of the house. It also raises the danger that the size of the house could again swell to unmanageable proportions. There are three obvious methods for limiting the number of appointees in the chamber. One is for the number of appointed members to be fixed—as in Canada. Another is to set a maximum number of members that can be appointed in each parliamentary session—this would be similar to the system in Italy. The third, and probably most practical, solution would be to end the system of life appointment and replace it by a fixed term for appointed

---

[43] For example the Mackay Commission set up by Conservative leader William Hague proposed two options, both of which included some elected and some appointed members (Mackay 1999). Others who have proposed that appointees could form part of the chamber include Richard and Welfare (1999) and Tyrie (1998). The Home Committee, set up in 1977 by Conservative leader Margaret Thatcher to make proposals on Lords reform also proposed a chamber comprising two-thirds elected and one-third appointed members. However, once the Conservatives entered government these recommendations were never acted upon.

members, allowing regular renewal—as used for the small number of appointees in Ireland.

Appointing Members

If appointed members are to be included in the upper house it is very important to the chamber's legitimacy that there is public support and trust in the appointment system. This is clearly lacking in the discredited Canadian Senate, for example, and partly accounts for the low esteem in which that chamber is held.

The way in which appointments are made will partly depend upon who is to be appointed. One important question is whether political appointments will continue to be made. One of the key arguments for inclusion of appointees is that this allows independent members to be brought into the house. If this is the primary reason for including an appointed element, there is a strong argument that all appointed members should be independent. Party representatives could then enter the chamber through election. The argument might be made that this would exclude many experienced politicians, such as retired MPs, who make an important contribution to the house. However in Italy, for example, such members have traditionally been placed on party lists for the upper house. The inclusion of *ex officio* members—as also used in Italy—could provide another solution. This is discussed below.

The appointment of independent members to a reformed upper house could be given to an Appointments Commission, as proposed in the White Paper on reform of the House of Lords.[44] An Appointments Commission is due to be created to make appointments to the transitional chamber, and it is important that this commission has public support. There are unfortunately no examples of similar commissions overseas for this purpose, from which we can learn. But the Canadian experience, and UK experience to date, suggests that the commission should be given a clear brief, and operate in as transparent a way as possible. The brief for the commission might include the requirement to seek to achieve balance in the house, in terms of gender, age, ethnicity, and geographical spread. It might also include the requirement to seek representatives of professions that are currently underrepresented, or expertise that is particularly desirable (e.g. science policy or human rights). In order to boost public support for the system, the commission might even advertise for members of the house, in the way that many other public appointments are now advertised. Such

---

[44] See Chapter 1.

advertisements could be used to call for people with particular expertise.

If it were felt desirable to continue to make political appointments, some fixed balance of independent and political appointees should be agreed. This would avoid the situation that exists in Canada, where independent members are only rarely appointed. It could therefore improve the credibility of the house.

Appointment to a Territorial Chamber

There is a possibility that appointees be included as part of a territorial chamber, or even make up the total membership of that chamber, as in Canada. Here again the Canadian experience brings a clear lesson: it is essential that any such appointments involve input from the nations and regions concerned.[45] The Canadian Senate lacks all credibility as a territorial chamber because all of its members are appointed by central government without reference to institutions in the provinces. Whether or not the appointed element of the chamber is intended to represent the nations and regions, it will be important to monitor appointments to ensure that they are representative of the whole of the UK.

Other Forms of Membership

Although direct election, indirect election, and appointment are the three primary mechanisms used for selecting members of second chambers, there are other methods that have either been proposed, or are in limited use. Three of these have been suggested as ways of ensuring that the chamber includes politically independent members. These three methods, discussed briefly below, are 'functional' (or vocational) representation, random selection, and *ex officio* membership.

'Functional' Representation

The White Paper on reform of the House of Lords refers to the possibility of including members representing 'functional constituencies' (Cabinet Office 1999). Such members would be chosen to represent particular professions, industries, or interest groups, rather than geographical areas or political parties. This is the form of representation used for most of the seats in the Irish Seanad, where it is

---

[45] Plaid Cymru have already proposed, in their evidence to the Royal Commission, that the Welsh Assembly be involved in a share of appointments if the chamber includes appointees.

referred to as 'vocational' representation.[46] Election in functional constituencies has the potential benefit of including a democratic element, whilst providing for independent members of the house. A vocational or functional element may also be included in an appointed system, or a house with *ex officio* members.

The vocational system employed in the Irish Seanad is widely seen as a failure. This is primarily because the electoral college used for the vocational seats comprises not members of functional groups, but elected councillors and members of parliament. Since most of these members represent the parties, the elections to the Seanad are not truly vocational, but are in reality just a form of indirect election of party representatives.

If a vocational system were adopted in the UK, it would surely not use the same electoral college as the Irish Seanad. Debate in Ireland has been continuous for over 60 years about the reform of the upper house, which is generally seen as unsatisfactory. However, it is interesting that few proposals have emerged in Ireland as to how the Seanad could be reformed to make it truly vocational. Michael Laver, who has acted as an adviser to the Irish government, has suggested that 'it would now be extremely contentious to attempt, in cold blood, to introduce an effective system of vocational representation in the Seanad' (1996: 533). For similar reasons, it has been suggested that corporate representation would be hard, at best, to build into the reform of the House of Lords:

in a nation as diverse as the UK, it would be very difficult to reach agreement on the corporate interests which should be entitled to representation (as well as the difficulties in representing people who are not members of any official body or grouping, such as unemployed people) quite aside from achieving the most appropriate balance of numbers between them and the inevitable imbalance in resources they would have available (Constitution Unit 1996: 65).

An almost identical argument could be applied to religious representation in the house, which currently exists through the 26 seats given to Anglican bishops. It is widely acknowledged that the representation of only one religious group in a multi-cultural Britain is outdated. However, it is difficult to envisage an agreement being reached on religious representation in a new chamber which fully satisfied all religious groups. Arguments about the relative number of seats to be given to Catholic bishops or Muslim leaders are likely to prove equally difficult as questions about the relative balance of employers and trade unions, or teachers and doctors, in a 'functional' or

---

[46] The history of this form of representation, and its application in Ireland, was discussed in Chapter 3.

vocational chamber. None of the other chambers considered here include seats reserved for religious representatives, although this applied in some cases in previous centuries.[47]

Random Selection

For completeness the option proposed by Barnett and Carty (1998) for a random membership of the upper house should be mentioned. This builds on the randomness of the traditional hereditary element in the house, but would extend it to citizens of both genders and all social classes. Members selected could also be balanced to ensure that there were fair numbers from each nation and region. This solution might be used to ensure that a proportion of members of the house were politically independent, and could have other advantages, including encouraging more people to engage with the work of the upper house. Although a similar method was used to form a council in ancient Athens, it is not currently in use in any second chamber. Its results in the UK are therefore not predictable on the basis of overseas experience.

Ex Officio Members

The final method that might be employed for membership of the house is the inclusion of *ex officio* members. These members would be neither elected nor appointed, but would gain membership of the house automatically, by virtue of their position.

There are two basic reasons for including *ex officio* members in the house. The first would be as a form of 'functional' representation, so that certain office holders—for example the Director General of the CBI and General Secretary of the TUC—would be given seats in the upper house as of right. This system is not employed in any of the chambers which have been studied, and could suffer from the difficulties of functional representation, already discussed above. It would also lead to a similar dual mandate problem to that which would apply to members elected from devolved assemblies. Holders of high office are unlikely to have sufficient time to attend the house on a regular basis.

The law lords are currently *ex officio* members of the house, although they keep their seats after retirement from office. If law lords were removed from the chamber as part of its reform, as many have proposed, this would result in a loss of legal expertise in the chamber. However, this might be compensated through other senior lawyers being given some form of *ex officio* membership of the house. One option would be for retired law lords to continue to be given *ex officio*

---

[47] This applied, for example, in Ireland and France—see Chapter 3.

seats in the new house. This would have the benefit of maintaining some continuity with tradition.

Another reason for including *ex officio* members could be to formalise the system whereby senior politicians are rewarded, after retiring from office, with a seat in the upper house. This system is used in some countries overseas, including Italy—where ex-Presidents of the Republic are given life membership of the Senato. It is a convention in the UK that ex-Prime Ministers are offered a seat in the House of Lords upon retirement from the Commons, and these members—and others who have served as senior ministers—are often valued members of the house. Such members might be lost to a house that was entirely elected, or where all appointed members were required to be independent. It therefore could be an option to formalise automatic membership of the upper house for ex- Prime Ministers, and perhaps for others such as ex-Chancellors of the Exchequer or Foreign Secretaries. Such a system might be seen by some as undemocratic, but could be a viable alternative to the continuation of political appointments.[48]

Prospects for a Mixed Chamber

Given the strengths and weaknesses of the different methods of composition discussed above, it is natural that many proposals fix on a solution that mixes two or more of these methods, in an attempt to get the benefits from each. Supporters of such proposals point out that the House of Lords is currently mixed—comprising hereditary and life members, plus *ex officio* law lords and bishops. The new Scottish Parliament, Welsh Assembly, and Greater London Assembly are also mixed, comprising some representatives elected in single member constituencies and others from party lists.[49] Mixed chambers are therefore already established within the UK political system.

There are various models of mixed chambers, and one option would be to combine directly and indirectly elected members in the upper house. This might be used, for example, to ensure that some members of the chamber were also members of devolved assemblies, whilst others had more time to devote to legislative work. This option has not worked well in Spain—where a similar model applies—but could perhaps be improved if genuine links were built with devolved

---

[48] A difficulty with these options, however, is that they would do nothing to improve the gender, class, or ethnic balance of the house—given the current profile of senior politicians and judges.

[49] A similar system was proposed by the Jenkins commission for the House of Commons: *Report of the Independent Commission on the Voting System*, Cm 4090-I, October 1998.

assemblies (as described in Chapter 13). An alternative would be to include indirectly elected members in some, but not all, of the chamber's work. Such a suggestion was made as part of a recently proposed reform package for the Italian upper house.[50] This would have the advantage of involving representatives of devolved assemblies in parliamentary work that was particularly relevant to the nations and regions—maybe including scrutiny of particular areas of legislation—without requiring a full-time presence from these members at Westminster. Under this arrangement indirectly elected members could not be pressurised by their party whips to attend the chamber more than was necessary, as they would be ineligible to vote on most bills.

Proposals for a mixed chamber more frequently combine a proportion of members who are elected (directly or indirectly) with a number of unelected members, who may be appointed or *ex officio*. Such proposals are intended to combine the benefits of a democratic chamber with the benefits of independent, and expert, members of the house. As discussed above, the inclusion of appointed or *ex officio* members could also be used to 'dilute' the legitimacy of an elected chamber, and reduce the risk that it would challenge the supremacy of the Commons.

The greatest potential difficulty in a new upper house that combines elected and appointed members is that it could become controversial whenever the appointed members decide the outcome of a vote. This has been raised, for example, by Bogdanor (1999). A similar situation applied towards the end of the life of the previous House of Lords, when commentators were quick to point out the occasions that the hereditary members were in this decisive position. Hereditary members were seen as less legitimate than life members, and it is possible that appointed members would bear the same stigma in a new chamber where most members had been elected. The nearest parallel for this situation amongst the chambers studied here is the Italian Senate, which includes a small number of appointed and *ex officio* members. Because there are so few of these members, and because most of them rarely attend, they tend not to affect the outcome of votes. On the one recent occasion when this happened, in 1994, it caused considerable controversy.[51] The President of Italy who retired in 1999 chose not to appoint any new members to the Senate, believing that inclusion of such individuals in the chamber was undemocratic. With the long tradition of appointed members in the House of Lords it is likely that there would be more tolerance in the UK for such an arrangement. However,

---

[50] This is described in Chapter 11.
[51] This incident is described in Chapter 4.

if appointed members decided the outcome of controversial votes, this tolerance could decline with time.

CONCLUSIONS

This chapter has attempted to set down some of the parameters within which the future membership of the upper house should be considered, based on overseas experience. As with the discussion about the role of the chamber in Chapter 13, it was not the intention to be prescriptive, or propose a specific model for the new upper house. Rather it was intended to suggest some general principles, and weigh up the pros and cons of different composition methods, based on experience from overseas. The principles proposed include:

- That the new chamber should be considerably smaller than the current House of Lords, which is extraordinarily large. Based on international experience a chamber around half the size of the House of Commons would be reasonable. It should be borne in mind that attendance in the new upper house is liable to be higher than it is currently.

- It would be advisable for the house to have a rolling membership, with members serving longer terms than MPs. If the chamber cannot be dissolved this potentially strengthens it, provides continuity and encourages independence. It also ensures that, in an elected chamber, members could never claim a newer mandate than the House of Commons.

- The party balance of the chamber will be critical in defining its behaviour. A chamber with a government majority would find it difficult to take a sufficiently detached view to operate successfully. However, a chamber controlled by the opposition could cause legislative deadlock unless its powers were very limited. The best outcome is probably a chamber where no party has overall control. However, this is difficult to guarantee unless a sizeable number of seats are reserved for independents. The alternative is for small parties to hold the balance of power.

- Inclusion of independent members in the chamber seems desirable. However, if independent members hold the balance of power in the chamber, they are liable to come under intense scrutiny. One consequence is that they will need to be far better resourced than they are now.

- It will be difficult to include 'expert' members in the new chamber, unless these members are retired from their professions, as the working hours of the house are increasing and pressure to attend regularly is likely to grow.

- Independence of mind amongst party representatives can be encouraged by factors such as long terms, rolling membership, and ending the appointment of ministers from the chamber. It may also be advisable to set a higher minimum age for membership of the upper house than for the Commons, to encourage a more mature membership. A minimum age of 30 to 40 is common overseas.

- If the chamber is to be more representative of the population, its members will need to be better resourced. Experience from other countries suggests that members of the upper house should earn the same salary as MPs, and also be provided with staff allowances and office space.

- If the chamber is to have a territorial role, consideration must be given to the distribution of seats between the nations and regions. The classic model would give each area the same number of seats, irrespective of population. This would base representation in the upper house on a different principle to that for the House of Commons, and reinforce the second chamber's subordinate role. However it would result in Northern Irish parties, in particular, being overrepresented.

- In a territorial chamber a transitional arrangement would also have to be found for those parts of England without devolved assemblies. This would need to be flexible enough to accommodate development of these assemblies, but also be able to last if they are not created.

This chapter then examined the different composition methods which could be employed in a new upper house, and considered the strengths and weaknesses of each. In summary, the following points were suggested:

Direct election

- A directly elected chamber would have public support, but must be carefully designed in order not to challenge the supremacy of the House of Commons.

- Such a chamber would be more likely to use its powers than the current chamber, particularly if controlled by the opposition. However, it would be potentially unstable to try to deal with this by giving the chamber weak formal powers.

- The electoral system would need to be different from that for the House of Commons, and not encourage constituency work. A chamber elected using the boundaries of nations and regions, using 'open' lists or the single transferable vote, would be feasible. Such a chamber could also take on a territorial role.

- In order to prevent the chamber challenging the supremacy of the Commons it would be advisable to either give each nation and region an equal number of seats, include a number of unelected members in the chamber, or both. A rolling membership would also help: elections could be timed to coincide either with general elections, or elections for devolved assemblies.

Indirect election

- An indirectly elected chamber would be more obviously territorial, and could have the benefit of not involving the public in another set of elections.

- It would be difficult for members of devolved assemblies to sit in the upper house, due to their workloads, but they could elect people to sit on their behalf who would be responsible for reporting to the assemblies.

- There are other difficulties, however, with indirect election. In particular it would be hard to devise a transitional arrangement for those parts of England without assemblies. Also, in London and Wales in particular, the pool of voters would be very small.

- It would be difficult to represent local government effectively in an indirectly elected chamber.

Appointment

- Experience from Canada suggests that a wholly appointed upper house, like the House of Lords to date, would have insufficient legitimacy to use its powers and would not command public respect. However, a smaller number of appointees could bring independent members to an otherwise party-dominated chamber.

- If the chamber does include appointees, there is a strong argument for requiring all these members to be independents. If party appointees are included, their number should be strictly limited.

- Appointments to the upper house could be made by an Appointments Commission, which must have public support. It could be given clear criteria for appointments, such as including currently underrepresented groups in the chamber.

- If appointees are included in the new chamber their number should be fixed, or able to fluctuate by only a few members. The open-ended nature of the current chamber's membership has a potential for political manipulation.

- If appointments are included in a territorially based upper house, it is essential that bodies based in the nations and regions are involved in the appointment process.

Other forms of membership

- Functional, or vocational, representation is not currently used successfully in any second chamber. It would prove very difficult to define the groups to be represented, and how seats should be shared between them, in such a system.

- Random selection of a number of members has also been suggested as a way of including independents, but this is even more untested.

- If there is a desire to keep up the tradition of including senior politicians in the chamber, political appointments could be avoided by including a small and clearly defined set of people, such as ex-Prime Ministers, as *ex officio* members. In order to retain the legal expertise in the chamber if the law lords were removed, retired law lords, or other senior lawyers, might also be included on an *ex officio* basis.

A mixed chamber

- If a mixed chamber was to include both directly and indirectly elected members, this must be considered carefully. One option would be for indirectly elected members to have limited rights to involvement in certain decisions with particular relevance to the nations and regions.

- Most proposals for a mixed chamber focus on including both elected and appointed members. However, it has been suggested that this would result in controversy if appointed members decided the outcome of votes. Limited experience from overseas suggests that this may be the case.

The final decision as to the membership of the reformed upper house must be driven by the functions which the chamber is required to perform. There is no perfect model of membership for the new upper house, but this chapter has sought to demonstrate that there are some options which are much more viable than others. If a broad consensus can be reached on what the new chamber is required to do, overseas experience has much to teach us about how that may be achieved.

15

Epilogue: Prospects for Reform

It is easier to get a constitutional [change] . . . on the political agenda than it is to win. The predominant pattern is one of frustrated demands (Banting and Simeon 1985: 25).

By the time this book is published, the Royal Commission on Reform of the House of Lords should have reported. Its recommendations are due to be sent to a joint parliamentary committee for consideration. At the same time the political parties will prepare their responses to the Royal Commission's conclusions, and state their intentions towards the long-term reform of the upper house. But what are the real prospects for reform?

The fundamental reshaping of a parliamentary chamber is a major exercise. No other country considered in this book has achieved such a change, apart from in times of crisis. The second chambers which have been discussed all owe their design to the drafting of a new constitution at a time of major upheaval—upon creation of the state in Canada and Australia, during post-war reconstruction in France, Germany, and Italy, following independence in Ireland, and after the fall of dictatorship in Spain. In other words the kind of major reform of parliament which the UK is currently contemplating normally takes place at a time of national crisis, restructuring, or both.

This suggests that the prospects for reform may not be good. Despite the frustrations with many second chambers overseas, experience shows that aspirations for reform are seldom realised.[1] Even the discredited Canadian Senate is still in very much its original form, following more than 100 years of reform debates. Likewise, the French Sénat remains representative of a bygone age, and the Spanish upper house awaits reform to bring it into line with the new devolved structure of the state, after almost 20 years.

There are many reasons why a second chamber may remain unreformed. Perhaps the most important is the attitude of government. Although many governments around the world have stated their commitment to upper house reform, to make the national parliament

---

[1] Some reasons for this were discussed in Chapter 11.

more effective, this is clearly against their own interests. Even true democrats in government will find it hard to prioritise a parliamentary reform which will involve their work being scrutinised more closely. For all the unpopularity of second chambers which are weak and ineffective, or suffer from problems of legitimacy, such chambers allow governments to get on with their work unimpeded. Lower house members, too, may be more comfortable with this situation, since it preserves their own status through preserving the superior status of the chamber where they sit. Meanwhile the public, while frustrated by the status quo, have many more pressing concerns on which they seek government action. Consequently governments and parliamentarians— not least members of upper houses themselves—may be publicly excused for their reluctance to progress upper house reform.

We need not rely on overseas experience to tell us that these factors are at play. They are precisely the factors which have delayed House of Lords reform for most of this century. There was an 88-year gap between the commitment in the 1911 Parliament Act to 'a second chamber constituted on a popular instead of a hereditary basis' and the first serious steps towards that conclusion. Consecutive governments have failed to grasp the nettle of House of Lords reform, and popular opinion has not required them to do so. The changes enacted by the 1997 Labour government ended—at last—the Conservative Party's dominance of the upper house. That was clearly in the interests of the government. It is questionable whether further reform of the upper house will prove to be so.

The House of Lords Act 1999 created a transitional chamber, consisting largely of appointees, plus law lords and bishops. Some, particularly the Conservative Party, have alleged that this transitional chamber will prove to be permanent. Overseas experience, once again, suggests that this may prove to be the case. As illustration, take the Italian Senato, created in 1948 to be composed 'on a regional basis'. Since regional assemblies had not yet been established it was agreed, in the interim, that the chamber would be directly elected using regional party lists. By the time the assemblies were finally put in place—in the 1970s—the transitional chamber had become permanent. Attempts are still being made to reform it to create a meaningful connection to devolved institutions. Not least of the obstacles are the 326 members of the existing 'transitional' upper house, who are not eager to be forced to find alternative employment. The same pattern may yet be duplicated in the UK.

The pace of recent constitutional change in Britain may however create a precedent for future reform. Reshaping the upper house is an ambitious aim, but perhaps no more ambitious than some of the changes which have already been achieved. If this momentum can be maintained—and particularly if the new upper house can be designed so that it cements the new constitutional settlement, and is flexible enough to respond to future developments—the prospects in the UK may be brighter than those overseas have proved to be. However, this will require true determination from all concerned—government, the political parties, members of the House of Commons, and the British public.

Bibliography

Atkins, A. (1990). 'Legislative and Executive Relations in the Republic of Ireland', in P. Norton (ed.), *Parliaments in Western Europe*. London: Frank Cass.

Banting, K. G. and Simeon, R. (1985). 'The Politics of Constitutional Change', in K. G. Banting and R. Simeon (eds.), *Redesigning the State: the Politics of Constitutional Change in Industrial Nations*. Toronto: University of Toronto Press.

Barnett, A. and Carty, P. (1998). *The Athenian Option*. London: Demos.

Beahan, M. (1996). 'Majorities and Minorities: Evolutionary Trends in the Australian Senate', *Papers on Parliament*, 27. Canberra: Senate.

Bean, C. S. and Wattenburg, M. P. (1998). 'Attitudes Towards Divided Government and Ticket-splitting in Australia and the United States', *Australian Journal of Political Science*. 33/1: 25–36.

Bennett, S. (1992). *Affairs of the State: Politics in the Australian States and Territories*. Sydney: Allen and Unwin.

Blackburn, R. and Plant. R. (eds.) (1999). *Constitutional Reform: The Labour Government's Constitutional Reform Agenda*. London: Longman.

Bogdanor, V. (1997). *Power to the People: A Guide to Constitutional Reform*. London: Victor Gollancz.

Bogdanor, V. (1999). 'Reform of the House of Lords: A Sceptical View', *Political Quarterly*. 70/4.

Bowler, S. and Denemark, D. (1993). 'Split Ticket Voting in Australia: Dealignment and Inconsistent Votes Reconsidered', in *Australian Journal of Political Science*. 28/1: 1–18.

Braunthal, G. (1972). *The West German Legislative Process*. Ithaca: Cornell University Press.

Brazier, R. (1998). *Constitutional Reform: Reshaping the British Political System*. Oxford: Oxford University Press.

Butler, D., Adonis, A. and Travers, T. (1994). *Failure in British Government: The Politics of the Poll Tax*. Oxford: Oxford University Press.

Cabinet Office (1999). *Modernising Parliament—Reforming the House of Lords*. London: The Stationery Office (Cm 4183).

Caminal Badia, M. (1996). 'Representacíon, Territorio y Plurinacionalidad: Una Propuesta Amimétrica Para un Senado de las Nacionalidades y Regiones', in F. Pau i Vall (ed.), *El Senado, Cámara de Representación Territorial*. Madrid: Editorial Tecnos.

Campbell, C. (1978). *The Canadian Senate: A Lobby from Within*. Toronto: Macmillan of Canada.

Carcassonne, G. (1988). 'France (1958): The Fifth Republic', in V. Bogdanor (ed.), *Constitutions in Democratic Politics*. Aldershot: Gower.

Carmichael, P. and Baker, A. (1999). 'Second Chambers—A Comparative Perspective', in B. Dickson and P. Carmichael, *The House of Lords: Its Parliamentary and Judicial Roles*. Oxford: Hart.

Chalmers, R. and Hutchison, J. (1983). *Inside Canberra: A Guide to Australian Federal Politics*. South Yarra, Victoria: Curry O'Neill Ross.

Chubb, B. (1992). *The Government and Politics of Ireland*. Harlow: Longman.

Closa, C. (1996). 'Spain: The Cortes and the EU—A Growing Together', in P. Norton (ed.), *National Parliaments and the European Union*. London: Frank Cass.

Cluzel, J. (1990). *Le Sénat dans la Société Française*. Paris: Economica.

Coakley, J. (1993). 'The Seanad Elections', in M. Gallagher and M. Laver (eds.), *How Ireland Voted 1992*. Limerick: PSAI Press.

Coakley, J. and Laver, M. (1997). 'Options for the Future of Seanad Éireann', in *The All-Party Oireachtas Committee on the Constitution, Second Progress Report: Seanad Éireann*. Dublin: Government of Ireland.

Coakley, J. and Manning, M. (1998). 'The Senate Elections', in M. Marsh and P. Mitchell (eds.), *How Ireland Voted 4: the General Election of 1997*. Limerick: PSAI Press.

Cody, H. (1995). 'Lessons from Australia in Canadian Senate Reform'. *Canadian Parliamentary Review*.

Constitution Unit (1996). *Reform of the House of Lords*. London: Constitution Unit.

Constitution Unit (1998a). *Checks and Balances in Single Chamber Parliaments: A Comparative Study*. London: Constitution Unit.

Constitution Unit (1998b). *Reforming the Lords: A Step by Step Guide*. London: Constitution Unit.

Coonan, H. (1999). *The Senate: Safeguard or Handbrake on Democracy*. Speech to Sydney Institute, 3 February.

Cotta, M. (1994). 'The Rise and Fall of the "Centrality" of the Italian Parliament: Transformation of the Executive-legislative Subsystem after the Second World War', in G. W. Copeland and S. C. Patterson (eds.), *Parliaments in the Modern World*. Michigan: University of Michigan Press.

CPI (1993). 'Relations Between Chambers in Bicameral Parliaments', *Constitutional and Parliamentary Information*, 166: 121–204.

CPI (1995*a*). 'The Parliamentary System of France', *Constitutional and Parliamentary Information*, 169: 3–41.

CPI (1995*b*). 'The Parliamentary System of Spain', *Constitutional and Parliamentary Information*, 170: 105–111.

Cumming Thom, A. (1988). 'The Powers of an Upper Chamber over Legislation'. *Constitutional and Parliamentary Information*, 153: 3–17.

D'Onofrio, F. (1979). 'Committees in the Italian Parliament', in J. Lees and M. Shaw (eds.), *Committees in Legislatures*. Oxford: Martin Robertson.

de Villiers, B. (1999). *National-Provincial Co-operation—the Potential Role of Provincial Interest Offices: The German Experience*, Konrad-Adenauer-Stiftung Occasional Papers. Johannesburg.

Delcamp, A. (1996). *The Senate inside the French Political System*. Paris: Sénat Service des Commissions.

Della Sala, V. (1993). 'The Permanent Committees of the Italian Chamber of Deputies: Parliament at Work?'. *Legislative Studies Quarterly*, 18/2: 157–183.

Della Sala, V. (1997). 'Italy: A Bridge Too Far?'. *Parliamentary Affairs*, 50/3: 396–409.

Democratic Audit (1999). *Making a Modern Senate: A New Democratic Second Chamber for Britain*. Colchester: Democratic Audit.

Derbyshire, J. D. and Derbyshire, I. (1996). *Political Systems of the World*. Oxford: Helicon.

Dickson, B. and Carmichael, P. (1999). *The House of Lords: Its Parliamentary and Judicial Roles*. Oxford: Hart.

Di Palma, G. and Cotta, M. (1986). 'Cadres, Peones and Entrepreneurs: Professional Identities in a Divided Parliament', in E. Suleiman (ed.), *Parliament and Parliamentarians*. London: Holmes and Meier.

Dinan, D. (1986). 'Constitution and Parliament', in B. Girvin and R. Sturm (eds.), *Politics and Society in Contemporary Ireland*. Aldershot: Gower.

Doherty, B. (1996). 'Seanad Éireann', in *Constitution Review Group Report 4: The National Parliament*. Dublin: Government of Ireland.

Dooge, J. (1987). 'The Role of the Seanad', in P. Lynch and J. Meenan (eds.), *Essays in Memory of Alexis FitzGerald*. Dublin: Incorporated Law Society of Ireland.

Doolan, B. (1994). *Constitutional Law and Constitutional Rights in Ireland*. Dublin: Gill and Macmillan.

Dooney, S. and O'Toole, J. (1992). *Irish Government Today*. Dublin: Gill and Macmillan.

Edinger, L. J. (1986). *West German Politics*. New York: Columbia University Press.

Elliott, C. (1997). 'Less than Optimal Outcomes: Fraser and Keating without the Numbers', *Legislative Studies*, 11/2: 35–45.

Emy, H. (1997). 'The Mandate and Responsible Government', *Australian Journal of Political Science*, 32/1: 65–78.

Evans, H. (1995). *Odgers' Australian Senate Practice*. Canberra: A.G.P.S. Also available on the internet and constantly updated at the following address: http://www.aph.gov.au/senate/pubs/html/index/htm.

Evans, H. (1997). 'Government and Parliament', in *The Second Keating Government*. Canberra: Institute of Public Administration.

Evans, H. (1999). 'The Howard Government and the Parliament', in G. Singleton (ed.), *The Howard Government*. Canberra: Institute of Public Administration (in press).

Forsey, E. (1982), 'The Canadian Senate', *The Parliamentarian*, 63/3: 270–6.

Forsey, E. (1988), 'Senate Reform', in R. J. Fleming (ed.), *Canadian Legislatures 1987–88*. Ottawa: Ampersand.

Franks, C. E. S. (1987). *The Parliament of Canada*. Toronto: University of Toronto Press.

Franks, C. E. S. (1999). 'Not Dead Yet, But Should It Be Resurrected? The Canadian Senate', in S. C. Patterson and A. Mughan (eds.), *Senates: Bicameralism in the Contemporary World*, Columbus, Ohio: Ohio State University Press.

Frears, J. (1990). 'The French Parliament: Loyal Workhorse, Poor Watchdog', in P. Norton (ed.), *Parliaments in Western Europe*, London: Frank Cass.

Fry, E. H. (1984). *Canadian Government and Politics in Comparative Perspective*. London: University Press of America.

Furlong, P. (1990). 'Parliament in Italian Politics', in P. Norton (ed.), *Parliaments in Western Europe*. London: Frank Cass.

Furlong, P. (1994). *Modern Italy: Representation and Reform*, London: Routledge.

Furlong, P. (1996). 'The Italian Parliament and European Integration—Responsibilities, Failures and Successes', in P. Norton (ed.), *National Parliaments and the European Union*. London: Frank Cass.

Gallagher, M. (1993*a*). 'The Constitution', in J. Coakley and M. Gallagher (eds.), *Politics in the Republic of Ireland*. Limerick: PSAI Press.

Gallagher, M. (1993*b*). 'Parliament', in J. Coakley and M. Gallagher (eds.), *Politics in the Republic of Ireland*. Limerick: PSAI Press.

Galligan, B. (1995). *A Federal Republic: Australia's Constitutional System of Government*. Cambridge: Cambridge University Press.

Gambetta, D. and Warner, S. (1996). 'The Rhetoric of Reform Revealed'. *Journal of Modern Italian Studies*, 1/3: 357–76.

Genieys, W. (1998). 'Autonomous Communities and the State in Spain', in Le Galès (ed.), *Regions in Europe*. London: Routledge.

Giol, J. C., Cotarelo, R., Garrido, D. L. and Subirats, J. (1990). 'By Consociationalism to a Majoritarian Parliamentary System: the Rise and Decline of the Spanish Cortes', in U. Liebert and M. Cotta (eds.), *Parliament and Democratic Consolidation in Southern Europe*. London: Pinter.

Government of Canada (1984). *Report of the Special Joint Committee of the Senate and the House of Commons on Senate Reform*. Ottawa: Canadian Government Publishing.

Government of Ireland (1996). *Report of the Constitution Review Group*. Dublin: Government of Ireland.

Government of Ireland (1997). *The All-Party Oireachtas Committee on the Constitution, Second Progress Report: Seanad Éireann*. Dublin: Government of Ireland.

Gwynn Morgan, D. (1990). *Constitutional Law of Ireland: The Law of the Executive Legislature and Judicature*. Dublin: The Round Hall Press.

Hamer, D. (1982). 'Towards a Valuable Senate', in M. James (ed.), *The Constitutional Challenge*. St. Leonards, NSW: Centre for Independent Studies.

Hansard Society (1992). *Making the Law: The Report of the Hansard Society Commission on the Legislative Process*. London: Hansard Society.

Hayward, J. E. S. (1983). *Governing France*. London: Weidenfeld & Nicholson.

Hazell, R. (ed.) (1999*a*). *Constitutional Futures: A History of the Next Ten Years*. Oxford: Oxford University Press.

Hazell, R. (1999*b*). 'The New Constitutional Settlement', in R. Hazell (ed.), *Constitutional Futures: A History of the Next Ten Years*. Oxford: Oxford University Press.

Hazell, R. and O'Leary, B. (1999). 'A Rolling Programme of Devolution: Slippery Slope or Safeguard of the Union?', in R. Hazell (ed.), *Constitutional Futures: A History of the Next Ten Years*. Oxford: Oxford University Press.

Heathcoat Amory, E. (1998). *Lords a' Leaping*. London: Centre for Policy Studies.

Hermet, G. (1988). 'Emerging from Dictatorship: The Role of the Constitution in Spain (1978) and Portugal (1976)' , in V. Bogdanor (ed.), *Constitutions in Democratic Politics*. Aldershot: Gower.

Heywood, P. (1995). *The Government and Politics of Spain*. Basingstoke: Macmillan.

Hine, D. (1988). 'Italy (1948): Condemned by its Constitution?', in V. Bogdanor (ed.), *Constitutions in Democratic Politics*. Aldershot: Gower.

Hine, D. (1993). *Governing Italy*. Oxford: Clarendon Press.

Hine, D. (1996). 'Federalism, Regionalism and the Unitary State: Contemporary Regional Pressures in Historical Perspective', in C. Levy (ed), *Italian Regionalism*. Oxford: Berg.

Hussey, G. (1993). *Ireland Today: Anatomy of a Changing State*. London: Viking.

IPPR (1991). *A Written Constitution for the United Kingdom*, London: IPPR.

Jackson, K. (1991). 'The Abolition of the New Zealand Upper House of Parliament', in L.D. Longley and D. M. Olson (eds.), *Two into One: The Politics and Processes of National Legislative Cameral Change*. San Francisco: Westview Press.

Jackson, R. J. and Jackson, D. (1998). *Politics in Canada*. Scarborough, Ontario: Prentice Hall Canada.

James, P. (1998). 'The Federal Framework', in P. James (ed.), *Modern Germany*. London: Routledge.

Jeffery, C. (1998). 'German Federalism in the 1990s: On the Road to a 'Divided Polity'?', in K. Larres (ed.), *Germany Since Unification*. Basingstoke: Macmillan.

Juberías, C. F. (1999). 'A House in Search of a Role', in S. C. Patterson and A. Mughan (eds.), *Senates: Bicameralism in the Contemporary World*, Columbus, Ohio: Ohio State University Press.

Keating, M. (1996). *Nations Against the State: The New Politics of Nationalism in Quebec, Catalonia and Scotland*. London: Macmillan.

Kolinsky, E. (1984). *Parties, Opposition and Society in West Germany*. New York: St Martin's Press.

Kunz, F. A. (1965). *The Modern Senate of Canada*. Toronto: University of Toronto Press.

Labour Party. (1993). *Report of the Working Party on Electoral Systems*. London: Labour Party.

Landes, R. (1987). *The Canadian Polity: A Comparative Introduction*. Scarborough, Ontario: Prentice Hall Canada.

Laundy, P. (1989). *Parliaments in the Modern World*. Aldershot: Dartmouth.

Laver, M. (1996). 'Notes on a new Irish Senate', in *Report of the Constitution Review Group*. Dublin: Government of Ireland.

Leonardy, U. (1997). 'Federalism and Parties in Germany: Organisational Joints between Constitutional and Political Structures', paper to 17th World Congress of the Political Science Association, Seoul.

Leonardy, U. (1999a). 'The Institutional Structures of German Federalism', in C. Jeffery (ed.), *Recasting German Federalism*. London: Pinter.

Leonardy, U. (1999b). 'German Federalism Towards 2000: To be Reformed or Deformed', in C. Jeffery (ed.), *Recasting German Federalism*. London: Pinter.

Lijphart, A. (1984). *Democracies: Patterns of Majoritarian and Consensus Government in Twenty-one Countries*. New Haven: Yale University Press.

Lodici, C. (1999). 'Parliamentary Autonomy: The Italian Senato', in S. C. Patterson and A. Mughan (eds.), *Senates: Bicameralism in the Contemporary World*, Columbus, Ohio: Ohio State University Press.

Loewenberg, G. (1966). *Parliament in the German Political System*. New York: Cornell University Press.

Loewenberg, G. and Patterson, S. C. (1979). *Comparing Legislatures*. Boston : Little, Brown.

Lucy, R. (1993). *The Australian Form of Government*. Melbourne: Macmillan.

Mackay, R. A. (1926). *The Unreformed Senate of Canada*. Oxford: Oxford University Press.

Mackay. (1999). *The Report of the Constituional Commission on Options for a New Second Chamber*. London: Mackay Commission.

Mastias, J. and Grangé, J. (1987). *Les Secondes Chambres du Parlement en Europe Occidentale*. Paris: Economica.

Mastias, J. (1999). 'A Problem of Identity: The French Sénat', in S. C. Patterson and A. Mughan (eds.), *Senates: Bicameralism in the Contemporary World*, Columbus, Ohio: Ohio State University Press.

Maus, D. (1993). 'Libres Propos sur le Sénat', *Pouvoirs*, 64: 89–97.

Mény, Y. (1998). *The French Political System*. Paris: La Documentation Française.

Mény, Y. and Knapp, A. (1998). *Government and Politics in Western Europe: Britain, France, Italy, Germany*. Oxford: Oxford University Press.

Mitchell, A. (1999). *Farewell My Lords*. London: Politico's.

Mitchell, J. and Seyd, B. (1999). 'Fragmentation in the Party and Political Systems', in R. Hazell (ed.), *Constitutional Futures: A History of the Next Ten Years*. Oxford: Oxford University Press.

Mughan, A. and Patterson, S. C. (1999). 'Senates: A Comparative Perspective', in S. C. Patterson and A. Mughan, *Senates*. Columbus, Ohio: Ohio State University Press.

Mulgan, R. (1996). 'The Australian Senate as a 'House of Review''. *Australian Journal of Political Science*, 31/2: 191–204.

Nealon, T. (1997). *Nealon's Guide to the 28th Dáil and Seanad: Election '97*. Dublin: Gill and Macmillan.

Nethercote, J. R. (1998). 'Australia's Adversarial Bicameralism', *The House Magazine*, 13 May 1998, Canberra.

Newton, M. T. (1997). *Institutions of Modern Spain*. Cambridge: Cambridge University Press.

Norris, P. (1996). 'Legislative Recruitment', in L. LeDuc, R. G. Niemi and P. Norris (eds.), *Comparing Democracies: Elections and Voting in Global Perspective*. London: Sage.

O'Halpin, E. (1996). 'Irish Parliamentary Culture and the European Union: Formalities to be Observed' in P. Norton (ed), *National Parliaments and the European Union*, London: Frank Cass.

Osmond, J. (1998). *Reforming the Lords and Changing Britain*. London: Fabian Society.

Padgett, S. and Burkett, T. (1986). *Political Parties and Elections in Germany*. London: C. Hurst and Co.

Parliament of the Commonwealth of Australia (1997). *Constitutional Change*. Report of the House of Representatives Standing Committee on Legal and Constitutional Affairs. Canberra: House of Representatives.

Pasquino, G. (1986). 'The Debate on Institutional Reform', in R. Leonardi and R. Nanetti (eds.), *Italian Politics: A Review, Volume. 1*. London: Pinter.

Pasquino, G. (1997). 'No Longer a 'Party State'?: Institutions, Power and the Problems of Italian Reform'. *West European Politics*, 20/1: 34–53.

Pasquino, G. (1998). 'Reforming the Italian Constitution'. *Journal of Modern Italian Studies*, 3/1: 42–54.

Patterson, S. C. and Mughan, A. (1999). 'Senates and the Theory of Bicameralism', in S. C. Patterson and A. Mughan (eds.), *Senates: Bicameralism in the Contemporary World*, Columbus, Ohio: Ohio State University Press.

Patzelt, W. J. (1999). 'The Very Federal House: The German Bundesrat', in S. C. Patterson and A. Mughan (eds.), *Senates: Bicameralism in the Contemporary World*, Columbus, Ohio: Ohio State University Press.

Pau i Vall, F. (ed.) (1996). *El Senado, Cámara de Representación Territorial*. Madrid: Editorial Tecnos.

Paxman, K. (1998). 'Referral of Bills to Senate Committees: An Evaluation', *Papers on Parliament*, 31. Canberra: Senate.

Placci, L. (1993). *Le Commissioni Parlamentari Bicamerali nella Crisi del Bicameralismo Italiano*. Milan: A.Giuffrè.

Power, G. (1996). *Reinventing Westminster*. London: Charter 88.

Power, G. (1998). *Representatives of the People?: The Constituency Role of MPs*. London: Fabian Society.

PSOE (1998). *La Estructura del Estado*. Madrid: PSOE.

Quarmby, K. (1997). *Straight to the Senate*. London: IPPR.

Reidy, A. (1999*a*). *The House of Lords: In Defence of Human Rights?*, London: Constitution Unit.

Reidy, A. (1999*b*). *A Human Rights Committee for Westminster*, London: Constitution Unit.

Rescigno, F. (1995). *Disfunzioni e Prospettive di Reforma del Bicameralismo Italiano: La Camera delle Regioni*. Milan: A.Giuffrè.

Richard, I. and Welfare, D. (1999). *Unfinished Business: Reforming the House of Lords*. London: Vintage.

Riddell, P. (1998). *Parliament Under Pressure*. London: Victor Gollancz.

Ripollés, M. R. (1999). 'The Spanish Senate', in *Dossier Prepared with Information of the Seminar, Spanish Senate*. Madrid: Senado.

Risse, H. (1998). 'The Bundesrat in the Legislative Process of the Federal Republic of Germany', in *Dossier Prepared with Information of the Seminar, Spanish Senate*. Madrid: Senado.

Rizzuto, F. (1996). 'The French Parliament and the EU: Loosening the Constitutional Straitjacket', in P. Norton (ed.), *National Parliaments and the European Union*. London: Frank Cass.

Rizzuto, F. (1997). 'France: Something of a Rehabilitation', *Parliamentary Affairs*, 50/3: 373–9.

Rousseau, D. (1995). 'Constitution et Conseil Constitutionnel', in *La Revue Administrative*, 286: 372–5.

Rush, M. (1983). 'Parliamentary Reform: The Canadian Experience', in D. Judge (ed.), *The Politics of Parliamentary Reform*. London: Heinemann.

Rush, M. (1990), 'The Canadian Parliament and Federalism', in M. Burgess (ed.), *Canadian Federalism: Past, Present, and Future*. Leicester: Leicester University Press.

Russell, M. (1998). *An Appointed Upper House: Lessons from Canada*. London: Constitution Unit.

Russell, M. (1999). *Resolving Disputes between the Chambers*. London: Constitution Unit.

Saalfeld, T. (1990). 'The West German Bundestag After 40 Years: The Role of Parliament in a 'Party Democracy''', in P. Norton (ed.), *Parliaments in Western Europe*. London: Frank Cass.

Saalfeld, T. (1996). 'The German Houses of Parliament and European Legislation', in P. Norton (ed.), *National Parliaments and the European Union*. London: Frank Cass.

Safran, W. (1998). *The French Polity*. New York: Addison Wesley Longman.

Sartori, G. (1997). *Comparative Constitutional Engineering : An Inquiry into Structures, Incentives, and Outcomes*. Basingstoke : Macmillan.

Schick, R. and Zeh, W. (1997). *The German Bundestag: Functions and Procedures*. Rheinbreitbach: Neue Darmstädter Verlagsanstalt.

Senate of Canada (1997). *The Senate Today*, Ottawa: Senate of Canada.

Senato della Repubblica (1997). *Progetto di Legge Costituzionale: Revisione della Parte Seconda della Costituzione*, Commissione Parlamentare per le Riforme Costituzionali. Rome: Senato della Repubblica (ref. 2583-A).

Seyd, B. (1999). *A Transitional House of Lords: The Numbers*. London: Constitution Unit.

Sharman, C. (1986). 'The Senate, Small Parties and the Balance of Power', *Politics*, 21/2: 20–3.

Sharman, C. (1987). 'Second Chambers', in H. Bavkis and W. Chandler (eds.), *Federalism and the Role of the State*. Toronto: University of Toronto Press.

Sharman, C. (1988). 'Constitutional Politics in Australia (1900)', in V. Bogdanor (ed.), *Constitutions in Democratic Politics*. Aldershot: Gower.

Sharman, C. (1990). 'Australia as a Compound Republic', *Politics*, 25/1: 1–5.

Sharman, C. (1998). 'The Senate and Good Government', Australian Senate Occasional Lecture Series, 11 December.

Shaw, M. (1979). 'Conclusion', in J. D. Lees and M. Shaw (eds.), *Committees in Legislatures*, Oxford: Martin Robertson.

Shell, D. (1992). *The House of Lords*. London: Harvester Wheatsheaf.

Shell, D. (1993). 'Conclusion', in D. Shell and D. Beamish (eds.), *The House of Lords at Work*. Oxford: Clarendon Press.

Shell, D. (1998). 'Bicameralism Reconsidered', seminar paper to Wroxton College, Oxford, August 1998.

Shell, D. (1998a). 'The Second Chamber Question', *Journal of Legislative Studies*, 4/2: 17–32.

Shell, D. (1999). 'To Revise and Deliberate: The British House of Lords', in S. C. Patterson and A. Mughan (eds.), *Senates: Bicameralism in the Contemporary World*, Columbus, Ohio: Ohio State University Press.

Shell, D. and Beamish, D. (eds.) (1993). *The House of Lords at Work*. Oxford: Clarendon Press.

Shell, D. and Giddings, P. (1999). *The Future of Parliament: Reform of the Second Chamber*. London: Hansard Society.

Smith, G. (1992). 'The Nature of the Unified State', in G. Smith, W. E. Paterson, P. H. Merkl and S. Padgett (eds.), *Developments in German Politics*. Basingstoke: Macmillan.

Smith, J. (1994). 'Legislatures', in T.C. Pocklington (ed.), *Representative Democracy*, Toronto: Harcourt Brace Canada.

Smith, P. (1996). ''A quoi sert le Sénat?' Reflections on French Bicameralism'. *Modern and Contemporary France*, NS4/1: 51–60.

Smith, P. (1998). 'La Vengeance du Général: The Centre, the Right and the Fall of René Monory', paper to Association for the Study of Modern and Contemporary France Annual Conference, University of Bradford.

Smith, P. (1999). ''La République Sénatoriale' The Second Chamber and the Fifth Republic', University of Nottingham.

Smith, R. (1994). 'Parliament', in J. Brett, J. Gillespie and M. Goot (eds.), *Developments in Australian Politics*. Melbourne: Macmillan.

Sontheimer, K. (1988). 'The Federal Republic of Germany (1949): Restoring the *Rechtsstaat*', in V. Bogdanor (ed.), *Constitutions in Democratic Politics*. Aldershot: Gower.

Soto, J. L. P. (1997). 'Spain: A Fledgling Parliament 1977–97'. *Parliamentary Affairs*, 50/3: 410–22.

Stevens, A. (1996). *The Government and Politics of France*. Basingstoke: Macmillan.

Stone, B. (1998). 'Small Parties and the Senate Revisited: The Consequences of the Enlargement of the Senate in 1984', *Australian Journal of Political Science.* 33/2: 211–218.

Sturm, R. (1992*a*). 'Government at the Centre', in G. Smith, W. E. Paterson, P. H. Merkl and S. Padgett (eds.), *Developments in German Politics.* Basingstoke: Macmillan.

Sturm, R. (1992*b*). 'The Changing Territorial Balance', in G. Smith, W. E. Paterson, P. H. Merkl and S. Padgett (eds.), *Developments in German Politics.* Basingstoke: Macmillan.

Tsebelis, G. and Money, J. (1997). *Bicameralism.* Cambridge: Cambridge University Press.

Tyrie, A. (1998). *Reforming the Lords: A Conservative Approach.* London: Conservative Policy Forum.

Uhr, J. (1989). 'The Canadian and Australian Senates: Comparing Federal Political Institutions', in B. Hodgins et. al., *Federalism in Canada and Australia.* Peterborough, Ontario : Frost Centre for Canadian Heritage and Development Studies, Trent University.

Uhr, J. (1998). *Deliberative Democracy in Australia.* Cambridge: Cambridge University Press.

Uhr, J. (1999). 'Generating Divided Government: The Australian Senate', in G. W. Copeland and S. C. Patterson (eds.), *Parliaments in the Modern World.* Michigan: University of Michigan Press.

Vera Santos, J. M. (1997). *Senado Territorial y Presencia de Notables.* Madrid: Senado.

Visiedo Mazón, F. J. (1997). *La Reforma del Senado: Territorialización del Senado.* Madrid: Senado.

Von Beyme, K. (1998). *The Legislator: German Parliament as a Centre of Political Decision-Making.* Aldershot: Ashgate.

Wheare, K. C. (1968). *Legislatures.* London: Oxford University Press.

White, R. (1990). *Voice of Region: The Long Journey to Senate Reform in Canada.* Toronto: Dundurn Press.

Wood, D. M. (1998). 'Legislators and Constituents', in G. T. Kurian (ed.), *World Encyclopedia of Parliaments.* Washington: Congressional Quarterly.

Ziller, G. (1982). 'The Bundesrat of the Federal Republic of Germany'. *The Parliamentarian.* 63: 277–80.

Index